Shojo Beat

The Magic Touch

Oyayubi kara Romance

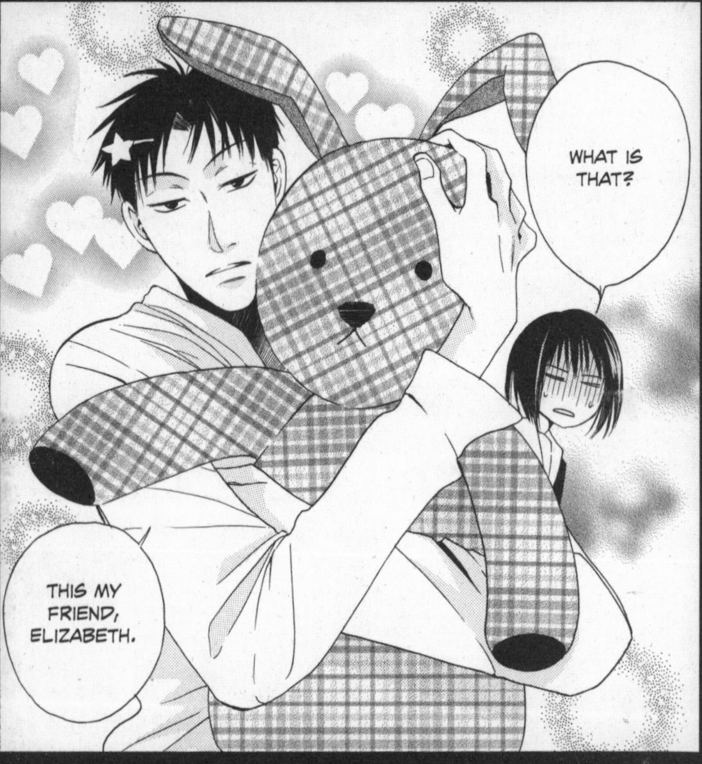
WHAT IS THAT?
THIS MY FRIEND, ELIZABETH.

Vol. 7

Story & Art by Izumi Tsubaki

The Magic Touch
Oyayubi kara Romance

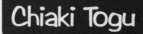

Story and Characters Introduction

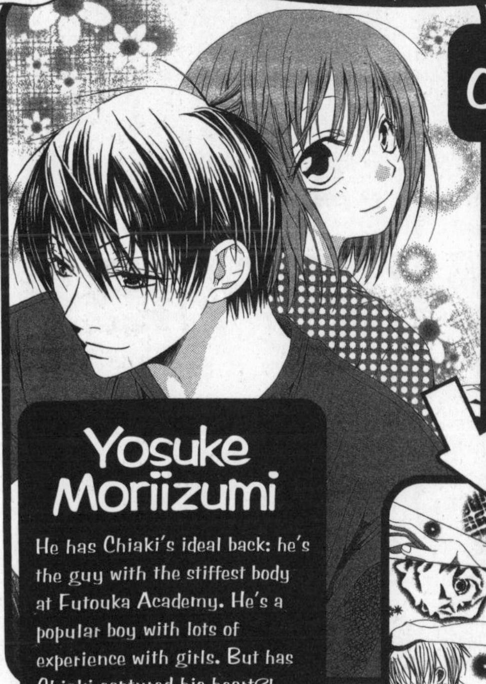

Chiaki Togu

The main character of this story. She's a first-year student in Futouka Academy's Massage Research Club and a rising star in the club.☆ She has an incredible passion and a great talent for massage! But she's normally quiet.

Yosuke Moriizumi

He has Chiaki's ideal back: he's the guy with the stiffest body at Futouka Academy. He's a popular boy with lots of experience with girls. But has Chiaki captured his heart?!

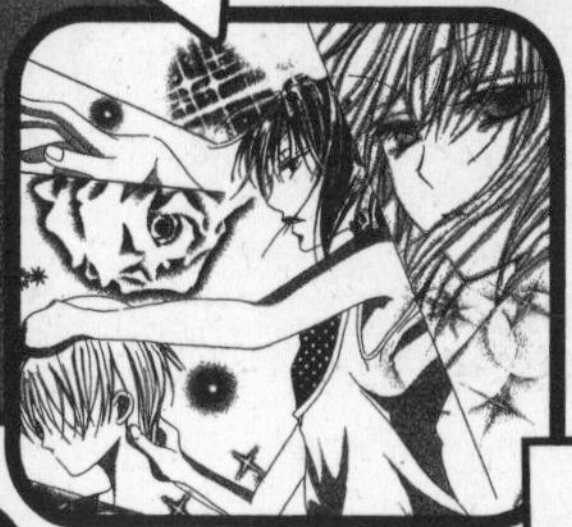

She suddenly changes when she becomes absorbed in massage!

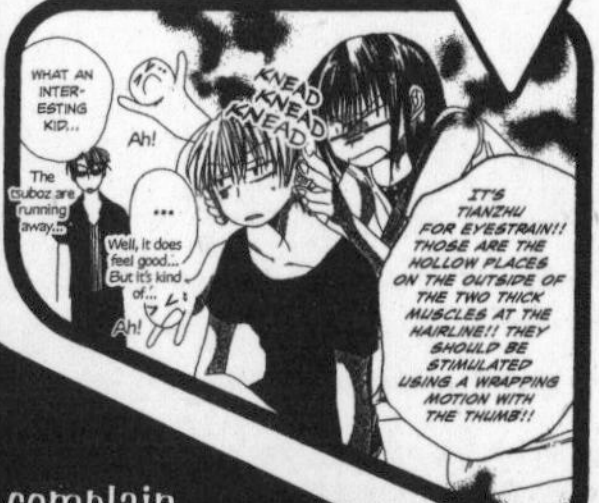
IT'S TIANZHU FOR EYESTRAIN!! THOSE ARE THE HOLLOW PLACES ON THE OUTSIDE OF THE TWO THICK MUSCLES AT THE HAIRLINE!! THEY SHOULD BE STIMULATED USING A WRAPPING MOTION WITH THE THUMB!!
KNEAD KNEAD KNEAD
Ah!
WHAT AN INTERESTING KID...
...
Well, it does feel good... But it's kind of...
The tsuboz are running away...
Ah!

And furthermore...

Tsuboz

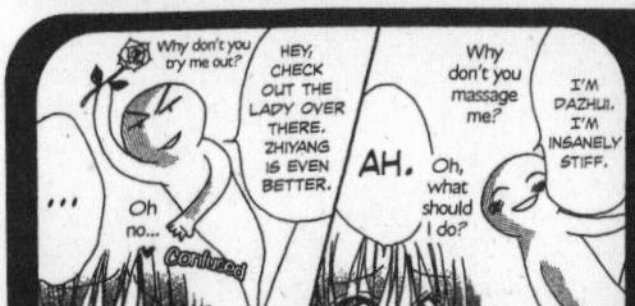
I'M DAZHUI. I'M INSANELY STIFF.
Why don't you massage me?
Oh, what should I do?
KA-THUMP KA-THUMP
AH.
HEY, CHECK OUT THE LADY OVER THERE. ZHIYANG IS EVEN BETTER.
Why don't you try me out?
Oh no...
confused
...
KA-THUMP KA-THUMP

Creatures (?!) that can be seen (maybe) by people who love massage the most. They come out from the tsubo and complain that "it's stiff here." ♥ For now, the only ones who can see them are Chiaki, Takeshi and Takeshi's mentor, Ohnuki.

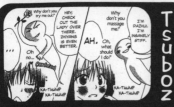

★ Futouka Academy Massage Research Club ★

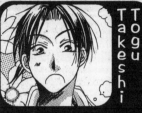

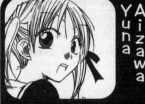

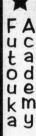

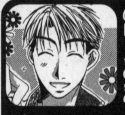

Yuna Aizawa

Chiaki's friend. She is very competent at massage. She has feelings for Togu Senpai!

Takeshi Togu

Chiaki's brother, who's a year older. He's living with his mentor right now as an apprentice. He's a master at gal games.

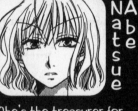

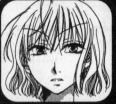

Natsue Abe

She's the treasurer for the Massage Research Club. She has a nice body, but she's ruthless when money is involved.

Chitose Harumi

He's the manager of the Massage Research Club. He's normally carefree. His family seems to be rich.

♥ The Story So Far ♥

★ Chiaki Togu is a first-year student in the Massage Research Club. One day, on her way to school, she encounters a truly "ideal" back.♥ She falls in love with it at first sight...

★ While searching for that boy with the stiffest back at her school, Chiaki finds Yosuke Moriizumi, the most popular boy at school. In response to Chiaki's pleas to "let me massage your back," he sets one condition: Chiaki must make him fall in love with her!

★ Despite many events and misunderstandings, the two start going out. They make progress, but things are sometimes awkward between Yosuke, a player who has broken many hearts, and Chiaki, who is extremely shy when she's not involved in massage.

★ Yosuke believes the fact that he "hates" women has to do with a missing childhood memory. In order to fill in that blank, he visits the town he used to live in and discovers a past that's a surprise even to him!

CONTENTS

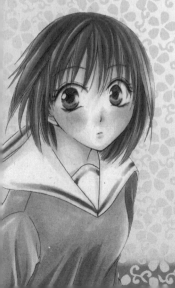

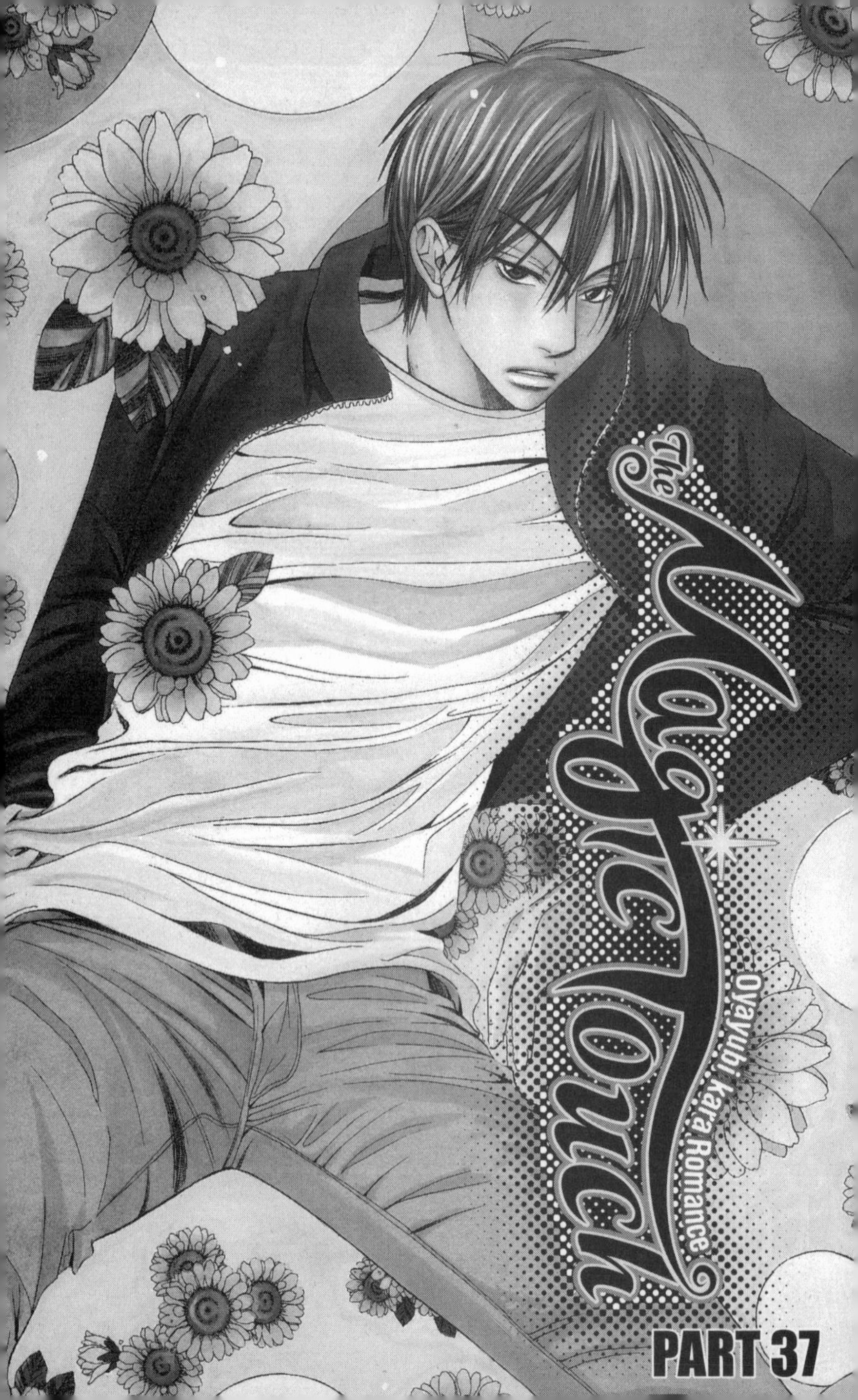
The Magic Touch
Oyayubi Kara Romance
PART 37

Chiaki Togu

Birthday: February 19

Blood Type: A

School: First-Year, Futouka Academy

Height: 155 cm

Hobby: Massage

Special Talent: Seeing the Tsuboz

Likes: Yosuke, Massage

Hates: Ghosts, Pepper

Siblings: Older Brother, Older Sister

Club in Middle School: Cooking Club

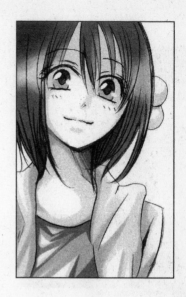

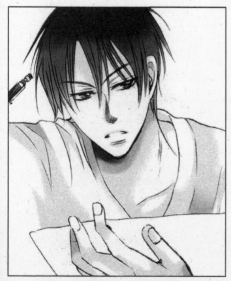

Yosuke Moriizumi

Birthday: May 28

Blood Type: A

School: First-Year, Futouka Academy

Height: 175 cm

Hobby: Computers, Reading

Special Talent: Good at Everything

Likes: Popcorn (Butter and Soy-Sauce Flavored)

Hates: Women Besides Chiaki

Siblings: Younger Brother

Club in Middle School: Soccer Club

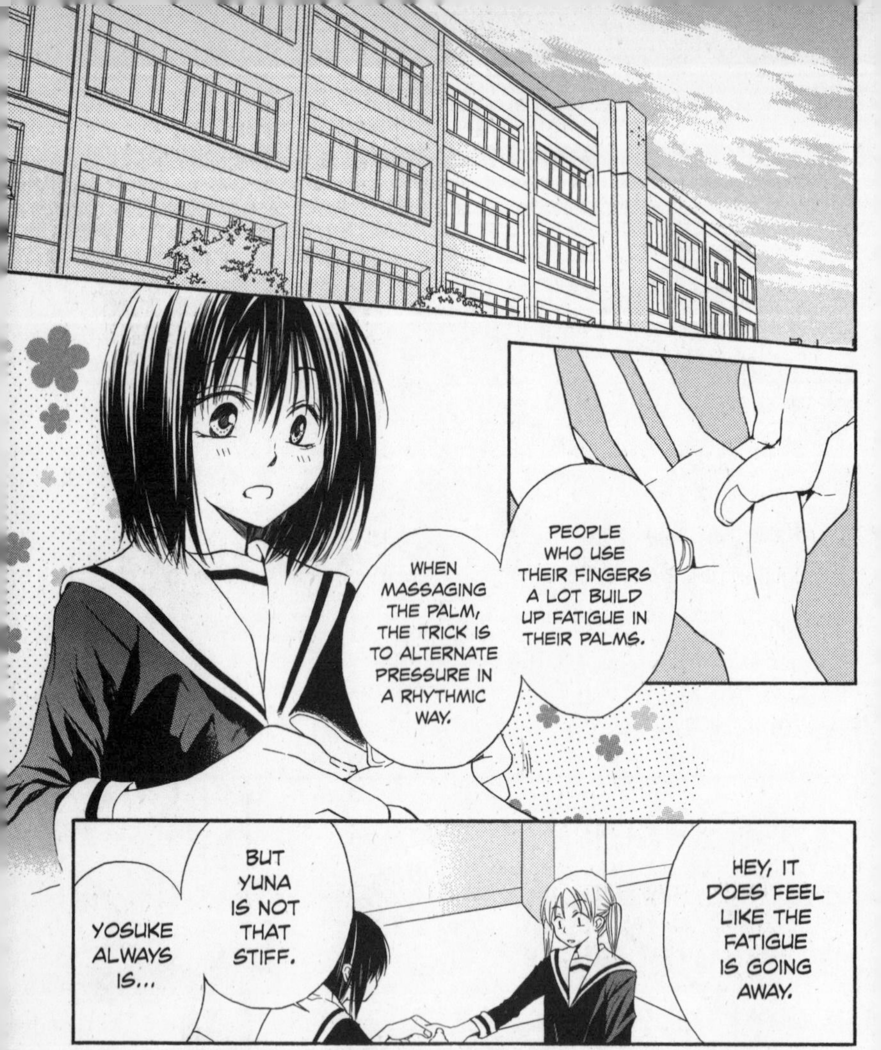
PEOPLE WHO USE THEIR FINGERS A LOT BUILD UP FATIGUE IN THEIR PALMS.
WHEN MASSAGING THE PALM, THE TRICK IS TO ALTERNATE PRESSURE IN A RHYTHMIC WAY.
HEY, IT DOES FEEL LIKE THE FATIGUE IS GOING AWAY.
BUT YUNA IS NOT THAT STIFF.
YOSUKE ALWAYS IS...

It's Volume 7.

Hello! It's been a while. This is Izumi Tsubaki. We've finally passed the middle of the story and entered the climax. This volume contains a series that focuses on Yosuke. The side columns will talk about how I've been doing recently, since I'm often asked in letters. (There's really not that much...) The cover includes Tanaka.

See you later then! I hope to see you again in volume 8.

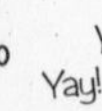
Yay!
Yay!
...even though it's at the beginning.
This is the postscript...

SPECIAL THANKS

My younger sister, my family, editor, Shiina, Kana... and you!
Thank you all!

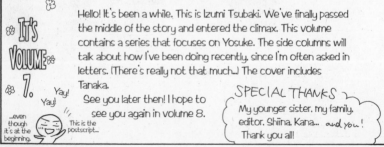

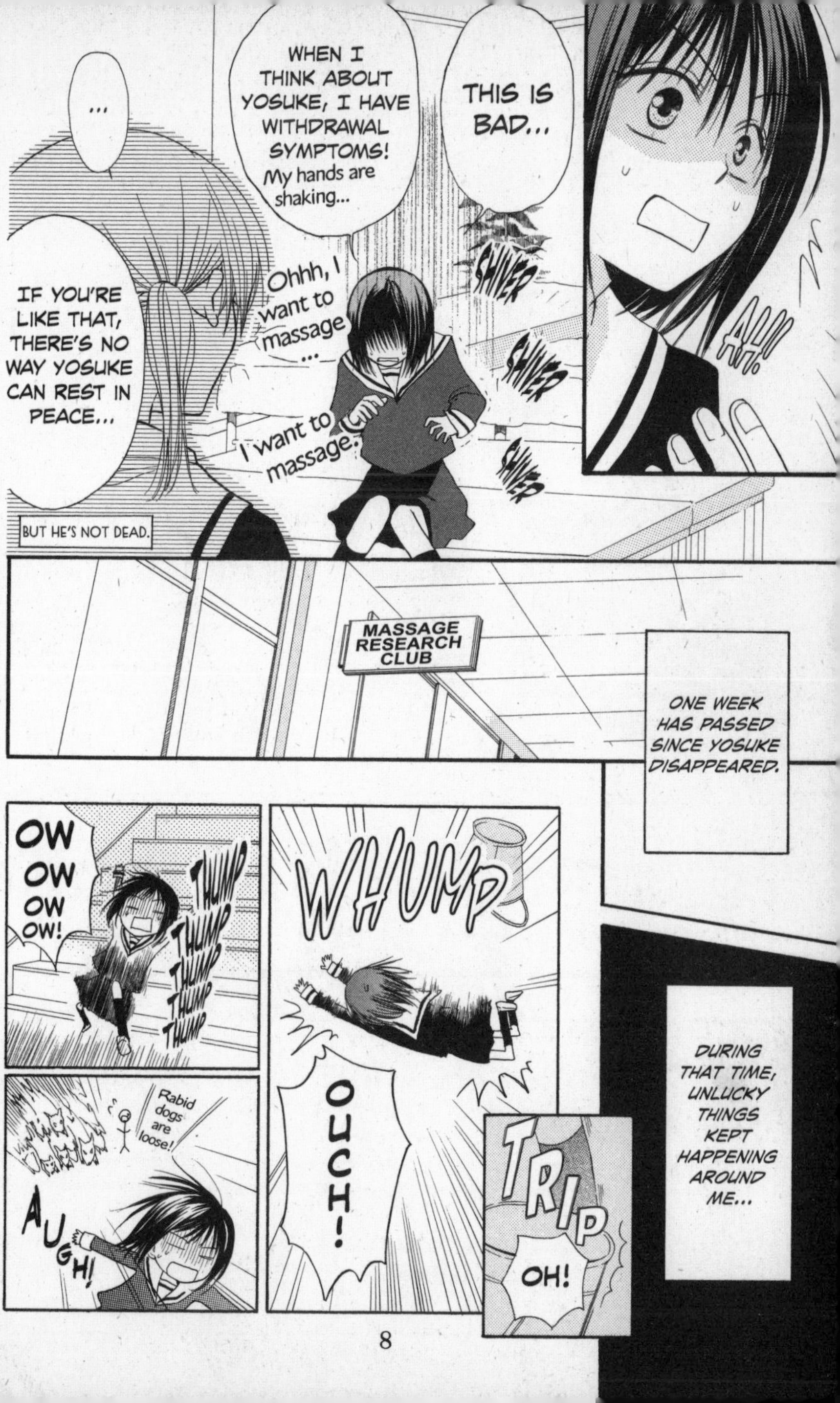
AH!!
THIS IS BAD...
WHEN I THINK ABOUT YOSUKE, I HAVE WITHDRAWAL SYMPTOMS! My hands are shaking...
SHIVER
Ohhh, I want to massage...
I want to massage.
SHIVER
SHIVER
...
IF YOU'RE LIKE THAT, THERE'S NO WAY YOSUKE CAN REST IN PEACE...
BUT HE'S NOT DEAD.
ONE WEEK HAS PASSED SINCE YOSUKE DISAPPEARED.
MASSAGE RESEARCH CLUB
DURING THAT TIME, UNLUCKY THINGS KEPT HAPPENING AROUND ME...
TRIP
OH!
WHUMP
OUCH!
THUMP THUMP THUMP THUMP THUMP
OW OW OW OW!
Rabid dogs are loose!
AUGH!

THIS MIGHT BE...

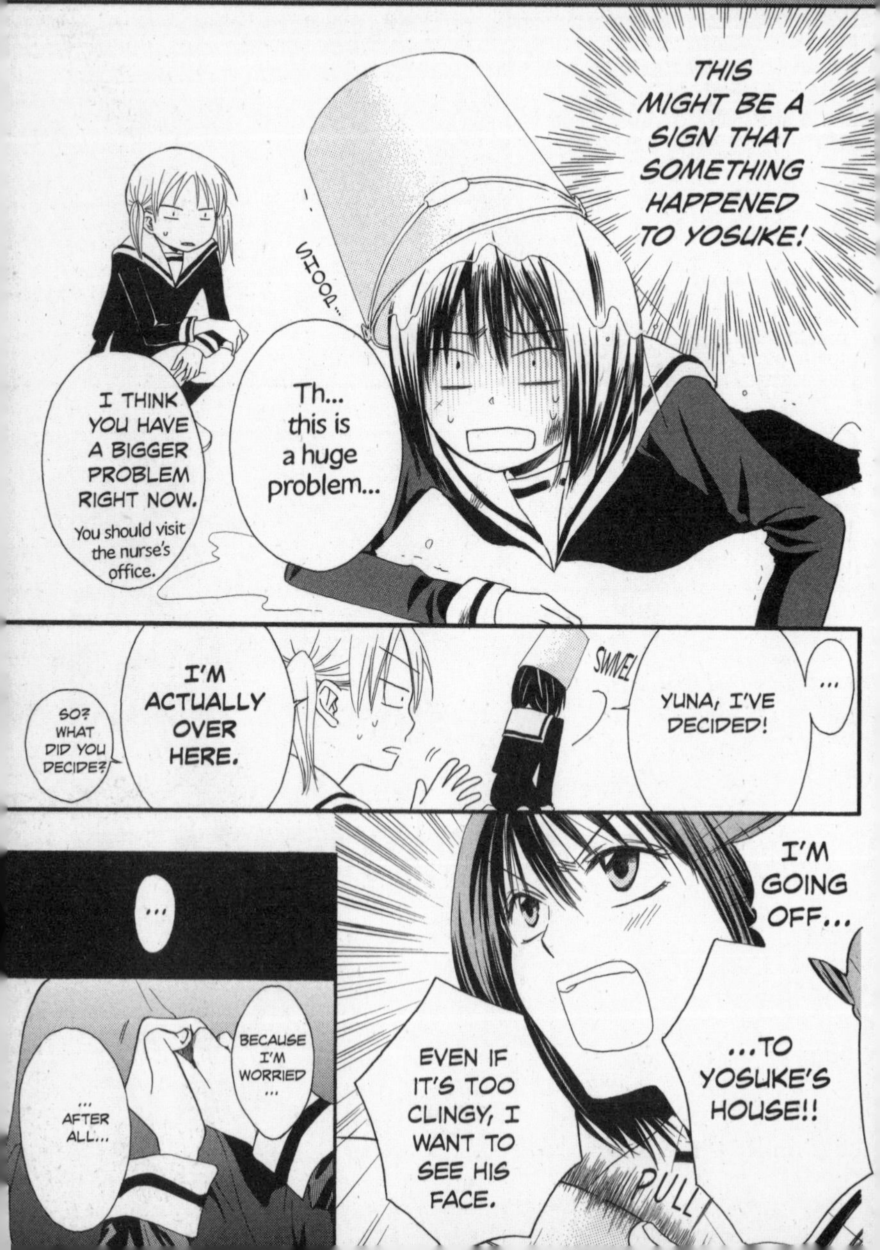
THIS MIGHT BE A SIGN THAT SOMETHING HAPPENED TO YOSUKE!
SHOOP...
Th... this is a huge problem...
I THINK YOU HAVE A BIGGER PROBLEM RIGHT NOW.
You should visit the nurse's office.
...
YUNA, I'VE DECIDED!
SWIVEL
I'M ACTUALLY OVER HERE.
SO? WHAT DID YOU DECIDE?
I'M GOING OFF...
...TO YOSUKE'S HOUSE!!
EVEN IF IT'S TOO CLINGY, I WANT TO SEE HIS FACE.
PULL
...
BECAUSE I'M WORRIED...
... AFTER ALL...

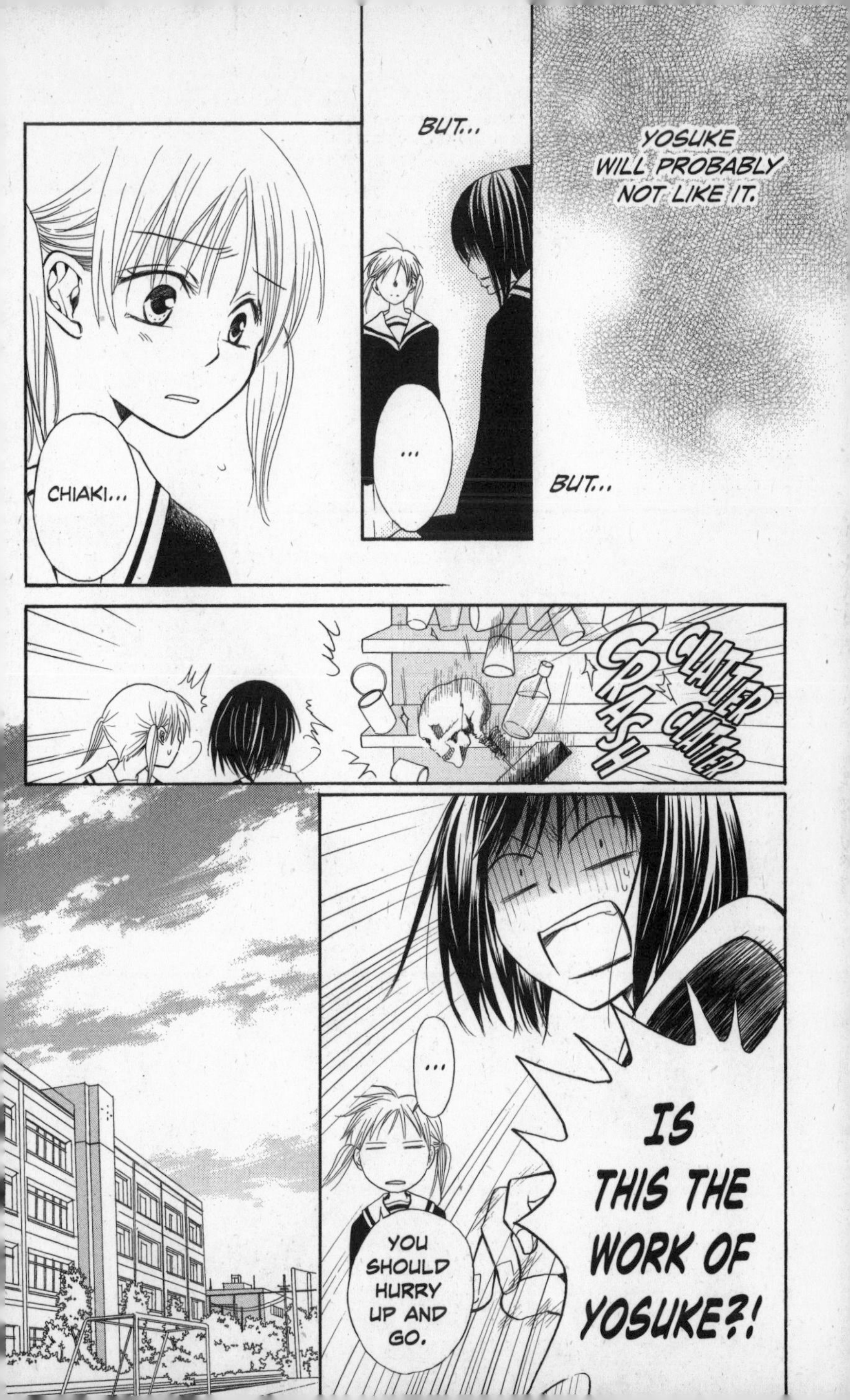
YOSUKE WILL PROBABLY NOT LIKE IT.
BUT...
BUT...
...
CHIAKI...
CLATTER CLATTER
CRASH
IS THIS THE WORK OF YOSUKE?!
...
YOU SHOULD HURRY UP AND GO.

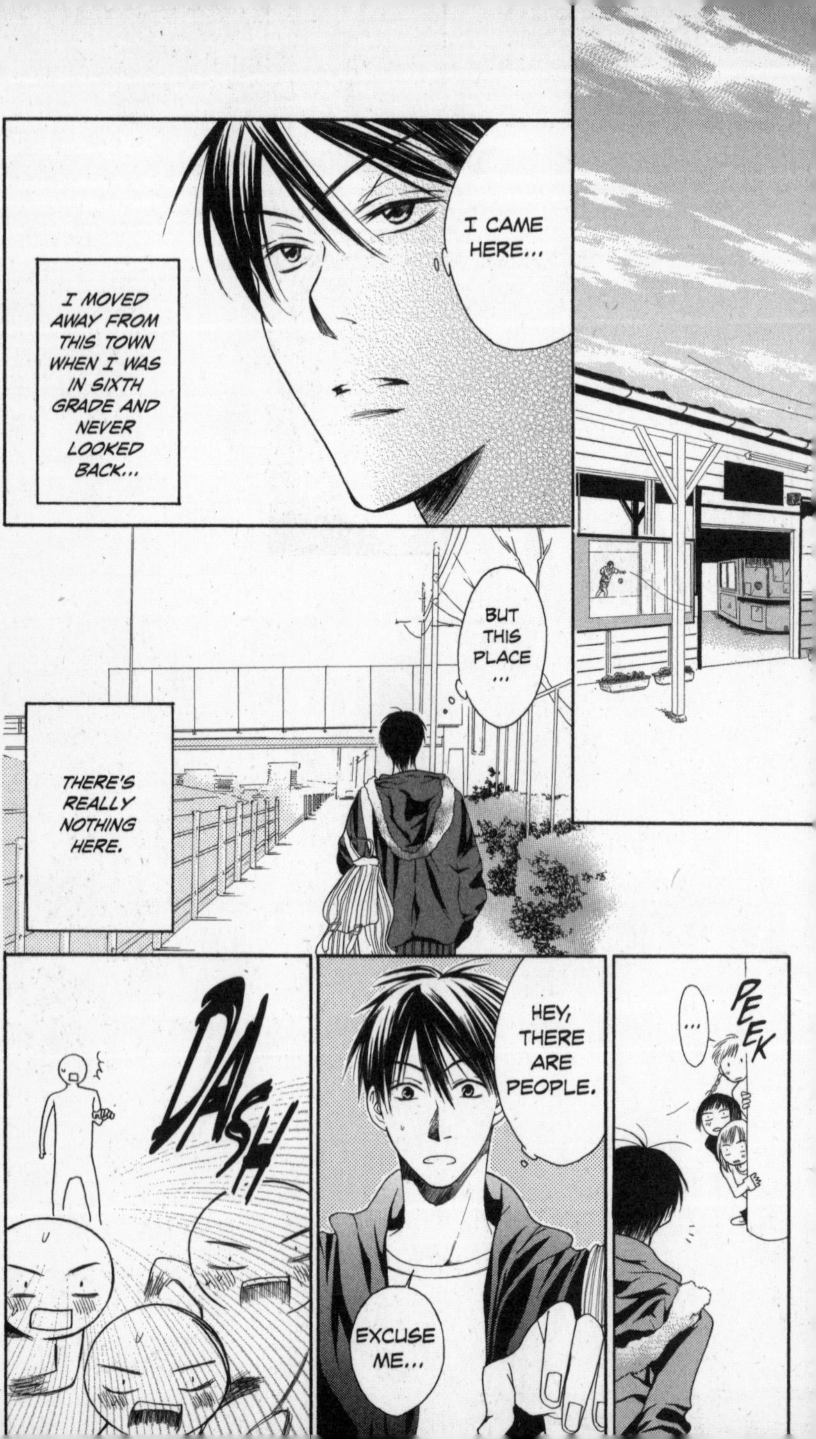
I CAME HERE...
I MOVED AWAY FROM THIS TOWN WHEN I WAS IN SIXTH GRADE AND NEVER LOOKED BACK...
BUT THIS PLACE...
THERE'S REALLY NOTHING HERE.
...
PEEK
HEY, THERE ARE PEOPLE.
EXCUSE ME...
DASH

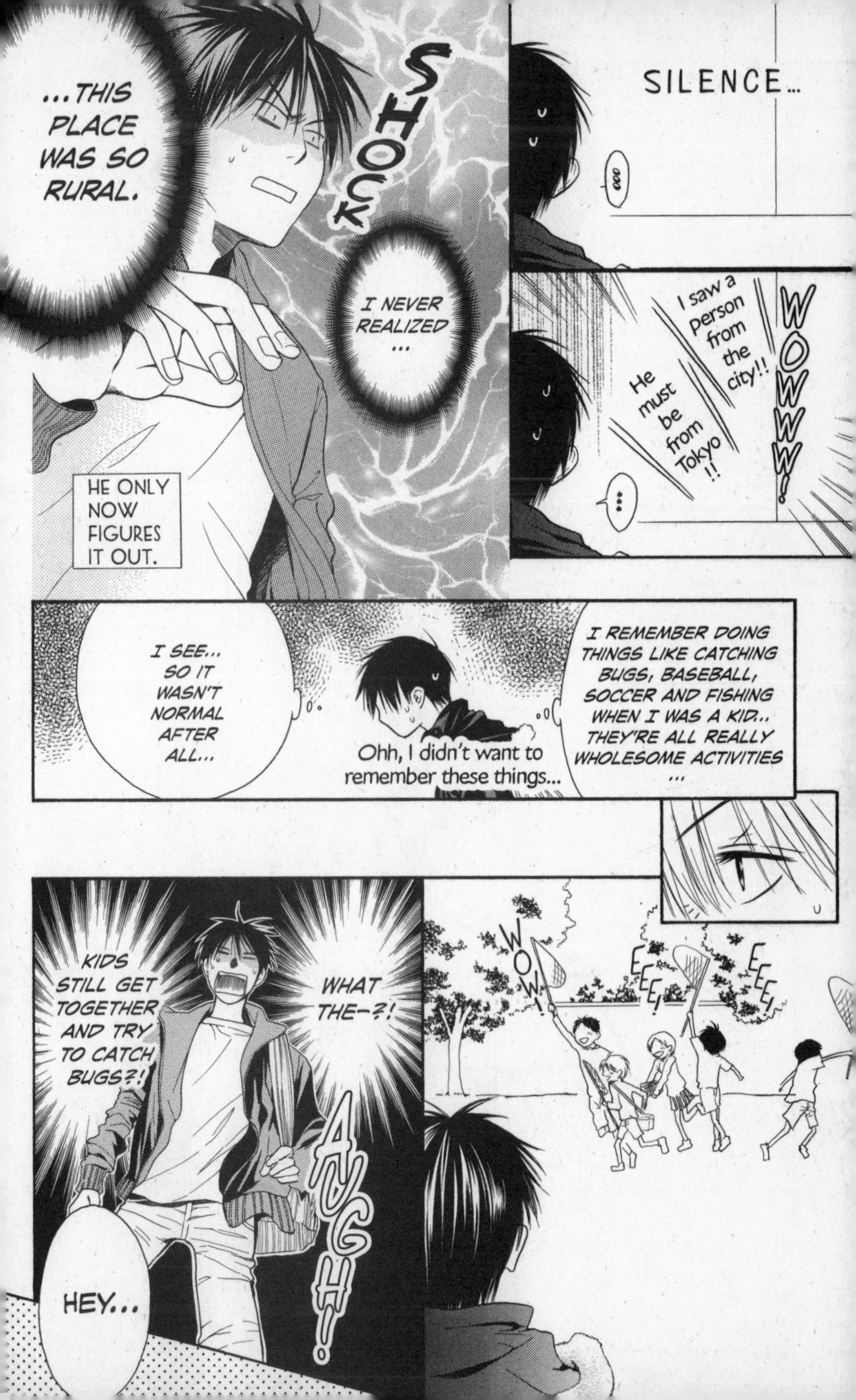
SILENCE...
...
WOWWW!
I saw a person from the city!!
He must be from Tokyo!!
...
SHOCK
I NEVER REALIZED...
...THIS PLACE WAS SO RURAL.
HE ONLY NOW FIGURES IT OUT.
I REMEMBER DOING THINGS LIKE CATCHING BUGS, BASEBALL, SOCCER AND FISHING WHEN I WAS A KID... THEY'RE ALL REALLY WHOLESOME ACTIVITIES...
Ohh, I didn't want to remember these things...
I SEE... SO IT WASN'T NORMAL AFTER ALL...
EEE!
EEE!
WOW!
WHAT THE-?!
KIDS STILL GET TOGETHER AND TRY TO CATCH BUGS?!
AUGH!!
HEY...

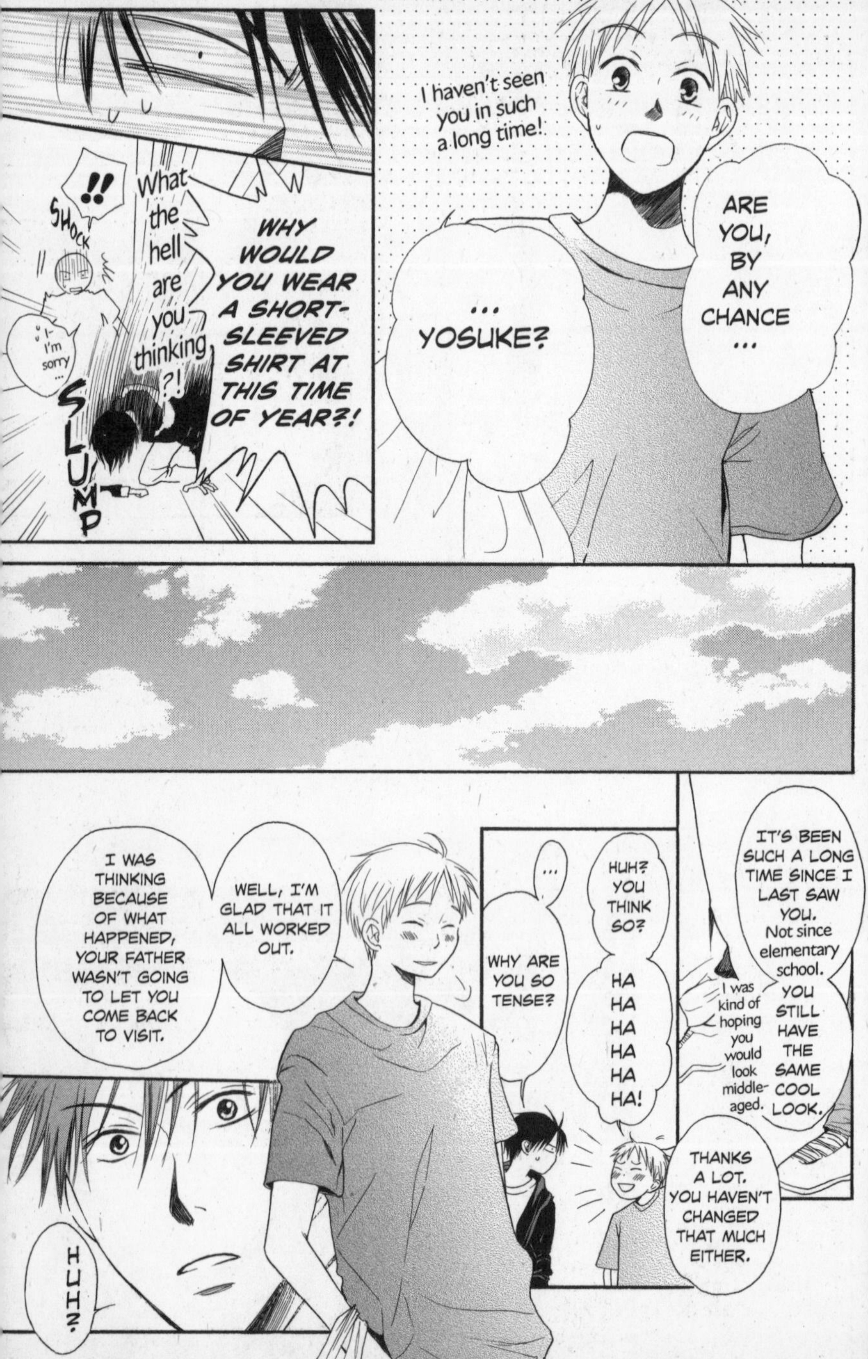
I haven't seen you in such a long time!
ARE YOU, BY ANY CHANCE ...
... YOSUKE?
WHY WOULD YOU WEAR A SHORT-SLEEVED SHIRT AT THIS TIME OF YEAR?!
What the hell are you thinking?!
!!
SHOCK
I-I'm sorry ...
SLUMP
IT'S BEEN SUCH A LONG TIME SINCE I LAST SAW YOU. Not since elementary school.
YOU STILL HAVE THE SAME COOL LOOK.
I was kind of hoping you would look middle-aged.
THANKS A LOT. YOU HAVEN'T CHANGED THAT MUCH EITHER.
HUH? YOU THINK SO?
HA HA HA HA HA HA!
...
WHY ARE YOU SO TENSE?
WELL, I'M GLAD THAT IT ALL WORKED OUT.
I WAS THINKING BECAUSE OF WHAT HAPPENED, YOUR FATHER WASN'T GOING TO LET YOU COME BACK TO VISIT.
HUH?

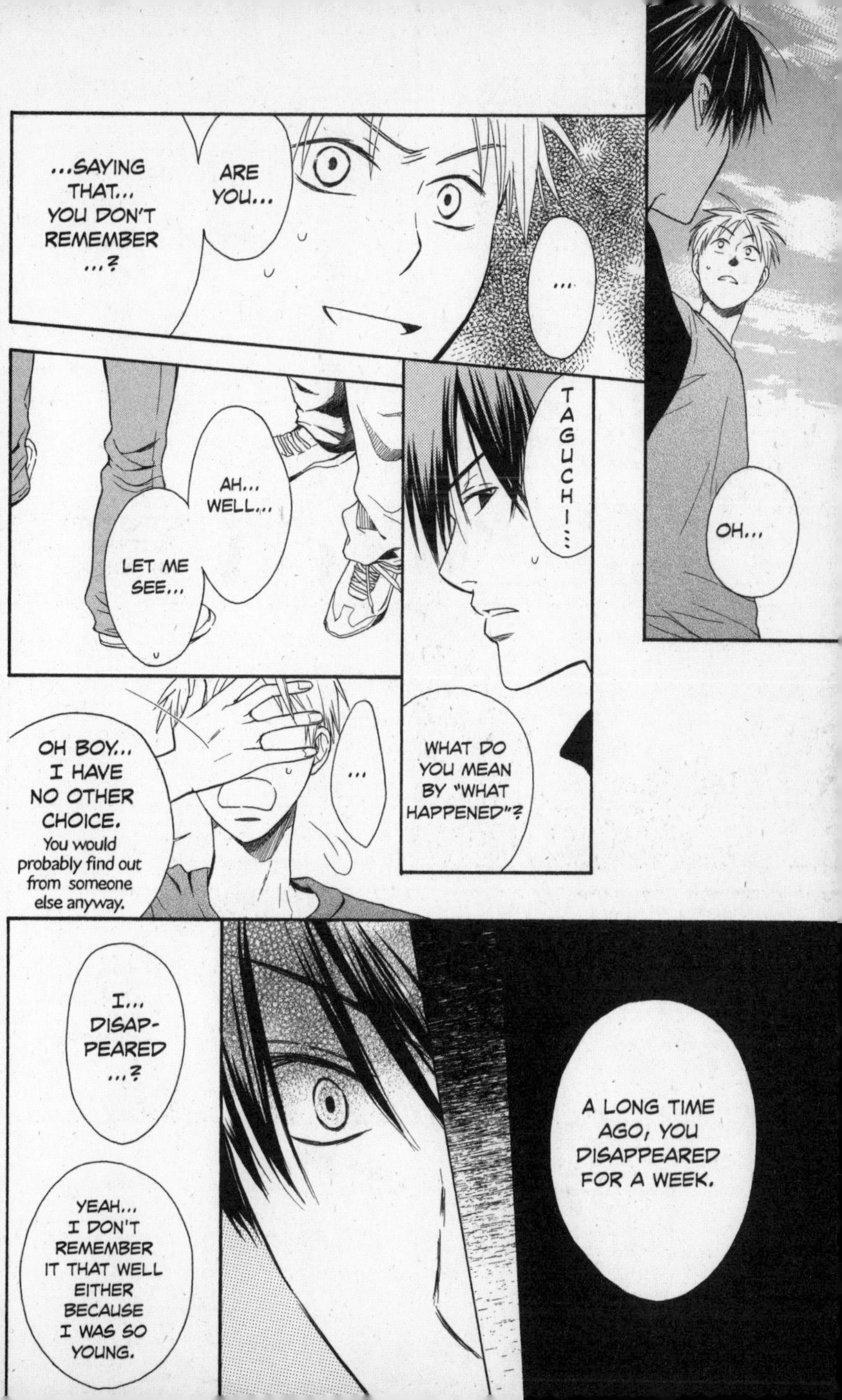
OH...
...
ARE YOU...
...SAYING THAT... YOU DON'T REMEMBER ...?
TAGUCHI...!
WHAT DO YOU MEAN BY "WHAT HAPPENED"?
AH... WELL...
LET ME SEE...
...
OH BOY... I HAVE NO OTHER CHOICE.
You would probably find out from someone else anyway.
A LONG TIME AGO, YOU DISAPPEARED FOR A WEEK.
I... DISAPPEARED ...?
YEAH... I DON'T REMEMBER IT THAT WELL EITHER BECAUSE I WAS SO YOUNG.

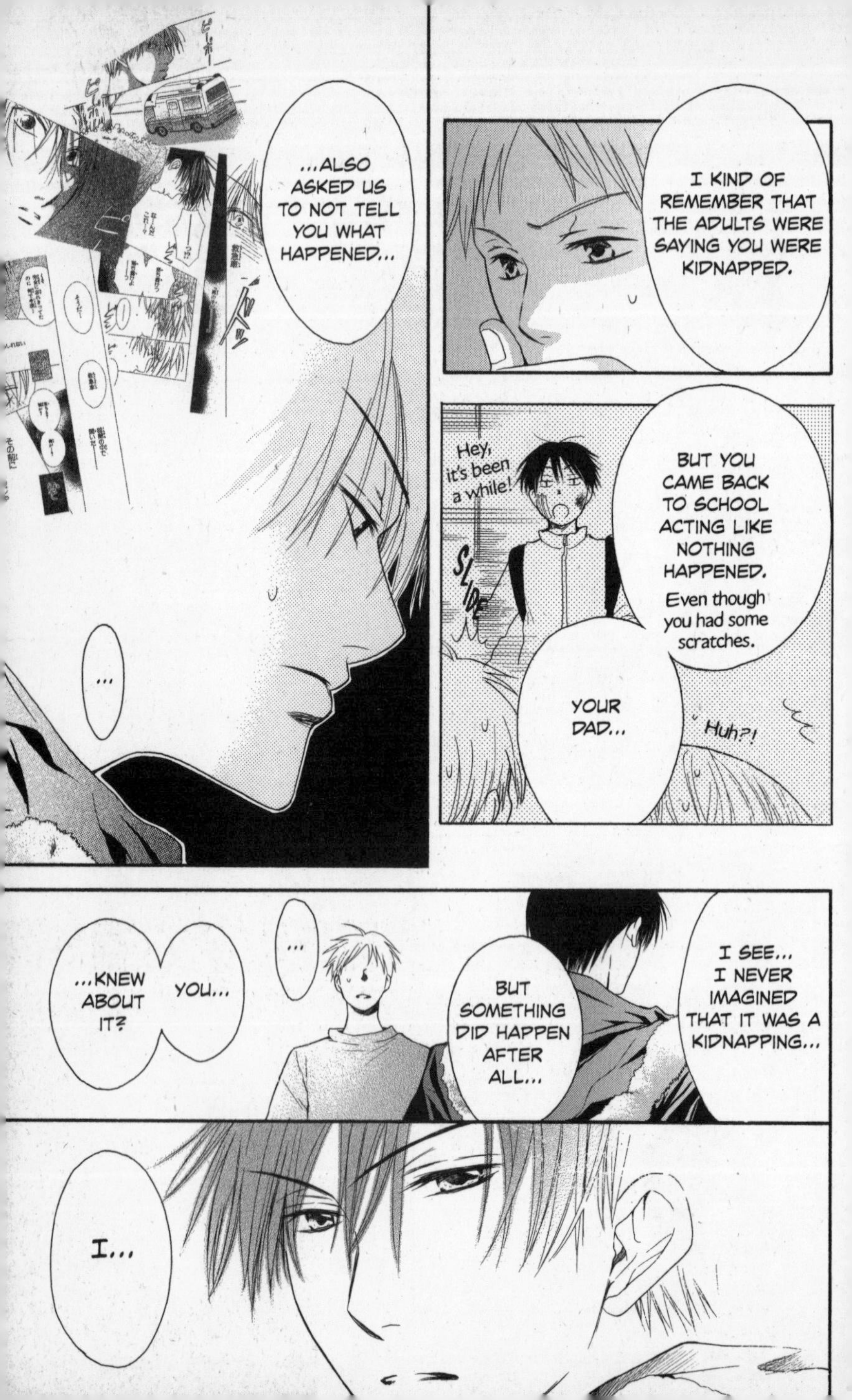
I KIND OF REMEMBER THAT THE ADULTS WERE SAYING YOU WERE KIDNAPPED.
BUT YOU CAME BACK TO SCHOOL ACTING LIKE NOTHING HAPPENED.
Hey, it's been a while!
SLIDE
Even though you had some scratches.
Huh?!
YOUR DAD...
...ALSO ASKED US TO NOT TELL YOU WHAT HAPPENED...
...
I SEE... I NEVER IMAGINED THAT IT WAS A KIDNAPPING...
BUT SOMETHING DID HAPPEN AFTER ALL...
...
YOU...
...KNEW ABOUT IT?
I...

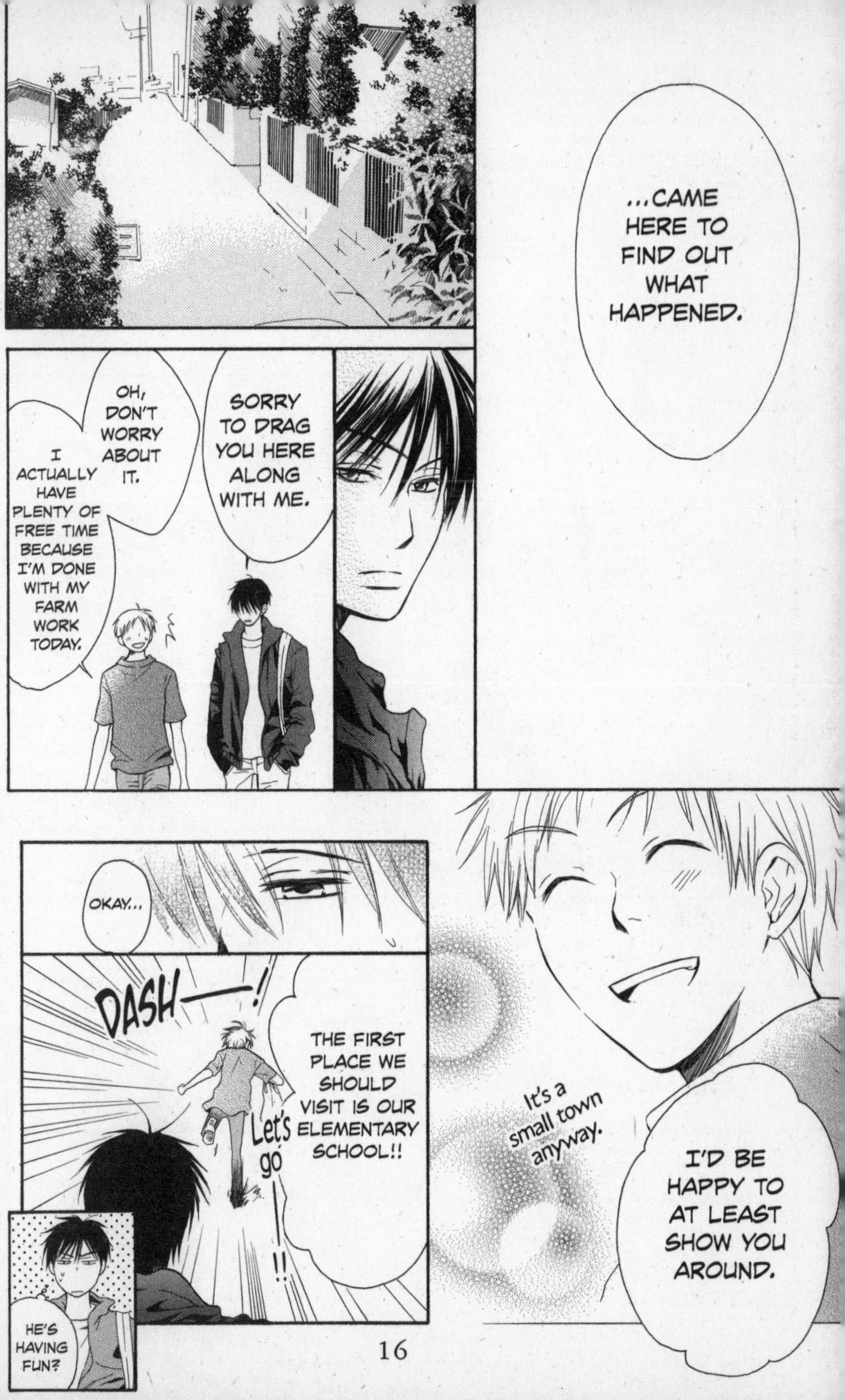
...CAME HERE TO FIND OUT WHAT HAPPENED.
SORRY TO DRAG YOU HERE ALONG WITH ME.
OH, DON'T WORRY ABOUT IT.
I ACTUALLY HAVE PLENTY OF FREE TIME BECAUSE I'M DONE WITH MY FARM WORK TODAY.
It's a small town anyway.
I'D BE HAPPY TO AT LEAST SHOW YOU AROUND.
OKAY...
THE FIRST PLACE WE SHOULD VISIT IS OUR ELEMENTARY SCHOOL!!
Let's go—!!
DASH—!
HE'S HAVING FUN?

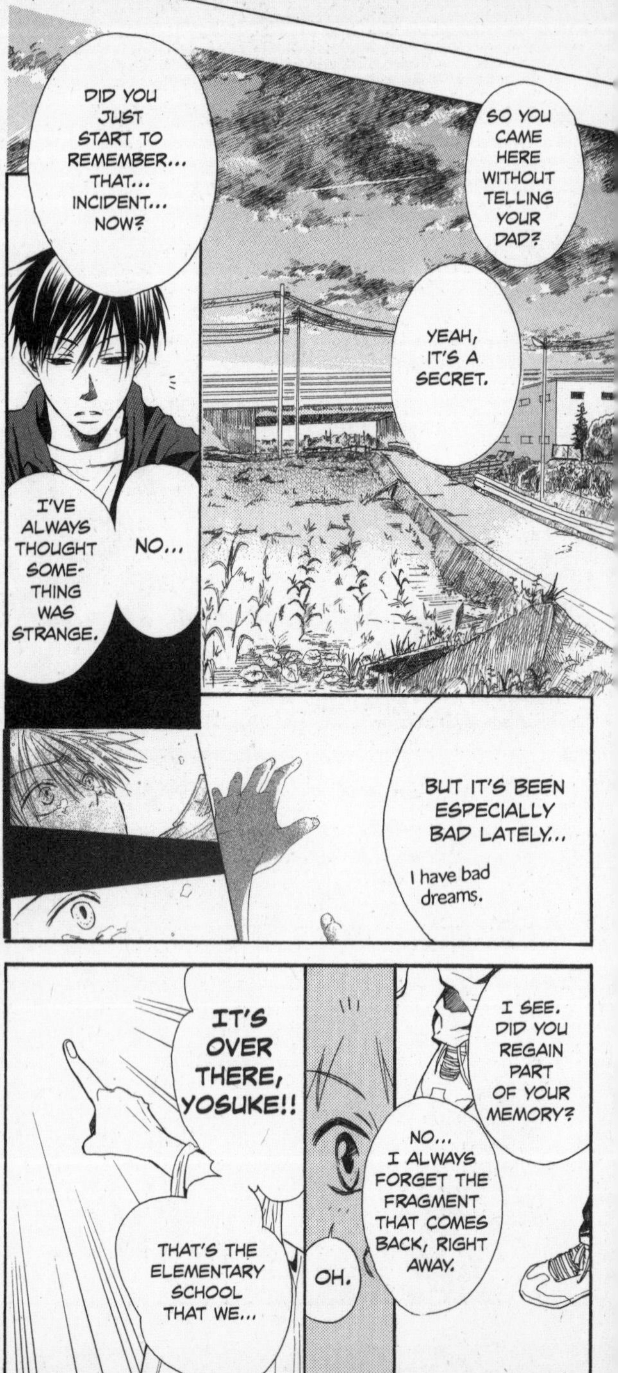
SO YOU CAME HERE WITHOUT TELLING YOUR DAD?
YEAH, IT'S A SECRET.
DID YOU JUST START TO REMEMBER... THAT... INCIDENT... NOW?
NO...
I'VE ALWAYS THOUGHT SOME-THING WAS STRANGE.
BUT IT'S BEEN ESPECIALLY BAD LATELY...
I have bad dreams.
I SEE. DID YOU REGAIN PART OF YOUR MEMORY?
NO... I ALWAYS FORGET THE FRAGMENT THAT COMES BACK, RIGHT AWAY.
OH.
IT'S OVER THERE, YOSUKE!!
THAT'S THE ELEMENTARY SCHOOL THAT WE...

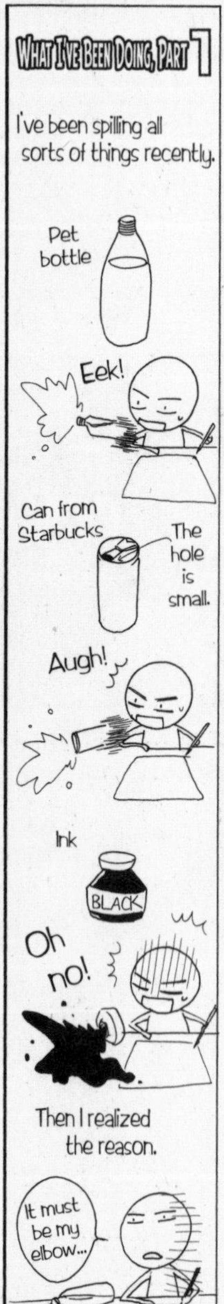
WHAT I'VE BEEN DOING, PART 1
I've been spilling all sorts of things recently.
Pet bottle
Eek!
Can from Starbucks
The hole is small.
Augh!
Ink
BLACK
Oh no!
Then I realized the reason.
It must be my elbow...

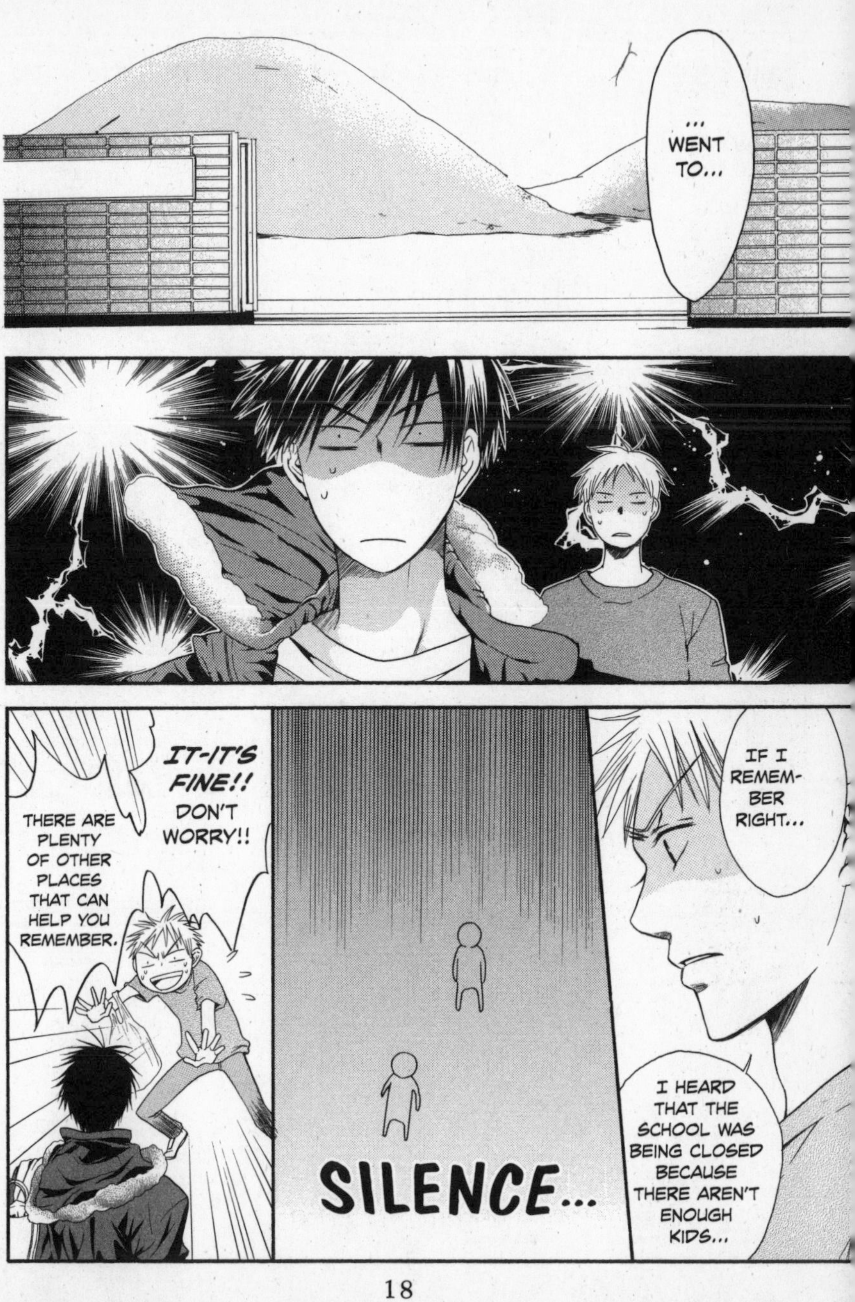
... WENT TO...
IF I REMEMBER RIGHT...
I HEARD THAT THE SCHOOL WAS BEING CLOSED BECAUSE THERE AREN'T ENOUGH KIDS...
SILENCE...
IT-IT'S FINE!! DON'T WORRY!!
THERE ARE PLENTY OF OTHER PLACES THAT CAN HELP YOU REMEMBER.

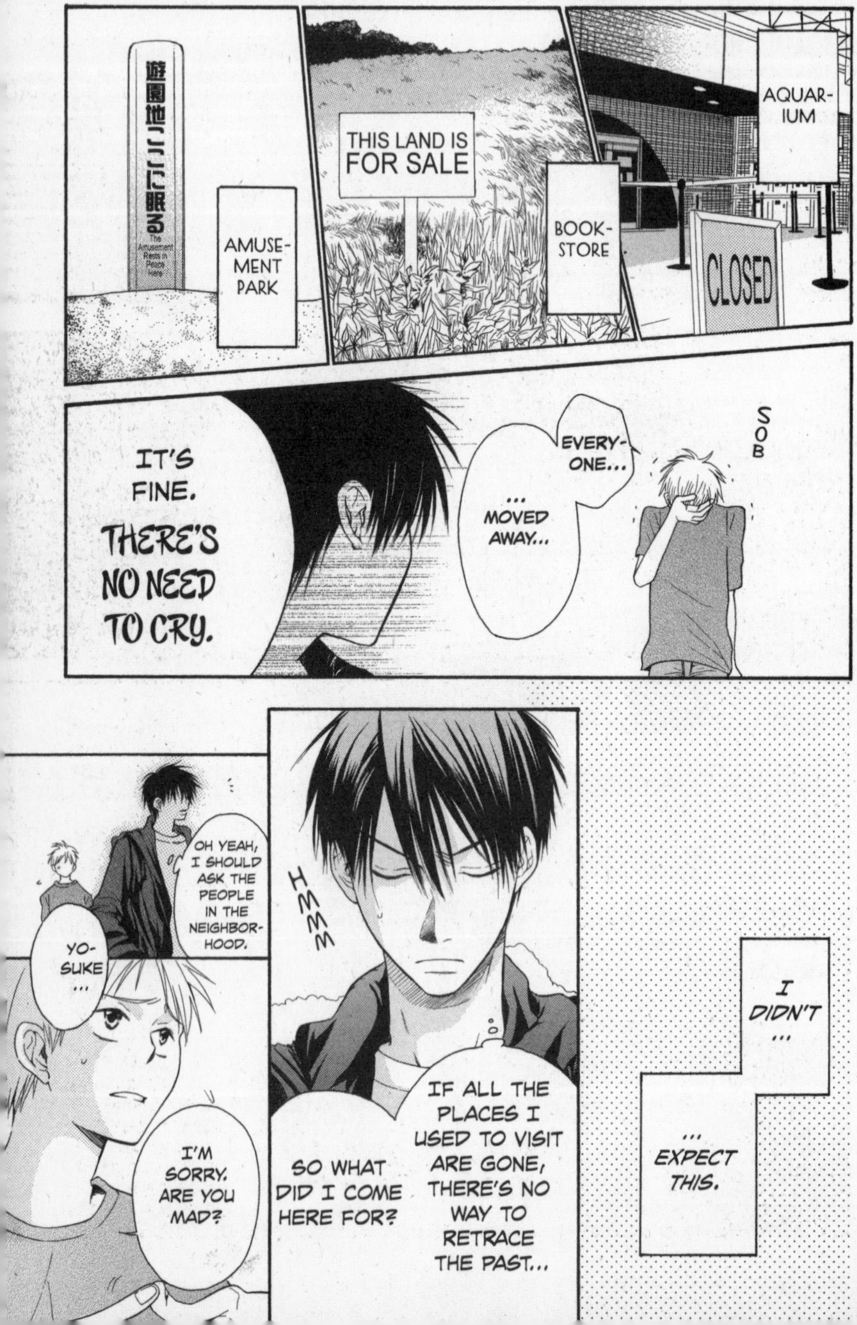
AQUAR-IUM
BOOK-STORE
CLOSED
THIS LAND IS FOR SALE
遊園地ここに眠る
The Amusement Rests in Peace Here
AMUSE-MENT PARK
SOB
EVERY-ONE... ...MOVED AWAY...
IT'S FINE.
THERE'S NO NEED TO CRY.
I DIDN'T...
...EXPECT THIS.
HMMM
IF ALL THE PLACES I USED TO VISIT ARE GONE, THERE'S NO WAY TO RETRACE THE PAST...
SO WHAT DID I COME HERE FOR?
OH YEAH, I SHOULD ASK THE PEOPLE IN THE NEIGHBOR-HOOD.
YO-SUKE...
I'M SORRY. ARE YOU MAD?

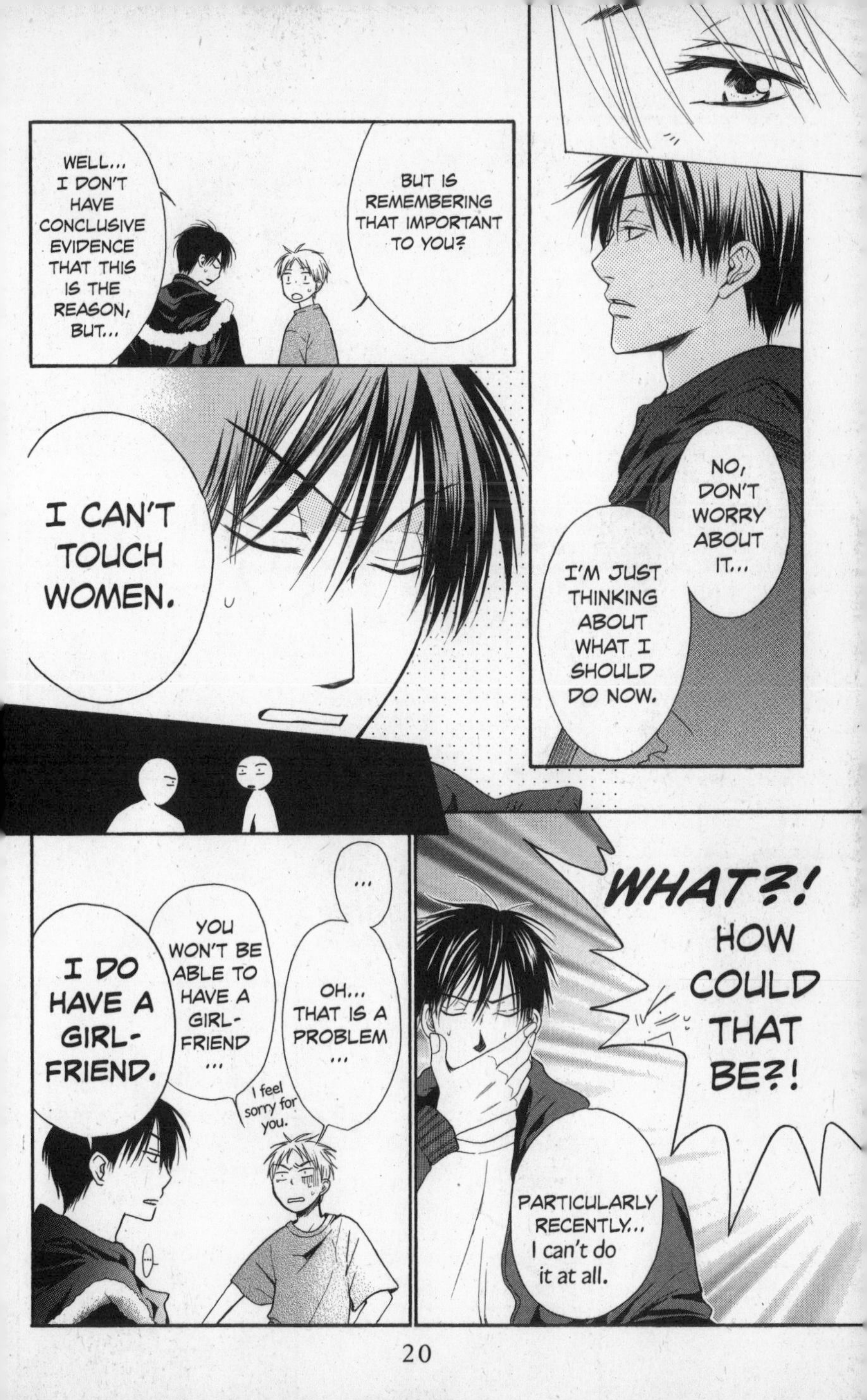
NO, DON'T WORRY ABOUT IT...
I'M JUST THINKING ABOUT WHAT I SHOULD DO NOW.
BUT IS REMEMBERING THAT IMPORTANT TO YOU?
WELL... I DON'T HAVE CONCLUSIVE EVIDENCE THAT THIS IS THE REASON, BUT...
I CAN'T TOUCH WOMEN.
WHAT?! HOW COULD THAT BE?!
PARTICULARLY RECENTLY... I can't do it at all.
...
OH... THAT IS A PROBLEM...
I feel sorry for you.
YOU WON'T BE ABLE TO HAVE A GIRL-FRIEND...
I DO HAVE A GIRL-FRIEND.
...

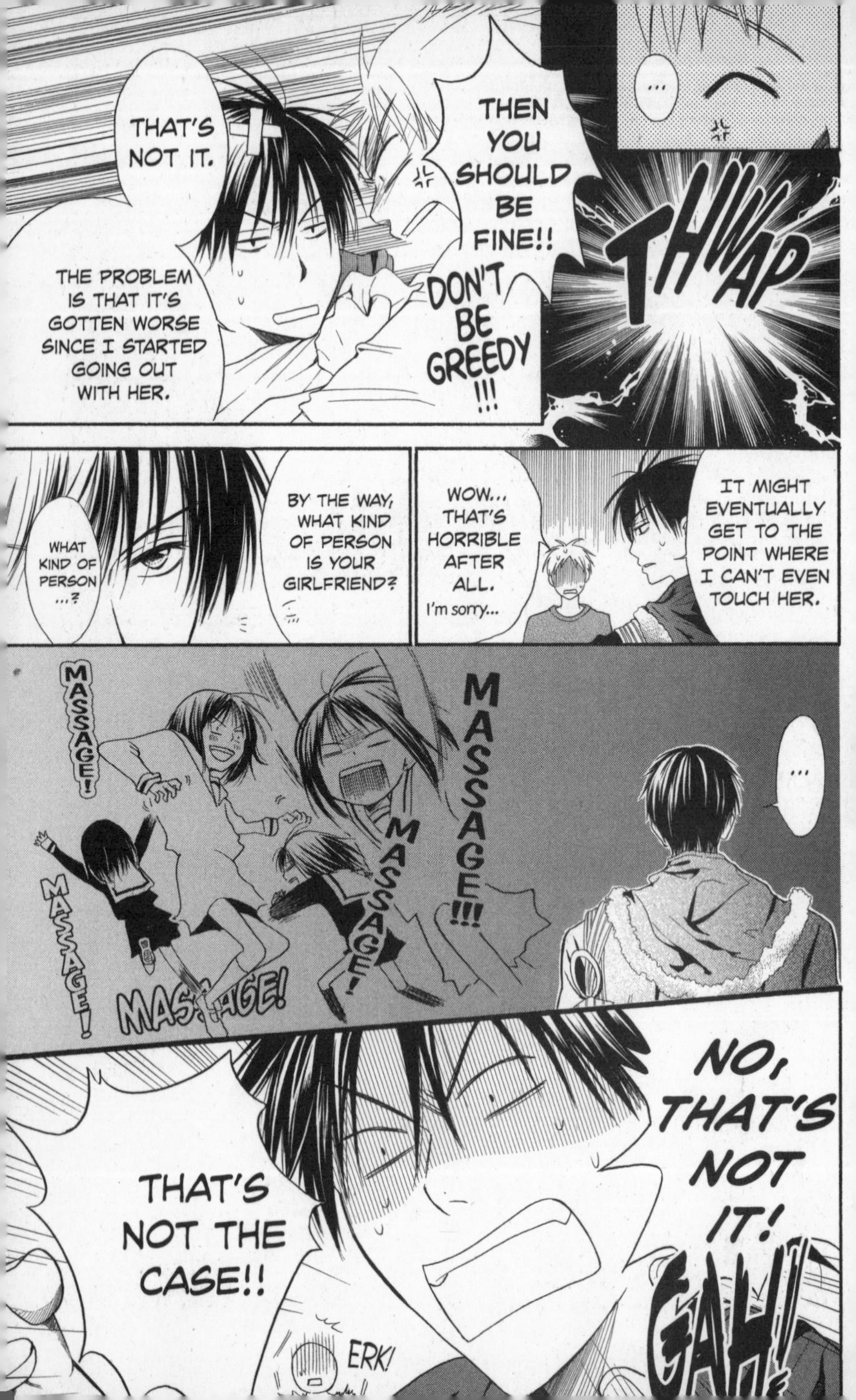
...
THWAP
THEN YOU SHOULD BE FINE!!
THAT'S NOT IT.
DON'T BE GREEDY!!!
THE PROBLEM IS THAT IT'S GOTTEN WORSE SINCE I STARTED GOING OUT WITH HER.
IT MIGHT EVENTUALLY GET TO THE POINT WHERE I CAN'T EVEN TOUCH HER.
WOW... THAT'S HORRIBLE AFTER ALL.
I'm sorry...
BY THE WAY, WHAT KIND OF PERSON IS YOUR GIRLFRIEND?
WHAT KIND OF PERSON ...?
...
MASSAGE!!!
MASSAGE!
MASSAGE!
MASSAGE!
MASSAGE!
NO, THAT'S NOT IT!
GAH!
THAT'S NOT THE CASE!!
ERK!

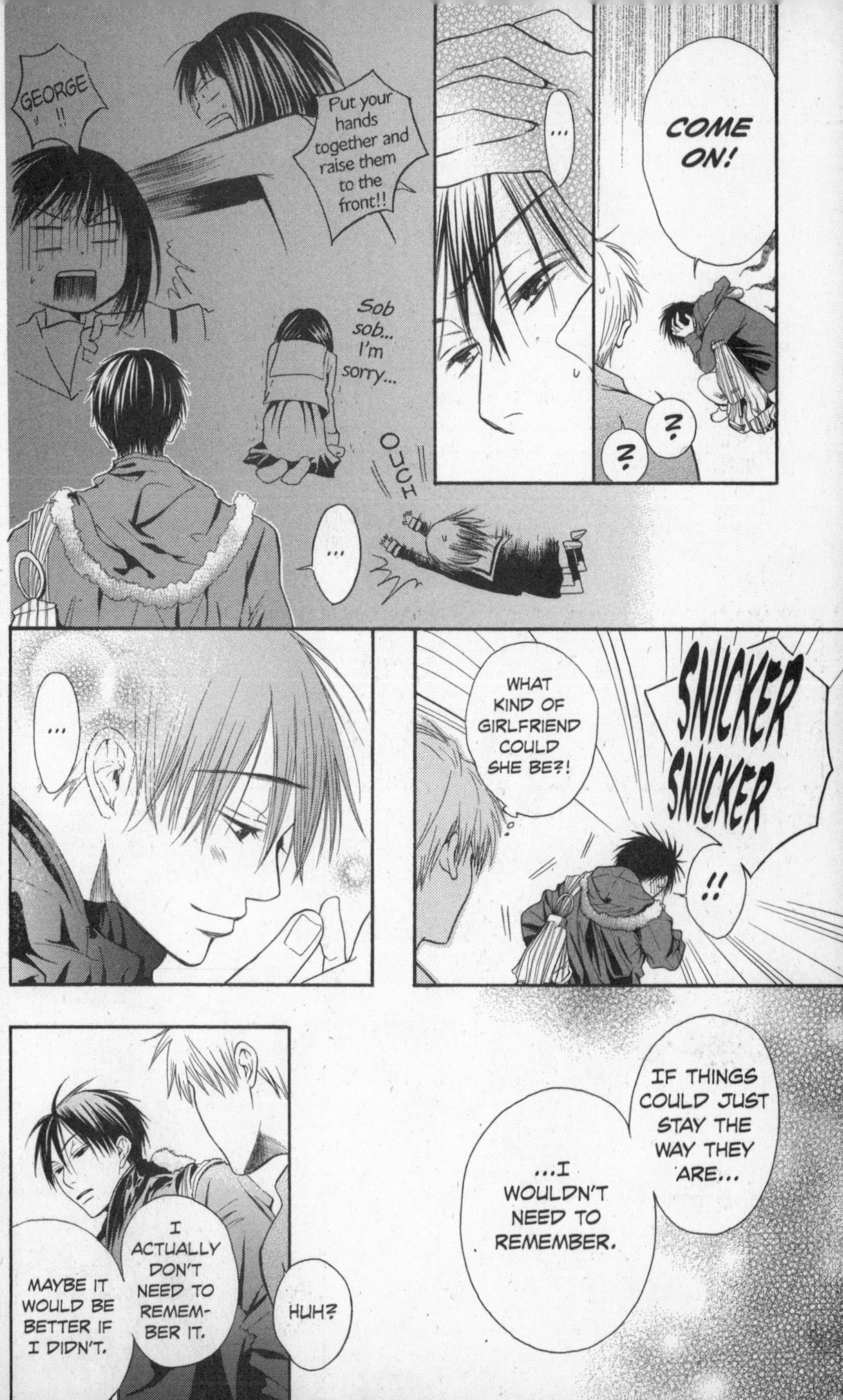
COME ON!
?
?
...
Put your hands together and raise them to the front!!
GEORGE !!
Sob sob... I'm sorry...
OUCH
...
SNICKER SNICKER
WHAT KIND OF GIRLFRIEND COULD SHE BE?!
!!
...
IF THINGS COULD JUST STAY THE WAY THEY ARE...
...I WOULDN'T NEED TO REMEMBER.
HUH?
I ACTUALLY DON'T NEED TO REMEMBER IT.
MAYBE IT WOULD BE BETTER IF I DIDN'T.

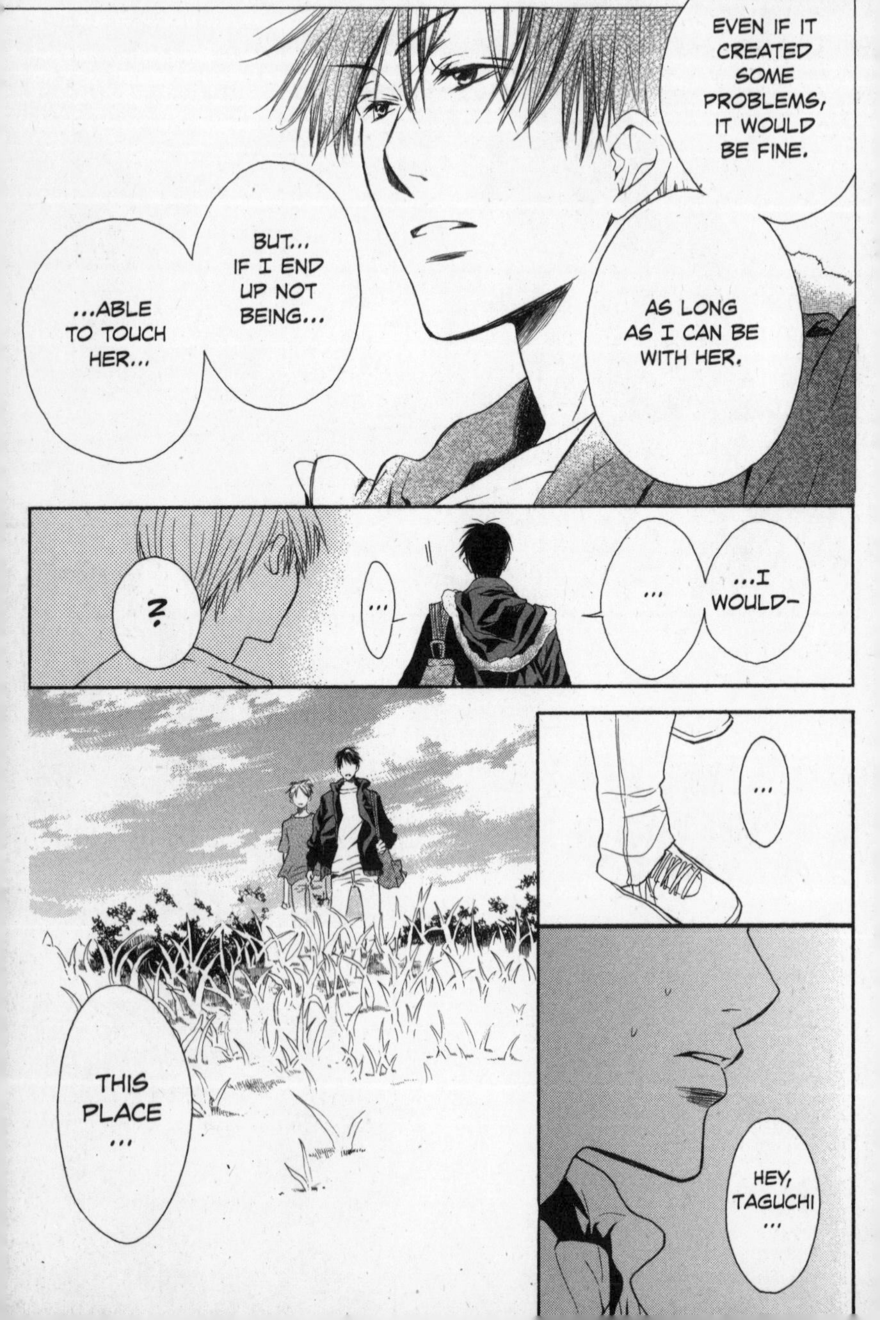
EVEN IF IT CREATED SOME PROBLEMS, IT WOULD BE FINE.
AS LONG AS I CAN BE WITH HER.
BUT... IF I END UP NOT BEING...
...ABLE TO TOUCH HER...
...I WOULD-
...
...
?
...
HEY, TAGUCHI ...
THIS PLACE ...

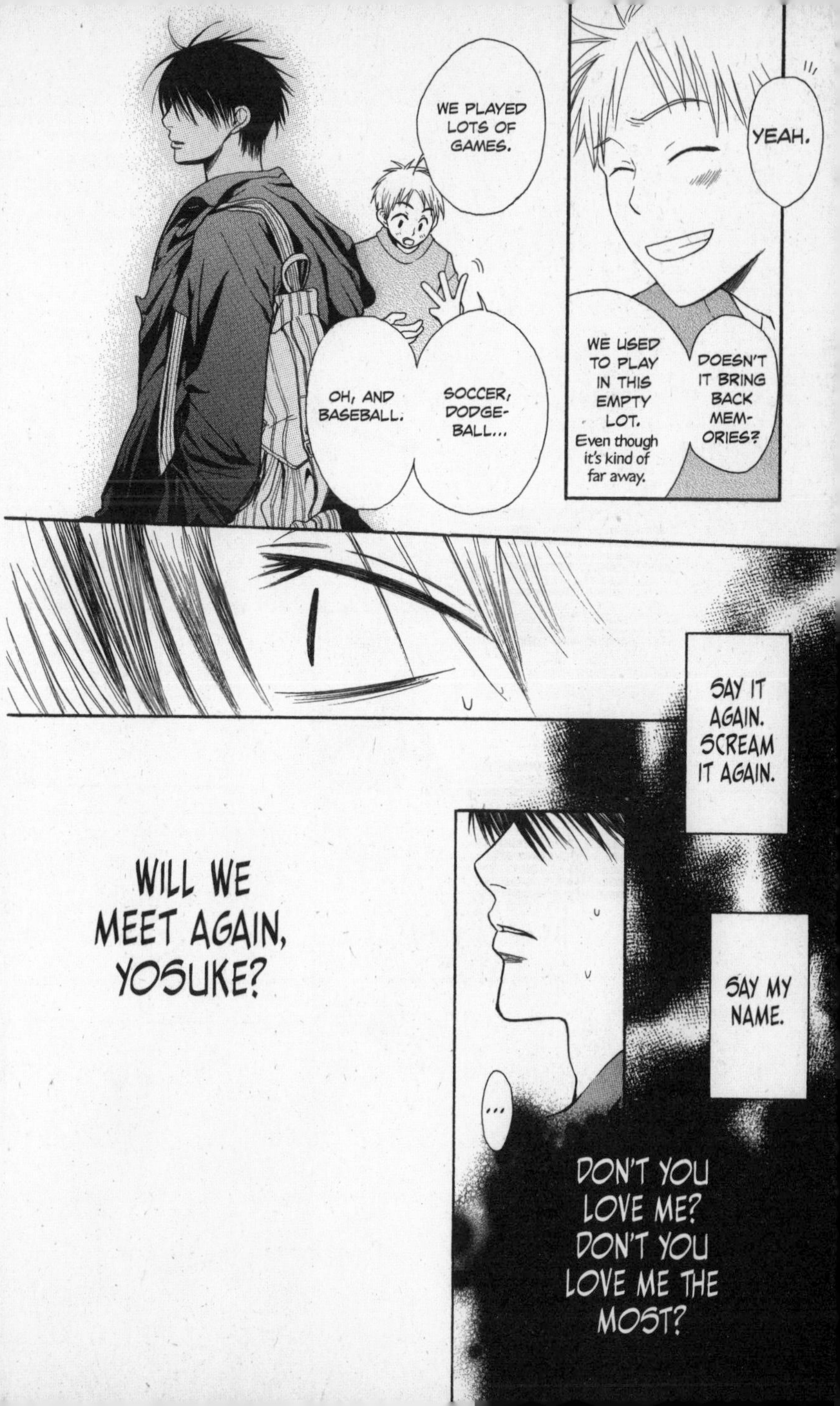
YEAH.
DOESN'T IT BRING BACK MEMORIES?
WE USED TO PLAY IN THIS EMPTY LOT. Even though it's kind of far away.
WE PLAYED LOTS OF GAMES.
SOCCER, DODGEBALL...
OH, AND BASEBALL.
SAY IT AGAIN. SCREAM IT AGAIN.
SAY MY NAME.
...
DON'T YOU LOVE ME? DON'T YOU LOVE ME THE MOST?
WILL WE MEET AGAIN, YOSUKE?

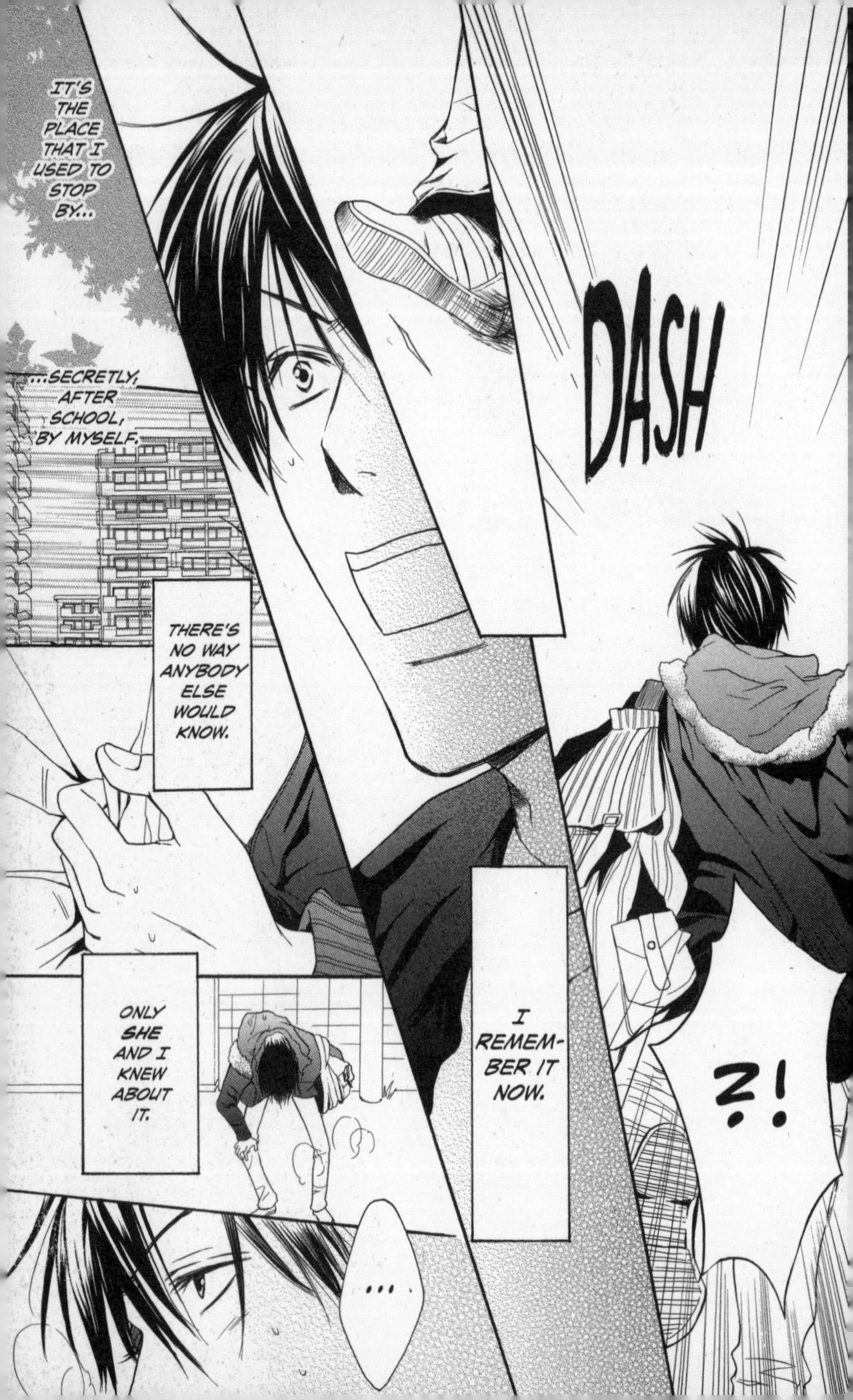
DASH
IT'S THE PLACE THAT I USED TO STOP BY...
...SECRETLY, AFTER SCHOOL, BY MYSELF.
THERE'S NO WAY ANYBODY ELSE WOULD KNOW.
?!
I REMEMBER IT NOW.
ONLY SHE AND I KNEW ABOUT IT.
...

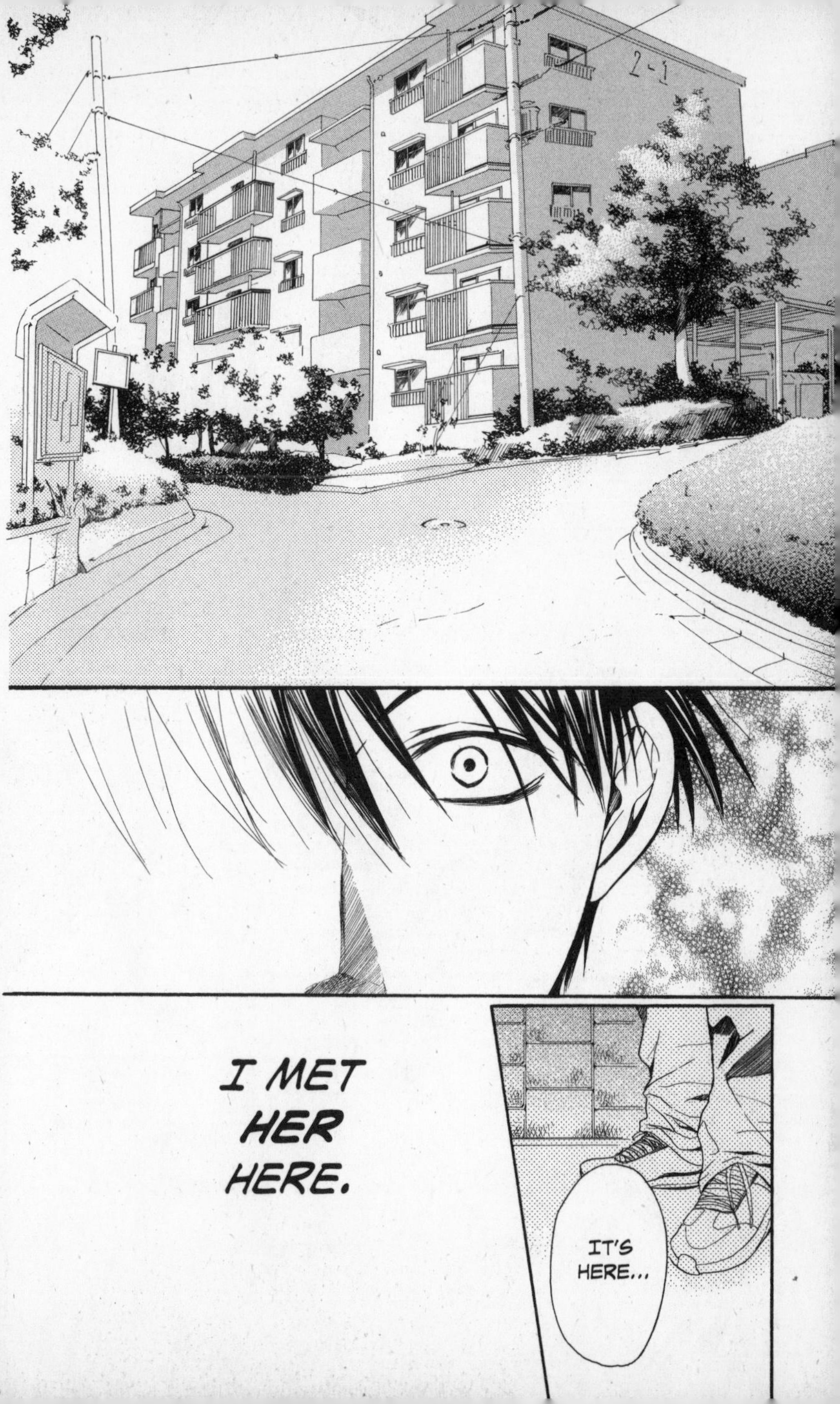
2-1
IT'S HERE...
I MET HER HERE.

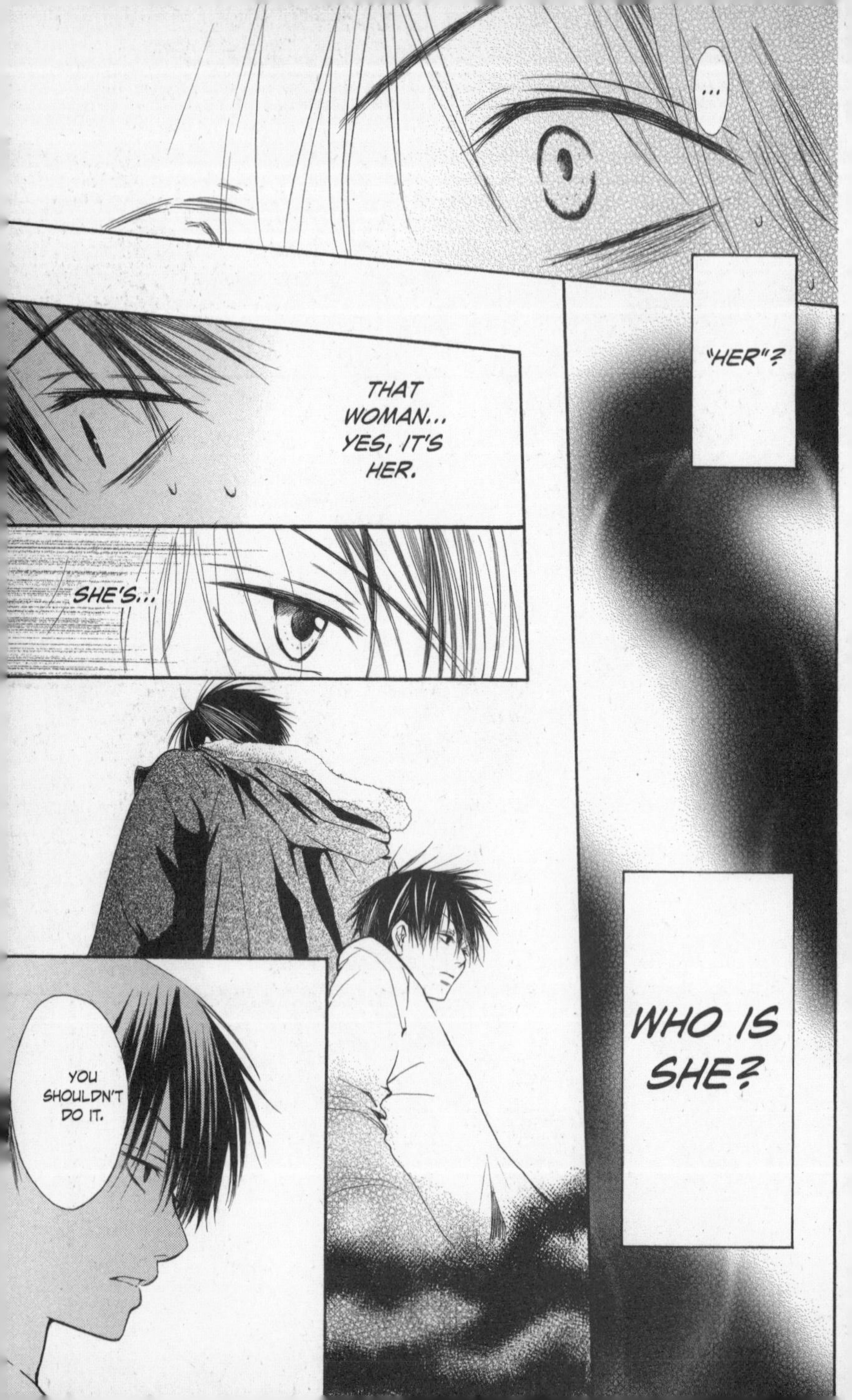
...
"HER"?
WHO IS SHE?
THAT WOMAN... YES, IT'S HER.
SHE'S...
YOU SHOULDN'T DO IT.

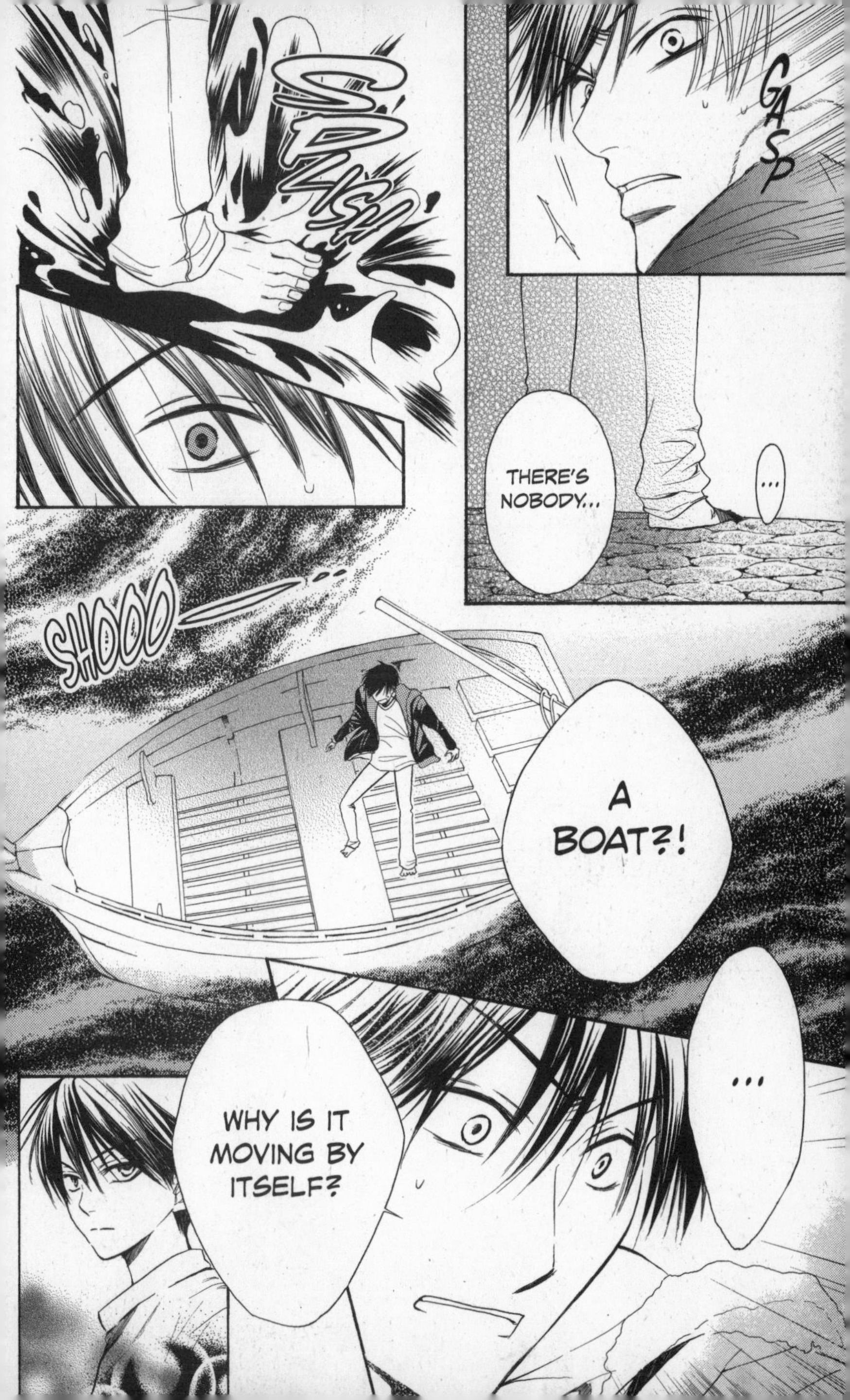
GASP
...
THERE'S NOBODY...
SPLASH
A BOAT?!
SHOOO
...
WHY IS IT MOVING BY ITSELF?

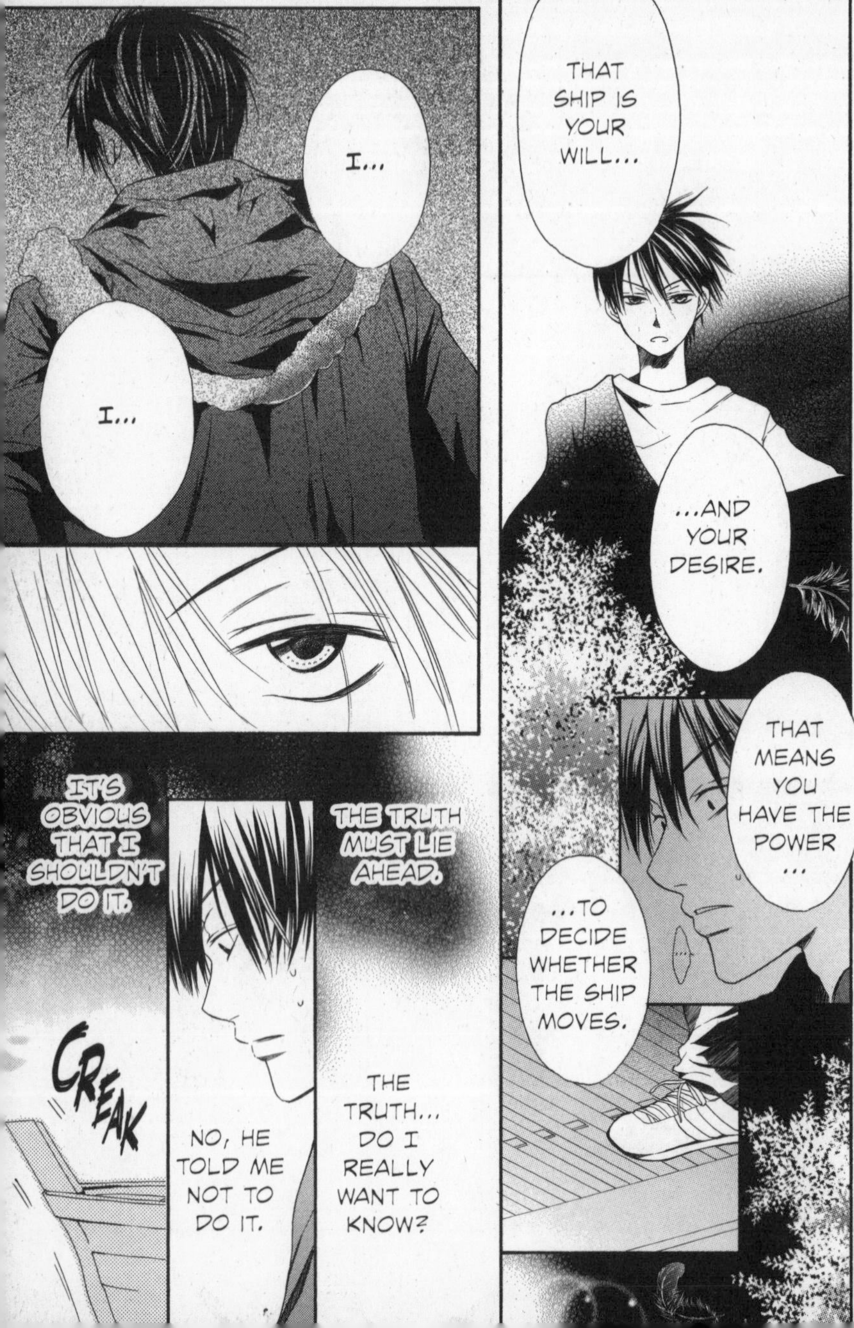
THAT SHIP IS YOUR WILL...
...AND YOUR DESIRE.
THAT MEANS YOU HAVE THE POWER ...
...TO DECIDE WHETHER THE SHIP MOVES.
I...
I...
THE TRUTH MUST LIE AHEAD.
IT'S OBVIOUS THAT I SHOULDN'T DO IT.
THE TRUTH... DO I REALLY WANT TO KNOW?
NO, HE TOLD ME NOT TO DO IT.
CREAK

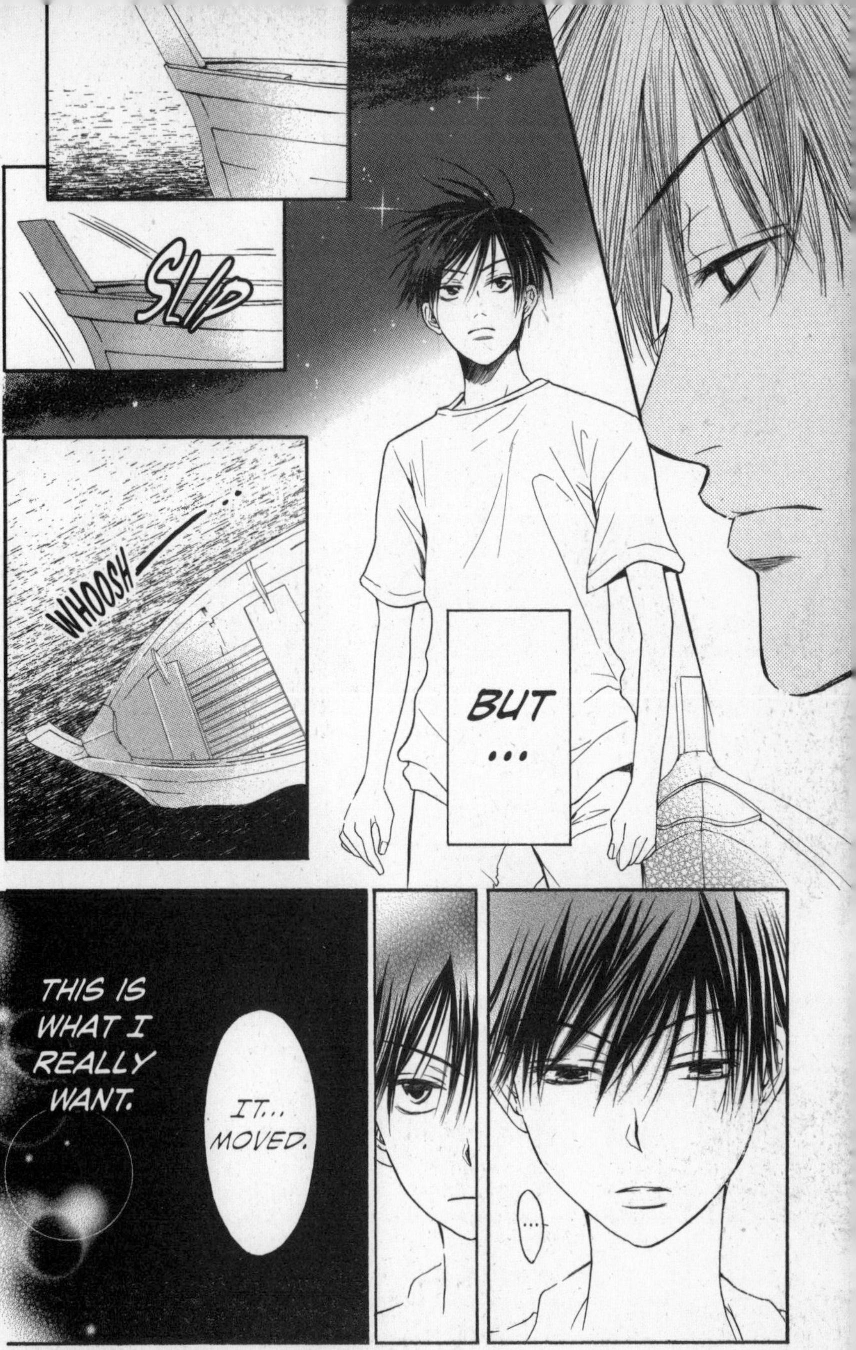
BUT...
SLID
WHOOSH
...
THIS IS WHAT I REALLY WANT.
IT... MOVED.

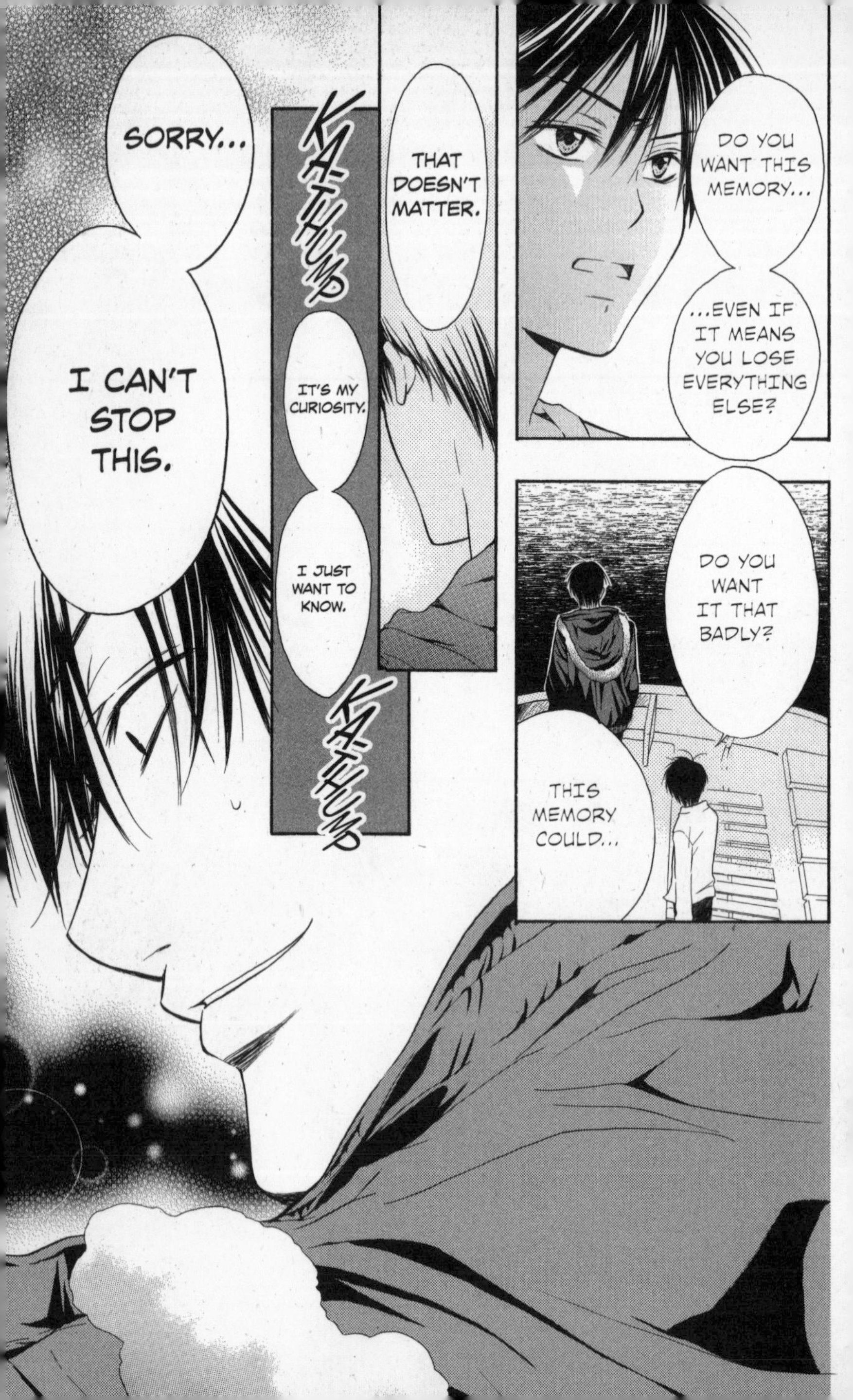
DO YOU WANT THIS MEMORY...
...EVEN IF IT MEANS YOU LOSE EVERYTHING ELSE?
THAT DOESN'T MATTER.
KATHUMP
IT'S MY CURIOSITY.
I JUST WANT TO KNOW.
KATHUMP
DO YOU WANT IT THAT BADLY?
THIS MEMORY COULD...
SORRY...
I CAN'T STOP THIS.

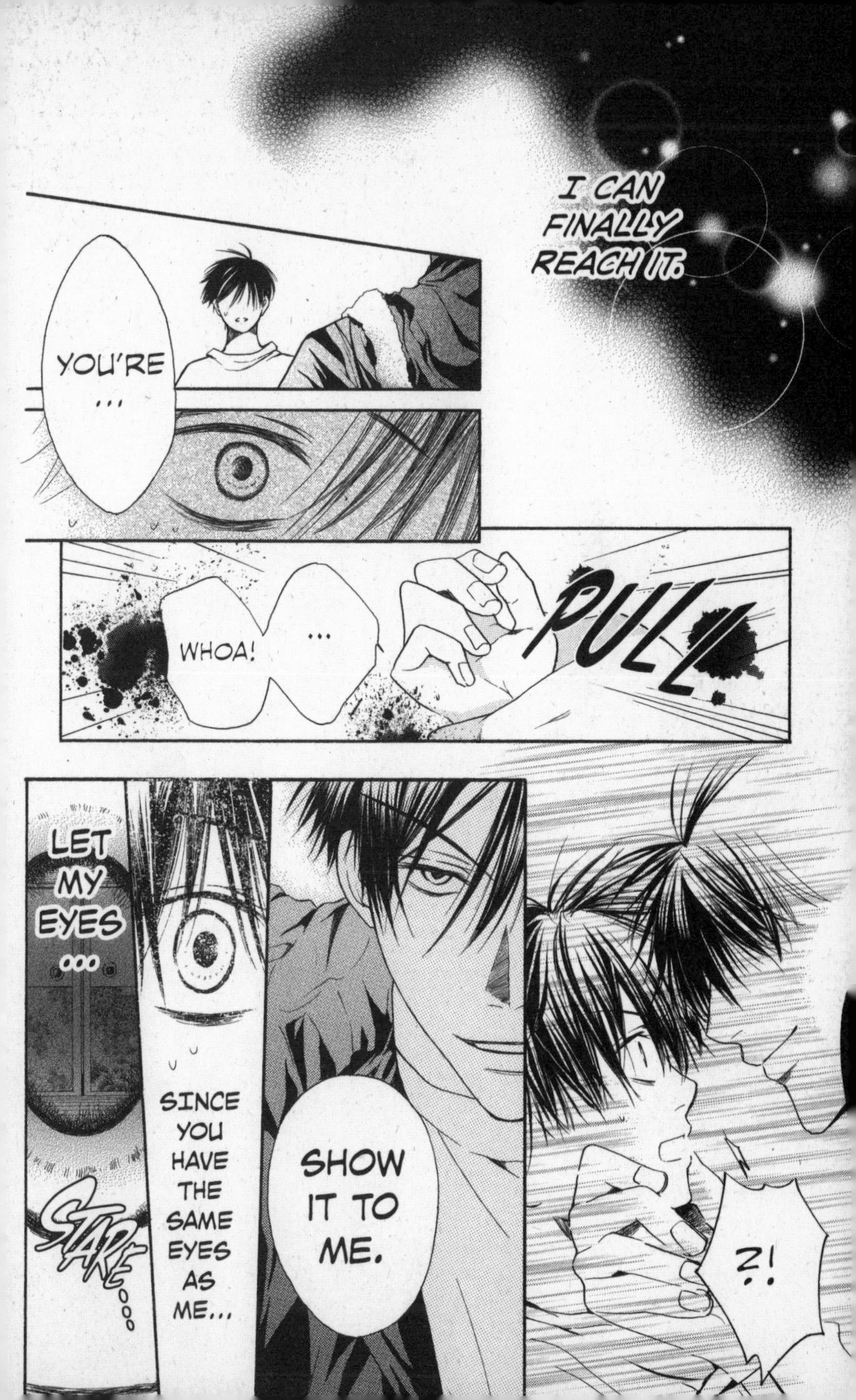
I CAN FINALLY REACH IT.
YOU'RE ...
PULL
...
WHOA!
?!
SHOW IT TO ME.
SINCE YOU HAVE THE SAME EYES AS ME...
LET MY EYES...
STARE

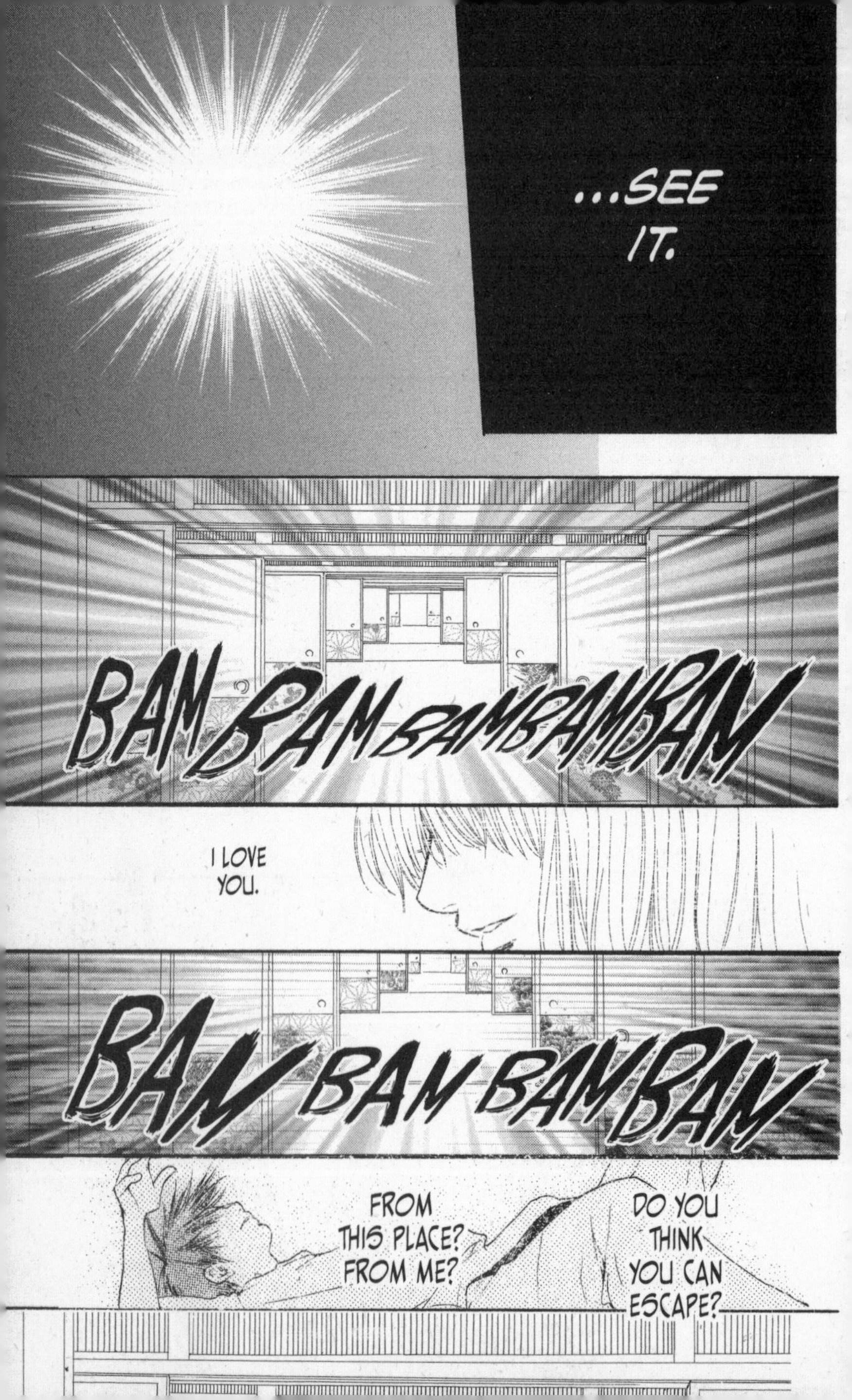
...SEE IT.
BAM BAM BAM BAM BAM
I LOVE YOU.
BAM BAM BAM BAM
DO YOU THINK YOU CAN ESCAPE?
FROM THIS PLACE? FROM ME?

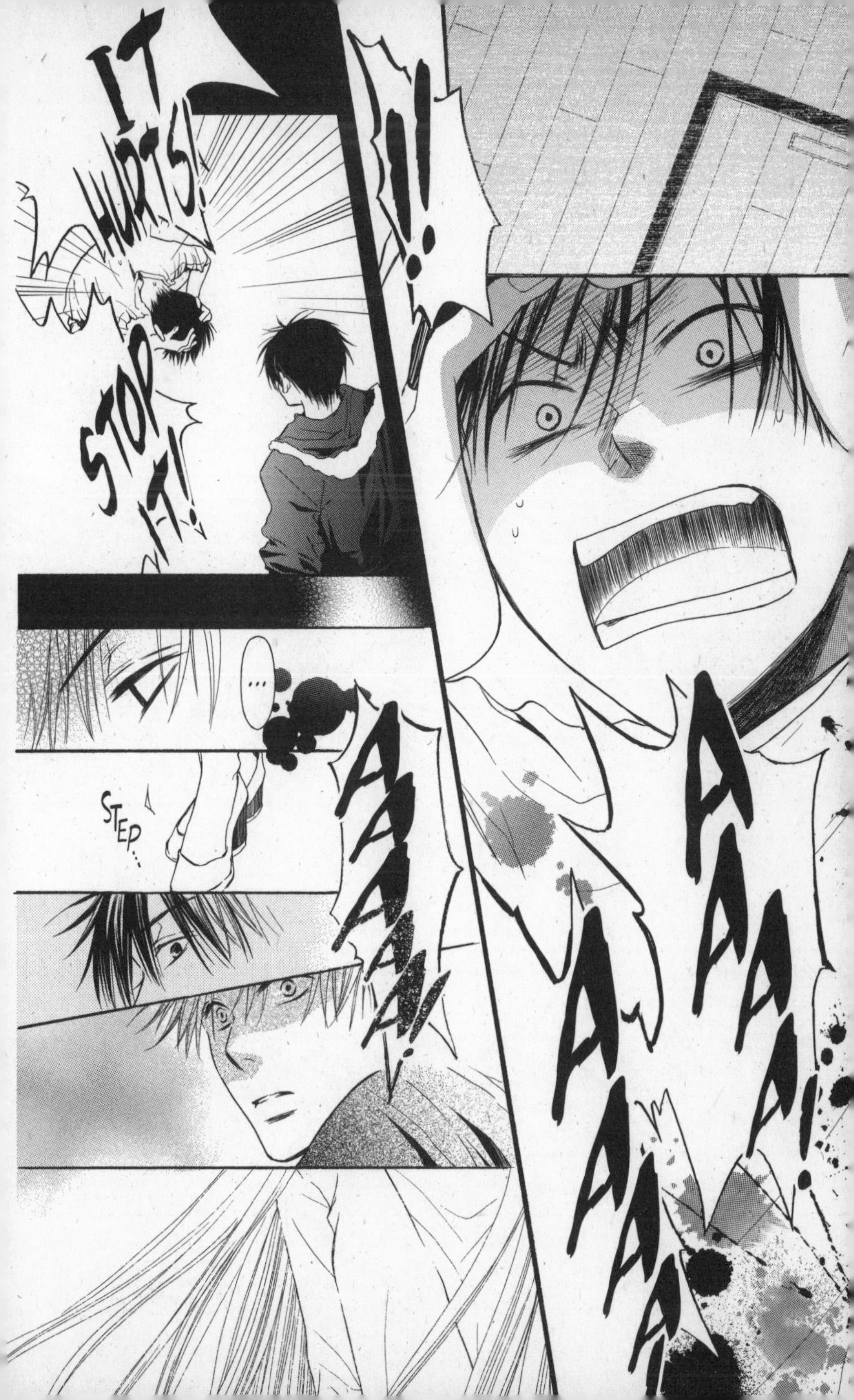
!!
AAAAAAAAA!
IT HURTS!
STOP IT!
...
AAAAAAA!
STEP...

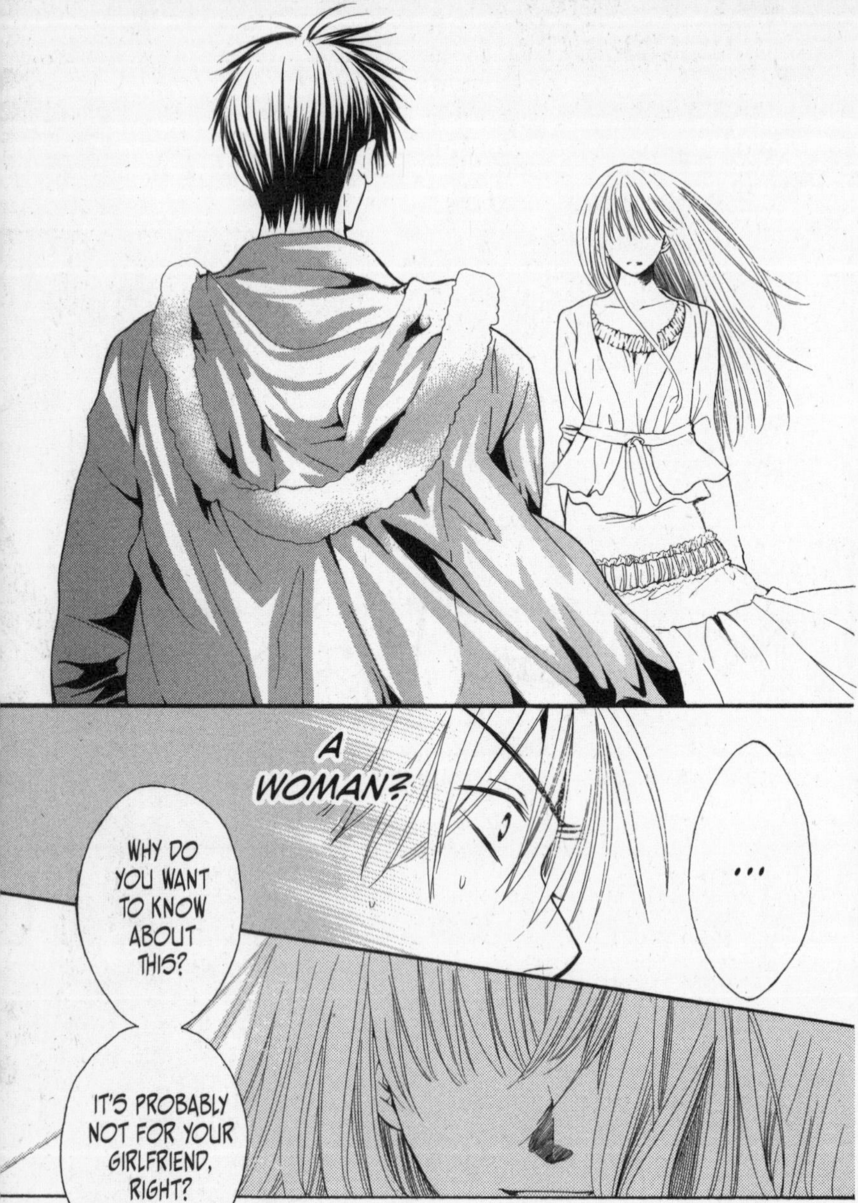
...
A WOMAN?
WHY DO YOU WANT TO KNOW ABOUT THIS?
IT'S PROBABLY NOT FOR YOUR GIRLFRIEND, RIGHT?

IN THE END, IT'S ONLY FOR YOURSELF.

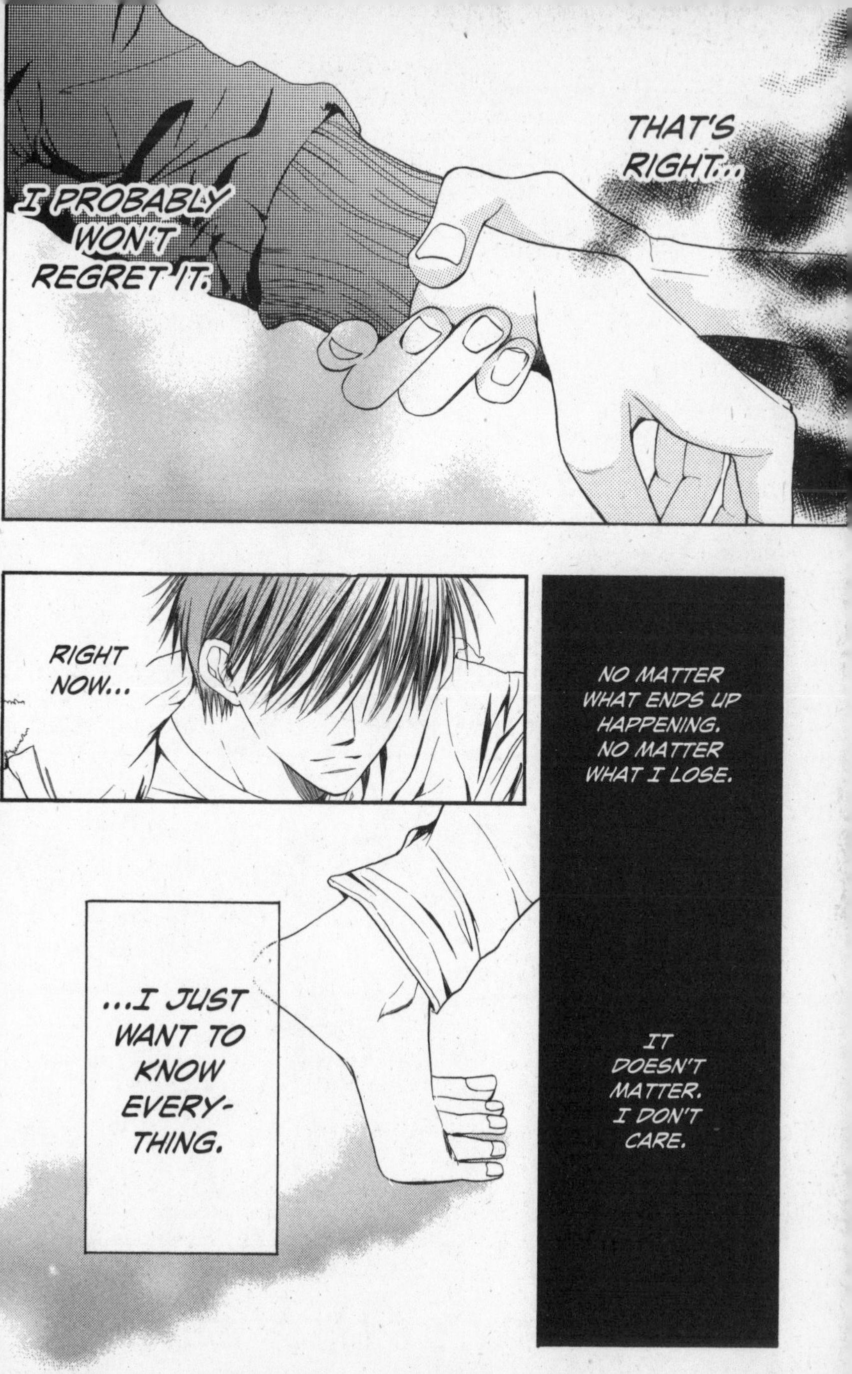
THAT'S RIGHT...
I PROBABLY WON'T REGRET IT.
NO MATTER WHAT ENDS UP HAPPENING. NO MATTER WHAT I LOSE.
IT DOESN'T MATTER. I DON'T CARE.
RIGHT NOW...
...I JUST WANT TO KNOW EVERY-THING.

The Magic Touch, Part 37/The End

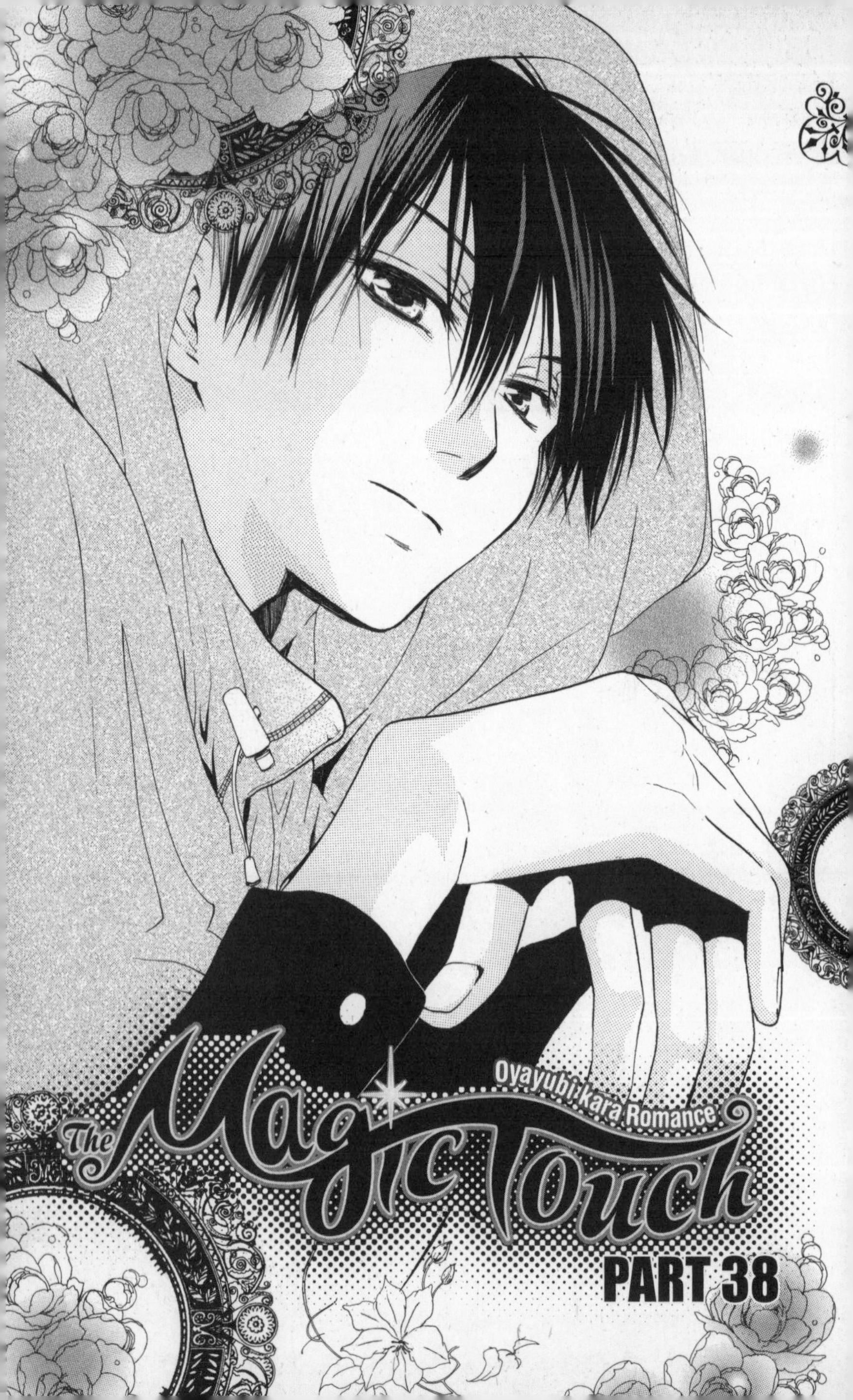
The Magic Touch
Oyayubi kara Romance
PART 38

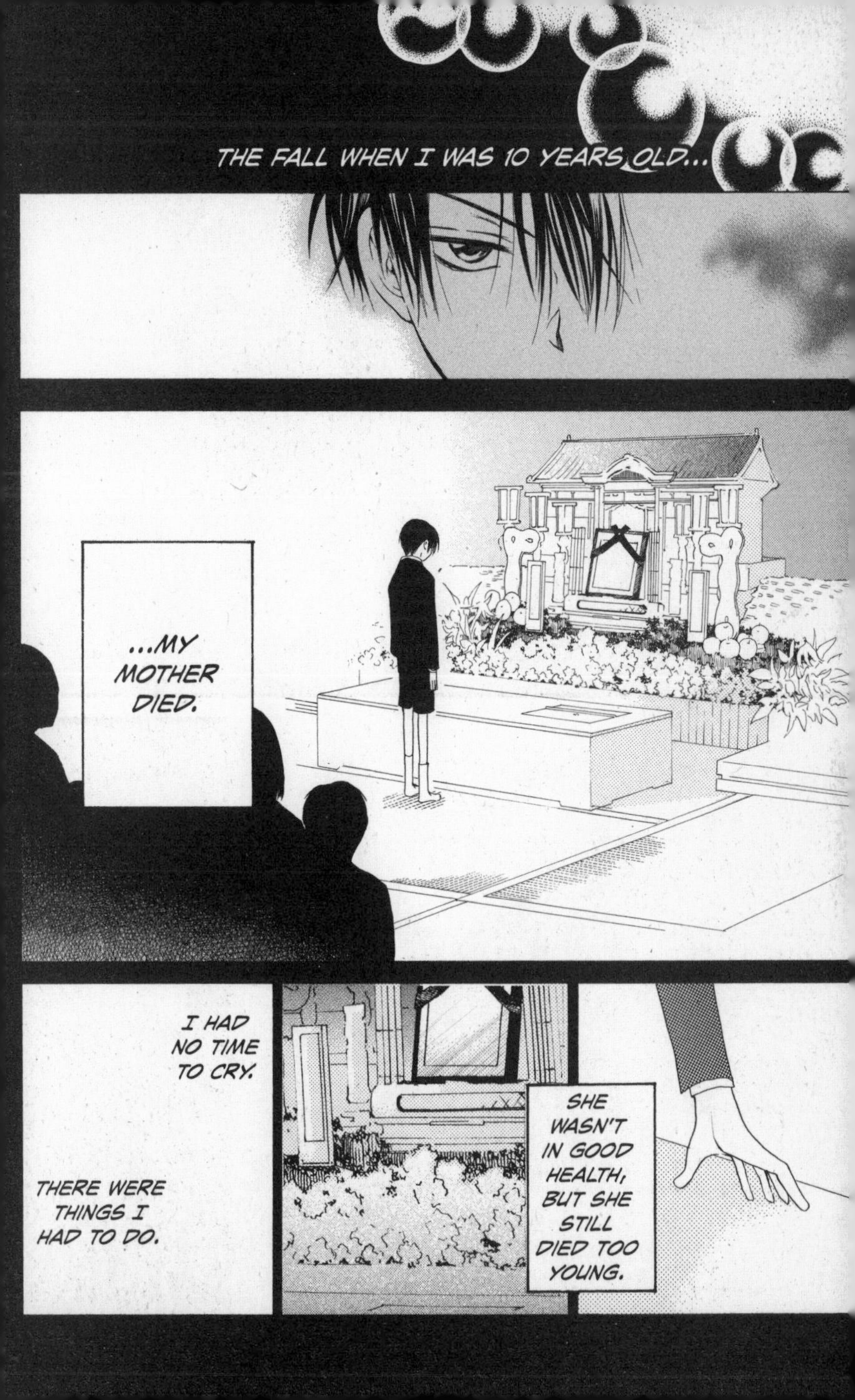
THE FALL WHEN I WAS 10 YEARS OLD...
...MY MOTHER DIED.
SHE WASN'T IN GOOD HEALTH, BUT SHE STILL DIED TOO YOUNG.
I HAD NO TIME TO CRY.
THERE WERE THINGS I HAD TO DO.

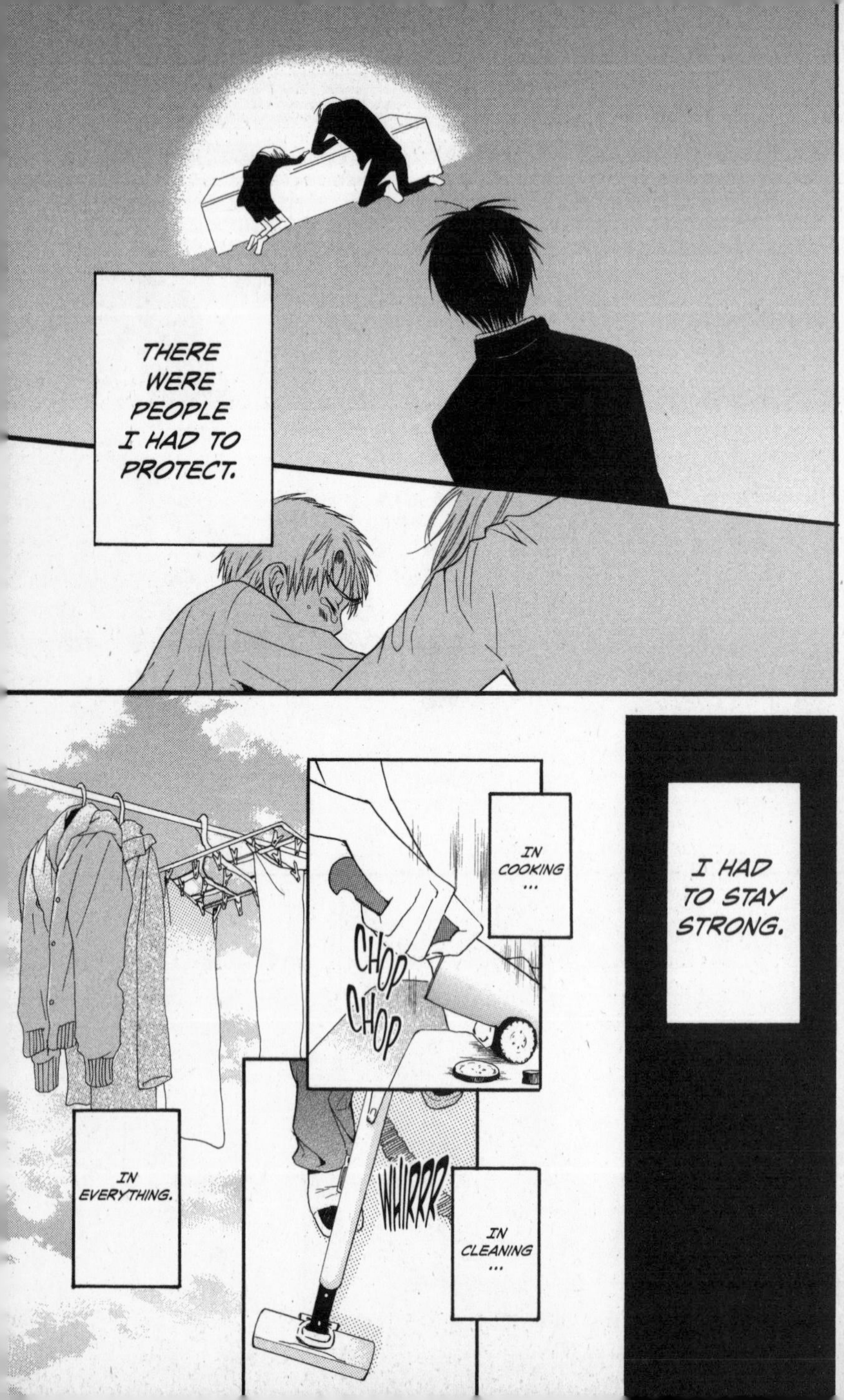
THERE WERE PEOPLE I HAD TO PROTECT.
I HAD TO STAY STRONG.
IN COOKING...
CHOP CHOP
IN CLEANING...
WHIRRR
IN EVERYTHING.

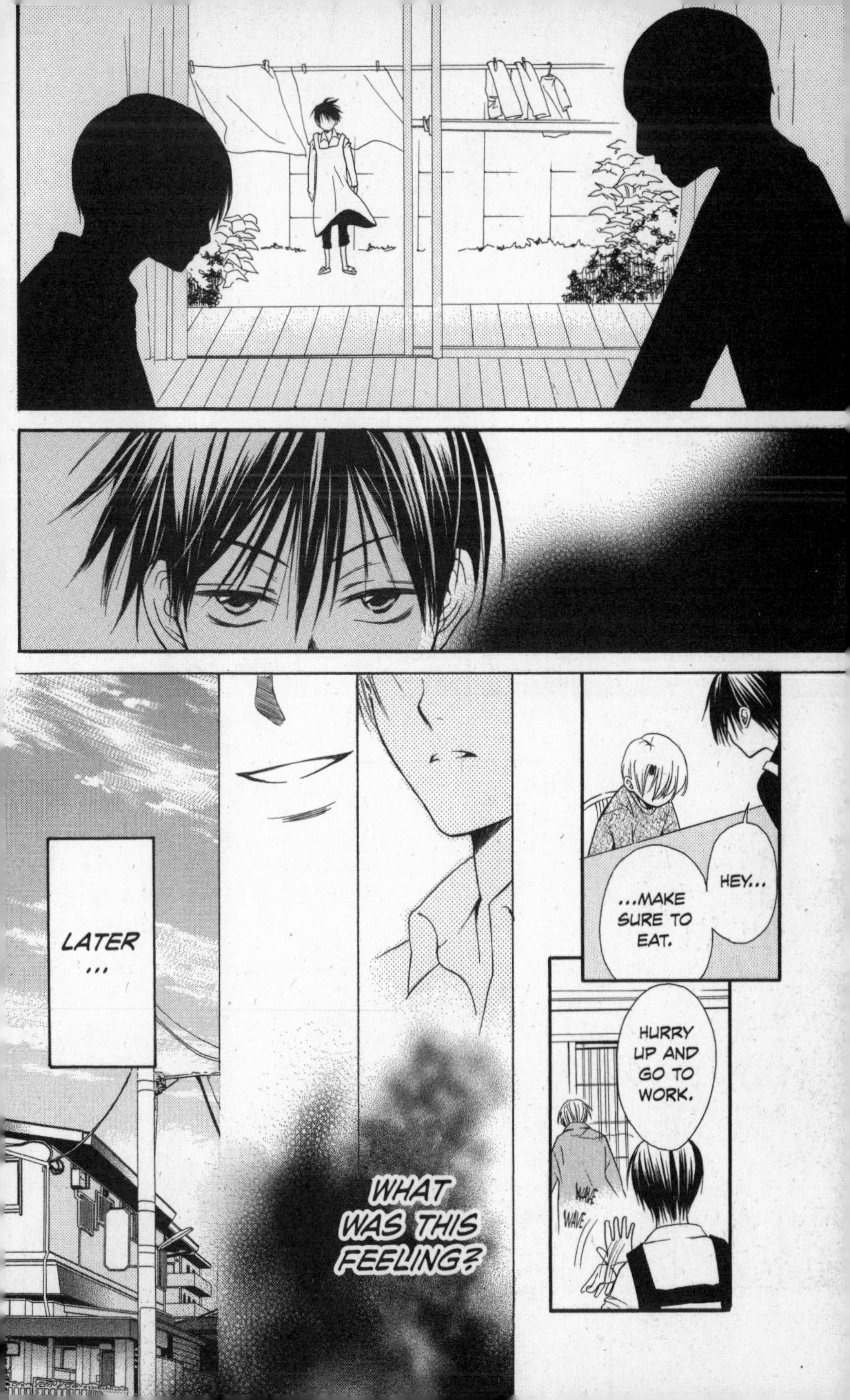
HEY...
...MAKE SURE TO EAT.
HURRY UP AND GO TO WORK.
WAVE
WAVE
WHAT WAS THIS FEELING?
LATER...

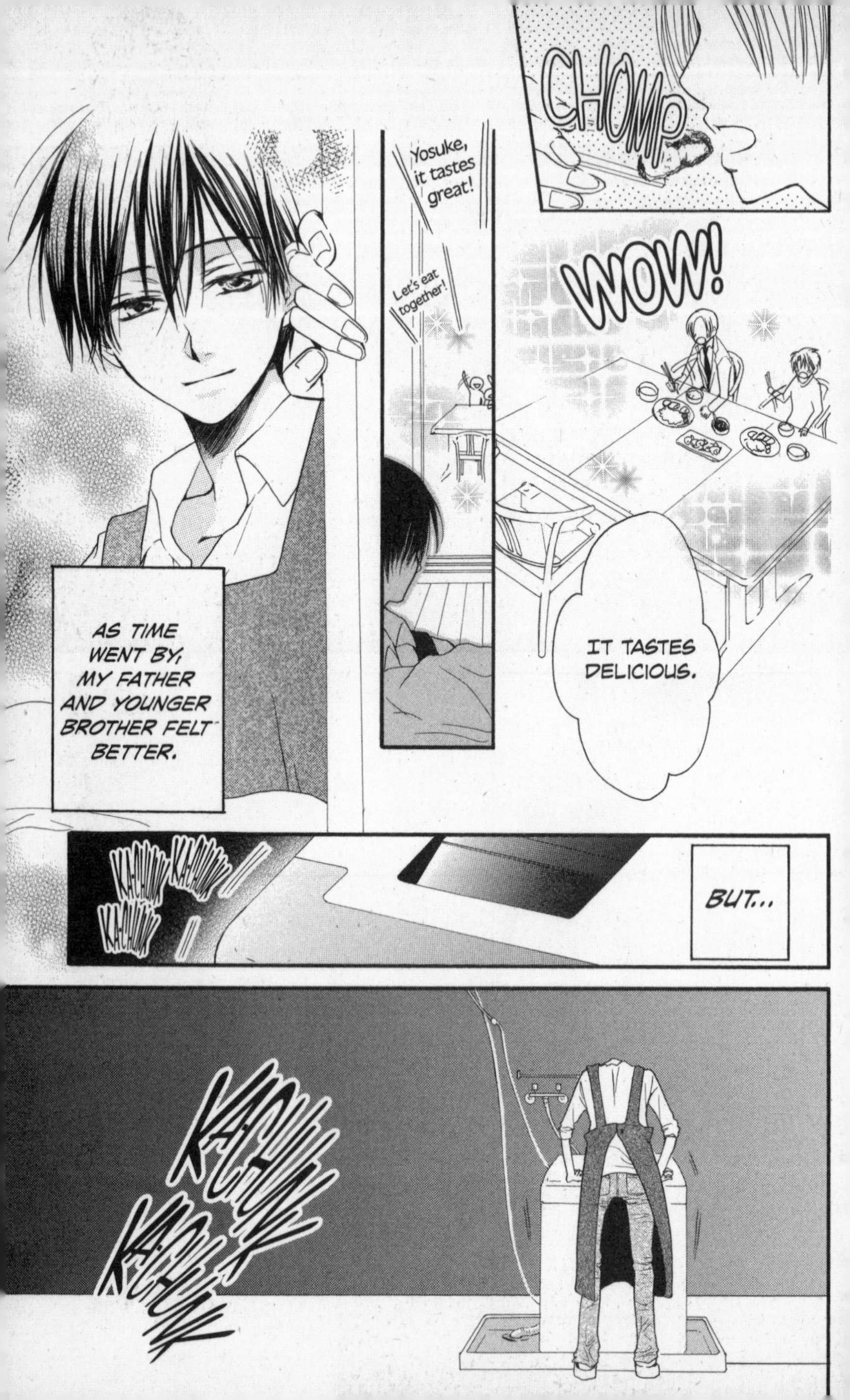
CHOMP
WOW!
IT TASTES DELICIOUS.
Yosuke, it tastes great!
Let's eat together!
AS TIME WENT BY, MY FATHER AND YOUNGER BROTHER FELT BETTER.
BUT...
KA-CHUNK KA-CHUNK
KA-CHUNK
KA-CHUNK
KA-CHUNK

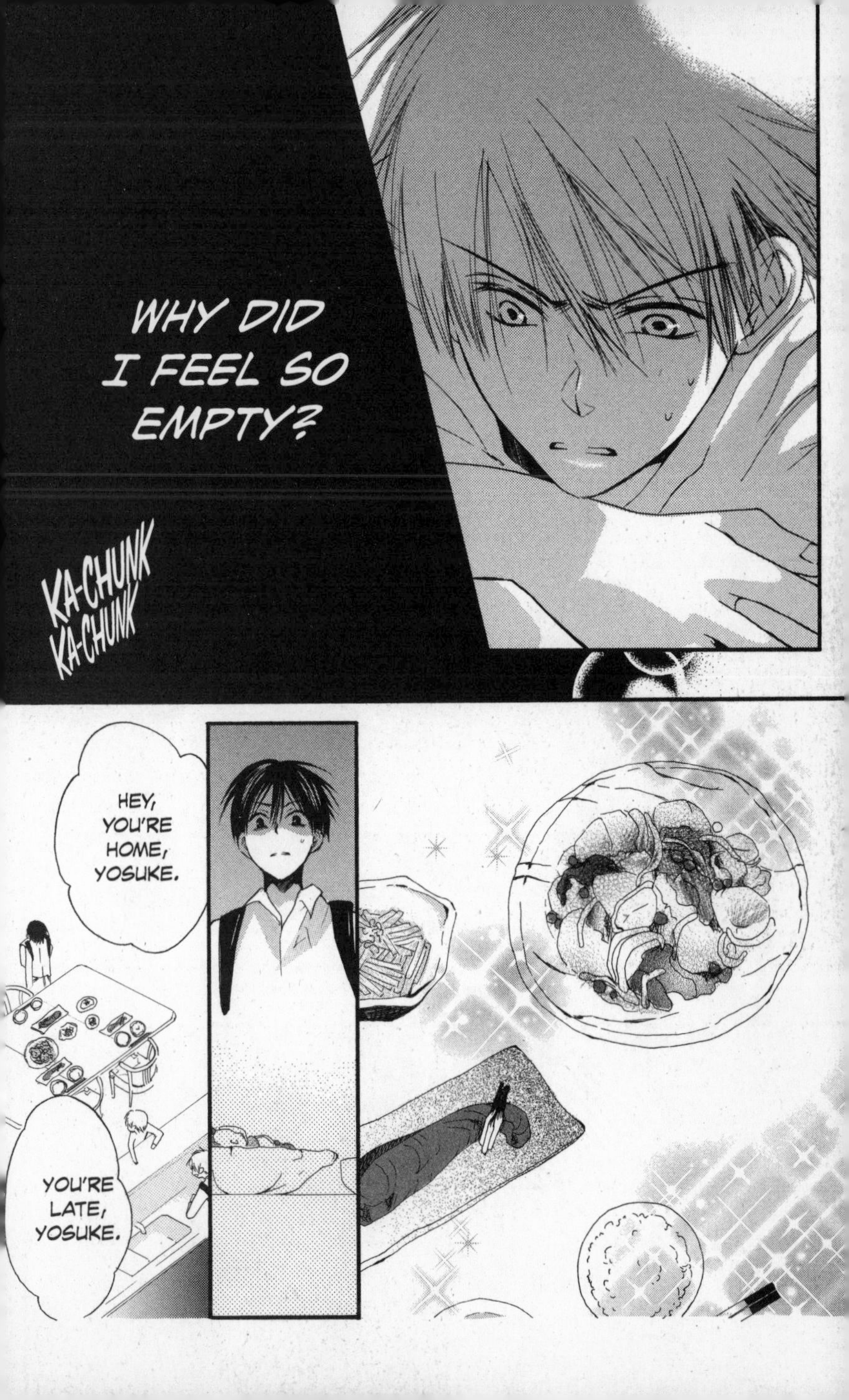
WHY DID I FEEL SO EMPTY?
KA-CHUNK KA-CHUNK
HEY, YOU'RE HOME, YOSUKE.
YOU'RE LATE, YOSUKE.

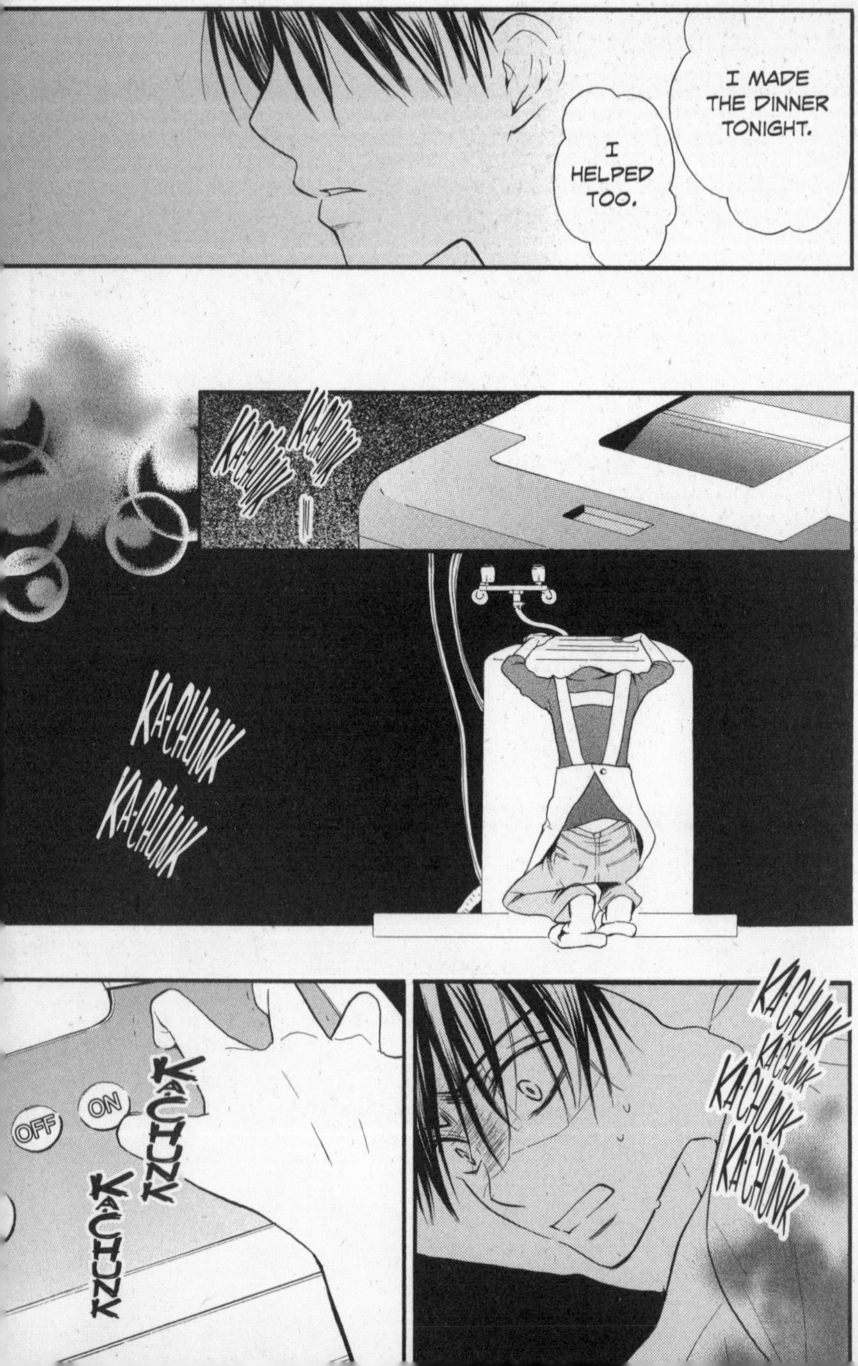
I MADE THE DINNER TONIGHT.
I HELPED TOO.
KA-CHUNK
KA-CHUNK
KA-CHUNK
KA-CHUNK
KA-CHUNK
KA-CHUNK
KA-CHUNK
KA-CHUNK
ON
OFF
KA-CHUNK
KA-CHUNK

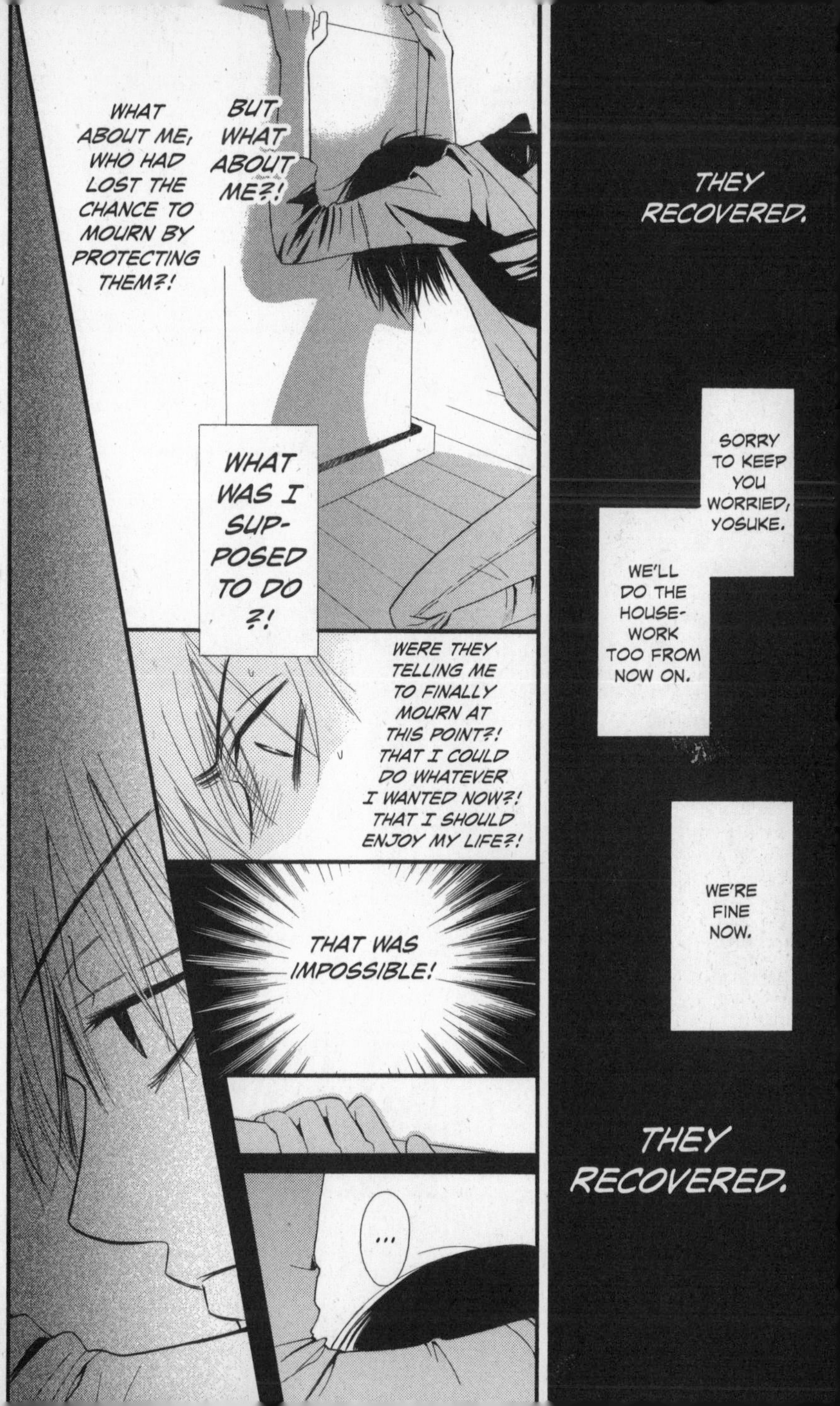
THEY RECOVERED.
SORRY TO KEEP YOU WORRIED, YOSUKE.
WE'LL DO THE HOUSE-WORK TOO FROM NOW ON.
WE'RE FINE NOW.
THEY RECOVERED.
BUT WHAT ABOUT ME?!
WHAT ABOUT ME, WHO HAD LOST THE CHANCE TO MOURN BY PROTECTING THEM?!
WHAT WAS I SUP-POSED TO DO?!
WERE THEY TELLING ME TO FINALLY MOURN AT THIS POINT?! THAT I COULD DO WHATEVER I WANTED NOW?! THAT I SHOULD ENJOY MY LIFE?!
THAT WAS IMPOSSIBLE!
...

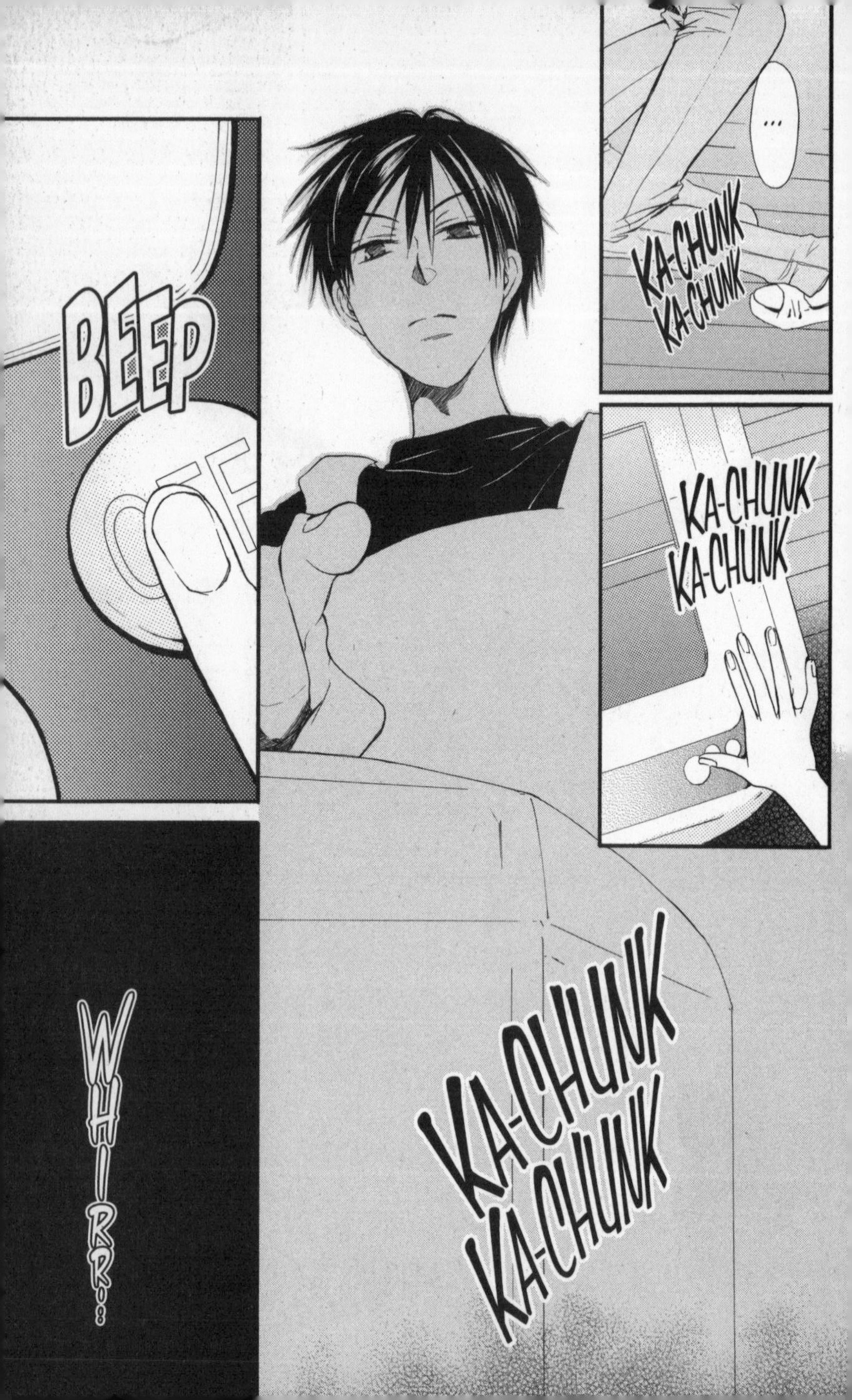
...
KA-CHUNK KA-CHUNK
KA-CHUNK KA-CHUNK
KA-CHUNK KA-CHUNK
BEEP
WHIRR..

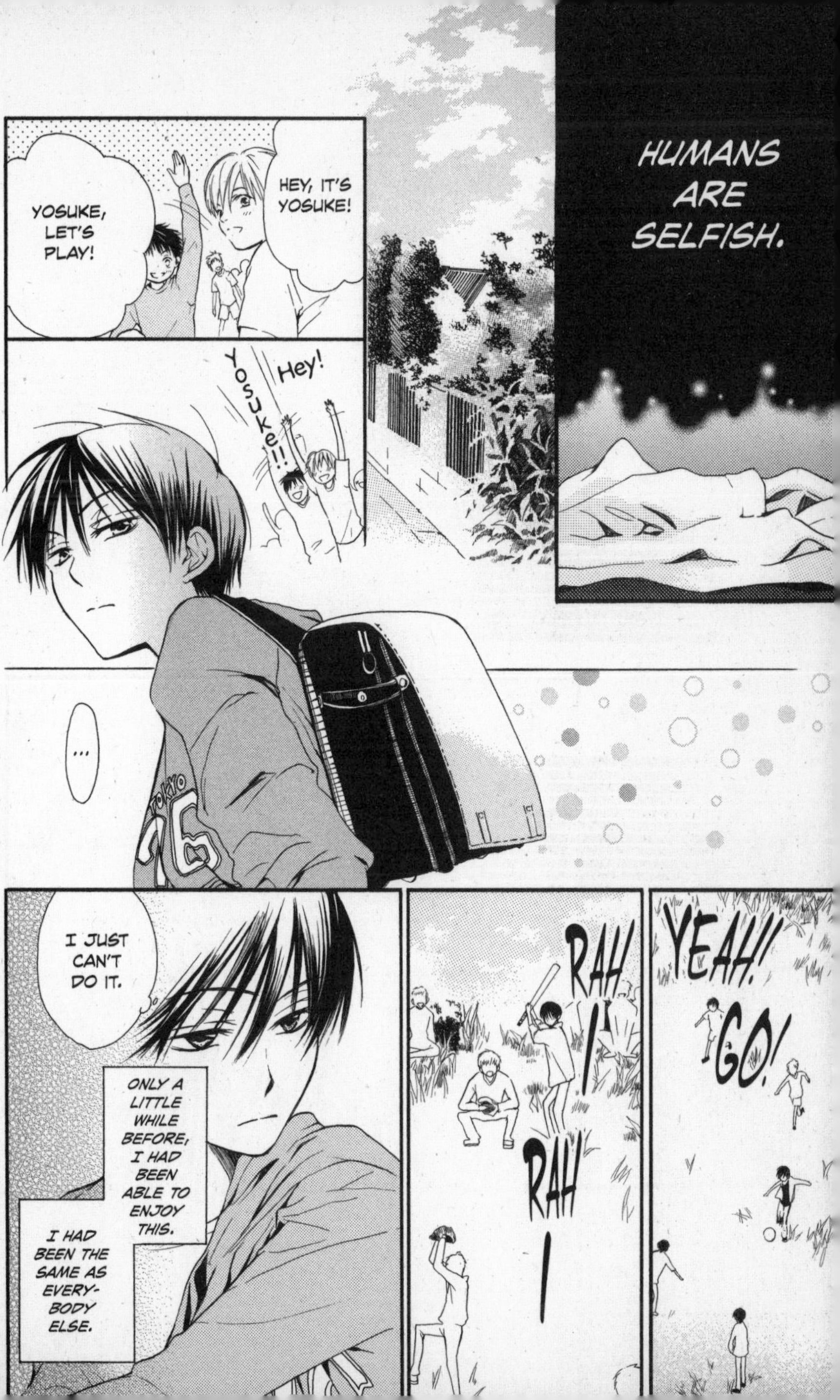
HUMANS ARE SELFISH.
HEY, IT'S YOSUKE!
YOSUKE, LET'S PLAY!
Hey!
YOSUKE!!
...
YEAH!!
GO!
RAH!
RAH!
I JUST CAN'T DO IT.
ONLY A LITTLE WHILE BEFORE, I HAD BEEN ABLE TO ENJOY THIS.
I HAD BEEN THE SAME AS EVERYBODY ELSE.

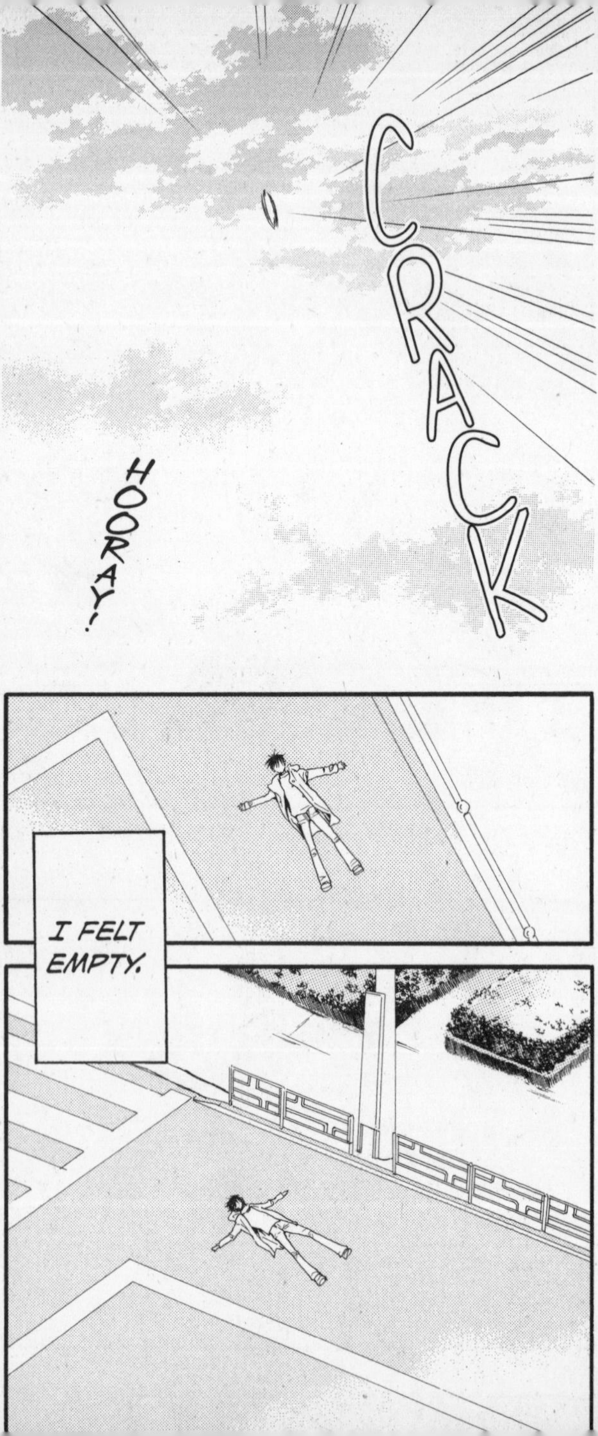
CRACK
HOORAY!
I FELT EMPTY.

2

I've been feeling my body deteriorate lately.

I can't sit in the traditional Japanese style even for five minutes.

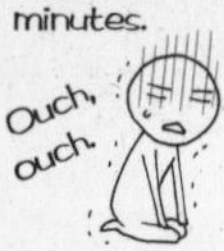
Ouch, ouch.

I can't even run for three minutes.

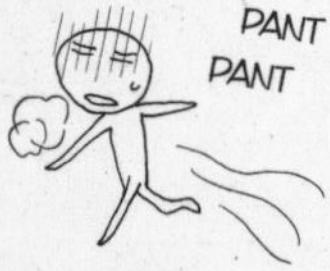
PANT
PANT

My jeans have become tight.

It won't fit...

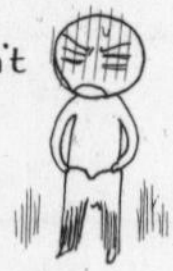

It's all because I got fat.

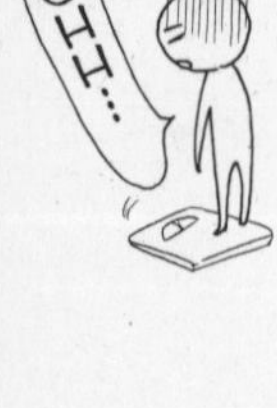
OHH...

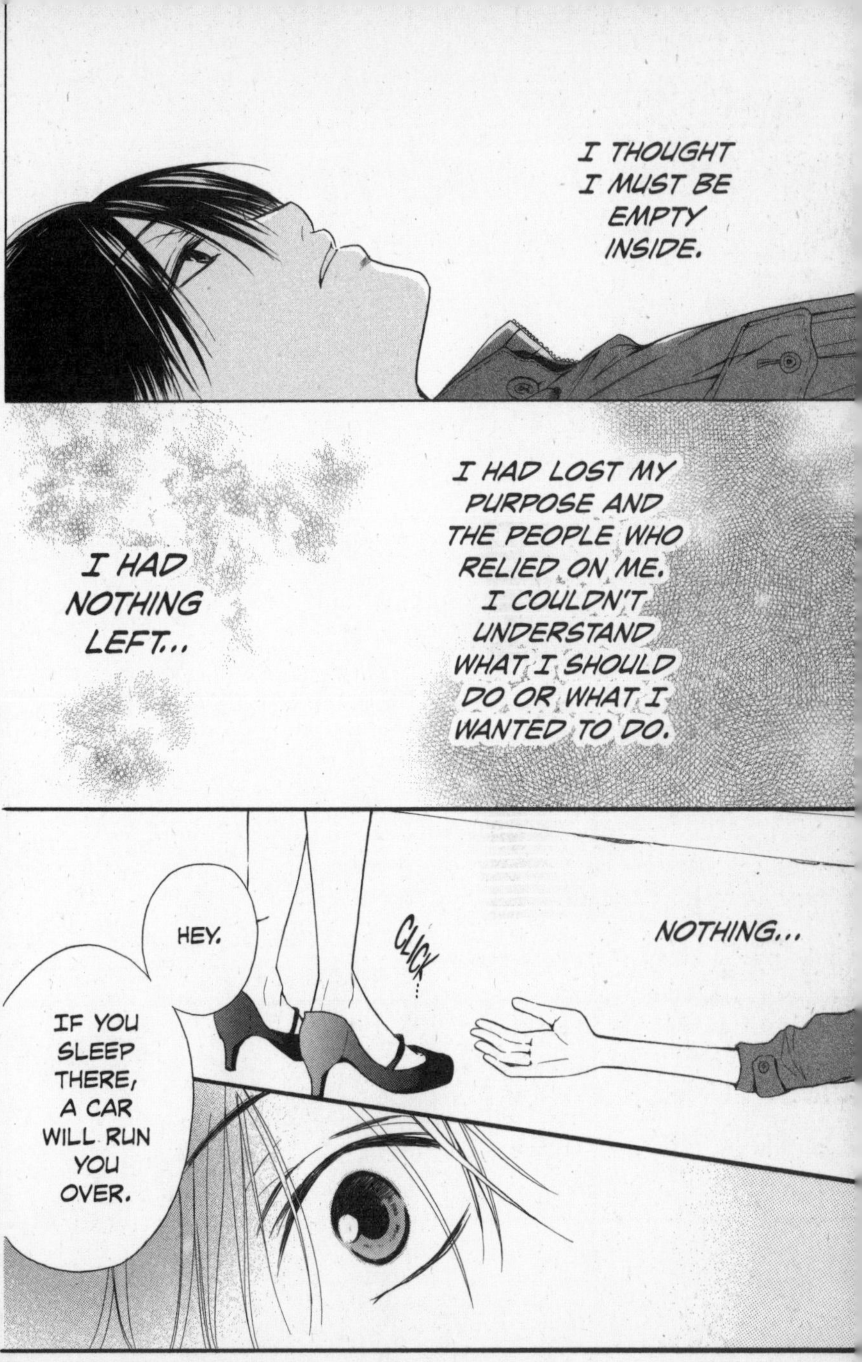
I THOUGHT I MUST BE EMPTY INSIDE.
I HAD LOST MY PURPOSE AND THE PEOPLE WHO RELIED ON ME. I COULDN'T UNDERSTAND WHAT I SHOULD DO OR WHAT I WANTED TO DO.
I HAD NOTHING LEFT...
NOTHING...
CLICK...
HEY.
IF YOU SLEEP THERE, A CAR WILL RUN YOU OVER.

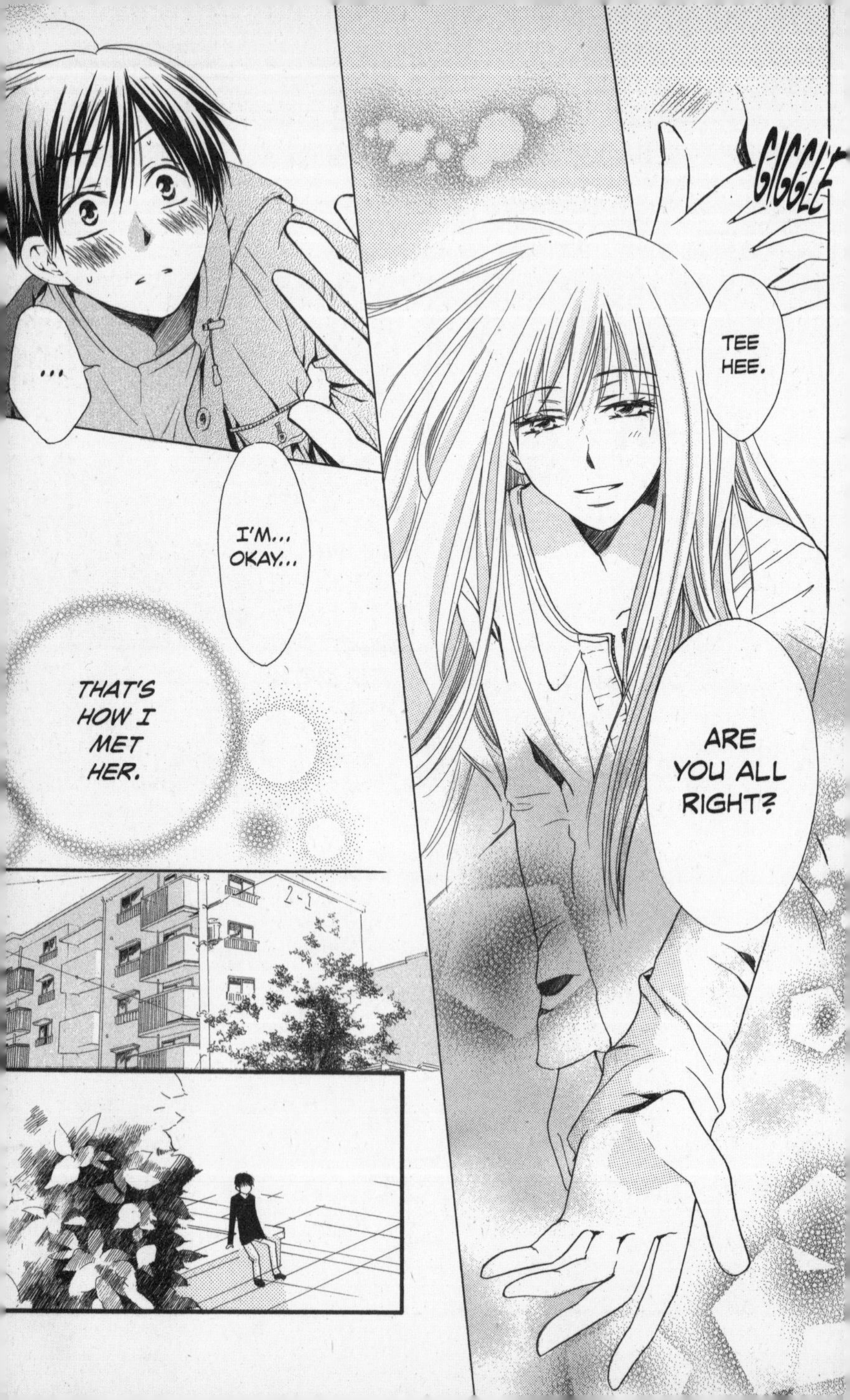
GIGGLE
TEE HEE.
ARE YOU ALL RIGHT?
...
I'M... OKAY...
THAT'S HOW I MET HER.

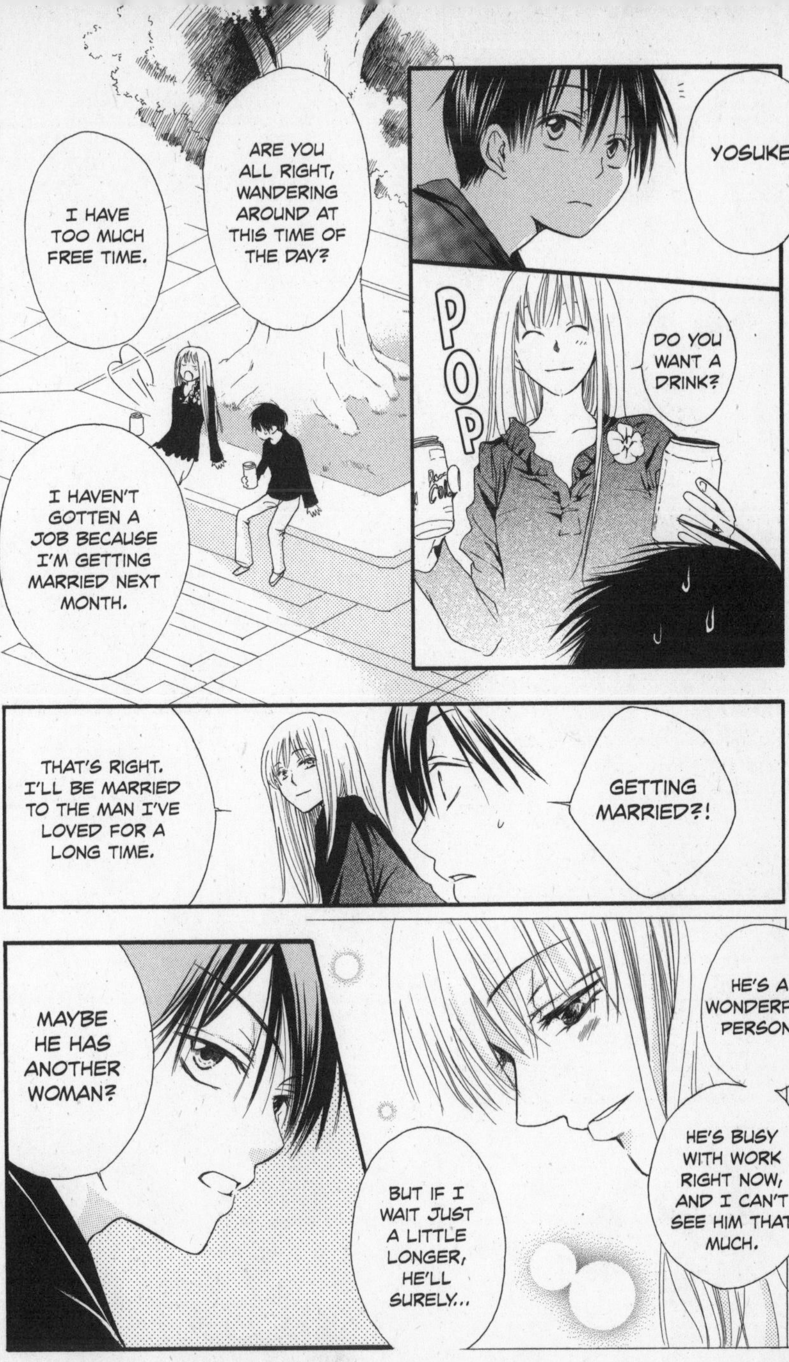
YOSUKE.
POP
DO YOU WANT A DRINK?
ARE YOU ALL RIGHT, WANDERING AROUND AT THIS TIME OF THE DAY?
I HAVE TOO MUCH FREE TIME.
I HAVEN'T GOTTEN A JOB BECAUSE I'M GETTING MARRIED NEXT MONTH.
GETTING MARRIED?!
THAT'S RIGHT. I'LL BE MARRIED TO THE MAN I'VE LOVED FOR A LONG TIME.
HE'S A WONDERFUL PERSON.
HE'S BUSY WITH WORK RIGHT NOW, AND I CAN'T SEE HIM THAT MUCH.
BUT IF I WAIT JUST A LITTLE LONGER, HE'LL SURELY...
MAYBE HE HAS ANOTHER WOMAN?

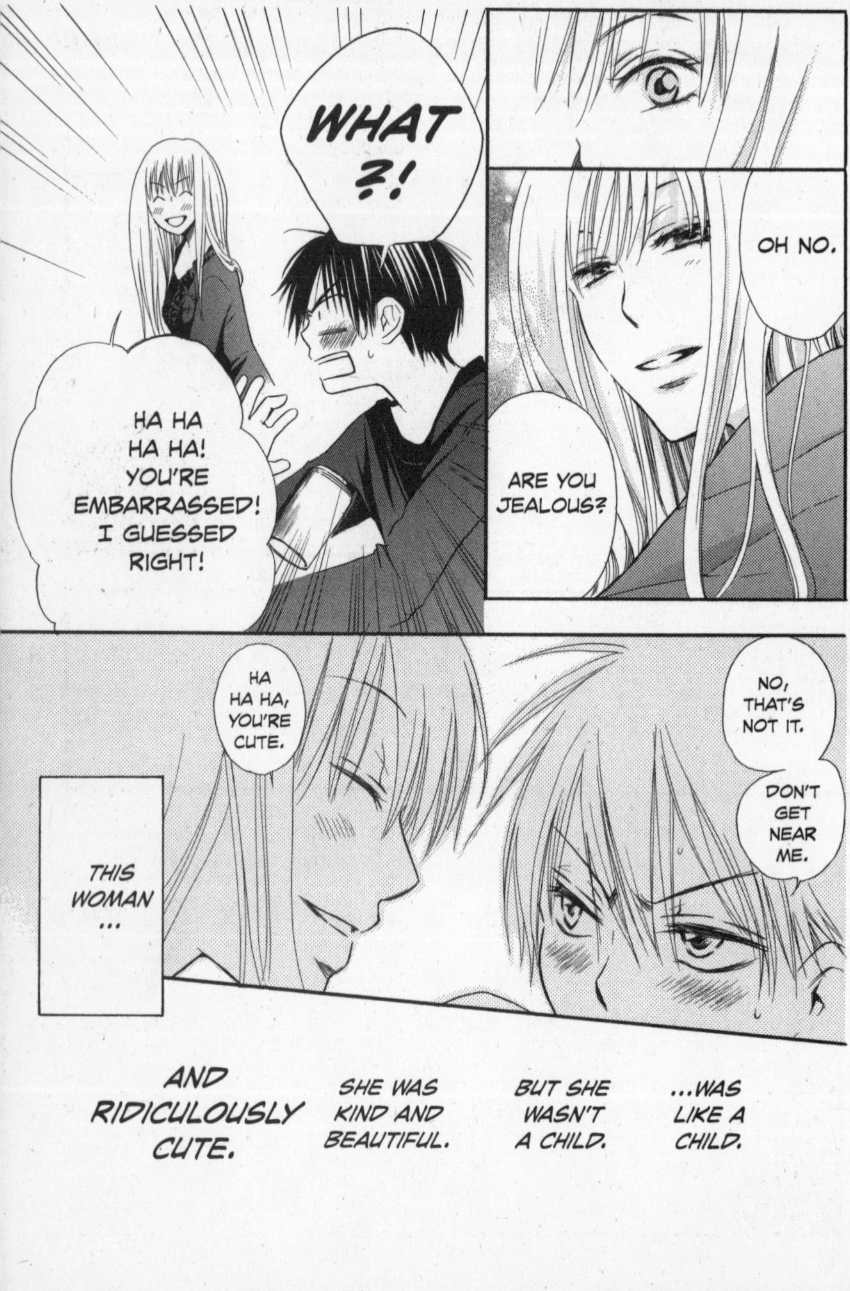
OH NO.
ARE YOU JEALOUS?
WHAT ?!
HA HA HA HA! YOU'RE EMBARRASSED! I GUESSED RIGHT!
NO, THAT'S NOT IT.
DON'T GET NEAR ME.
HA HA HA, YOU'RE CUTE.
THIS WOMAN ...
...WAS LIKE A CHILD.
BUT SHE WASN'T A CHILD.
SHE WAS KIND AND BEAUTIFUL.
AND RIDICULOUSLY CUTE.

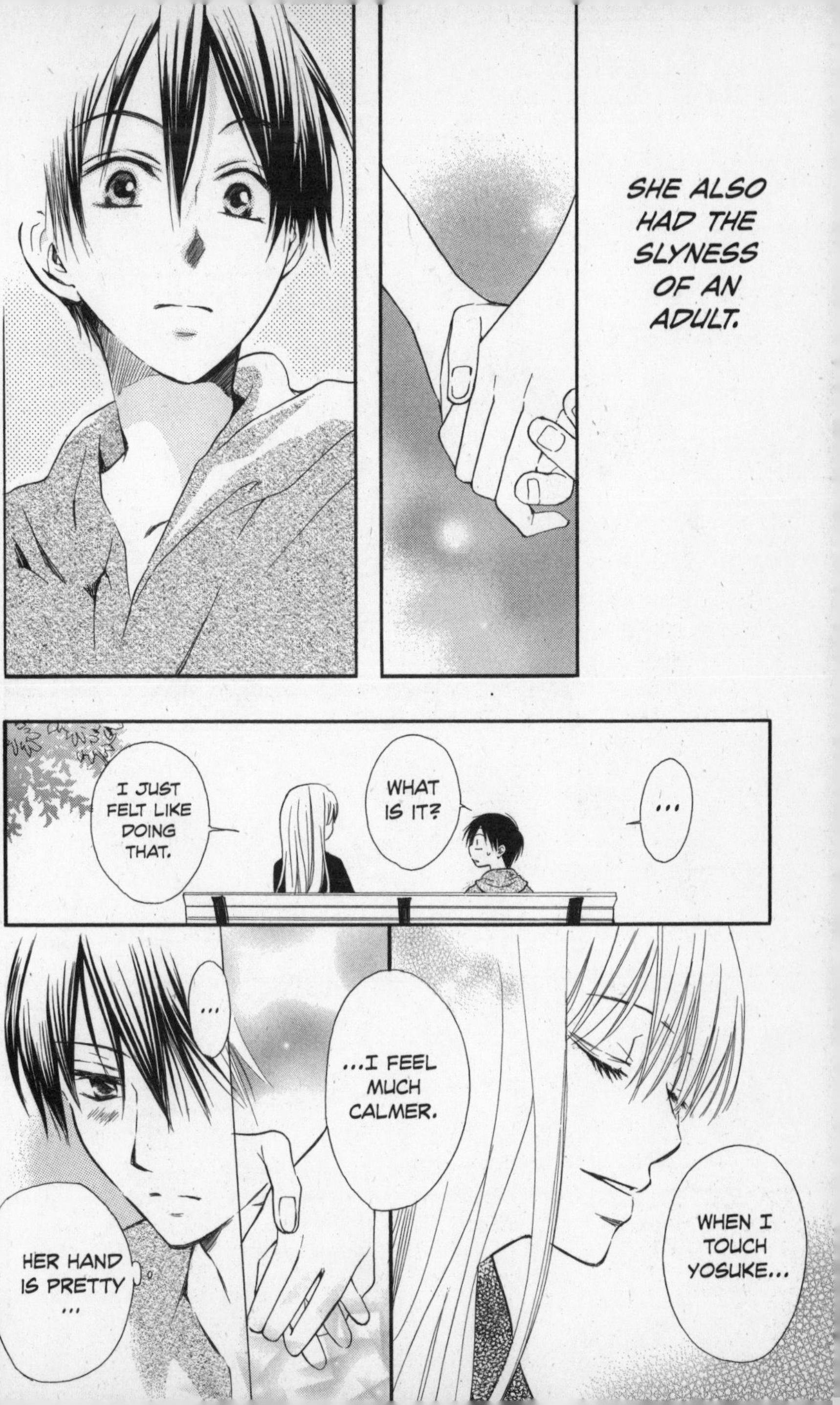
SHE ALSO HAD THE SLYNESS OF AN ADULT.
...
WHAT IS IT?
I JUST FELT LIKE DOING THAT.
WHEN I TOUCH YOSUKE...
...I FEEL MUCH CALMER.
...
HER HAND IS PRETTY...

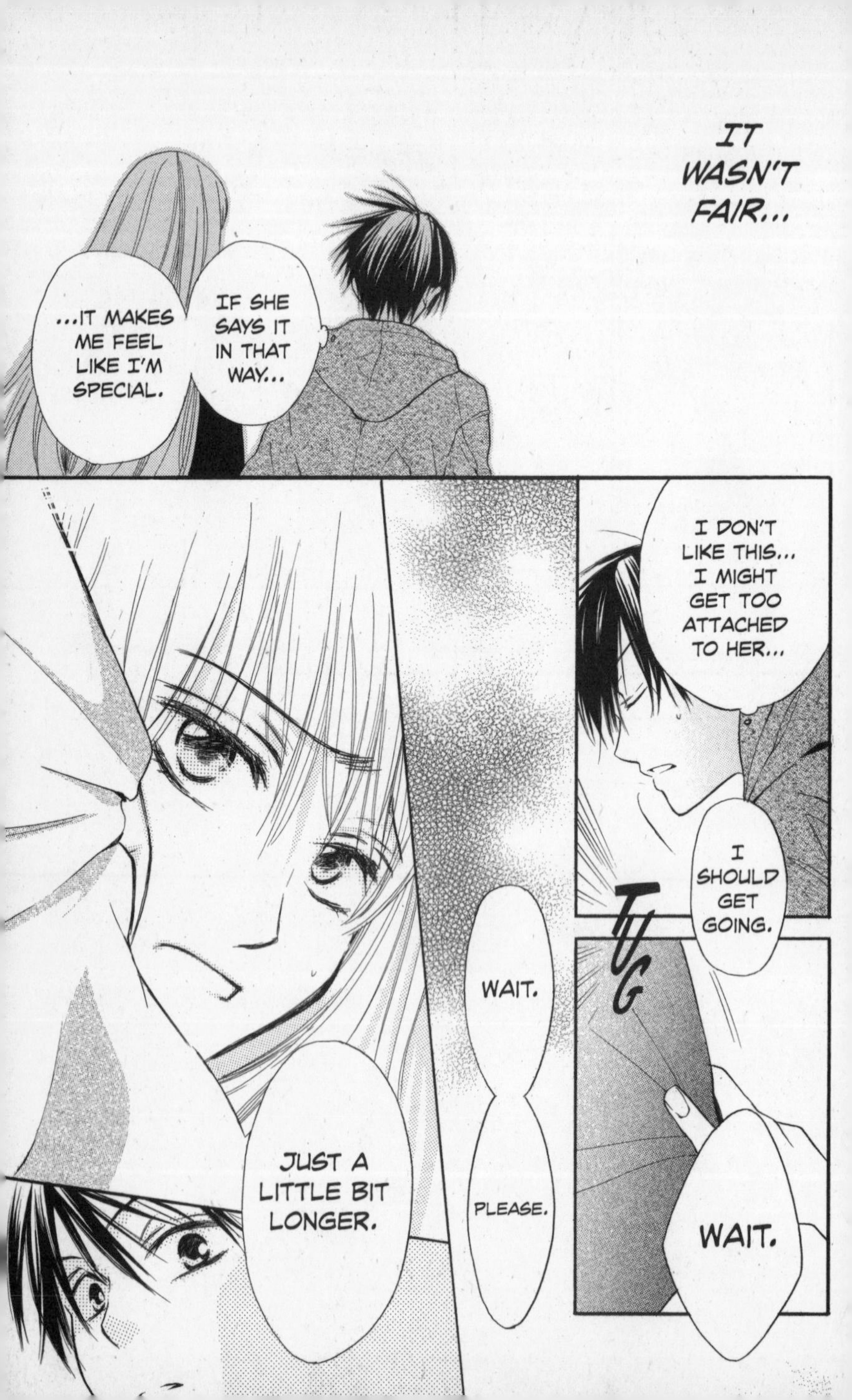
IT WASN'T FAIR...
IF SHE SAYS IT IN THAT WAY...
...IT MAKES ME FEEL LIKE I'M SPECIAL.
I DON'T LIKE THIS... I MIGHT GET TOO ATTACHED TO HER...
I SHOULD GET GOING.
TUG
WAIT.
WAIT.
PLEASE.
JUST A LITTLE BIT LONGER.

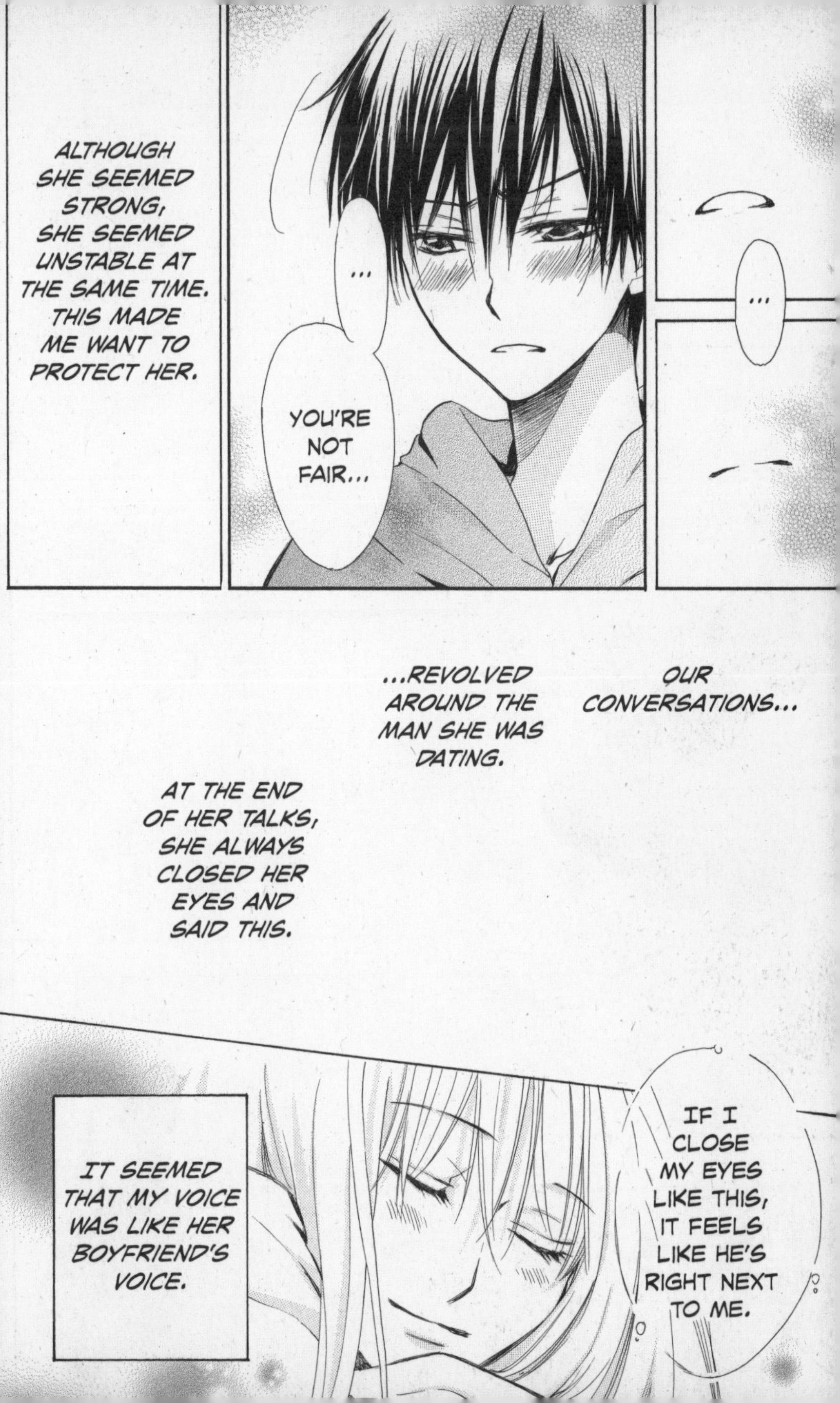
...
...
YOU'RE NOT FAIR...
ALTHOUGH SHE SEEMED STRONG, SHE SEEMED UNSTABLE AT THE SAME TIME. THIS MADE ME WANT TO PROTECT HER.
OUR CONVERSATIONS...
...REVOLVED AROUND THE MAN SHE WAS DATING.
AT THE END OF HER TALKS, SHE ALWAYS CLOSED HER EYES AND SAID THIS.
IF I CLOSE MY EYES LIKE THIS, IT FEELS LIKE HE'S RIGHT NEXT TO ME.
IT SEEMED THAT MY VOICE WAS LIKE HER BOYFRIEND'S VOICE.

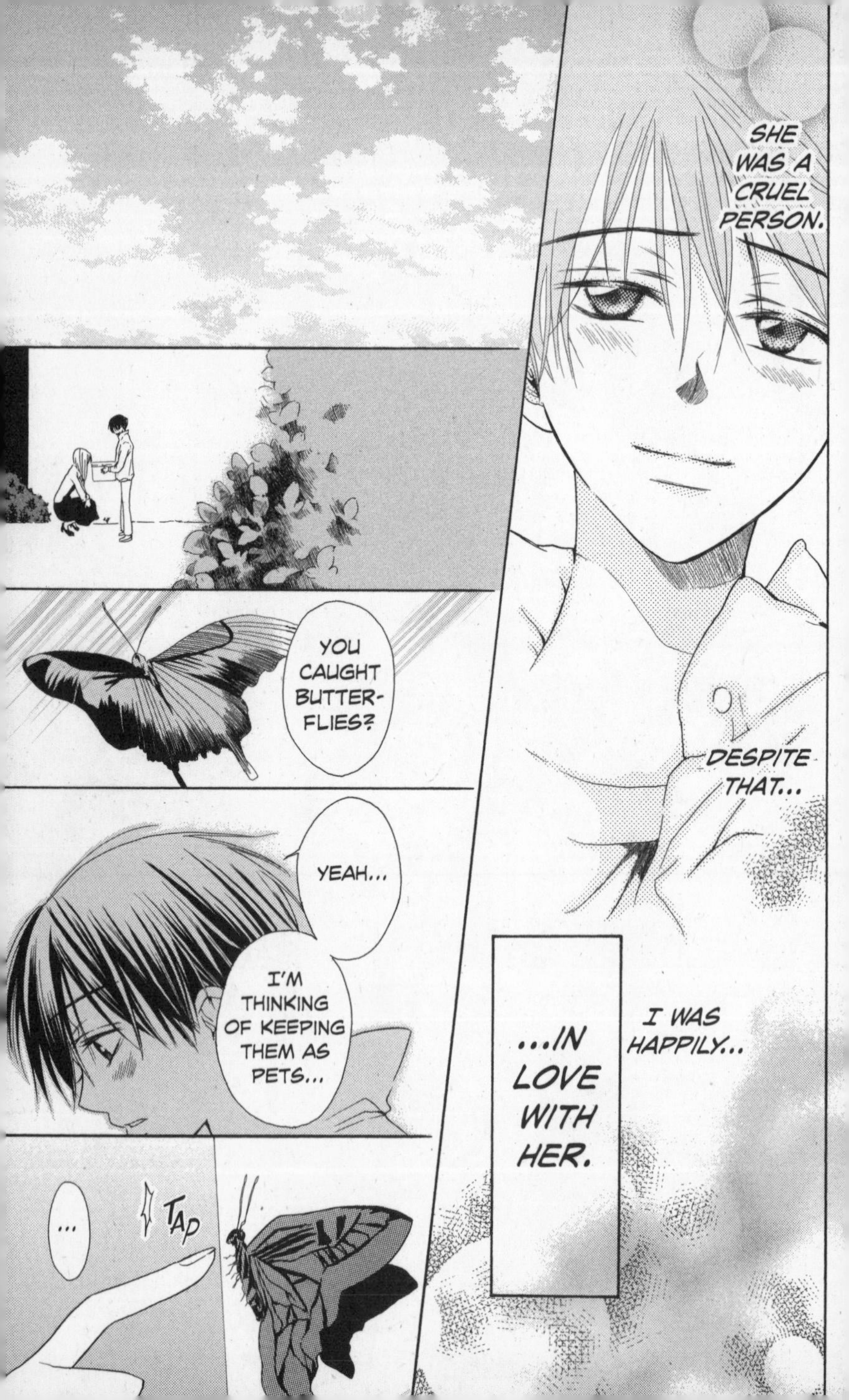
SHE WAS A CRUEL PERSON.
DESPITE THAT...
I WAS HAPPILY...
...IN LOVE WITH HER.
YOU CAUGHT BUTTER-FLIES?
YEAH...
I'M THINKING OF KEEPING THEM AS PETS...
...
TAP

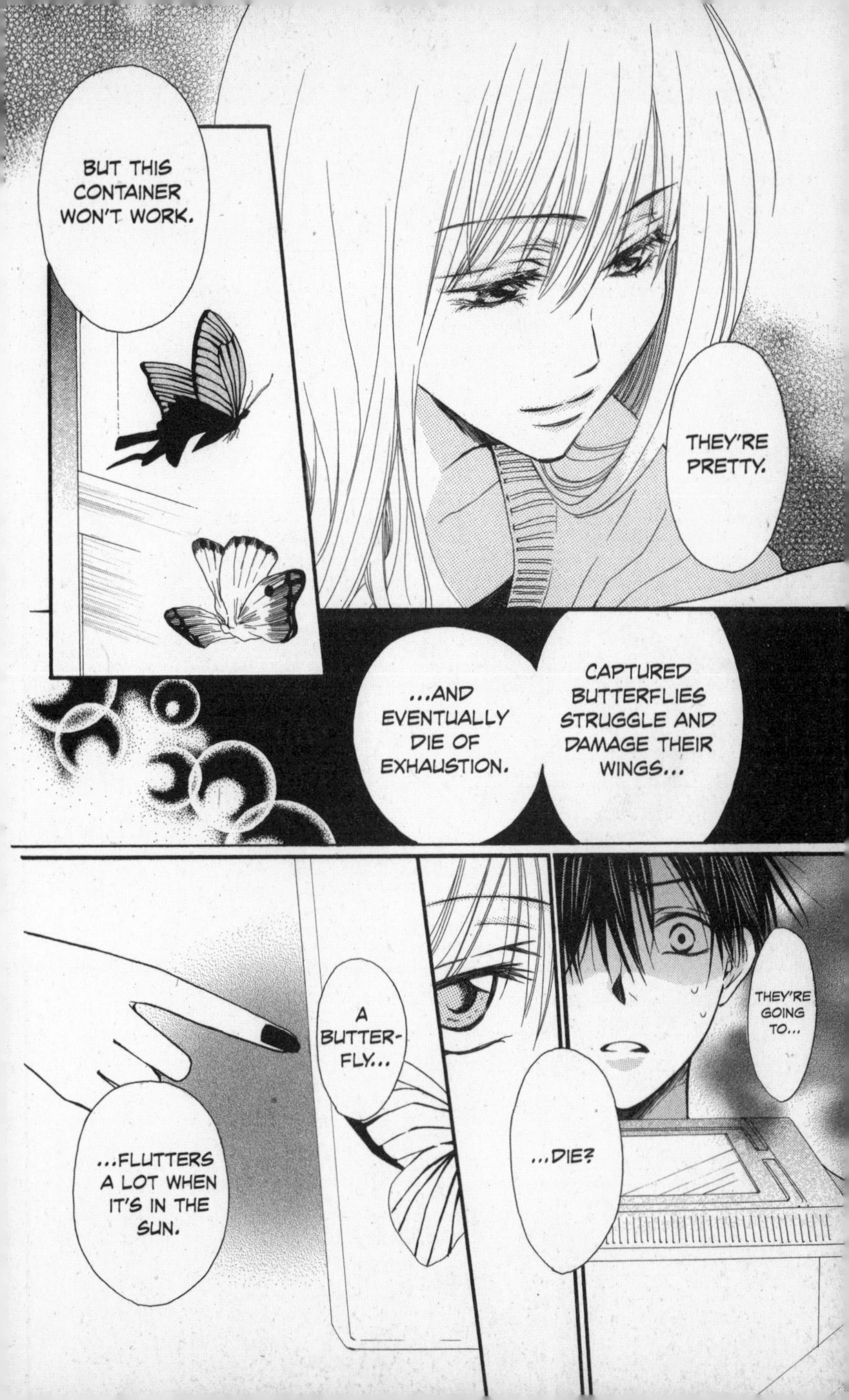
THEY'RE PRETTY.
BUT THIS CONTAINER WON'T WORK.
CAPTURED BUTTERFLIES STRUGGLE AND DAMAGE THEIR WINGS...
...AND EVENTUALLY DIE OF EXHAUSTION.
THEY'RE GOING TO...
...DIE?
A BUTTER-FLY...
...FLUTTERS A LOT WHEN IT'S IN THE SUN.

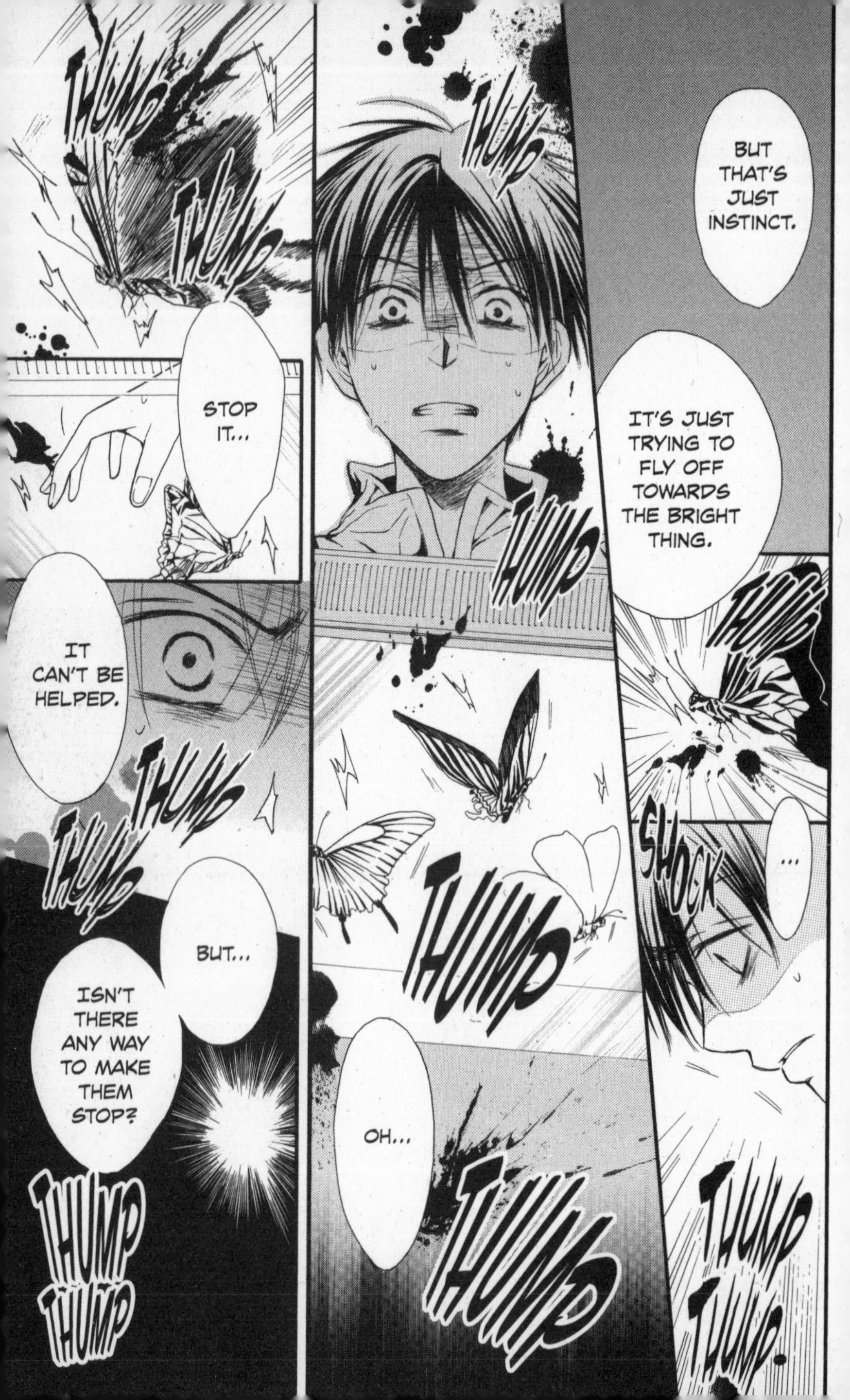
BUT THAT'S JUST INSTINCT.
IT'S JUST TRYING TO FLY OFF TOWARDS THE BRIGHT THING.
THUMP
SHOCK
...
THUMP THUMP
THUMP
THUMP
THUMP
OH...
THUMP
THUMP
THUMP
STOP IT...
IT CAN'T BE HELPED.
THUMP THUMP
BUT...
ISN'T THERE ANY WAY TO MAKE THEM STOP?
THUMP THUMP

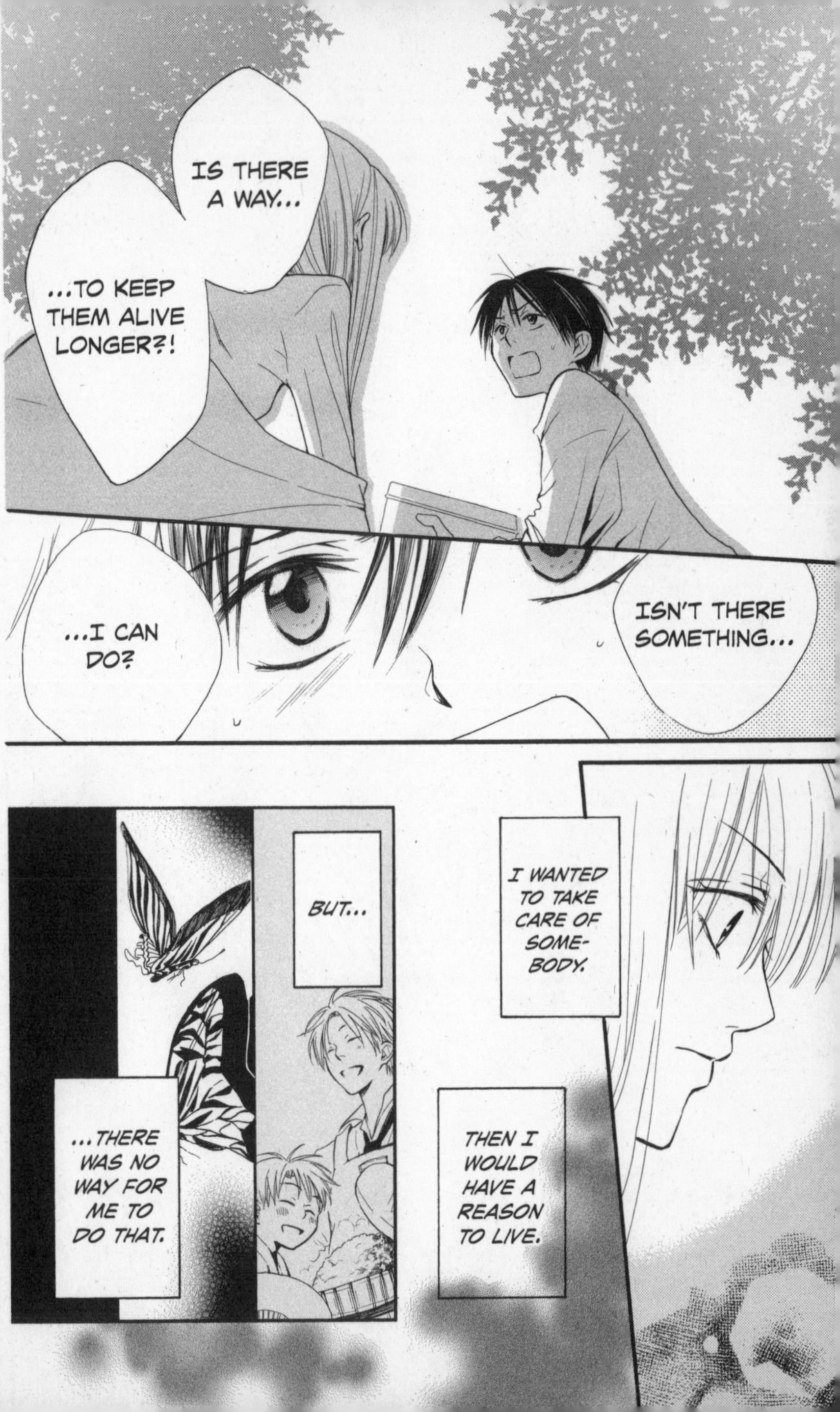
IS THERE A WAY...
...TO KEEP THEM ALIVE LONGER?!
ISN'T THERE SOMETHING...
...I CAN DO?
I WANTED TO TAKE CARE OF SOME-BODY.
THEN I WOULD HAVE A REASON TO LIVE.
BUT...
...THERE WAS NO WAY FOR ME TO DO THAT.

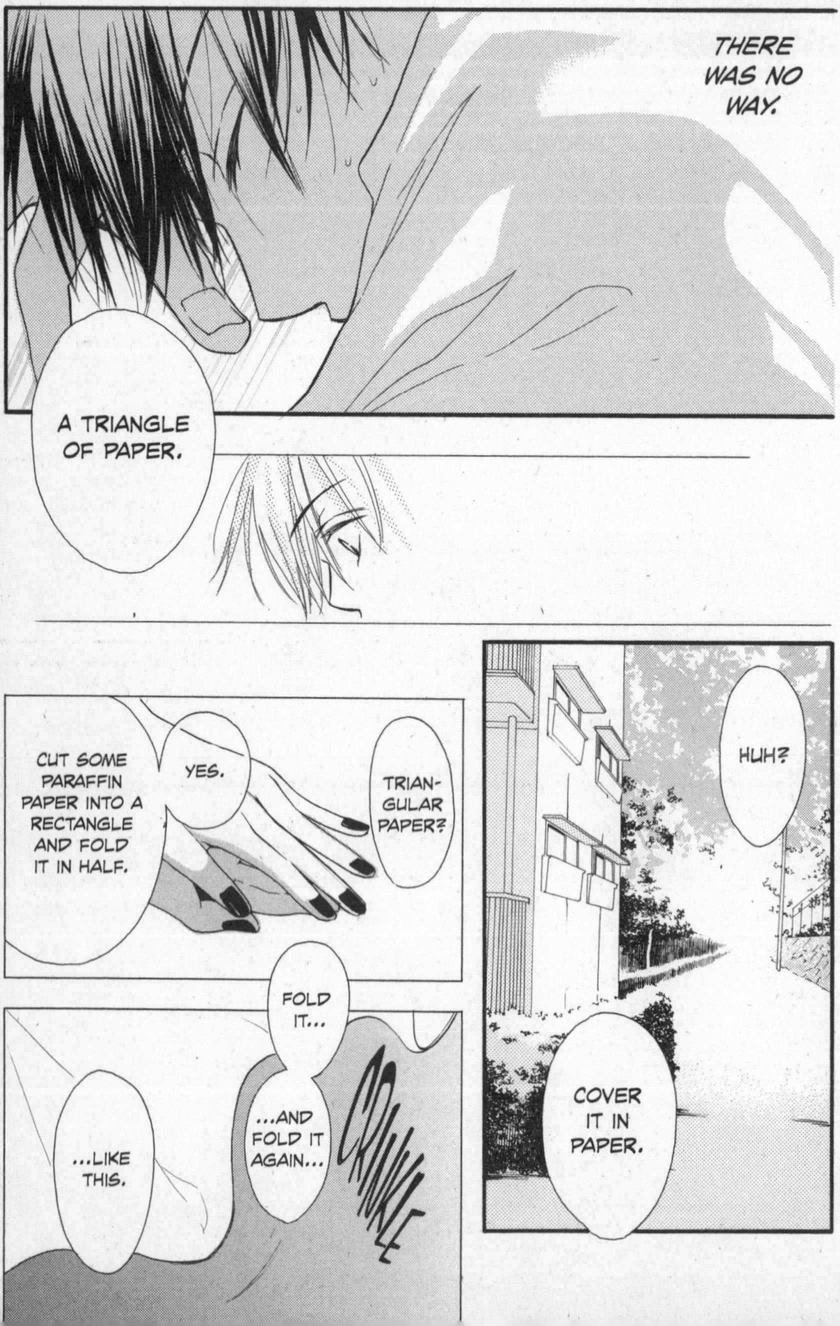
THERE WAS NO WAY.
A TRIANGLE OF PAPER.
HUH?
COVER IT IN PAPER.
TRIAN-GULAR PAPER?
YES.
CUT SOME PARAFFIN PAPER INTO A RECTANGLE AND FOLD IT IN HALF.
FOLD IT...
...AND FOLD IT AGAIN...
CRINKLE
...LIKE THIS.

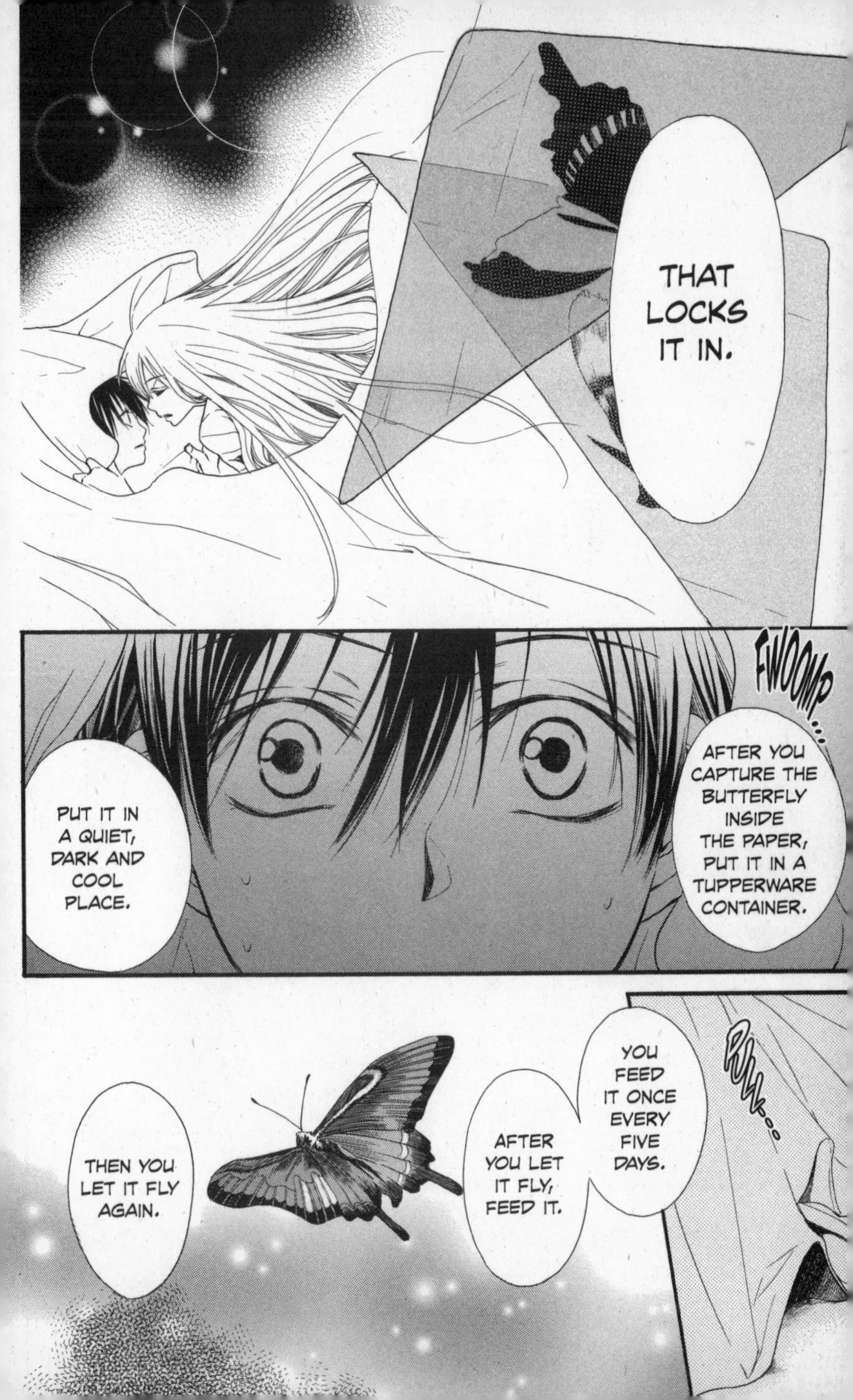
THAT LOCKS IT IN.
FWOOMP...
AFTER YOU CAPTURE THE BUTTERFLY INSIDE THE PAPER, PUT IT IN A TUPPERWARE CONTAINER.
PUT IT IN A QUIET, DARK AND COOL PLACE.
YOU FEED IT ONCE EVERY FIVE DAYS.
AFTER YOU LET IT FLY, FEED IT.
THEN YOU LET IT FLY AGAIN.

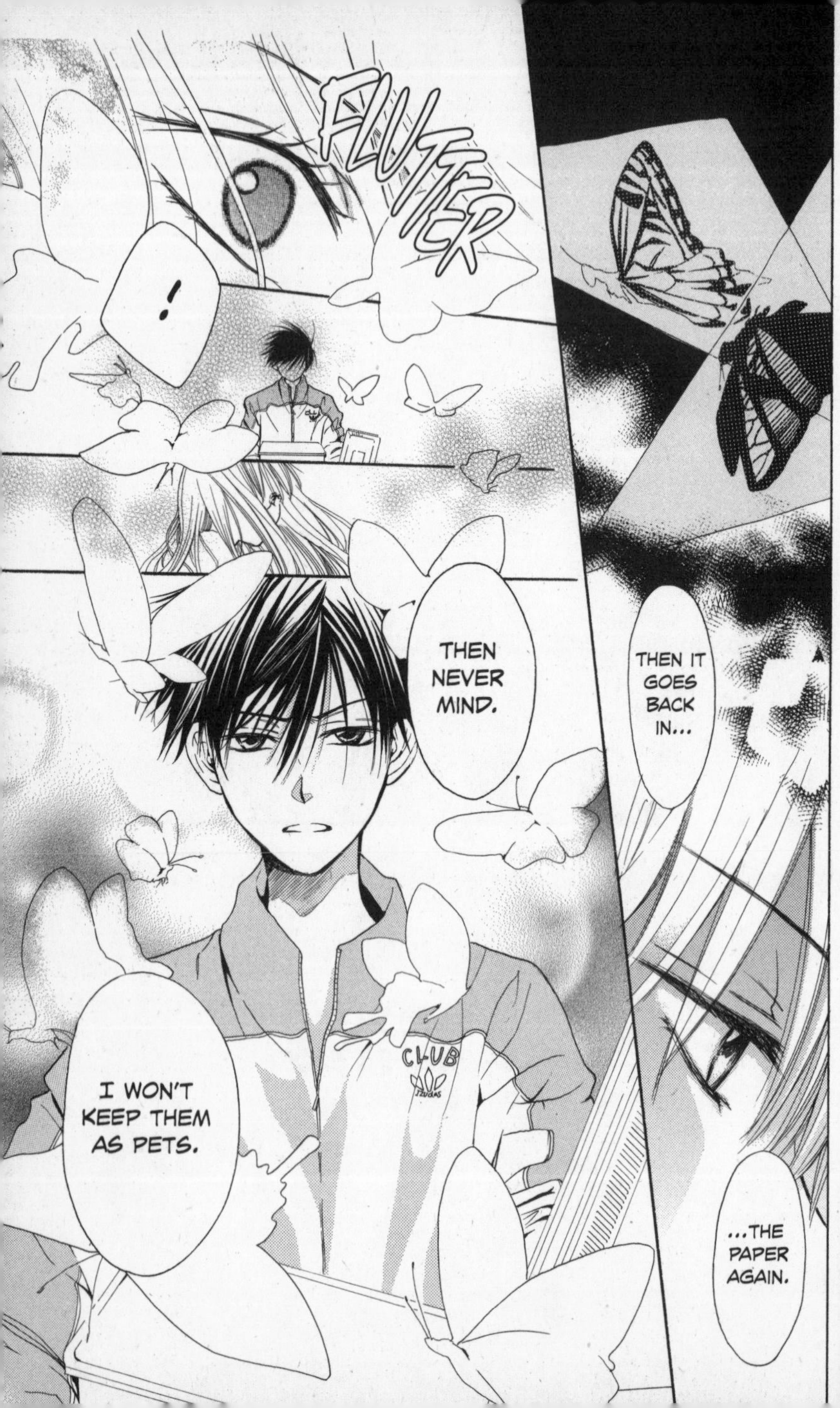
THEN IT GOES BACK IN...
...THE PAPER AGAIN.
FLUTTER
!
THEN NEVER MIND.
I WON'T KEEP THEM AS PETS.

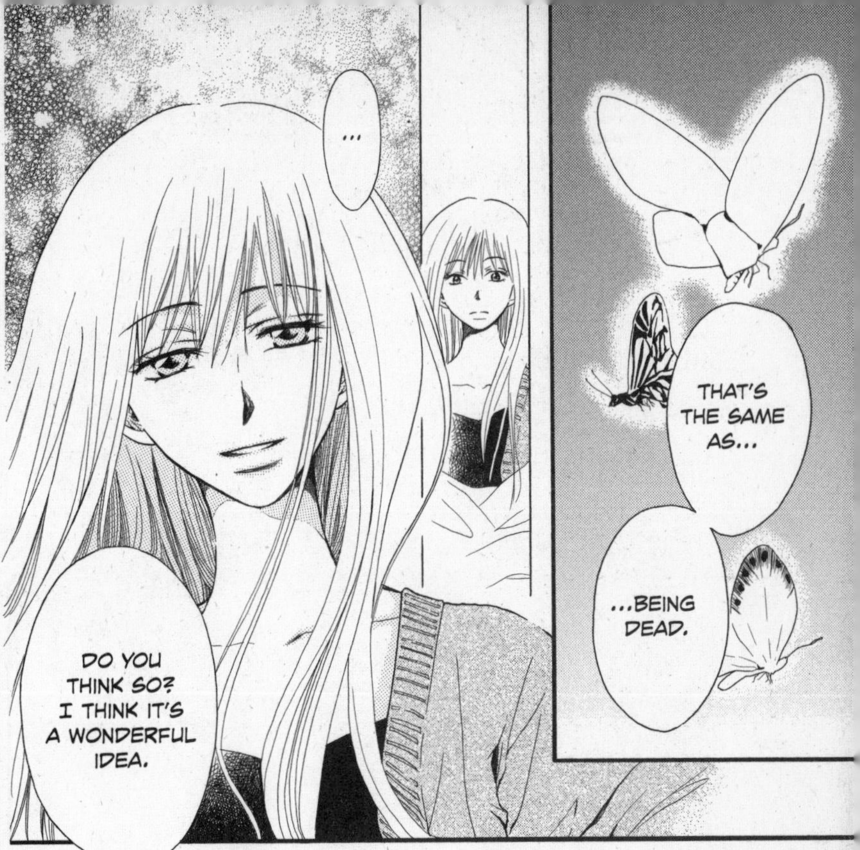
THAT'S THE SAME AS...
...BEING DEAD.
...
DO YOU THINK SO? I THINK IT'S A WONDERFUL IDEA.

SOMETIMES, SHE WAS VERY CRUEL.

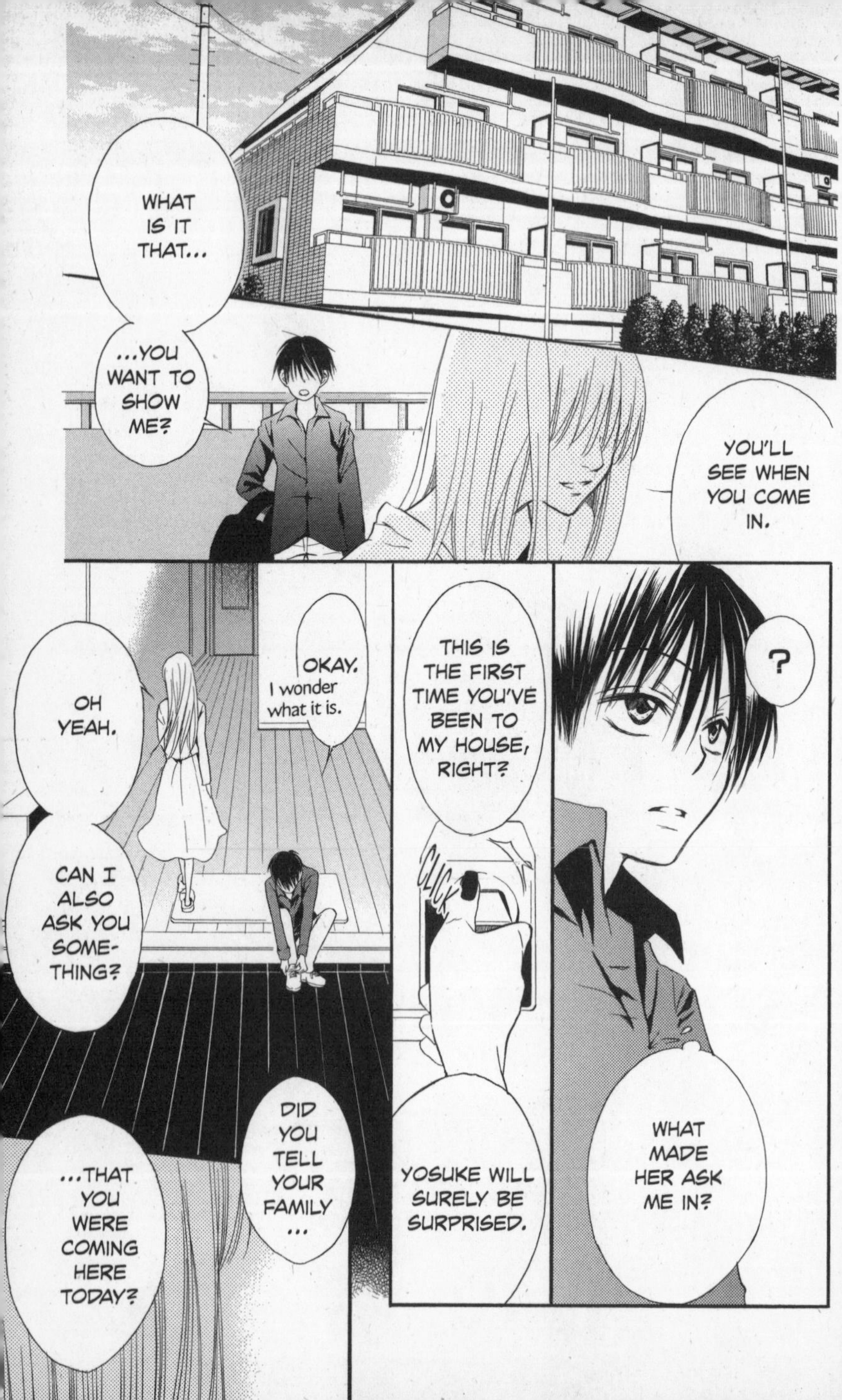
WHAT IS IT THAT...
...YOU WANT TO SHOW ME?
YOU'LL SEE WHEN YOU COME IN.
?
WHAT MADE HER ASK ME IN?
THIS IS THE FIRST TIME YOU'VE BEEN TO MY HOUSE, RIGHT?
CLICK
YOSUKE WILL SURELY BE SURPRISED.
OKAY.
I wonder what it is.
OH YEAH.
CAN I ALSO ASK YOU SOMETHING?
DID YOU TELL YOUR FAMILY...
...THAT YOU WERE COMING HERE TODAY?

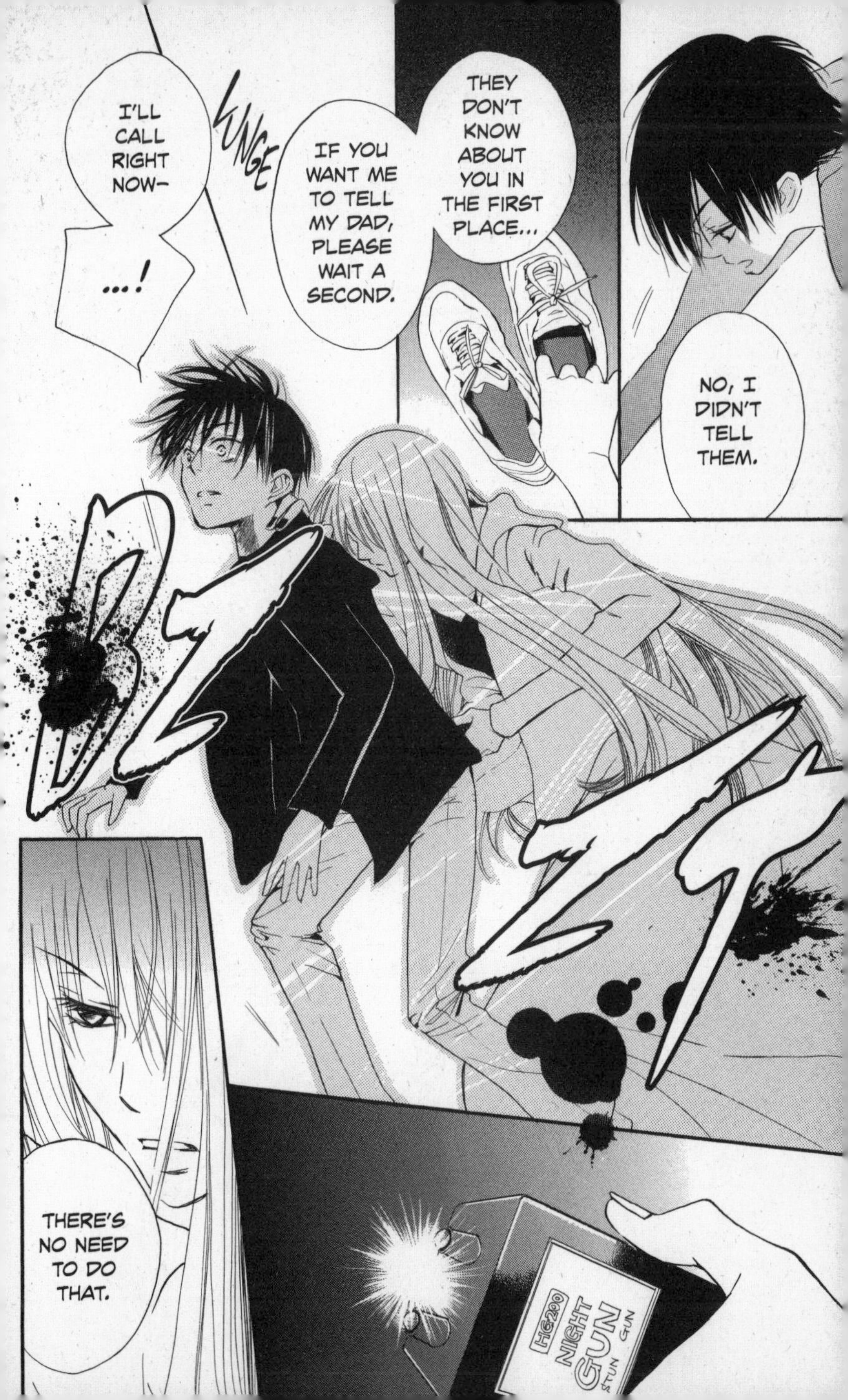
NO, I DIDN'T TELL THEM.
THEY DON'T KNOW ABOUT YOU IN THE FIRST PLACE...
IF YOU WANT ME TO TELL MY DAD, PLEASE WAIT A SECOND.
LUNGE
I'LL CALL RIGHT NOW–
...!
HG-200 NIGHT GUN STUN GUN
THERE'S NO NEED TO DO THAT.

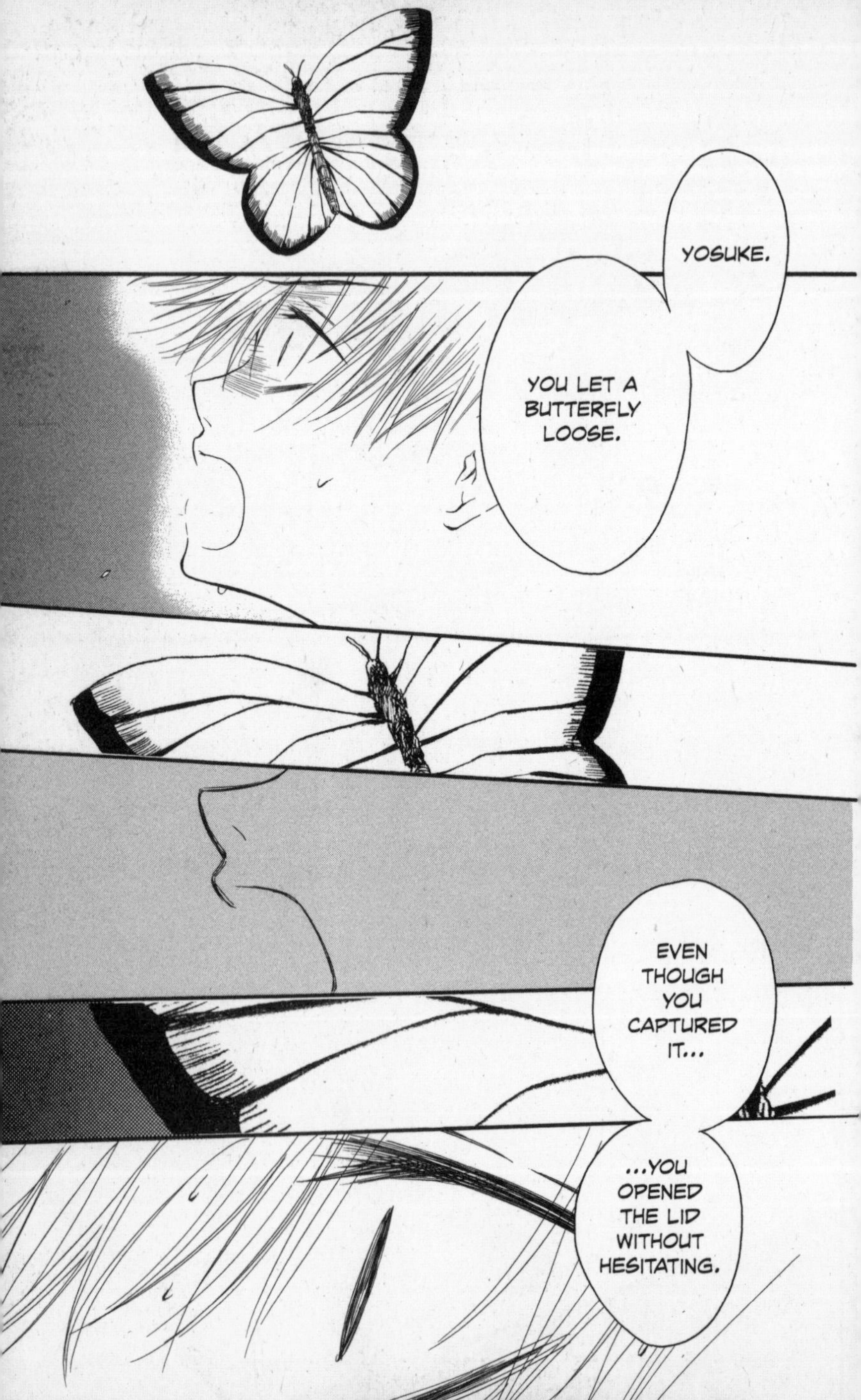
YOSUKE.
YOU LET A BUTTERFLY LOOSE.
EVEN THOUGH YOU CAPTURED IT...
...YOU OPENED THE LID WITHOUT HESITATING.

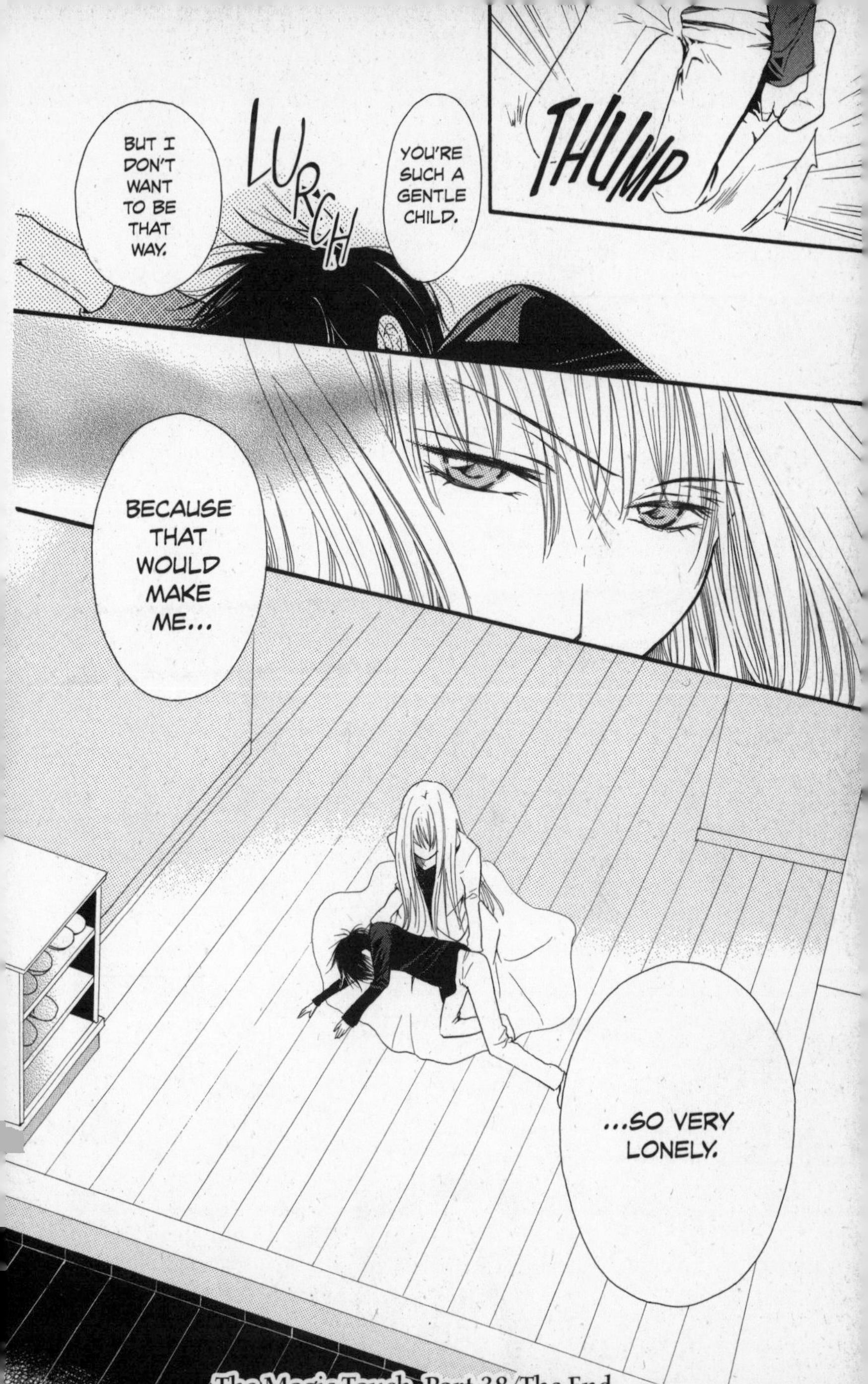
THUMP
LURCH
YOU'RE SUCH A GENTLE CHILD.
BUT I DON'T WANT TO BE THAT WAY.
BECAUSE THAT WOULD MAKE ME...
...SO VERY LONELY.

The Magic Touch, Part 38/The End

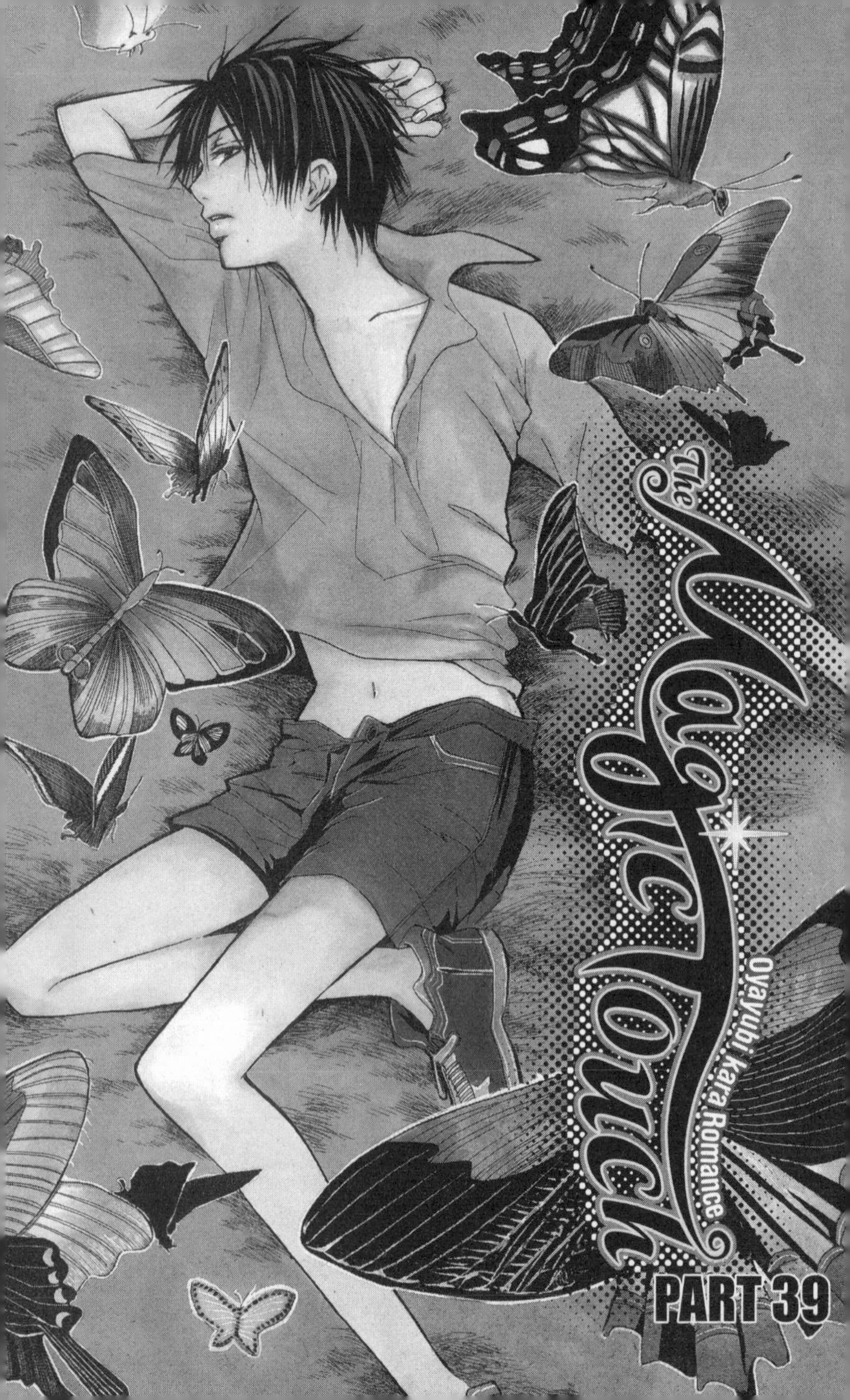
The Magic Touch
Oyayubi Kara Romance
PART 39

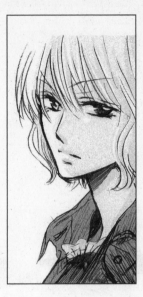

Natsue Abe

Birthday: November 25

Blood Type: AB

School: Third-Year (Treasurer), Futouka Academy

Height: 170 cm

Hobby: Sexual Harassment

Special Talents: Treasury Duties, Eating Lunch in Class
Before Lunch Time, Slot Machines at
Pachinko Parlors (this is illegal)

Likes: Honest People, Good-Looking Boys, English Tea

Hates: Gossip Magazines, People, Gym Class

Siblings: Older Sister

Club in Middle School: None

Chitose Harumi

Birthday: October 28

Blood Type: O

School: Third-Year, Futouka Academy

Height: 181 cm

Hobby: Sports, Collecting Sweat Suits, Shopping

Special Talents: Science and Mathematics

Likes: Ramune Soda, Music, Radio

Hates: Winter

Siblings: None

Club in Middle School: None

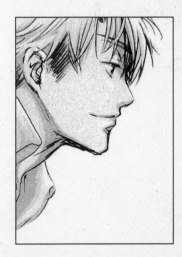

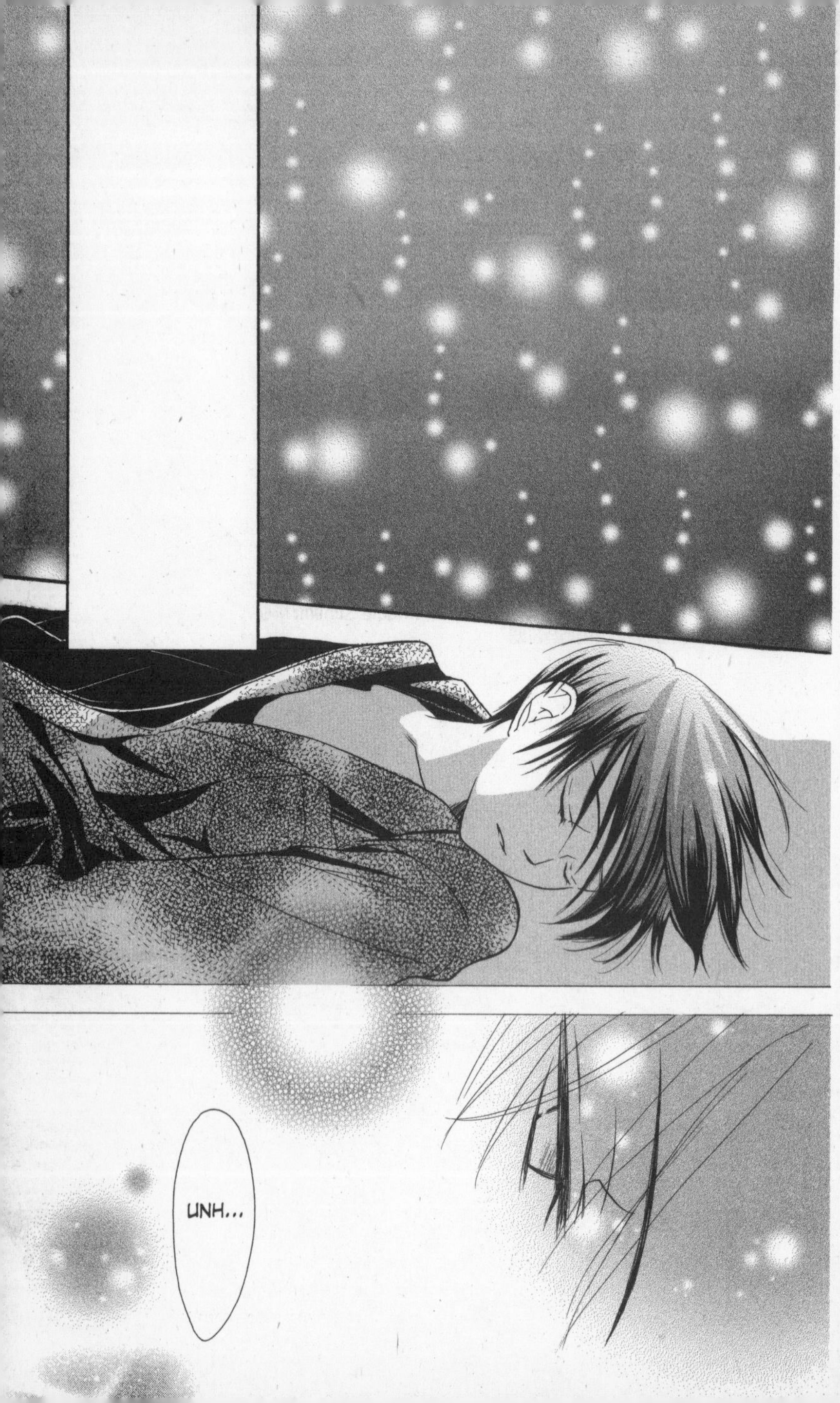
UNH...

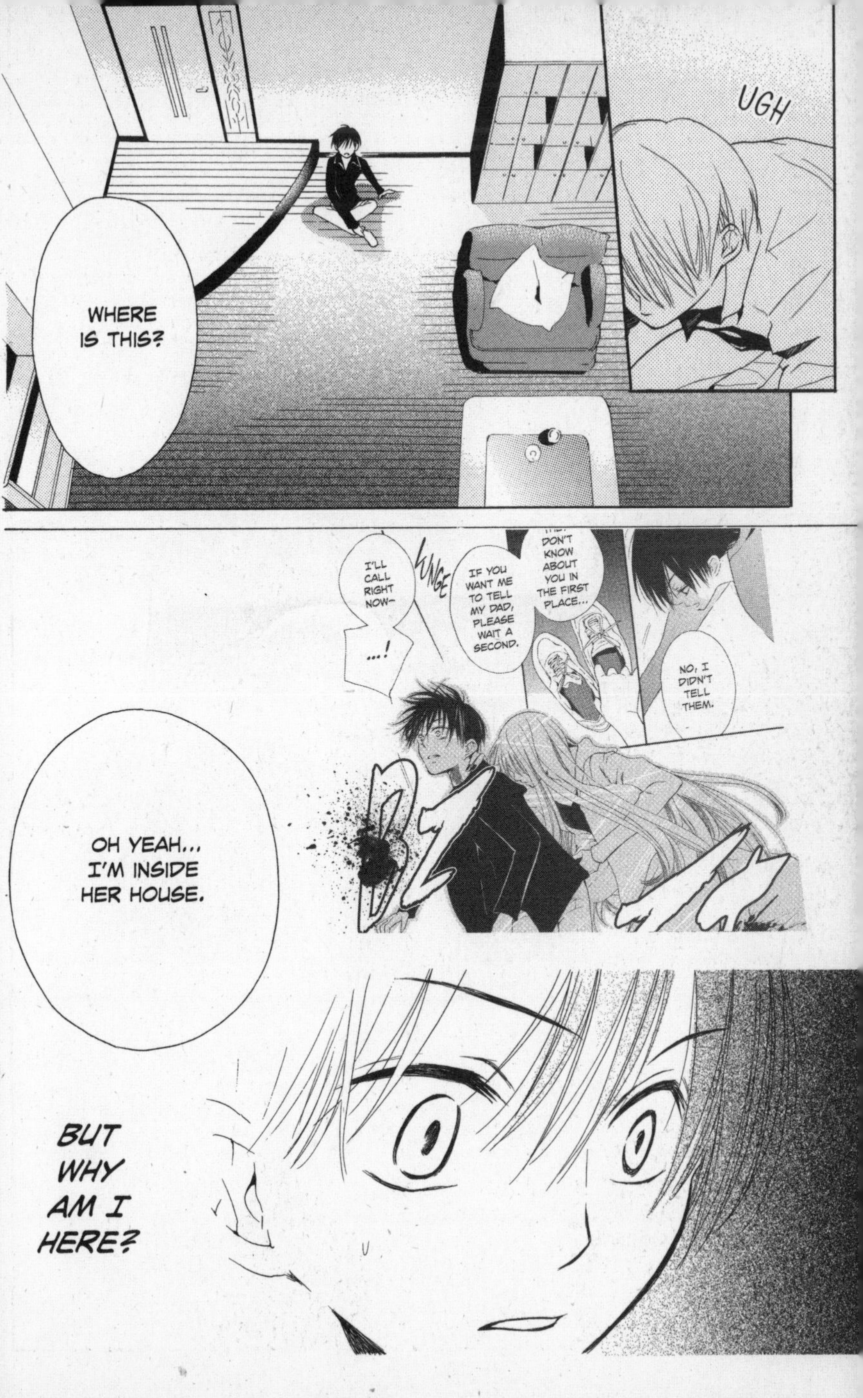
UGH
WHERE IS THIS?
DON'T KNOW ABOUT YOU IN THE FIRST PLACE...
NO, I DIDN'T TELL THEM.
IF YOU WANT ME TO TELL MY DAD, PLEASE WAIT A SECOND.
I'LL CALL RIGHT NOW—
LUNGE
...!
OH YEAH... I'M INSIDE HER HOUSE.
BUT WHY AM I HERE?

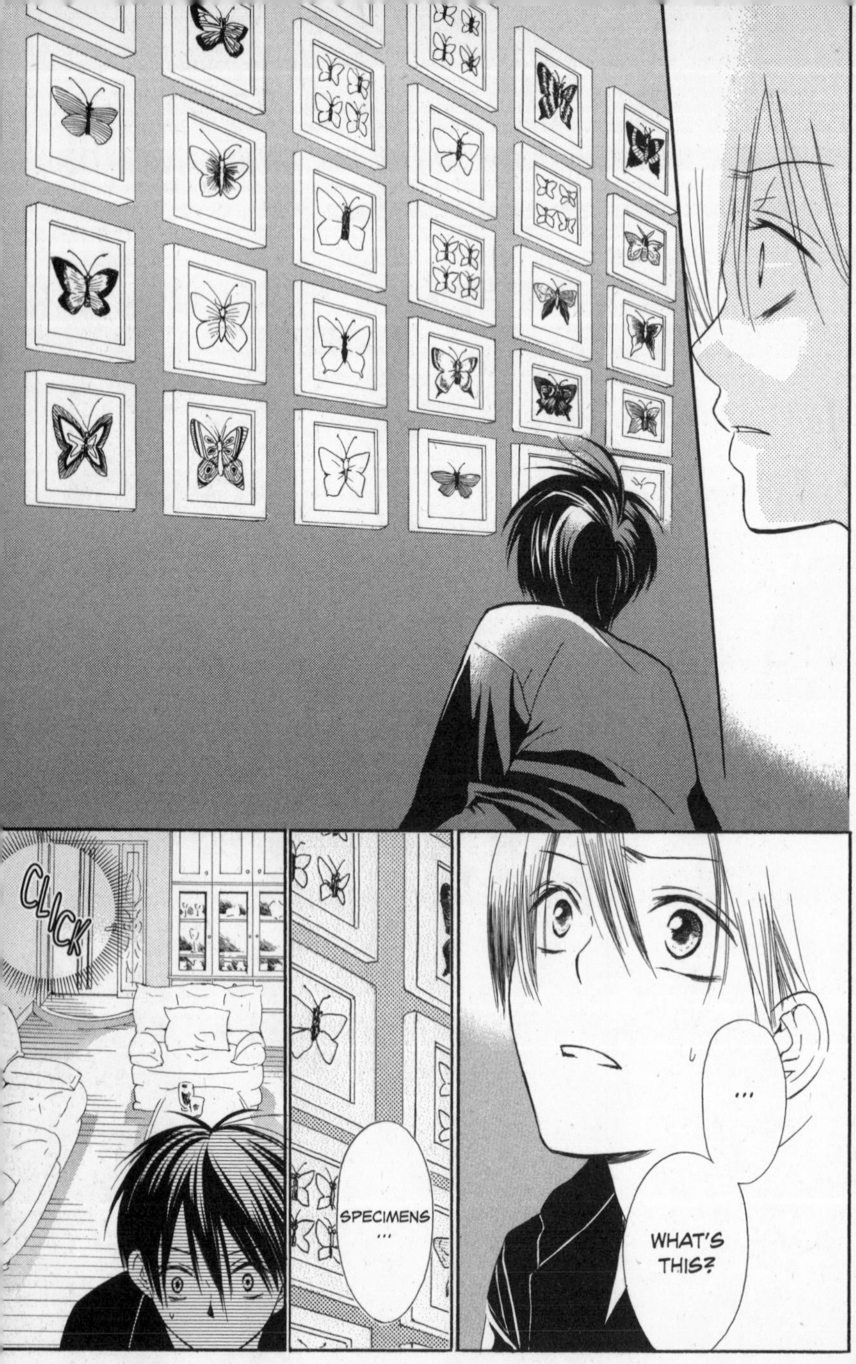
...
WHAT'S THIS?
SPECIMENS ...
CLICK

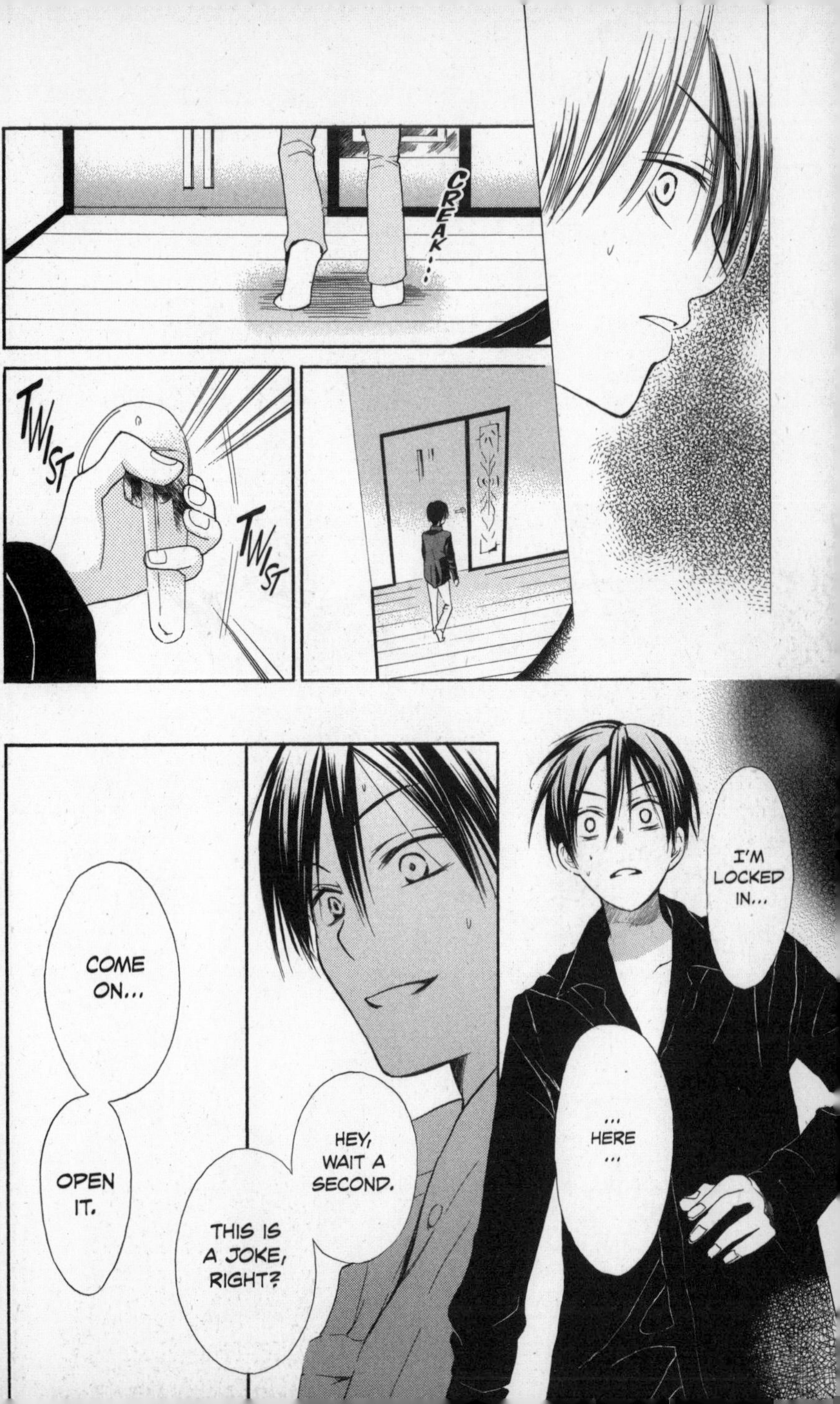
CREAK...
TWIST
TWIST
I'M LOCKED IN...
...HERE...
HEY, WAIT A SECOND.
THIS IS A JOKE, RIGHT?
COME ON...
OPEN IT.

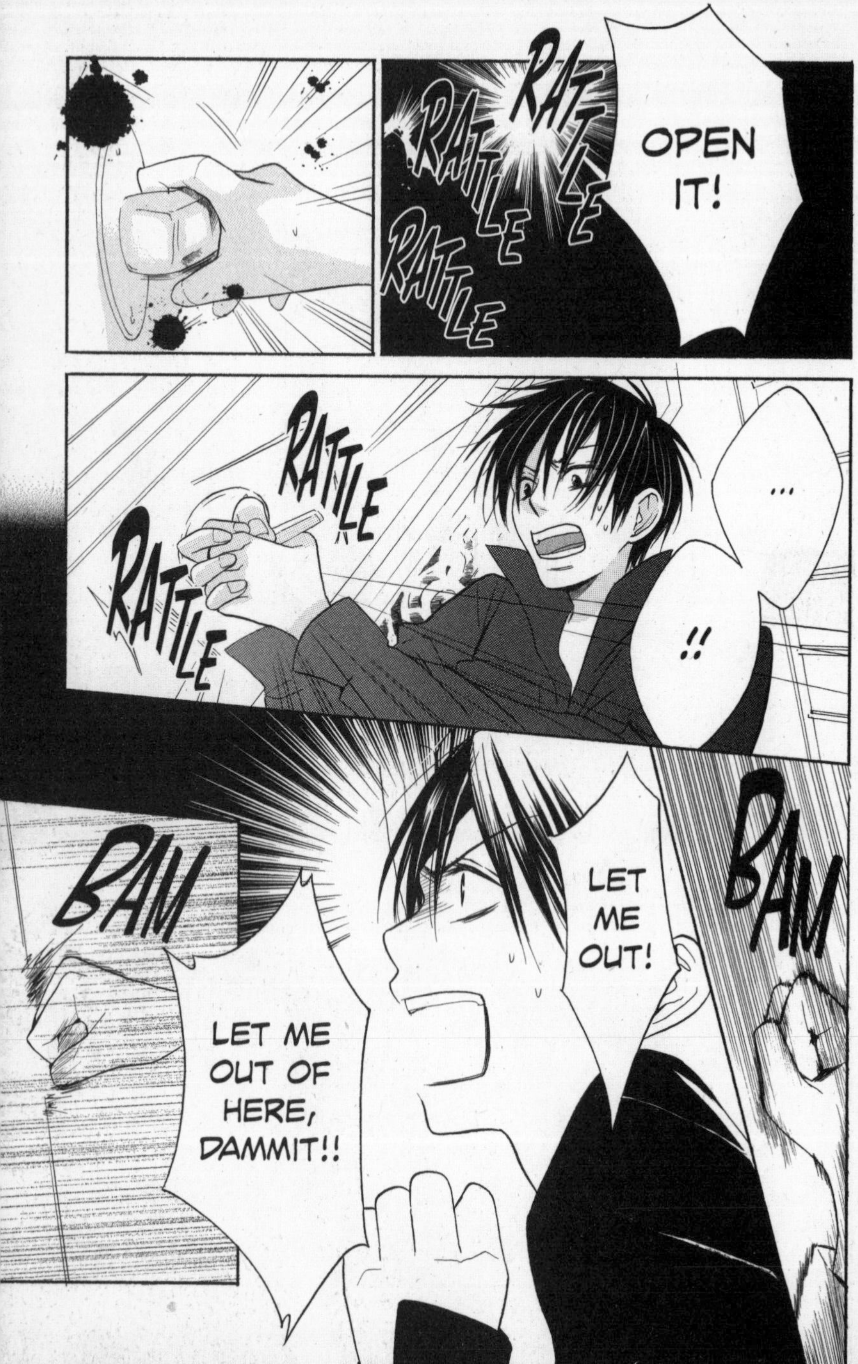
OPEN IT!
RATTLE
RATTLE
RATTLE
...
!!
RATTLE
RATTLE
BAM
LET ME OUT!
LET ME OUT OF HERE, DAMMIT!!
BAM

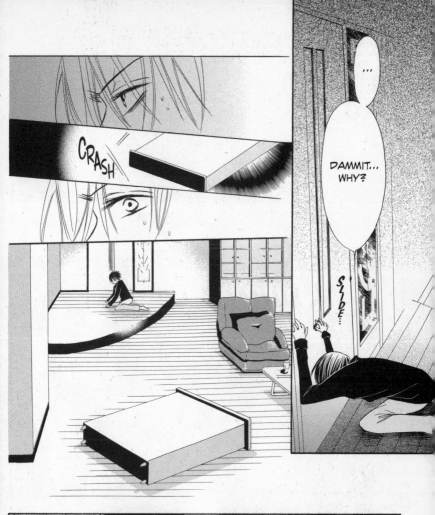

...

DAMMIT... WHY?

CRASH

SLIDE...

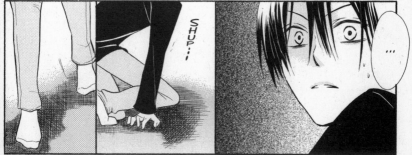

SHUP!!

...

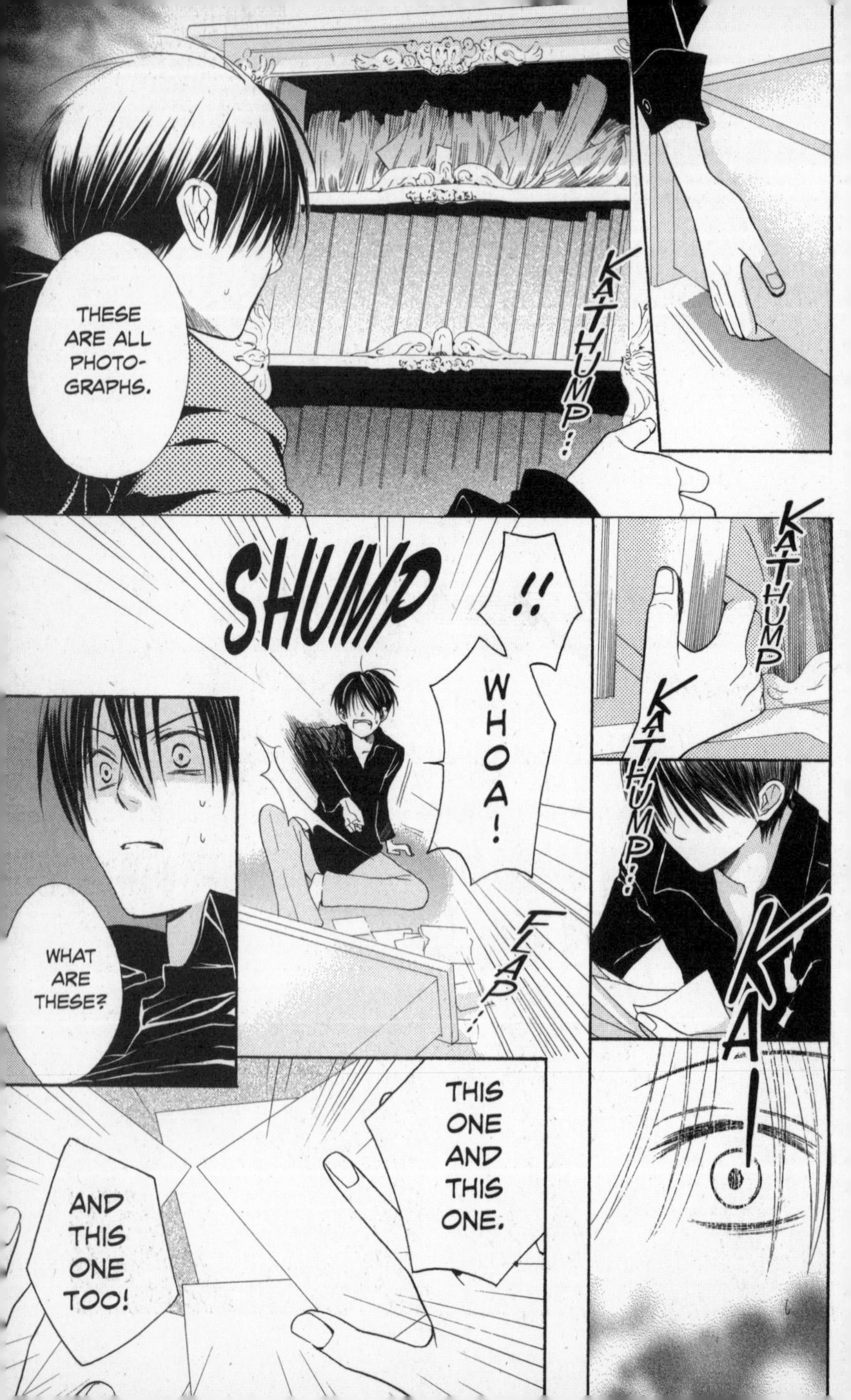
KATHUMP..
THESE ARE ALL PHOTO-GRAPHS.
KATHUMP
KATHUMP..
KA!
SHUMP
!!
WHOA!
FLAP..
WHAT ARE THESE?
THIS ONE AND THIS ONE.
AND THIS ONE TOO!

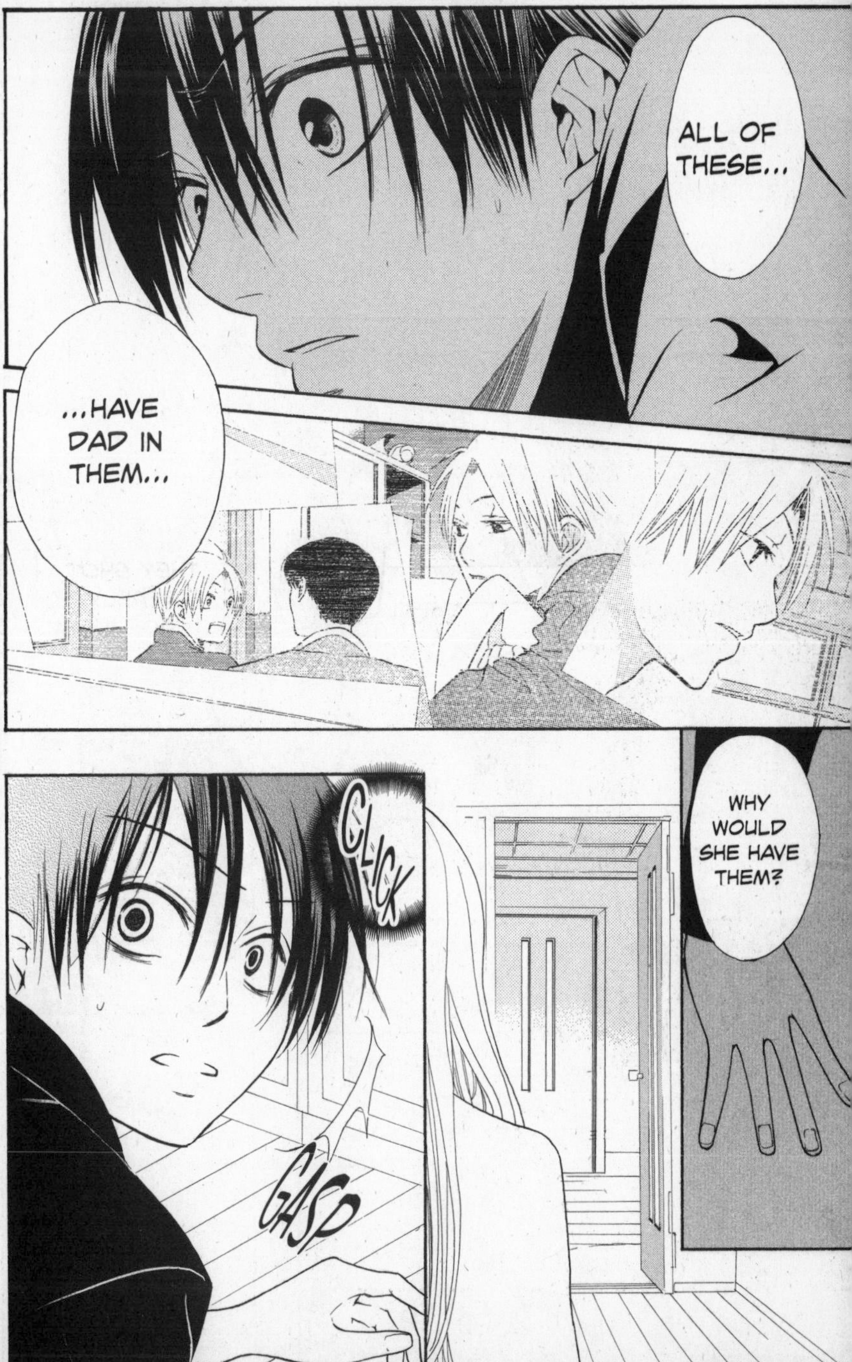
ALL OF THESE...
...HAVE DAD IN THEM...
WHY WOULD SHE HAVE THEM?
CLICK
GASP

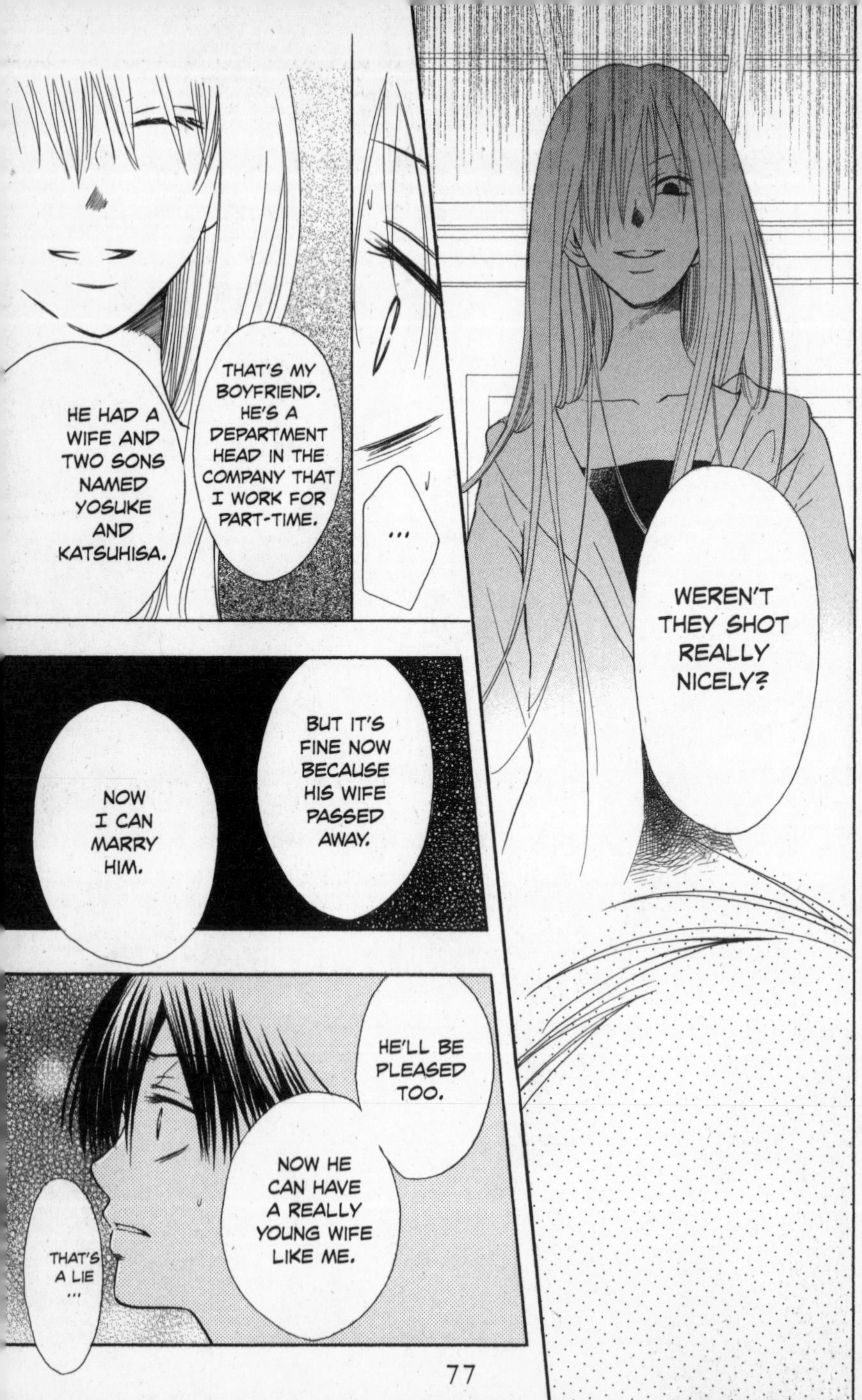
WEREN'T THEY SHOT REALLY NICELY?
...
THAT'S MY BOYFRIEND. HE'S A DEPARTMENT HEAD IN THE COMPANY THAT I WORK FOR PART-TIME.
HE HAD A WIFE AND TWO SONS NAMED YOSUKE AND KATSUHISA.
BUT IT'S FINE NOW BECAUSE HIS WIFE PASSED AWAY.
NOW I CAN MARRY HIM.
HE'LL BE PLEASED TOO.
NOW HE CAN HAVE A REALLY YOUNG WIFE LIKE ME.
THAT'S A LIE ...

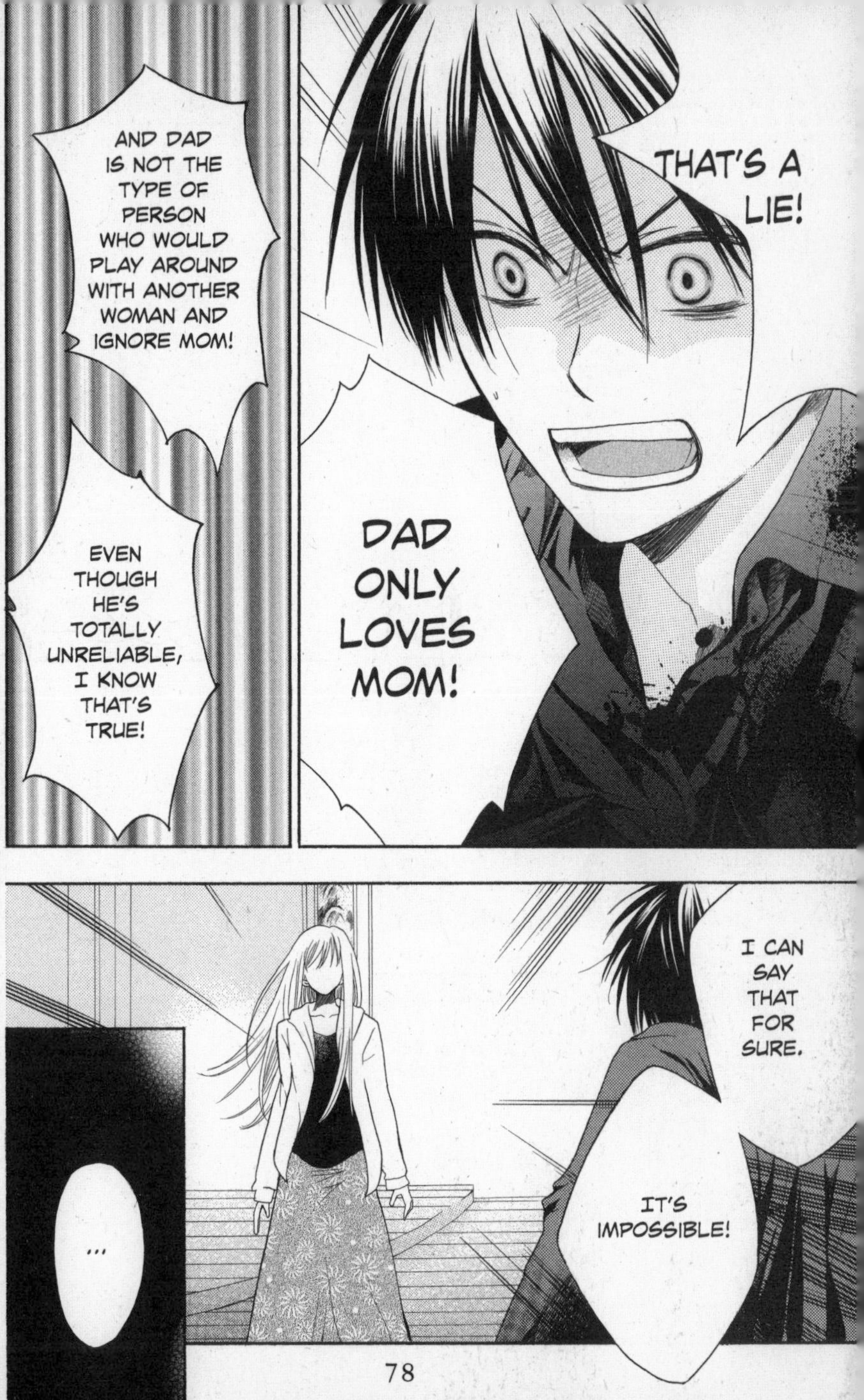
THAT'S A LIE!
DAD ONLY LOVES MOM!
AND DAD IS NOT THE TYPE OF PERSON WHO WOULD PLAY AROUND WITH ANOTHER WOMAN AND IGNORE MOM!
EVEN THOUGH HE'S TOTALLY UNRELIABLE, I KNOW THAT'S TRUE!
I CAN SAY THAT FOR SURE.
IT'S IMPOSSIBLE!
...

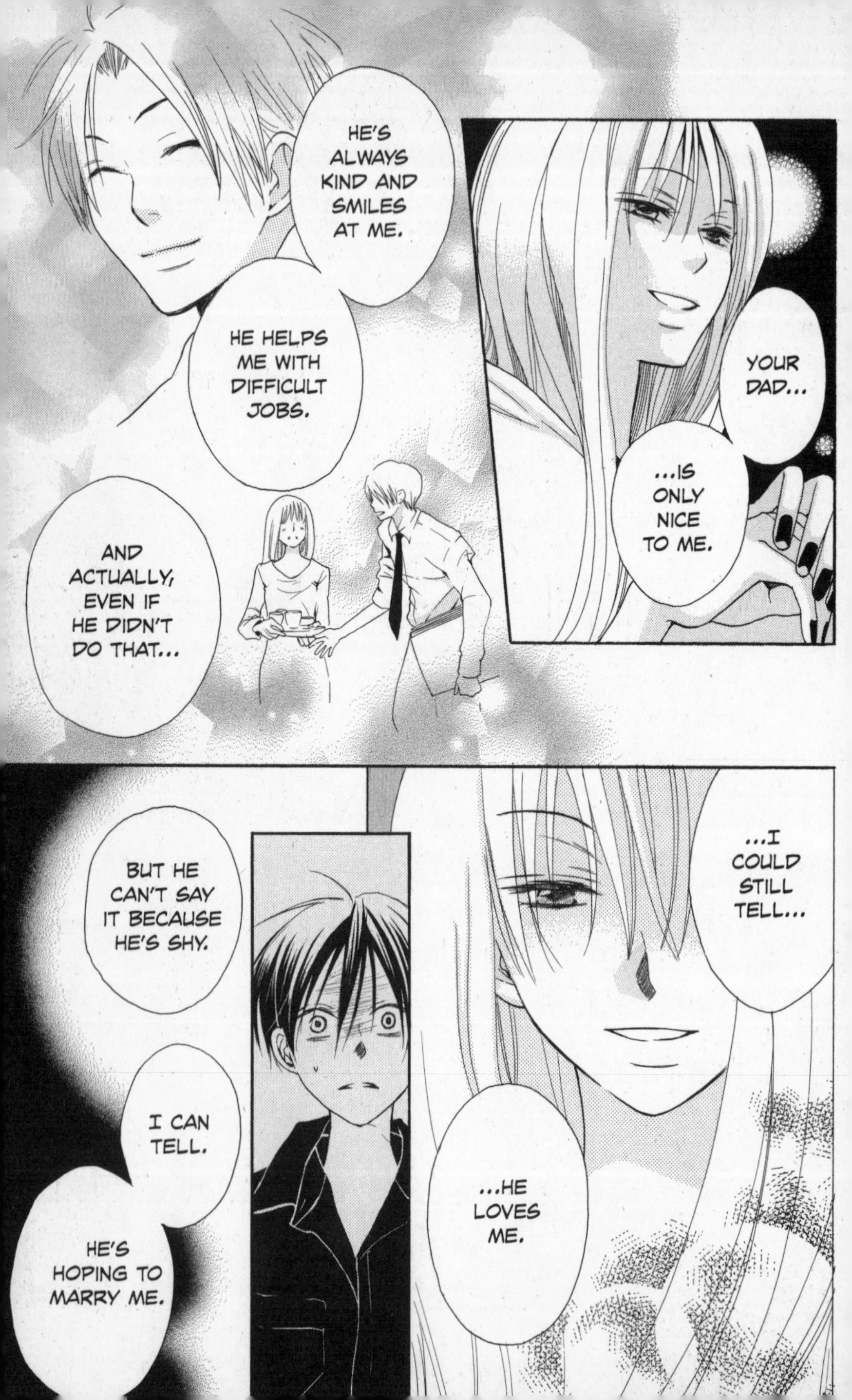
YOUR DAD...
...IS ONLY NICE TO ME.
HE'S ALWAYS KIND AND SMILES AT ME.
HE HELPS ME WITH DIFFICULT JOBS.
AND ACTUALLY, EVEN IF HE DIDN'T DO THAT...
...I COULD STILL TELL...
...HE LOVES ME.
BUT HE CAN'T SAY IT BECAUSE HE'S SHY.
I CAN TELL.
HE'S HOPING TO MARRY ME.

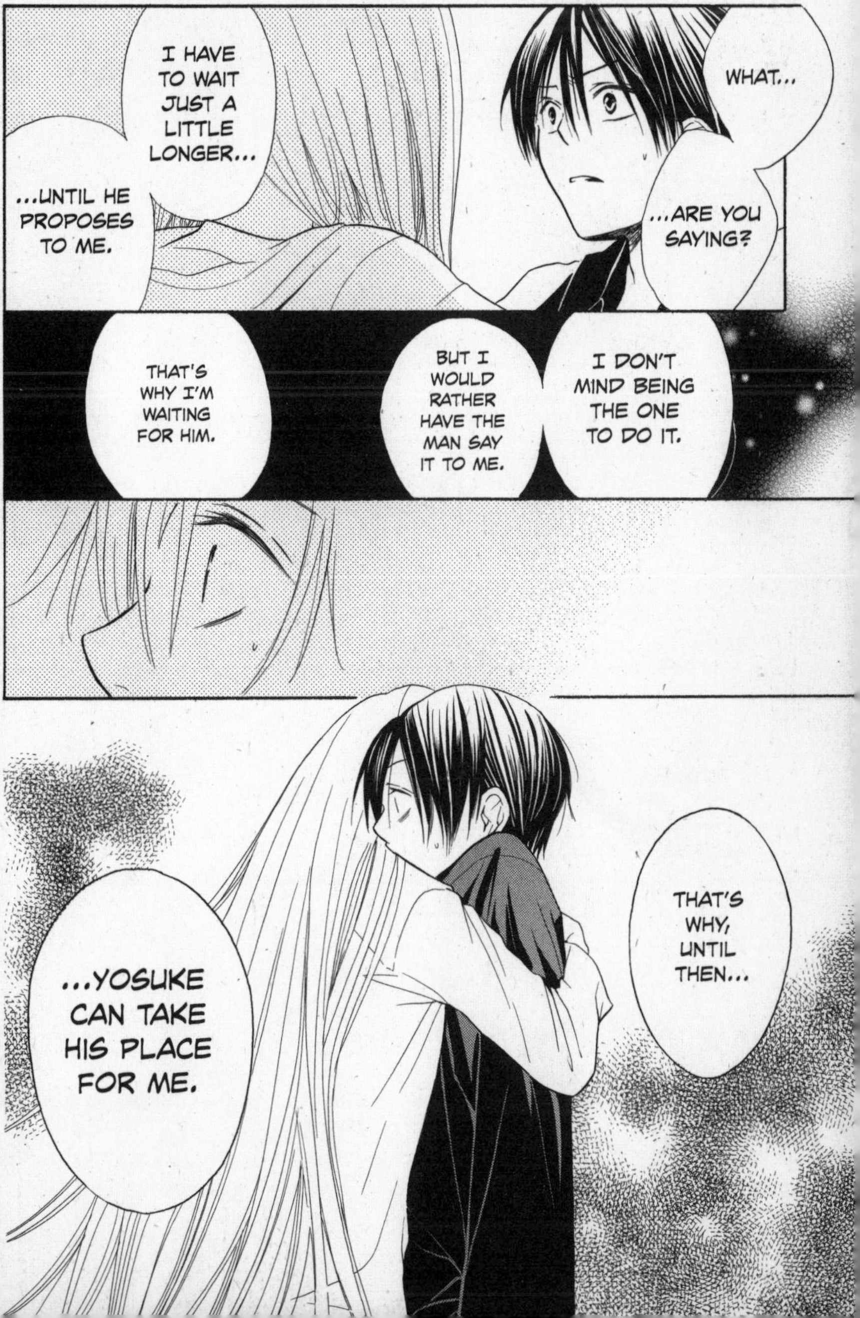
WHAT...
...ARE YOU SAYING?
I HAVE TO WAIT JUST A LITTLE LONGER...
...UNTIL HE PROPOSES TO ME.
I DON'T MIND BEING THE ONE TO DO IT.
BUT I WOULD RATHER HAVE THE MAN SAY IT TO ME.
THAT'S WHY I'M WAITING FOR HIM.
THAT'S WHY, UNTIL THEN...
...YOSUKE CAN TAKE HIS PLACE FOR ME.

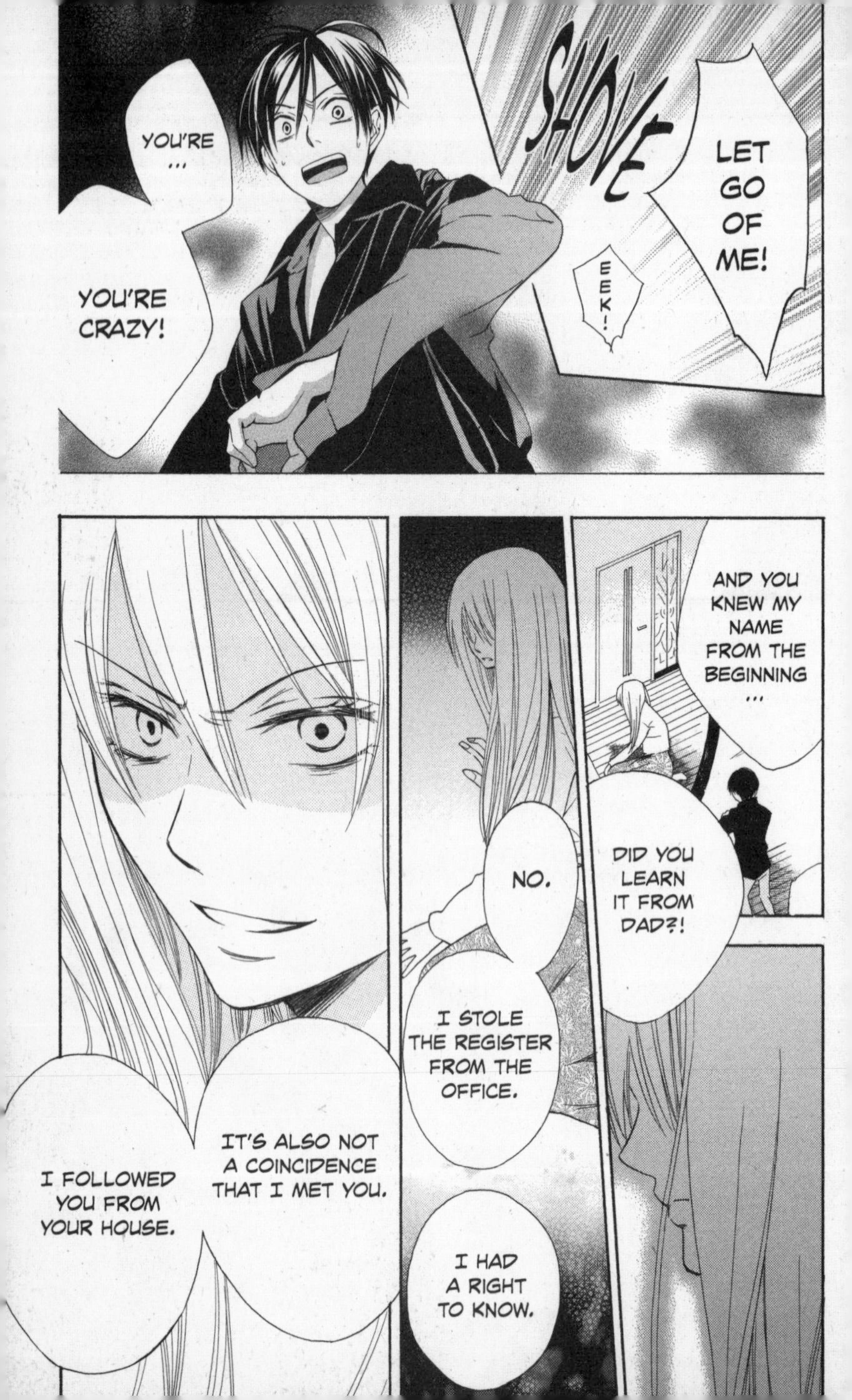
LET GO OF ME!
SHOVE
EEK!
YOU'RE ...
YOU'RE CRAZY!
AND YOU KNEW MY NAME FROM THE BEGINNING ...
DID YOU LEARN IT FROM DAD?!
NO.
I STOLE THE REGISTER FROM THE OFFICE.
I HAD A RIGHT TO KNOW.
IT'S ALSO NOT A COINCIDENCE THAT I MET YOU.
I FOLLOWED YOU FROM YOUR HOUSE.

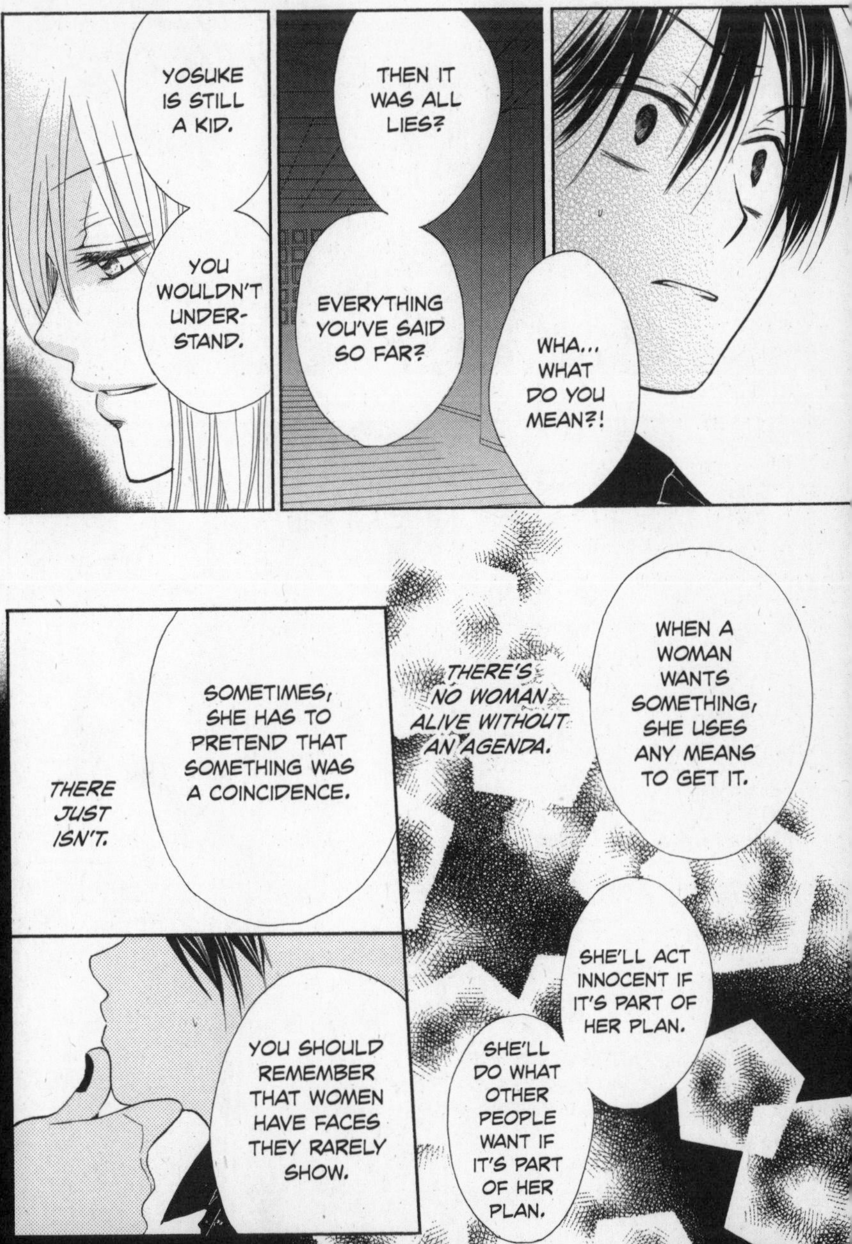
WHA... WHAT DO YOU MEAN?!
THEN IT WAS ALL LIES?
EVERYTHING YOU'VE SAID SO FAR?
YOSUKE IS STILL A KID.
YOU WOULDN'T UNDERSTAND.
WHEN A WOMAN WANTS SOMETHING, SHE USES ANY MEANS TO GET IT.
THERE'S NO WOMAN ALIVE WITHOUT AN AGENDA.
SHE'LL ACT INNOCENT IF IT'S PART OF HER PLAN.
SHE'LL DO WHAT OTHER PEOPLE WANT IF IT'S PART OF HER PLAN.
SOMETIMES, SHE HAS TO PRETEND THAT SOMETHING WAS A COINCIDENCE.
THERE JUST ISN'T.
YOU SHOULD REMEMBER THAT WOMEN HAVE FACES THEY RARELY SHOW.

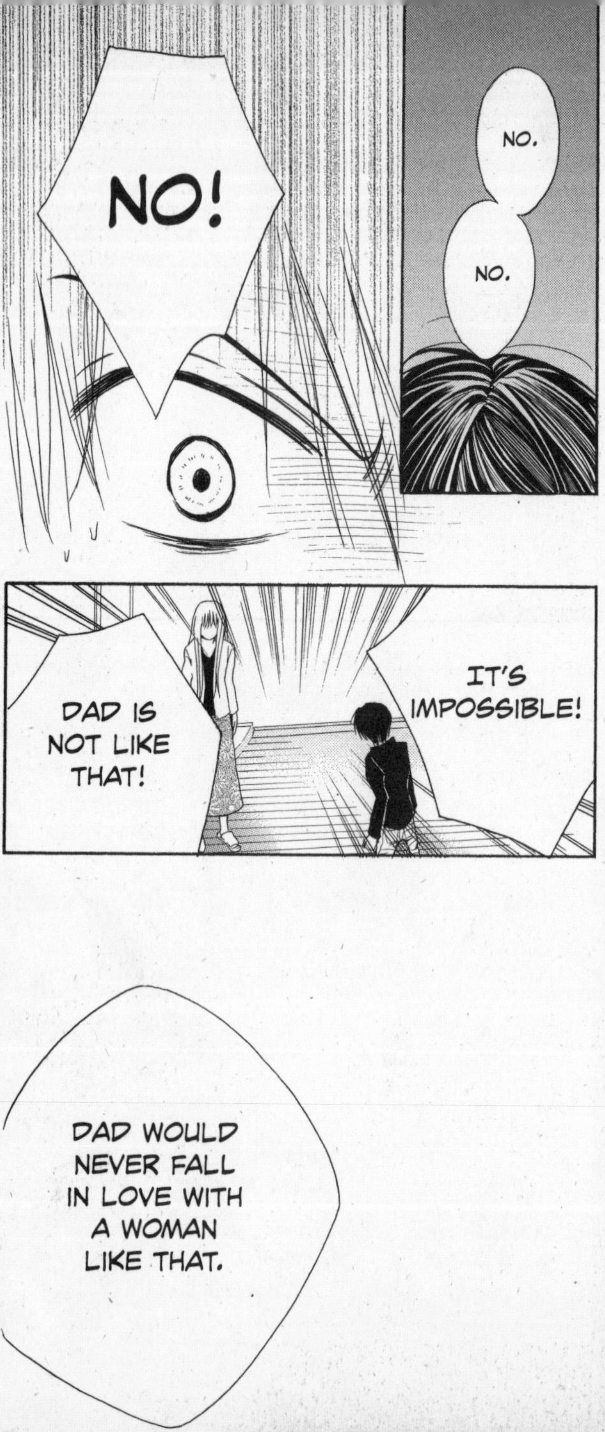
NO.
NO.
NO!
IT'S IMPOSSIBLE!
DAD IS NOT LIKE THAT!
DAD WOULD NEVER FALL IN LOVE WITH A WOMAN LIKE THAT.

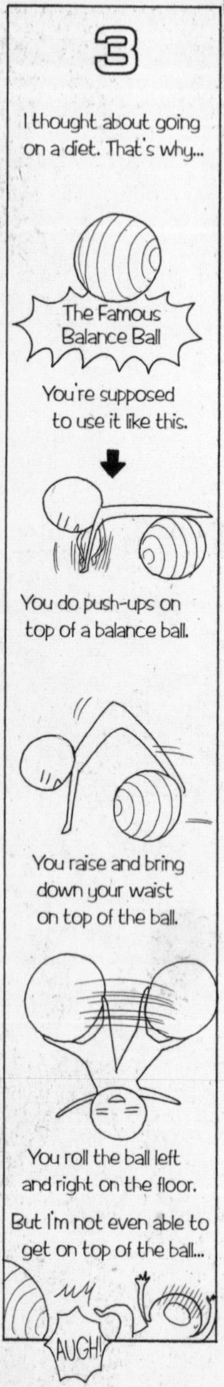
3
I thought about going on a diet. That's why...
The Famous Balance Ball
You're supposed to use it like this.
You do push-ups on top of a balance ball.
You raise and bring down your waist on top of the ball.
You roll the ball left and right on the floor.
But I'm not even able to get on top of the ball...
AUGH!

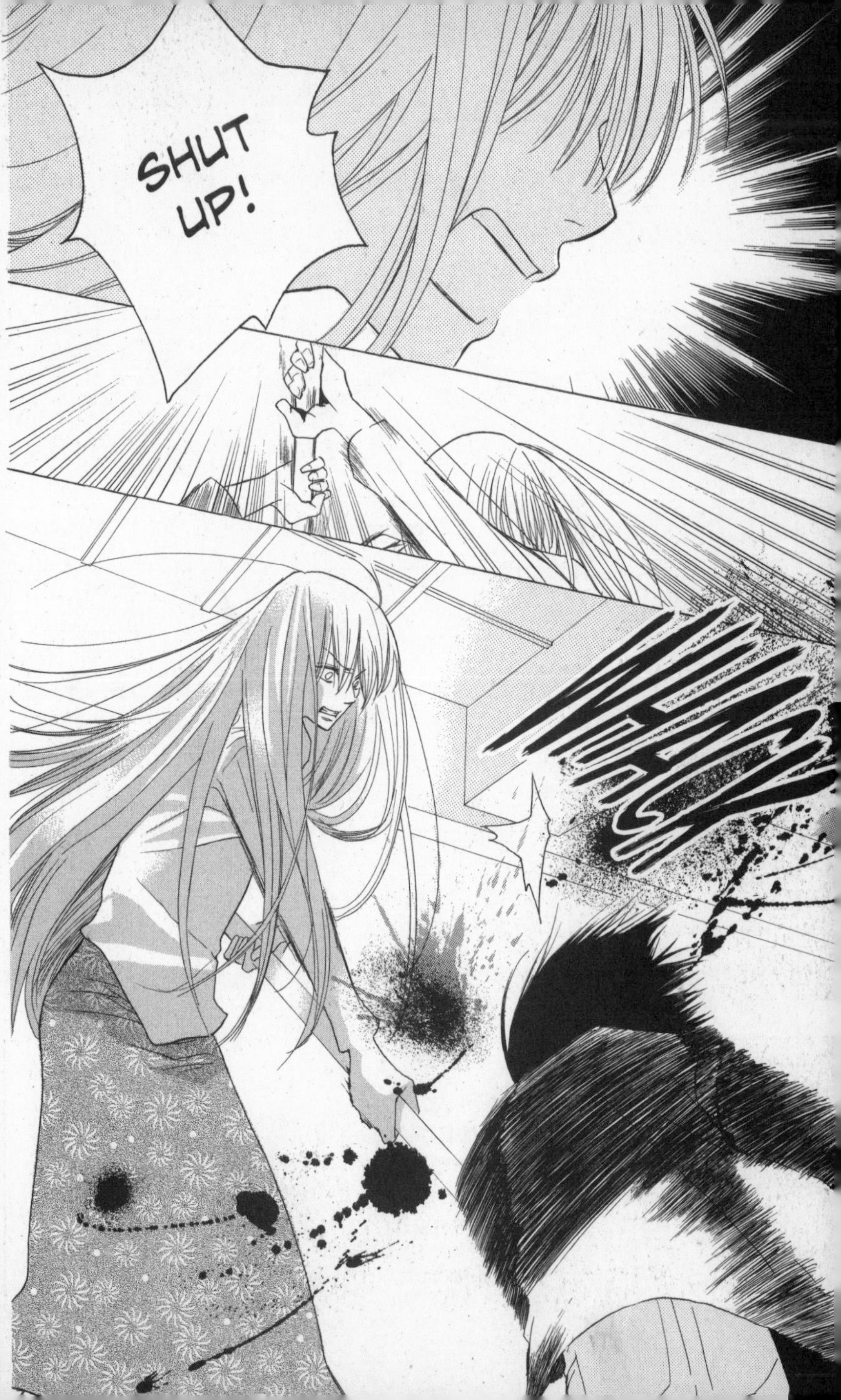
SHUT UP!

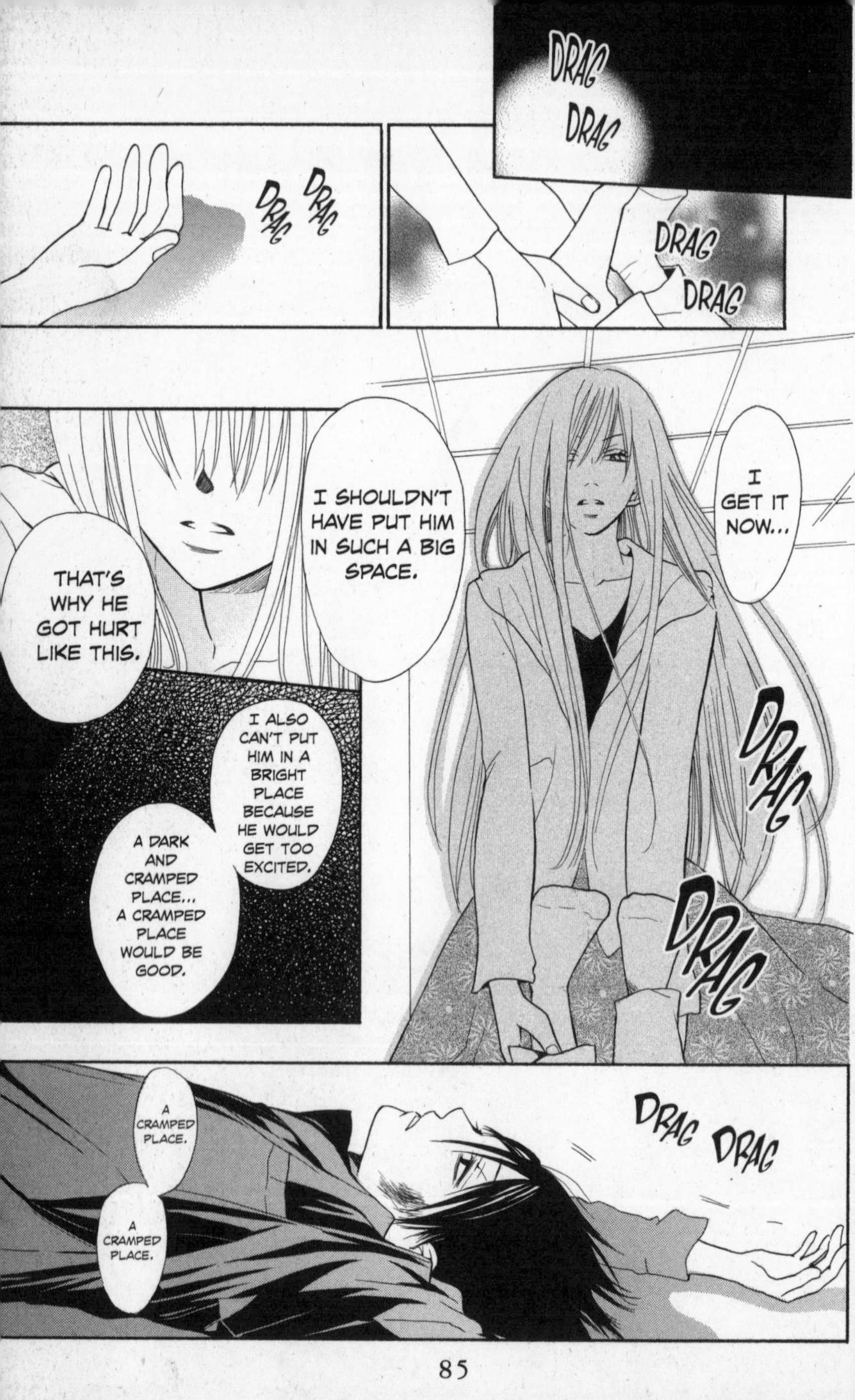
DRAG
DRAG
DRAG
DRAG
DRAG
DRAG
I GET IT NOW...
DRAG
DRAG
I SHOULDN'T HAVE PUT HIM IN SUCH A BIG SPACE.
THAT'S WHY HE GOT HURT LIKE THIS.
I ALSO CAN'T PUT HIM IN A BRIGHT PLACE BECAUSE HE WOULD GET TOO EXCITED.
A DARK AND CRAMPED PLACE... A CRAMPED PLACE WOULD BE GOOD.
DRAG DRAG
A CRAMPED PLACE.
A CRAMPED PLACE.

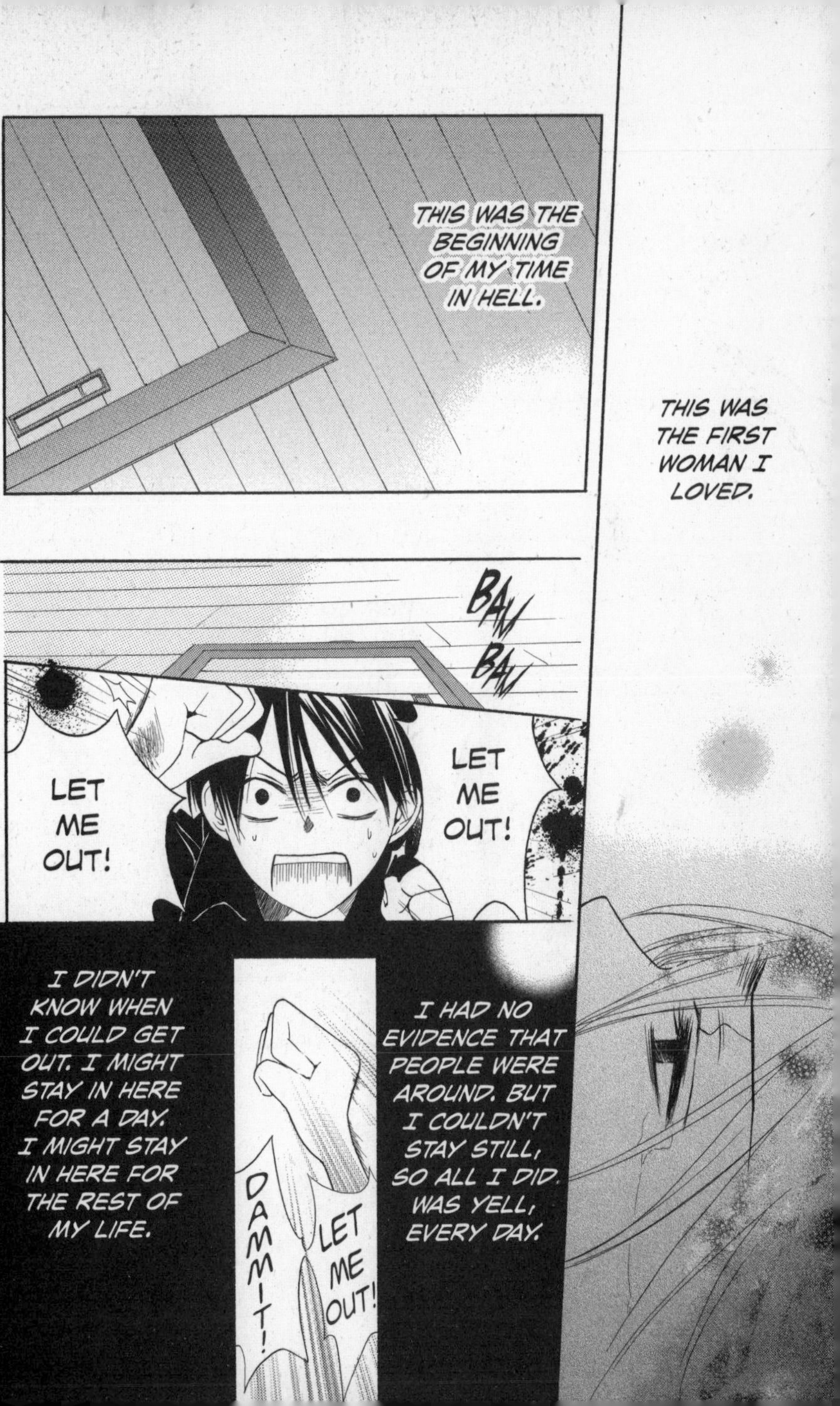
THIS WAS THE FIRST WOMAN I LOVED.
THIS WAS THE BEGINNING OF MY TIME IN HELL.
BAM BAM
LET ME OUT!
LET ME OUT!
I HAD NO EVIDENCE THAT PEOPLE WERE AROUND. BUT I COULDN'T STAY STILL, SO ALL I DID WAS YELL, EVERY DAY.
LET ME OUT!
DAMMIT!
I DIDN'T KNOW WHEN I COULD GET OUT. I MIGHT STAY IN HERE FOR A DAY. I MIGHT STAY IN HERE FOR THE REST OF MY LIFE.

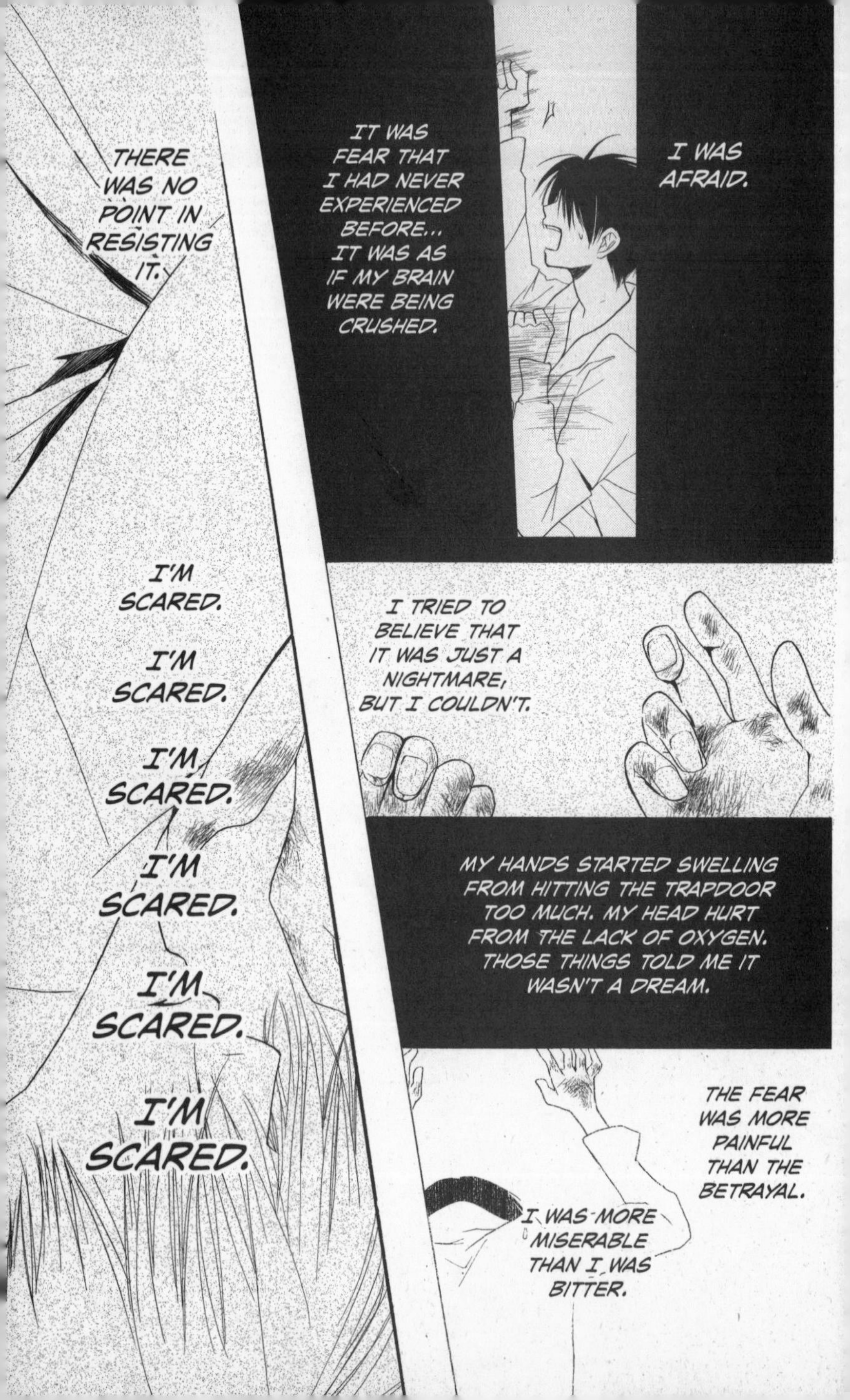
I WAS AFRAID.
IT WAS FEAR THAT I HAD NEVER EXPERIENCED BEFORE... IT WAS AS IF MY BRAIN WERE BEING CRUSHED.
I TRIED TO BELIEVE THAT IT WAS JUST A NIGHTMARE, BUT I COULDN'T.
MY HANDS STARTED SWELLING FROM HITTING THE TRAPDOOR TOO MUCH. MY HEAD HURT FROM THE LACK OF OXYGEN. THOSE THINGS TOLD ME IT WASN'T A DREAM.
THE FEAR WAS MORE PAINFUL THAN THE BETRAYAL.
I WAS MORE MISERABLE THAN I WAS BITTER.
THERE WAS NO POINT IN RESISTING IT.
I'M SCARED.
I'M SCARED.
I'M SCARED.
I'M SCARED.
I'M SCARED.
I'M SCARED.

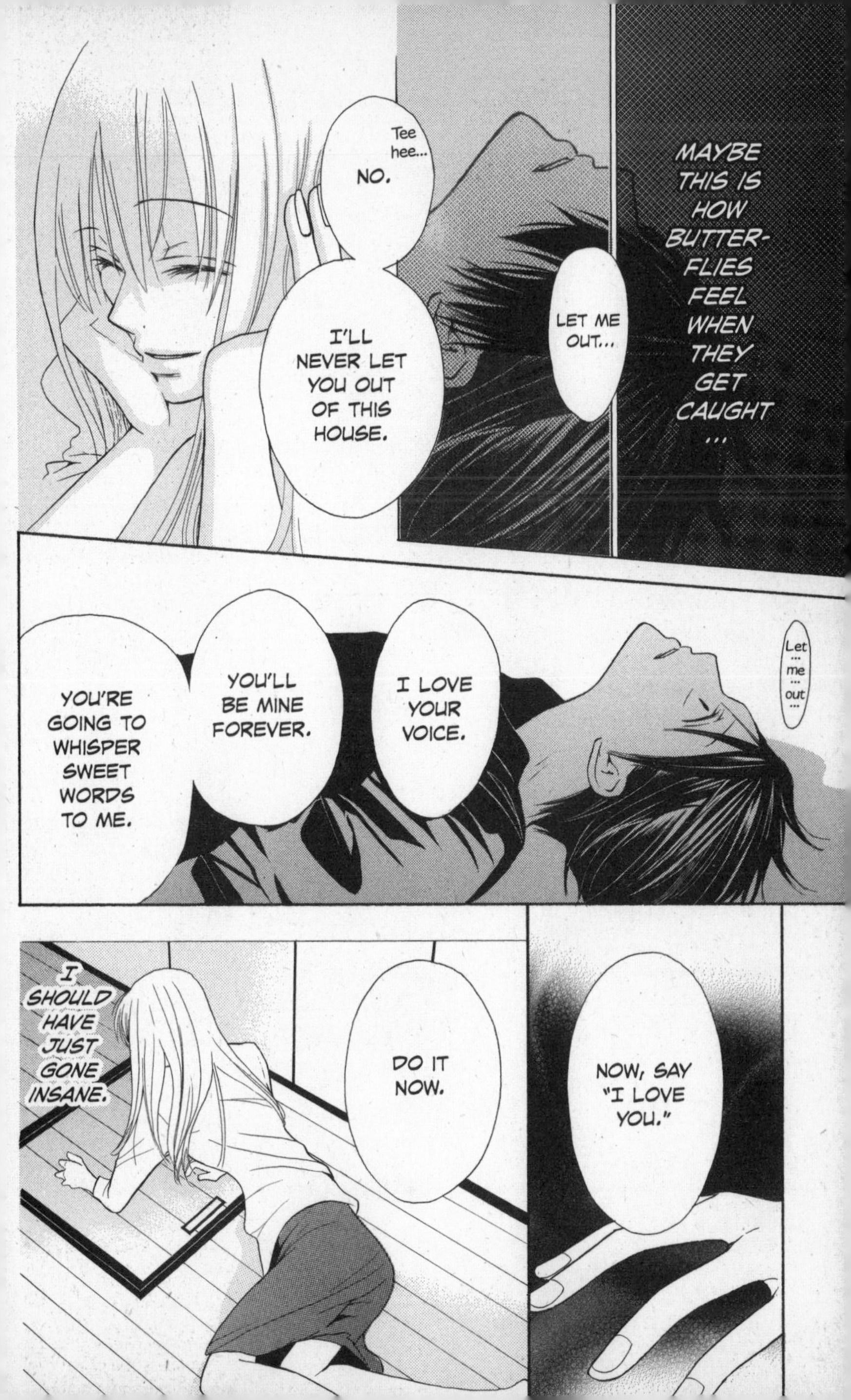
MAYBE THIS IS HOW BUTTER-FLIES FEEL WHEN THEY GET CAUGHT...
LET ME OUT...
Tee hee...
NO.
I'LL NEVER LET YOU OUT OF THIS HOUSE.
Let... me... out...
I LOVE YOUR VOICE.
YOU'LL BE MINE FOREVER.
YOU'RE GOING TO WHISPER SWEET WORDS TO ME.
NOW, SAY "I LOVE YOU."
DO IT NOW.
I SHOULD HAVE JUST GONE INSANE.

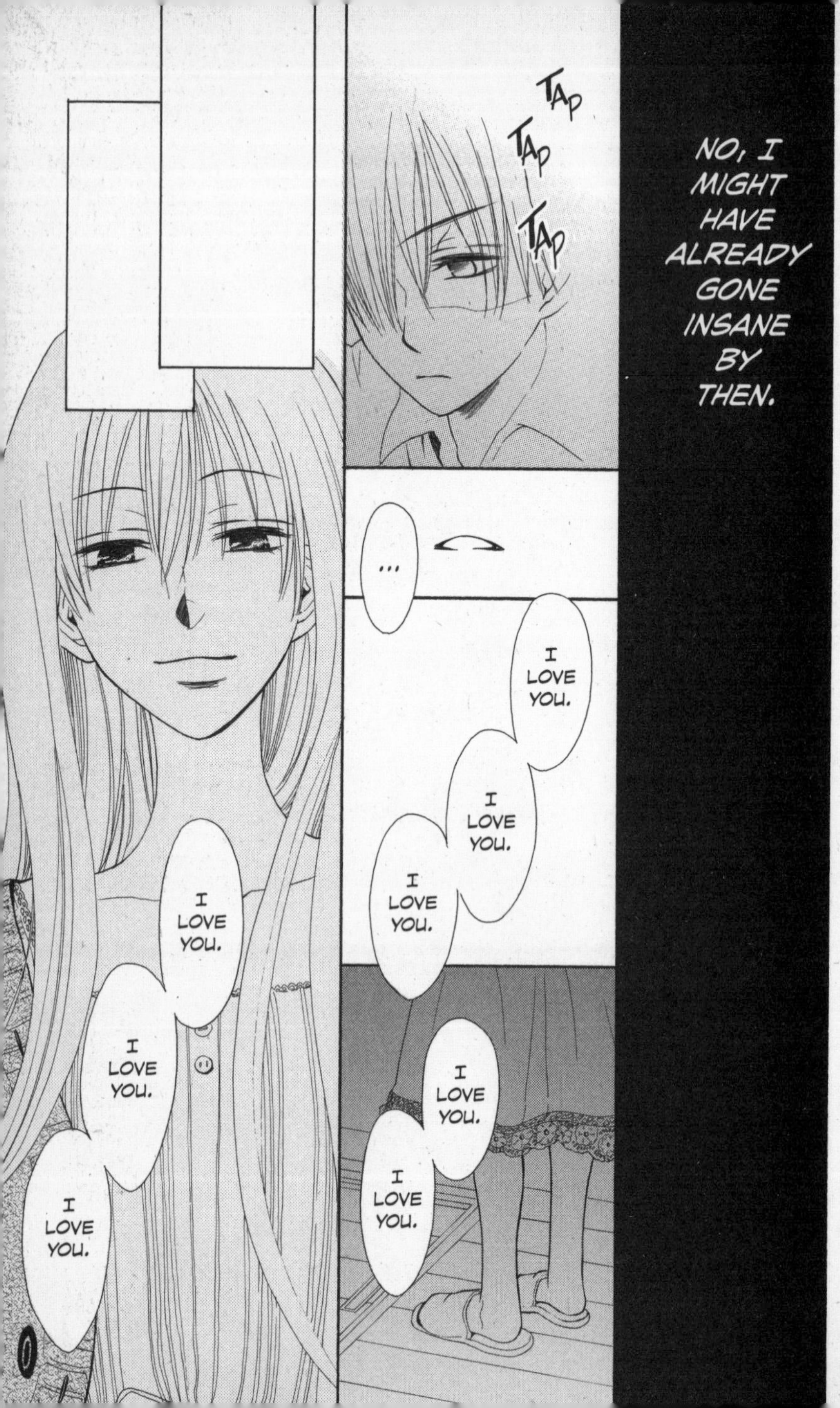
NO, I MIGHT HAVE ALREADY GONE INSANE BY THEN.
TAP
TAP
TAP
...
I LOVE YOU.
I LOVE YOU.
I LOVE YOU.
I LOVE YOU.
I LOVE YOU.
I LOVE YOU.
I LOVE YOU.
I LOVE YOU.

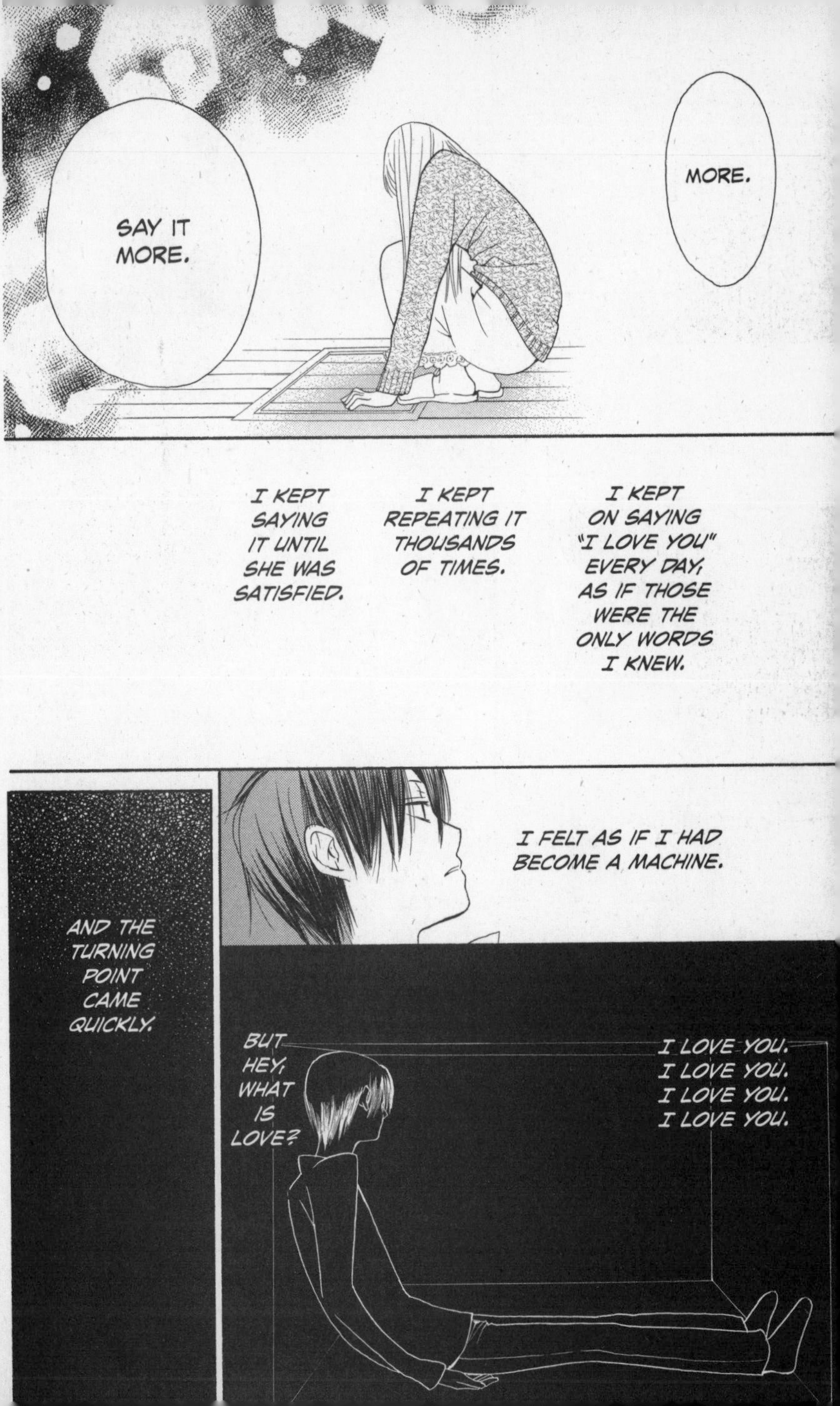
MORE.
SAY IT MORE.
I KEPT ON SAYING "I LOVE YOU" EVERY DAY, AS IF THOSE WERE THE ONLY WORDS I KNEW.
I KEPT REPEATING IT THOUSANDS OF TIMES.
I KEPT SAYING IT UNTIL SHE WAS SATISFIED.
I FELT AS IF I HAD BECOME A MACHINE.
I LOVE YOU.
I LOVE YOU.
I LOVE YOU.
I LOVE YOU.
BUT HEY, WHAT IS LOVE?
AND THE TURNING POINT CAME QUICKLY.

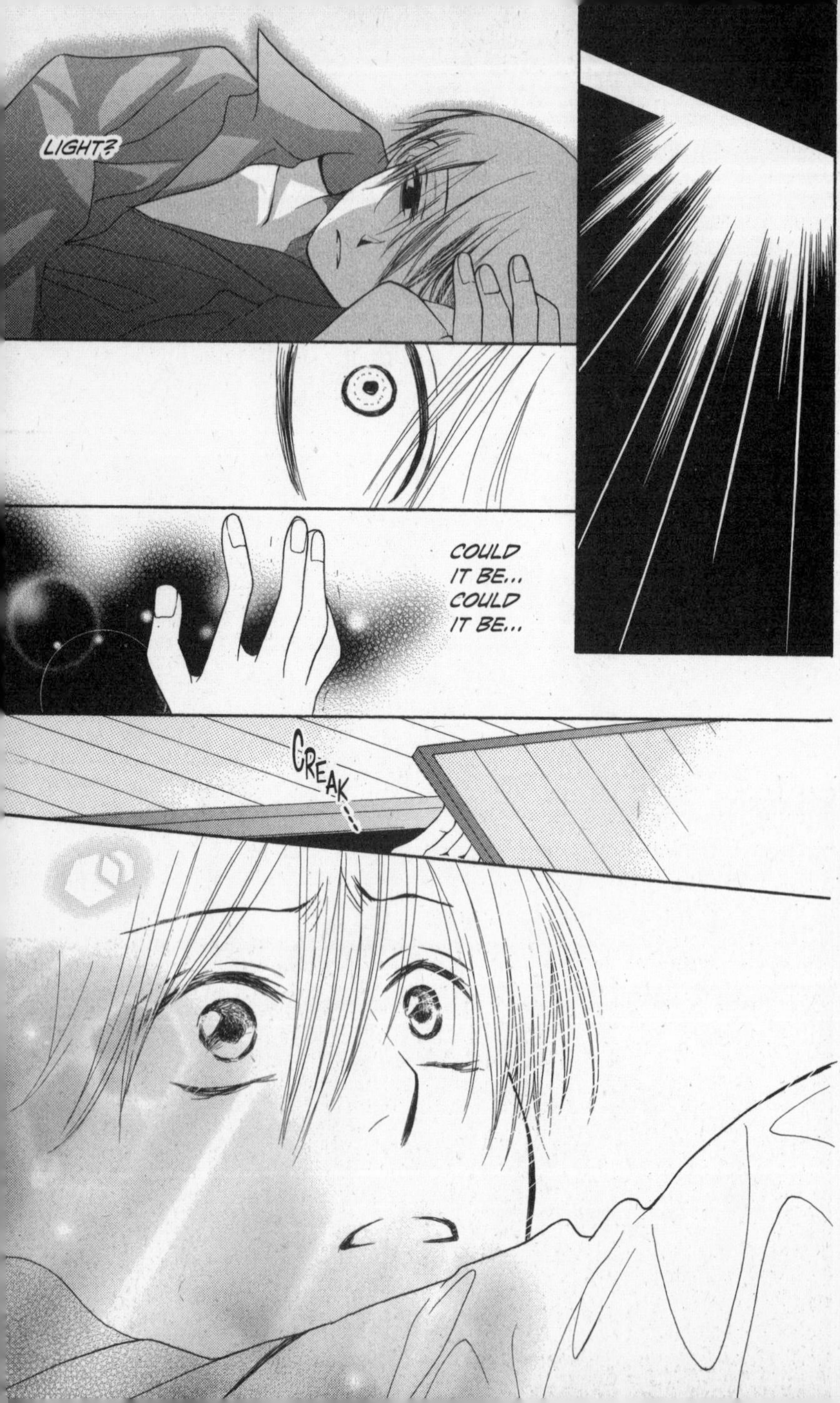
LIGHT?
COULD IT BE... COULD IT BE...
CREAK

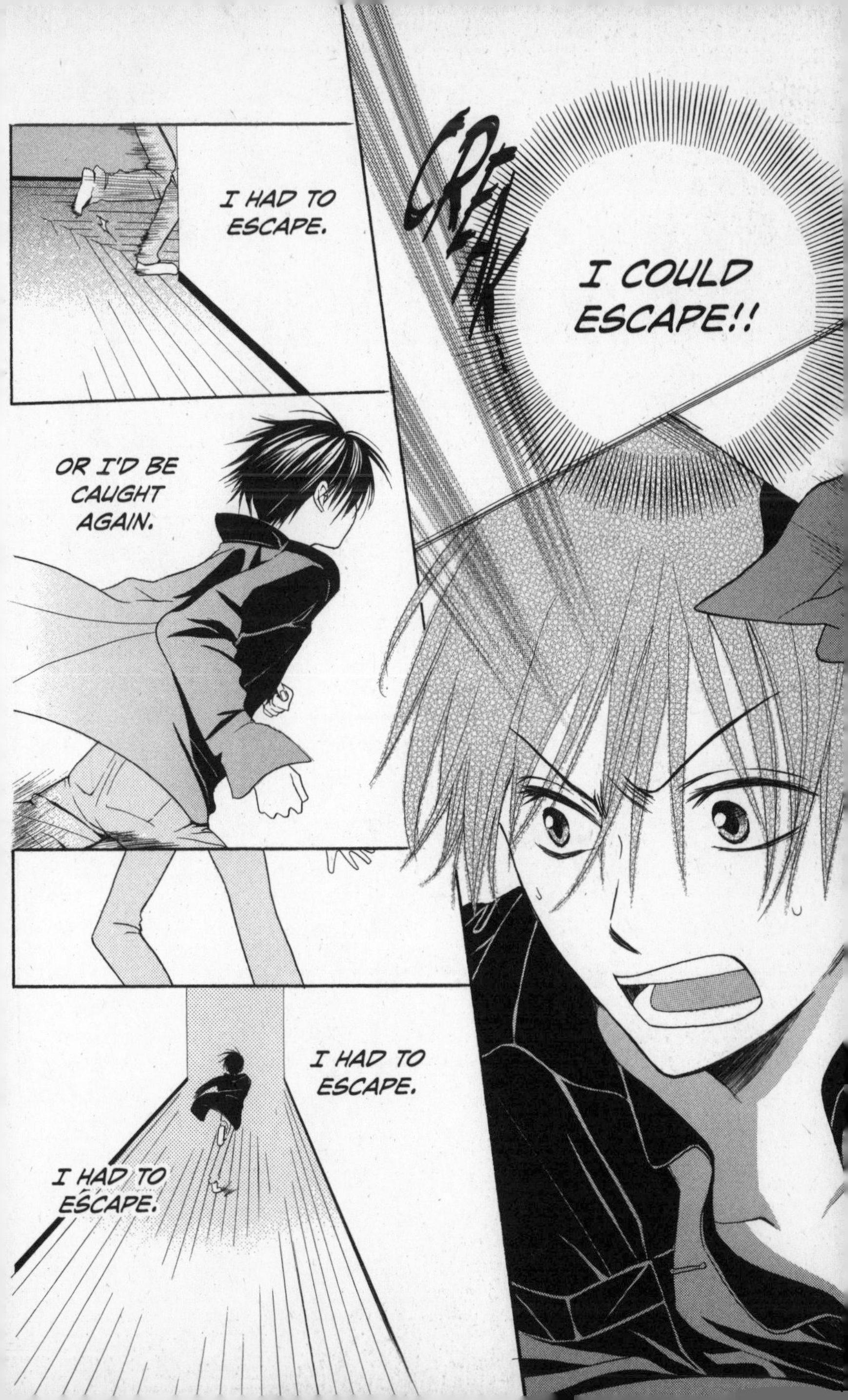
CREAK
I COULD ESCAPE!!
I HAD TO ESCAPE.
OR I'D BE CAUGHT AGAIN.
I HAD TO ESCAPE.
I HAD TO ESCAPE.

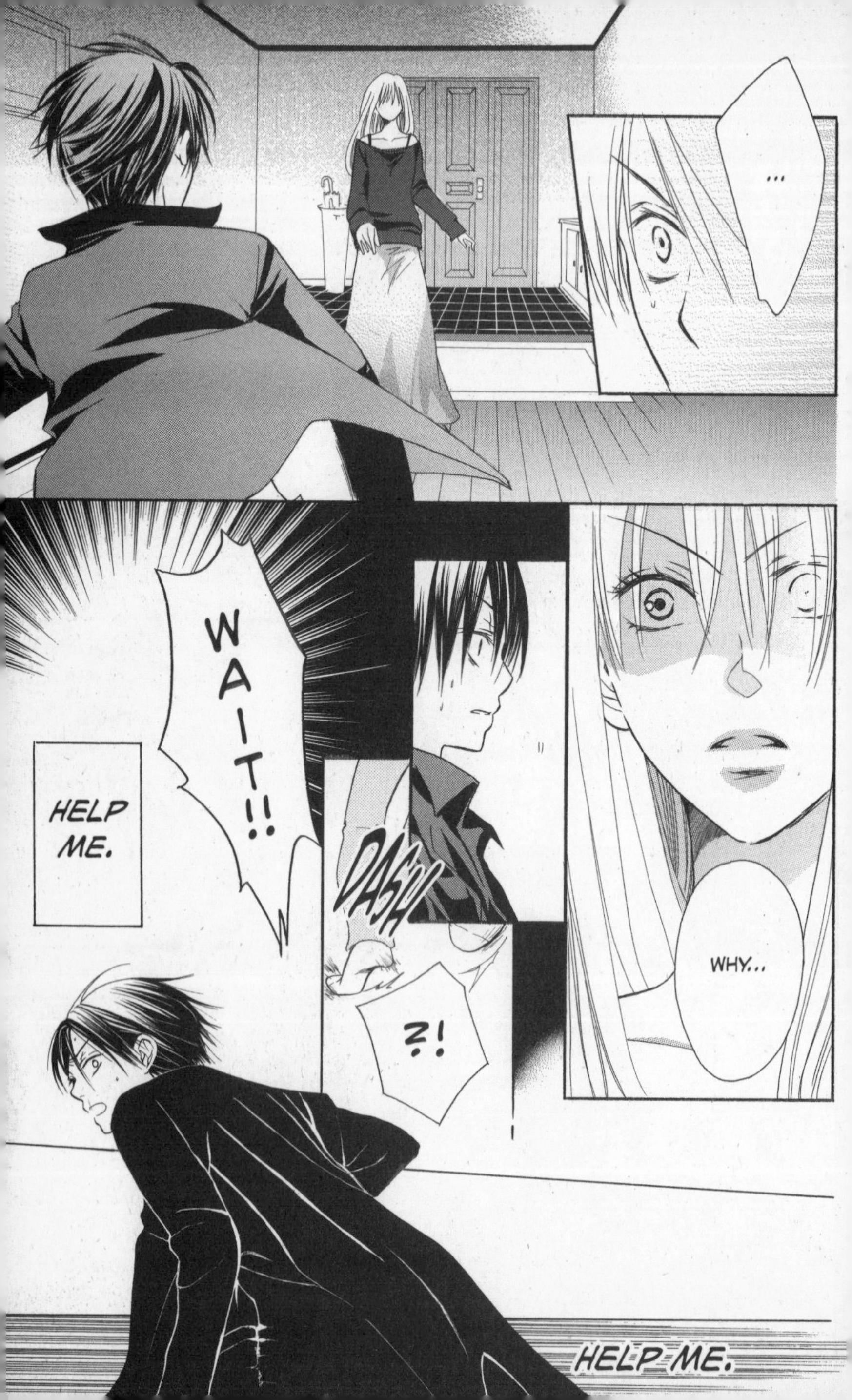
...
WHY...
DASH
?!
WAIT!!
HELP ME.
HELP ME.

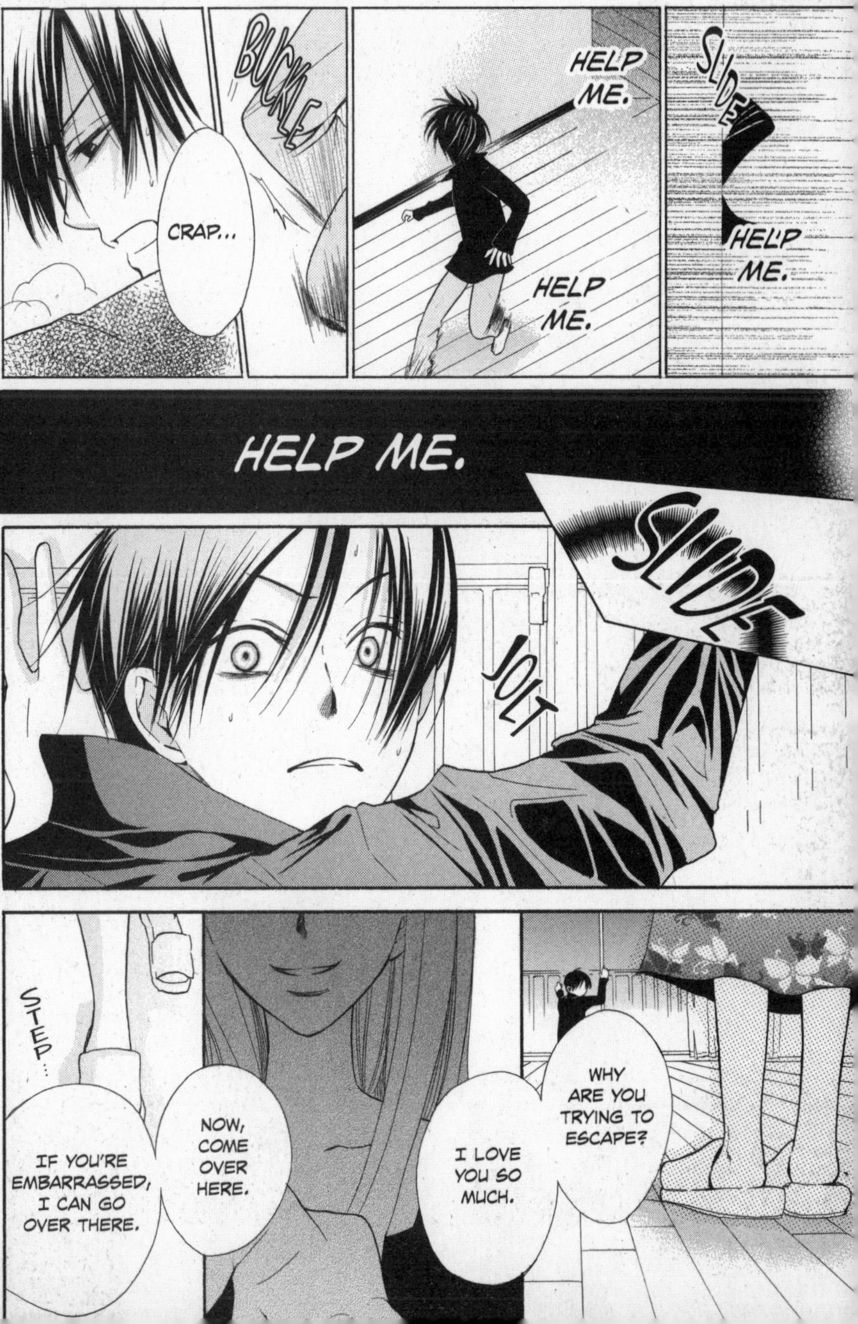
SLIDE
HELP ME.
HELP ME.
HELP ME.
BUCKLE
CRAP...
HELP ME.
SLIDE
JOLT
WHY ARE YOU TRYING TO ESCAPE?
I LOVE YOU SO MUCH.
NOW, COME OVER HERE.
STEP...
IF YOU'RE EMBARRASSED, I CAN GO OVER THERE.

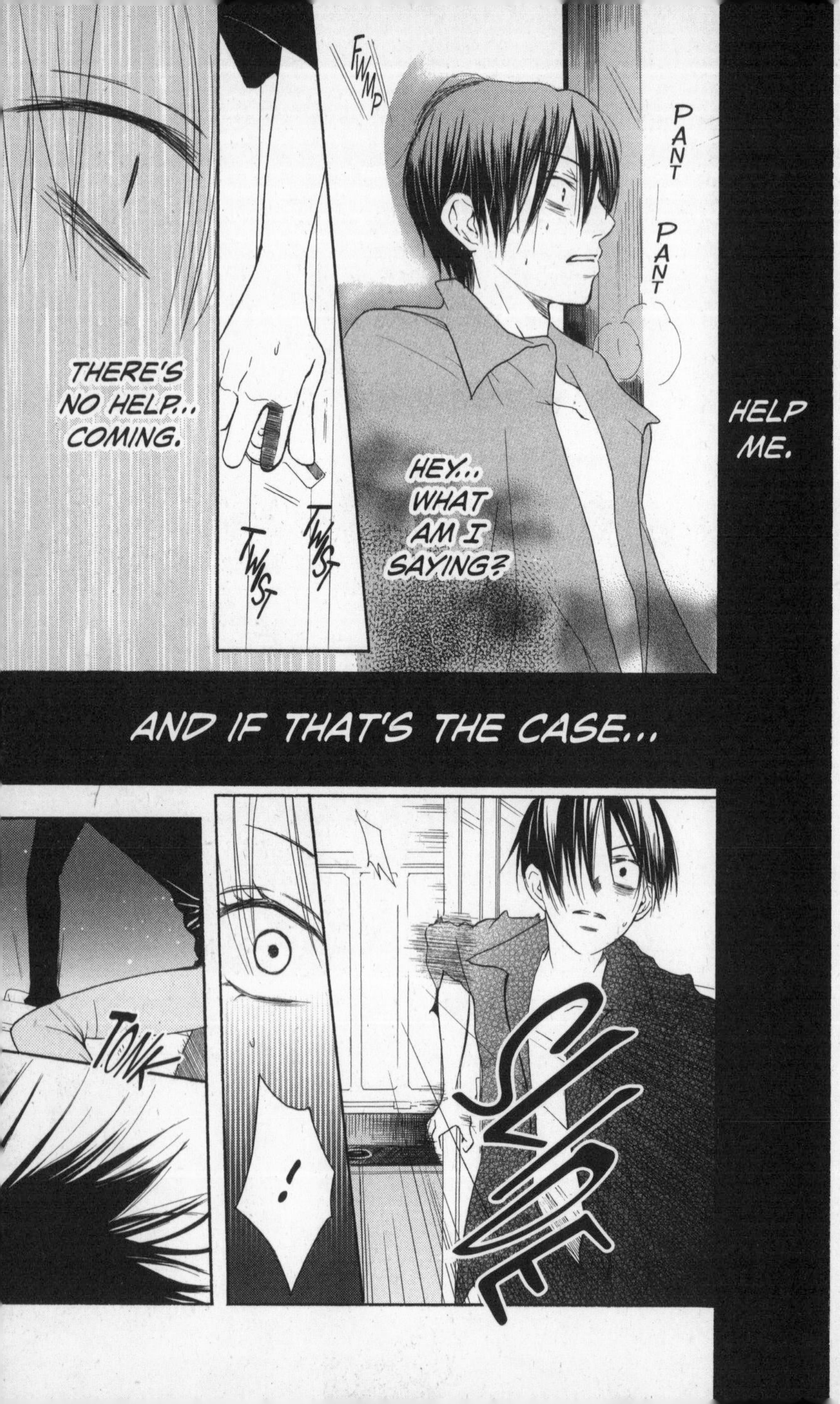
HELP ME.
PANT PANT
FWWMP
HEY... WHAT AM I SAYING?
TWIST TWIST
THERE'S NO HELP... COMING.
AND IF THAT'S THE CASE...
SLIDE
!
TONK

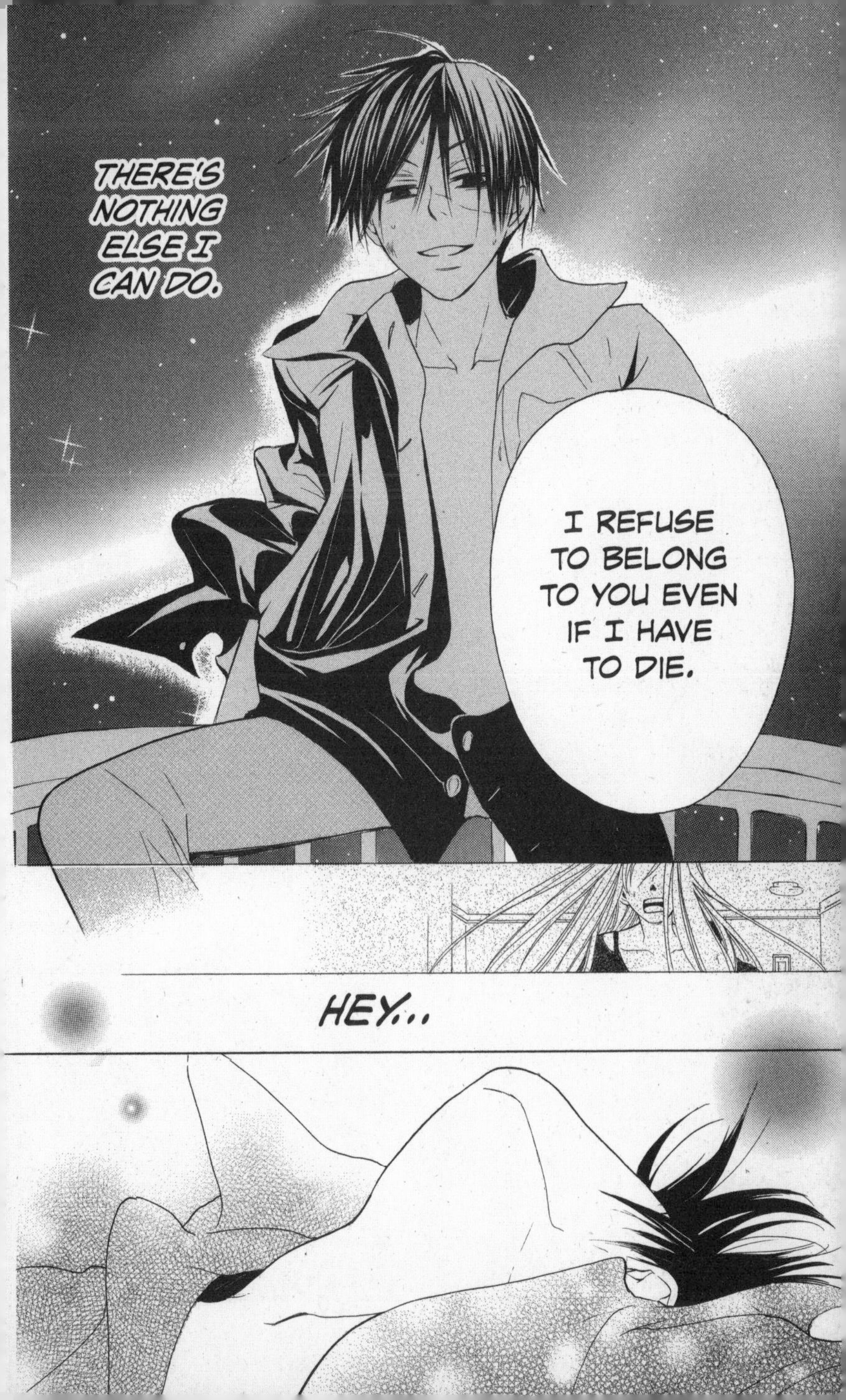
THERE'S NOTHING ELSE I CAN DO.
I REFUSE TO BELONG TO YOU EVEN IF I HAVE TO DIE.
HEY...

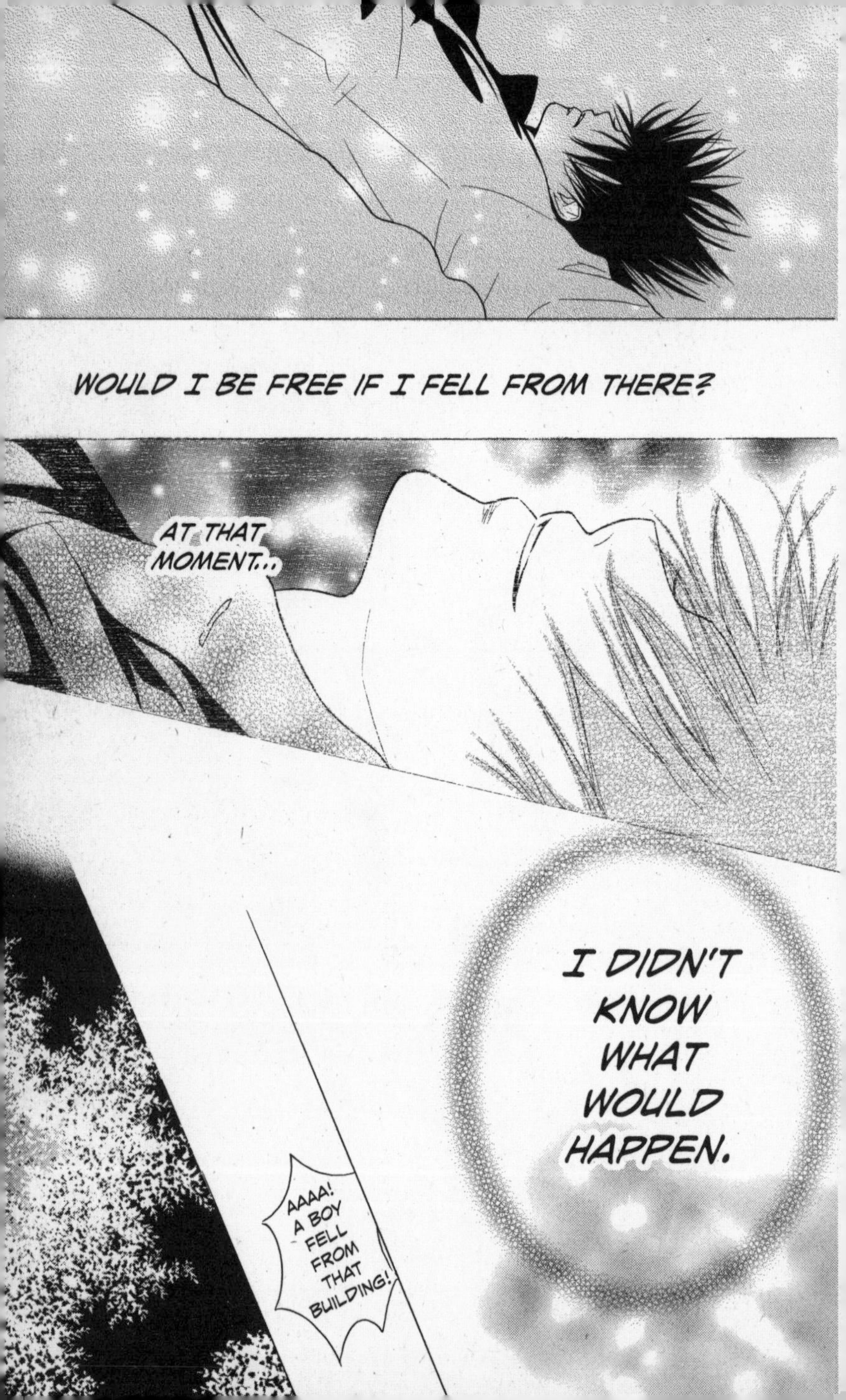
WOULD I BE FREE IF I FELL FROM THERE?
AT THAT MOMENT...
I DIDN'T KNOW WHAT WOULD HAPPEN.
AAAA! A BOY FELL FROM THAT BUILDING!

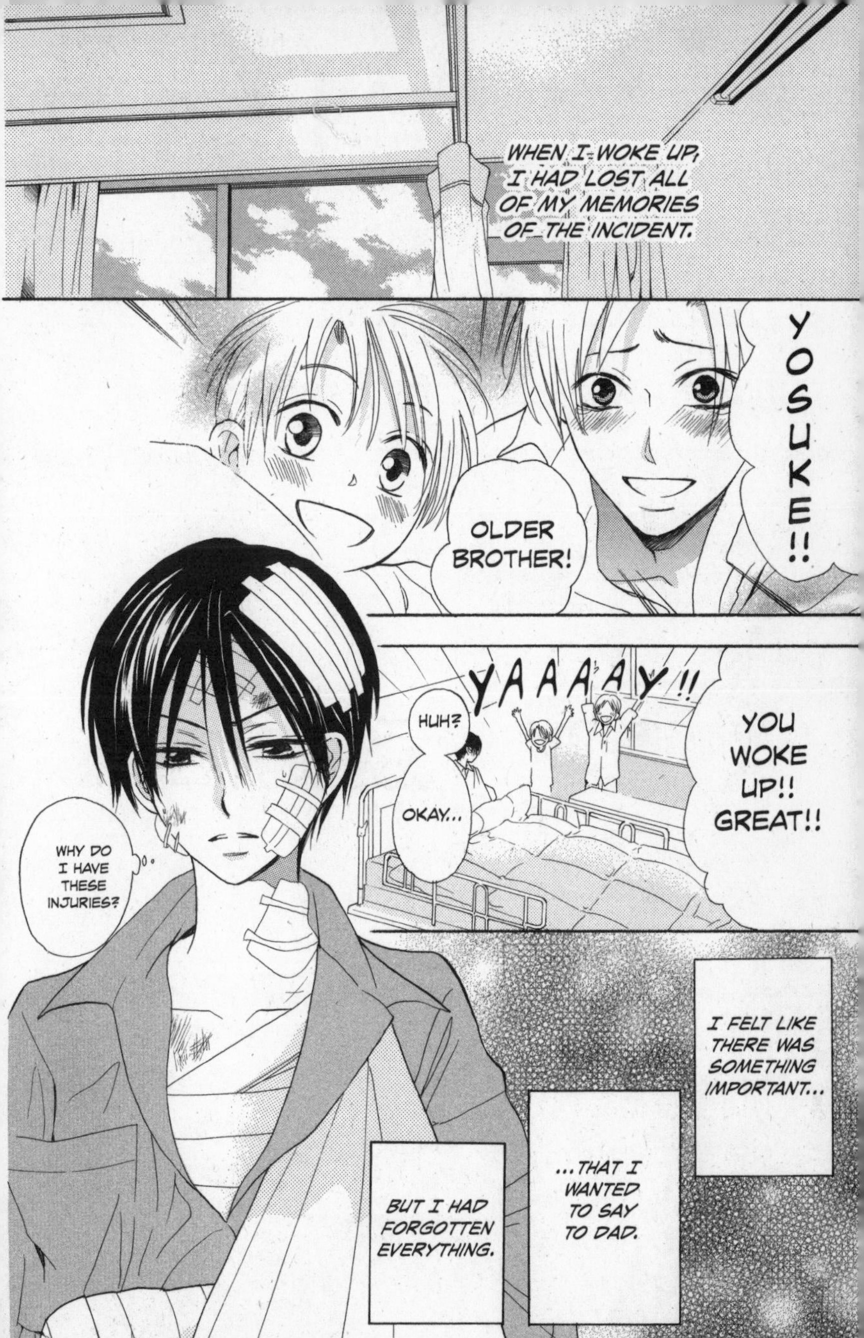
WHEN I WOKE UP, I HAD LOST ALL OF MY MEMORIES OF THE INCIDENT.
YOSUKE!!
OLDER BROTHER!
YOU WOKE UP!! GREAT!!
YAAAAY!!
HUH?
OKAY...
WHY DO I HAVE THESE INJURIES?
I FELT LIKE THERE WAS SOMETHING IMPORTANT...
...THAT I WANTED TO SAY TO DAD.
BUT I HAD FORGOTTEN EVERYTHING.

The Magic Touch, Part 39/The End

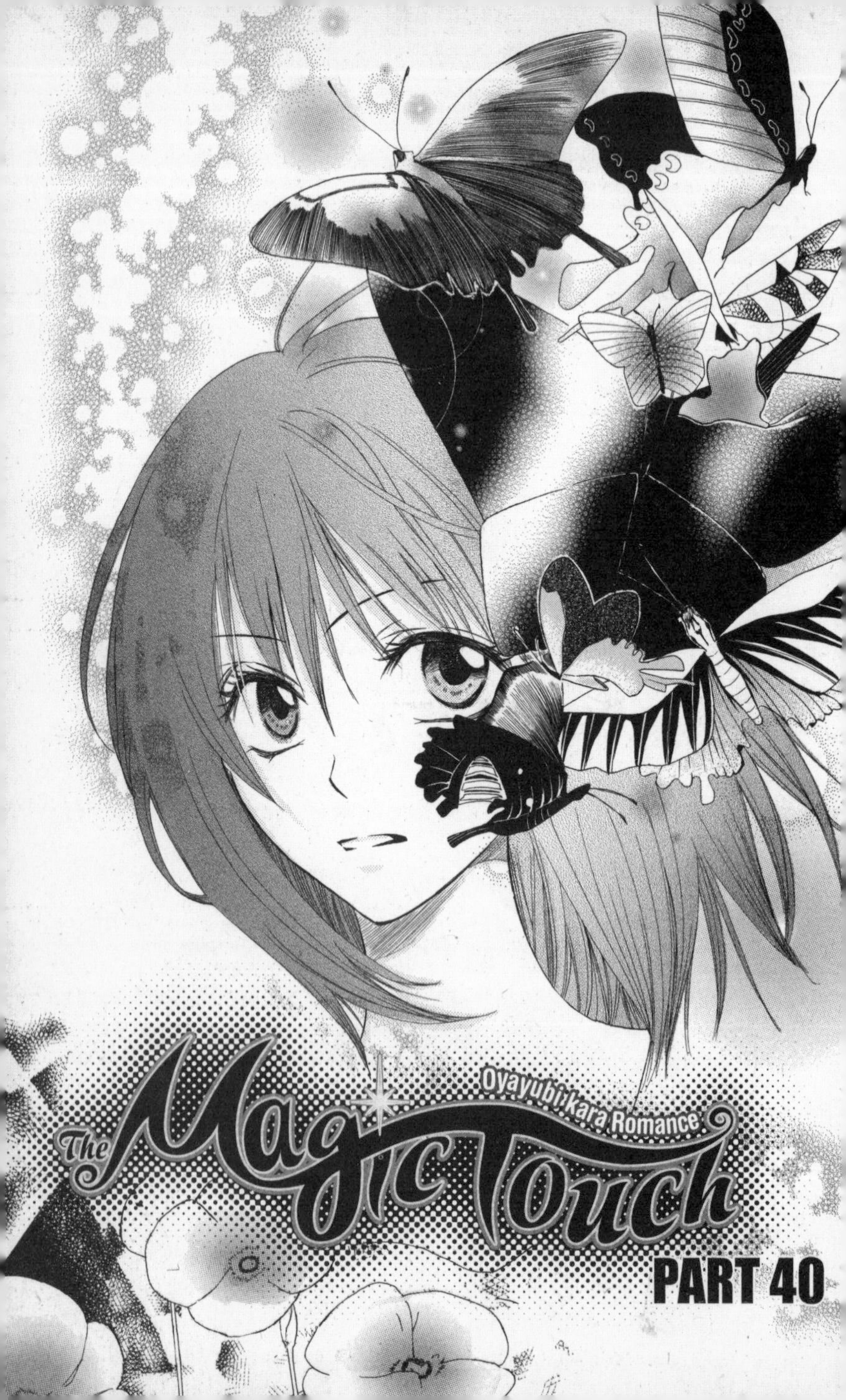
The Magic Touch
Oyayubi Kara Romance
PART 40

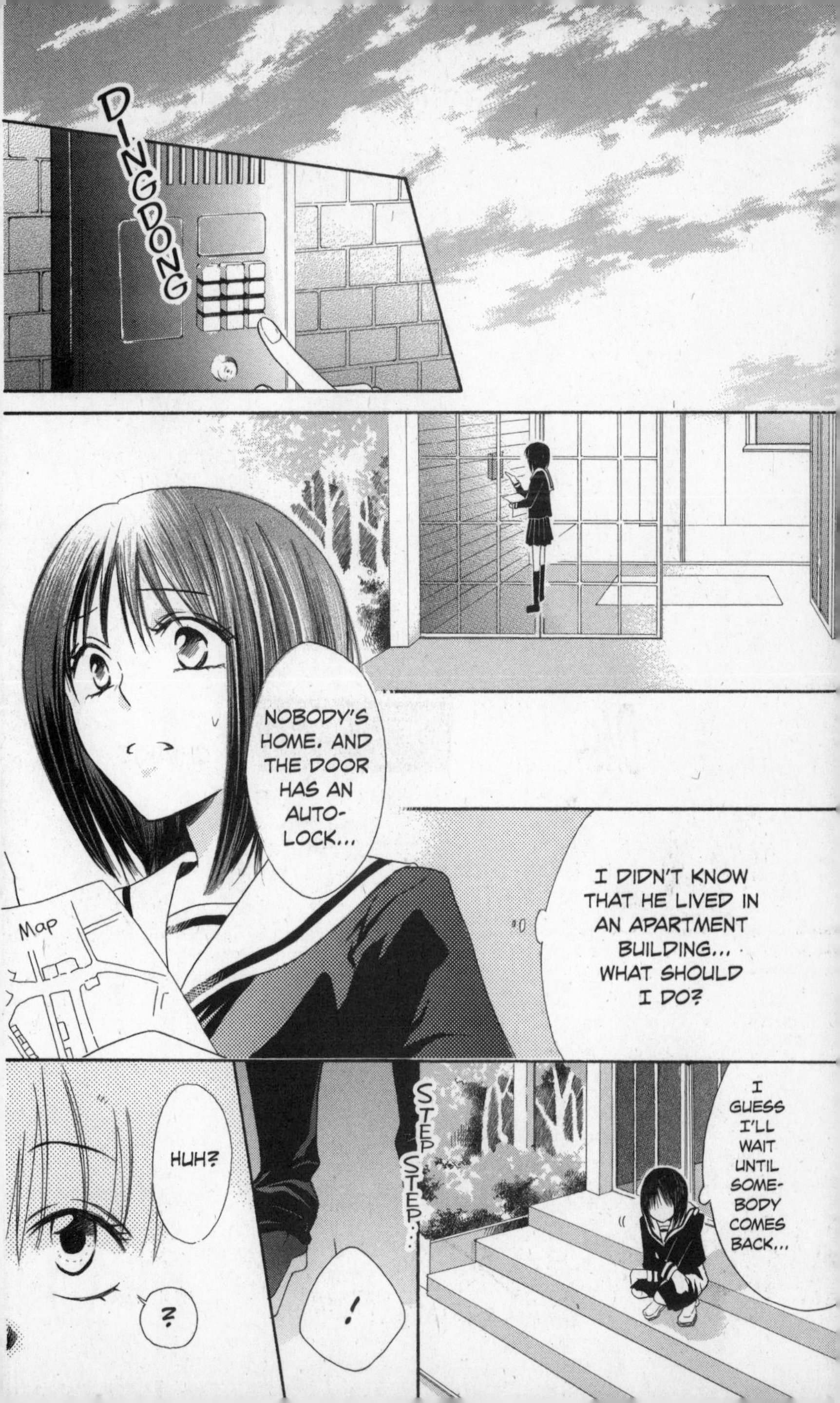
DINGDONG
I DIDN'T KNOW THAT HE LIVED IN AN APARTMENT BUILDING... WHAT SHOULD I DO?
NOBODY'S HOME. AND THE DOOR HAS AN AUTO-LOCK...
Map
I GUESS I'LL WAIT UNTIL SOME-BODY COMES BACK...
STEP STEP...
HUH?
!
?

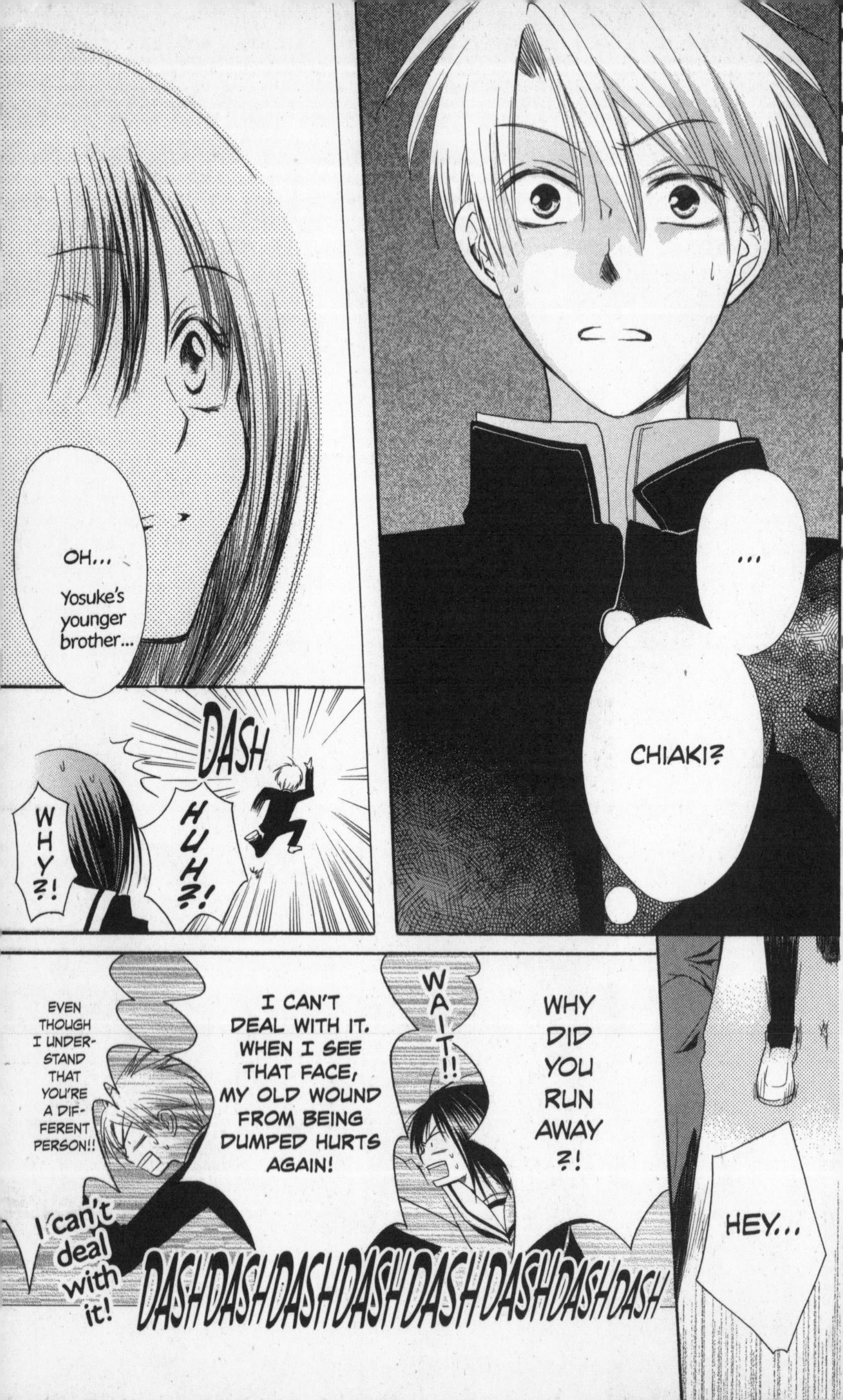
...
CHIAKI?
OH... Yosuke's younger brother...
DASH
HUH?!
WHY?!
HEY...
WHY DID YOU RUN AWAY?!
WAIT!!
I CAN'T DEAL WITH IT. WHEN I SEE THAT FACE, MY OLD WOUND FROM BEING DUMPED HURTS AGAIN!
EVEN THOUGH I UNDER-STAND THAT YOU'RE A DIF-FERENT PERSON!!
I can't deal with it!
DASH DASH DASH DASH DASH DASH DASH DASH

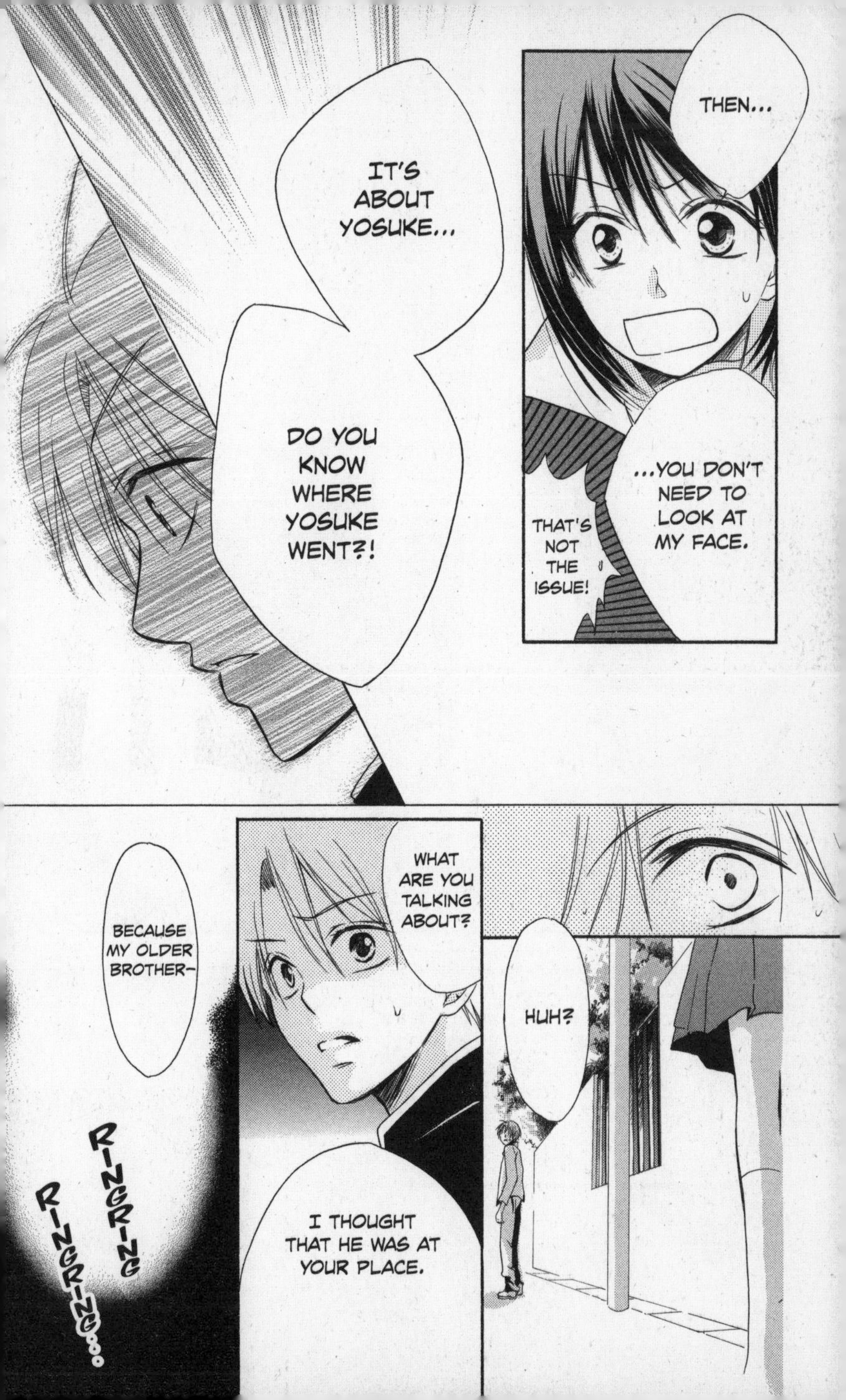
THEN...
...YOU DON'T NEED TO LOOK AT MY FACE.
THAT'S NOT THE ISSUE!
IT'S ABOUT YOSUKE...
DO YOU KNOW WHERE YOSUKE WENT?!
HUH?
WHAT ARE YOU TALKING ABOUT?
I THOUGHT THAT HE WAS AT YOUR PLACE.
BECAUSE MY OLDER BROTHER-
RINGRING
RINGRING...

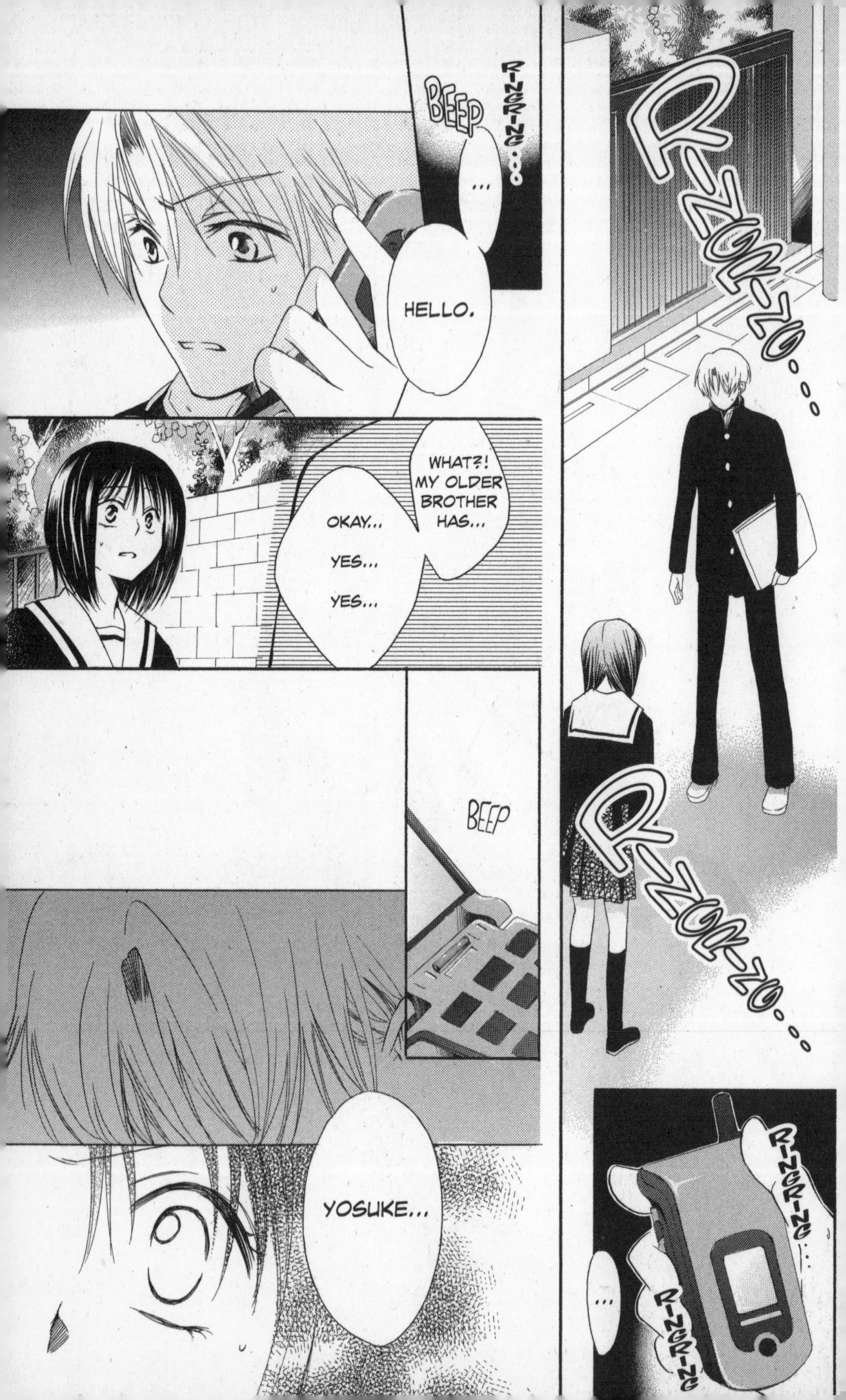
RINGRING...
...
RINGRING
RINGRING...
BEEP
...
HELLO.
WHAT?! MY OLDER BROTHER HAS...
OKAY...
YES...
YES...
BEEP
YOSUKE...

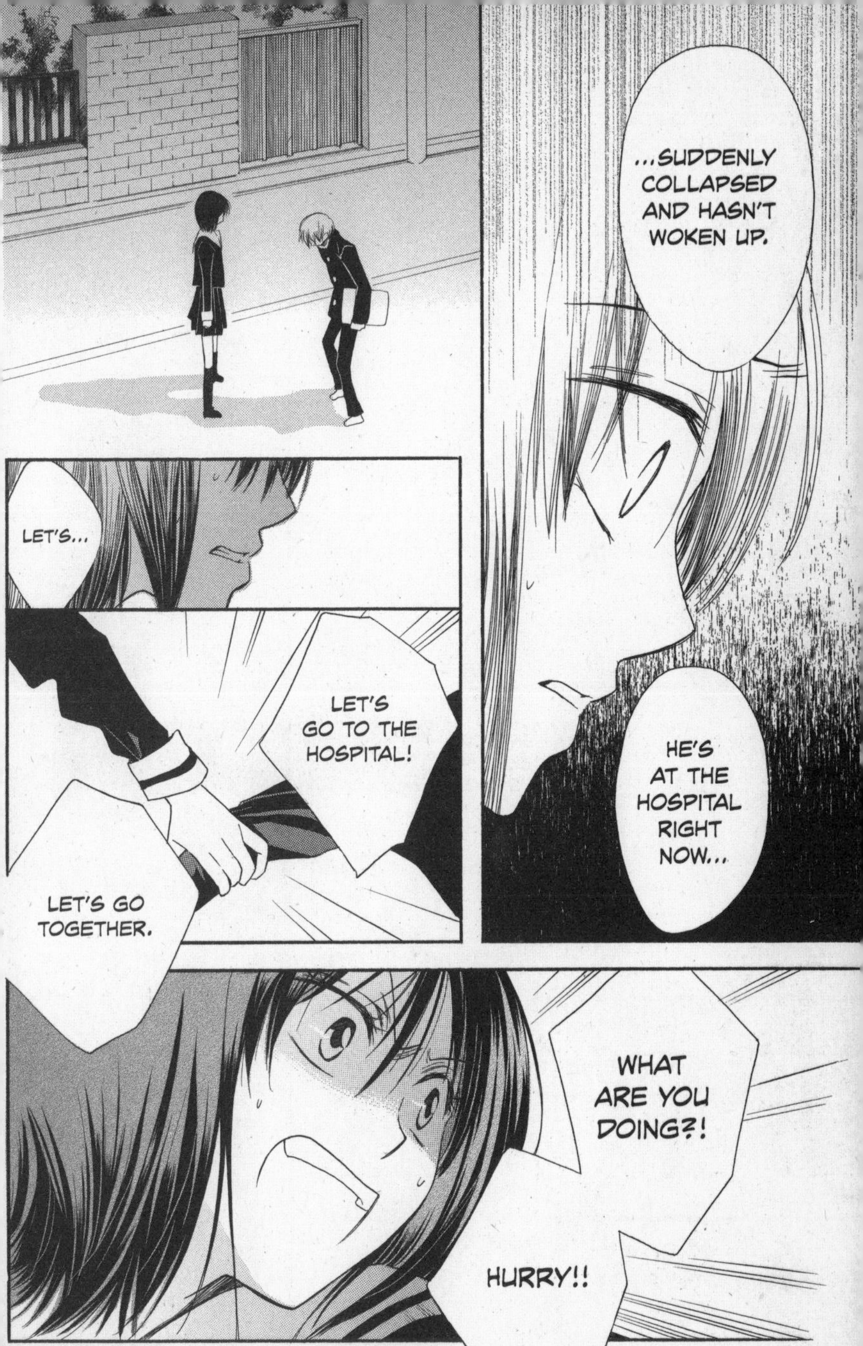
...SUDDENLY COLLAPSED AND HASN'T WOKEN UP.
HE'S AT THE HOSPITAL RIGHT NOW...
LET'S...
LET'S GO TO THE HOSPITAL!
LET'S GO TOGETHER.
WHAT ARE YOU DOING?!
HURRY!!

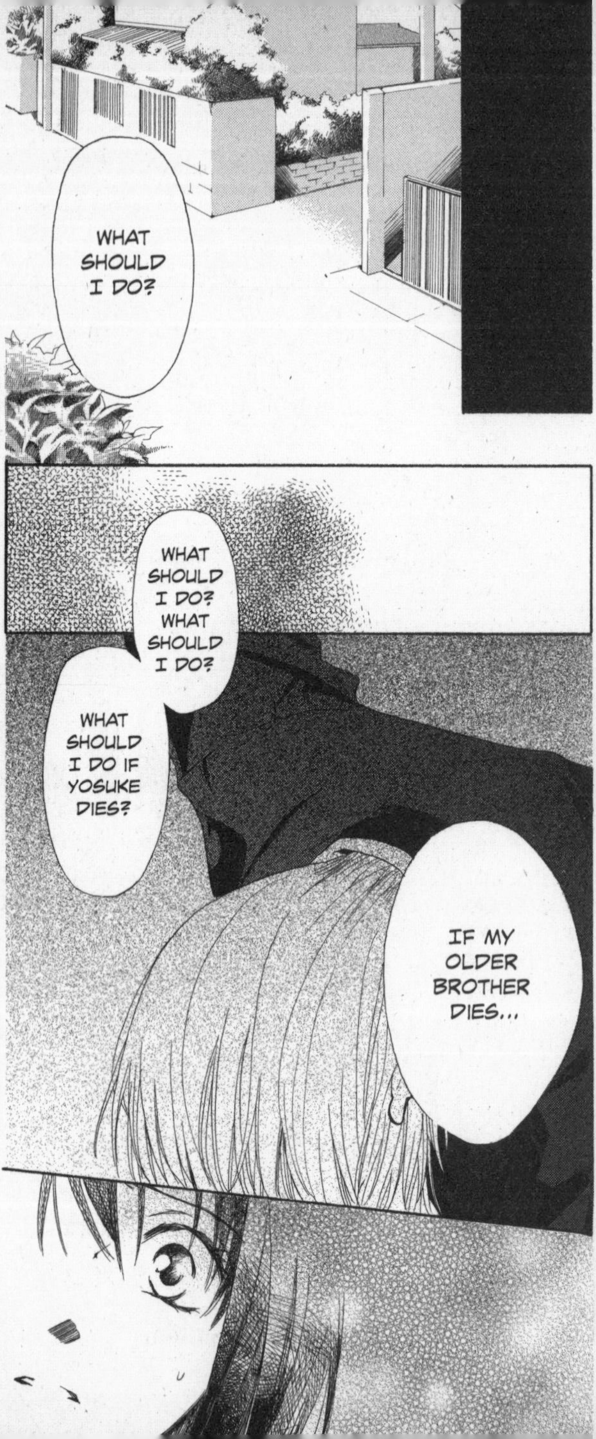
WHAT SHOULD I DO?
WHAT SHOULD I DO? WHAT SHOULD I DO?
WHAT SHOULD I DO IF YOSUKE DIES?
IF MY OLDER BROTHER DIES...

4

I saw on TV that they have a balance ball tournament.

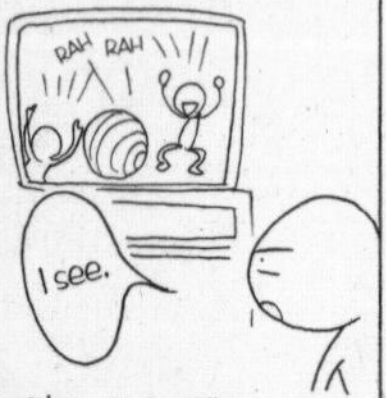
RAH RAH
I see.

It's really fun. They even have names for their moves.

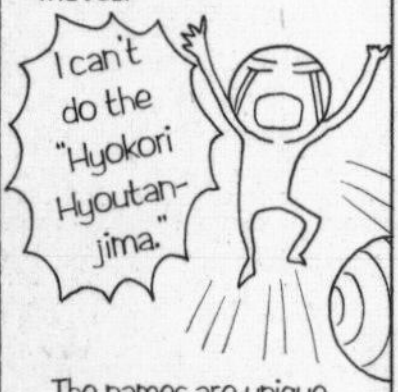
I can't do the "Hyokori Hyoutan-jima."

The names are unique.

Oh!

Maybe I can do a manga about balance ball!

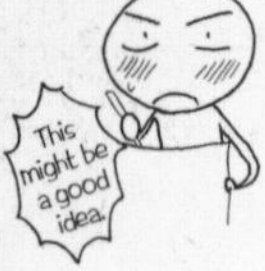
This might be a good idea.

The main character is a girl who can't do sports but has exceptional balance.

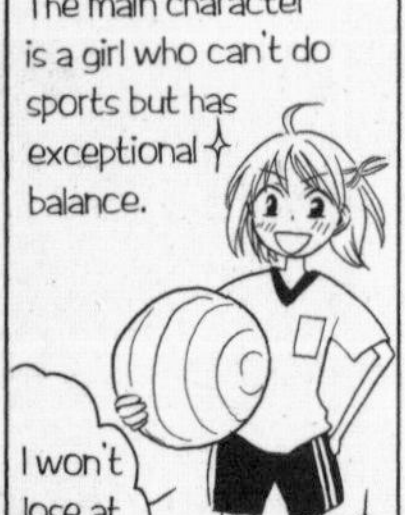
I won't lose at this!

Continued...

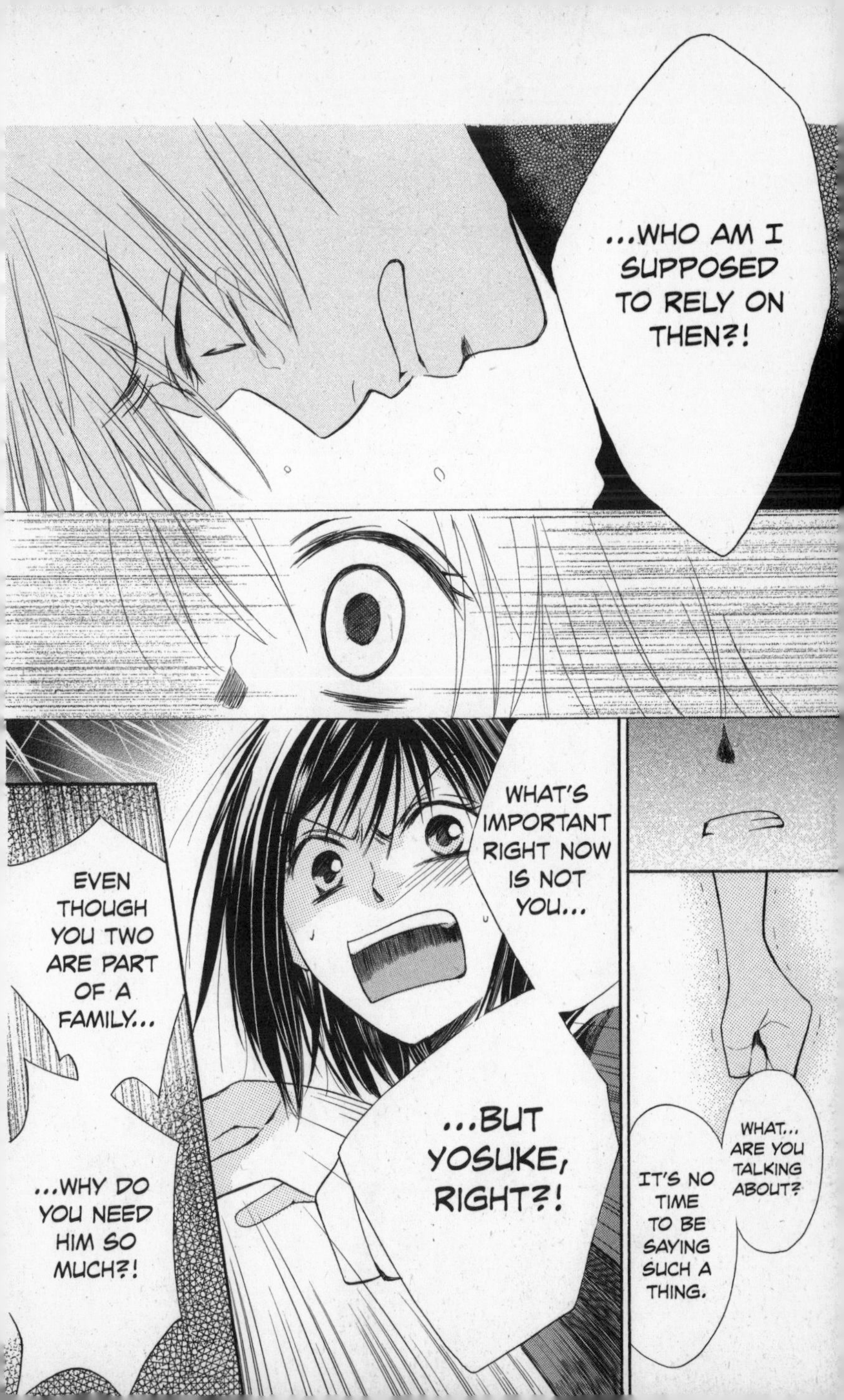
...WHO AM I SUPPOSED TO RELY ON THEN?!
WHAT... ARE YOU TALKING ABOUT?
IT'S NO TIME TO BE SAYING SUCH A THING.
WHAT'S IMPORTANT RIGHT NOW IS NOT YOU...
EVEN THOUGH YOU TWO ARE PART OF A FAMILY...
...BUT YOSUKE, RIGHT?!
...WHY DO YOU NEED HIM SO MUCH?!

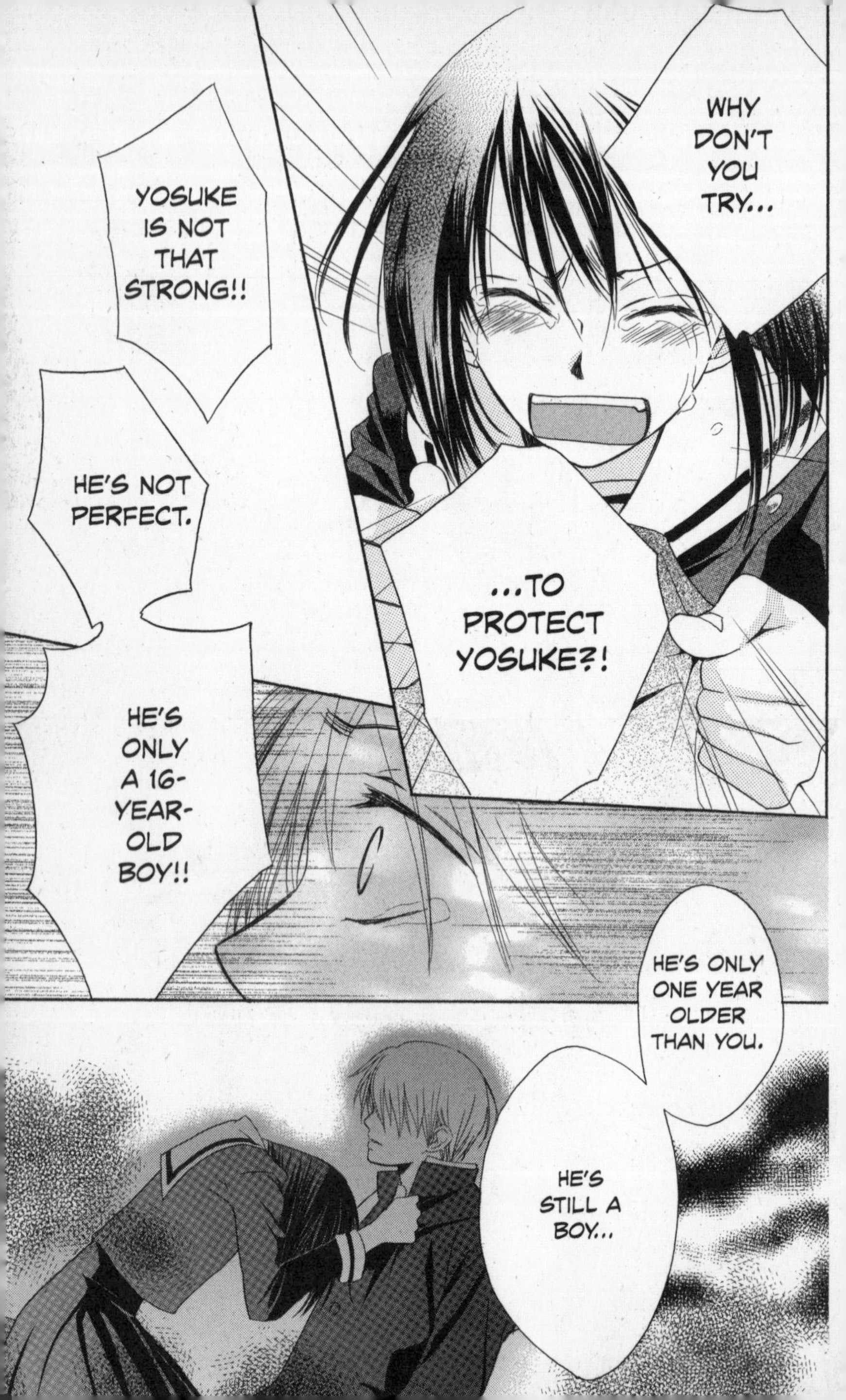
WHY DON'T YOU TRY...
...TO PROTECT YOSUKE?!
YOSUKE IS NOT THAT STRONG!!
HE'S NOT PERFECT.
HE'S ONLY A 16-YEAR-OLD BOY!!
HE'S ONLY ONE YEAR OLDER THAN YOU.
HE'S STILL A BOY...

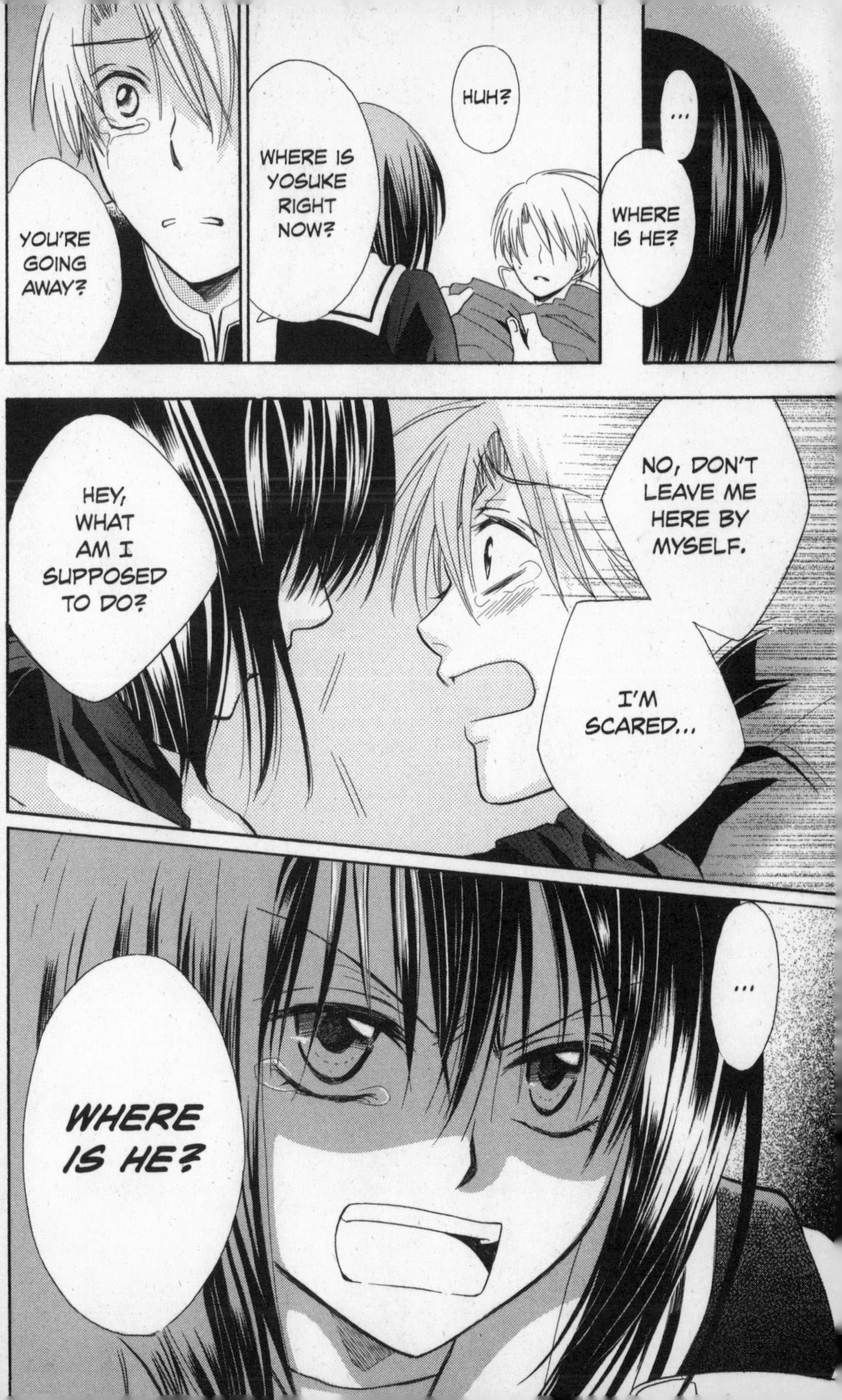
...
WHERE IS HE?
HUH?
WHERE IS YOSUKE RIGHT NOW?
YOU'RE GOING AWAY?
NO, DON'T LEAVE ME HERE BY MYSELF.
I'M SCARED...
HEY, WHAT AM I SUPPOSED TO DO?
...
WHERE IS HE?

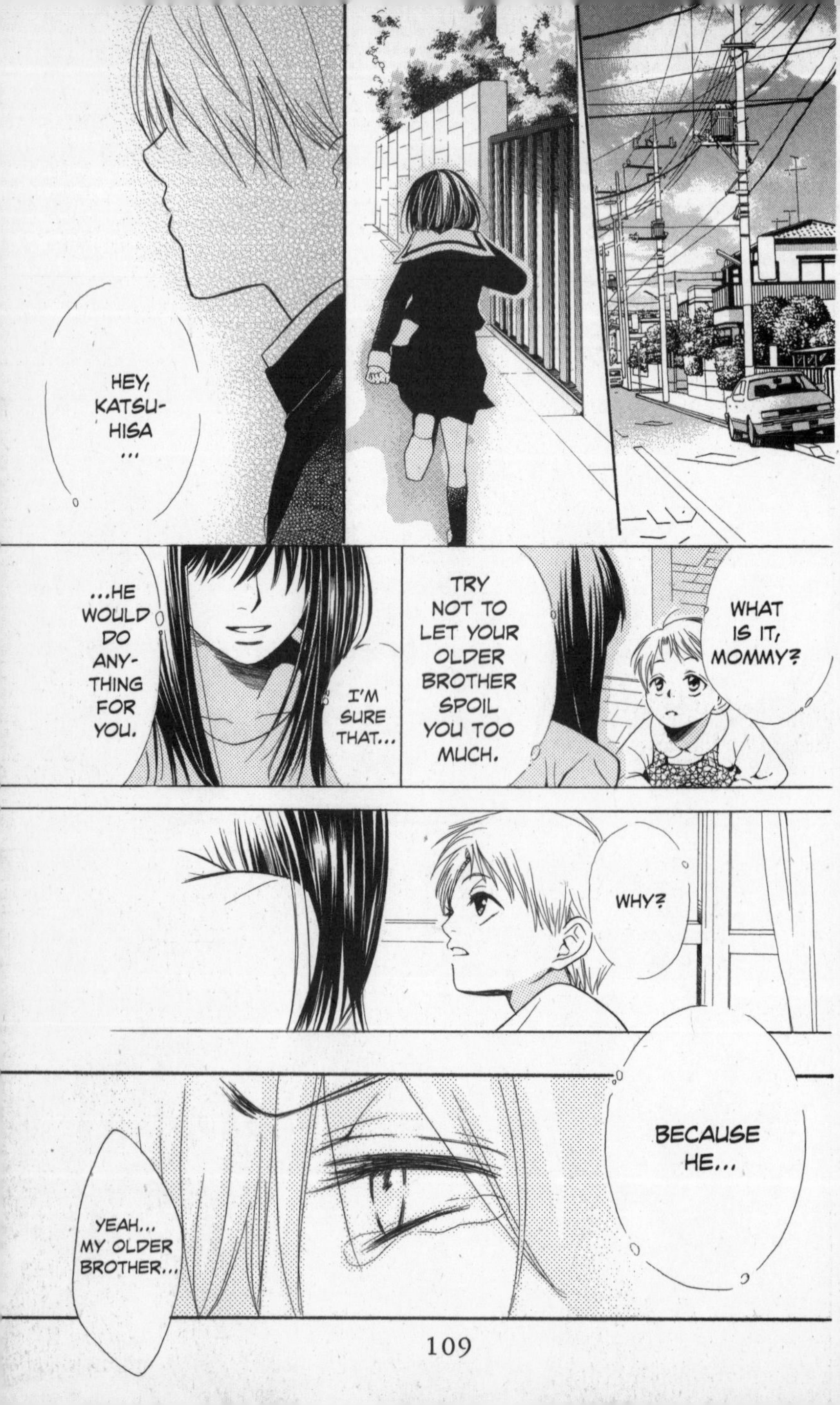
HEY, KATSU-HISA ...
WHAT IS IT, MOMMY?
TRY NOT TO LET YOUR OLDER BROTHER SPOIL YOU TOO MUCH.
I'M SURE THAT...
...HE WOULD DO ANY-THING FOR YOU.
WHY?
BECAUSE HE...
YEAH... MY OLDER BROTHER...

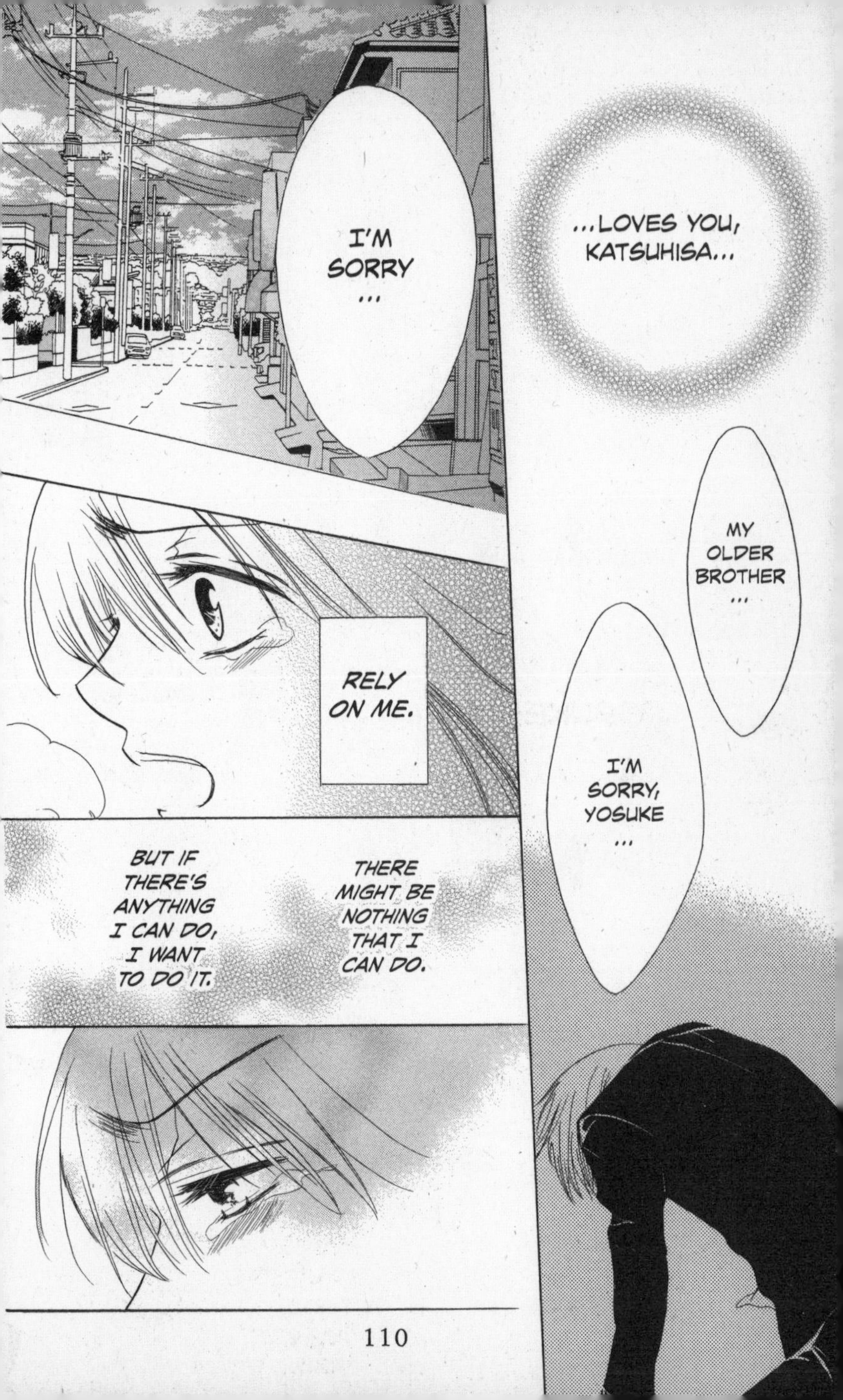
...LOVES YOU, KATSUHISA...
MY OLDER BROTHER ...
I'M SORRY, YOSUKE ...
I'M SORRY ...
RELY ON ME.
THERE MIGHT BE NOTHING THAT I CAN DO.
BUT IF THERE'S ANYTHING I CAN DO, I WANT TO DO IT.

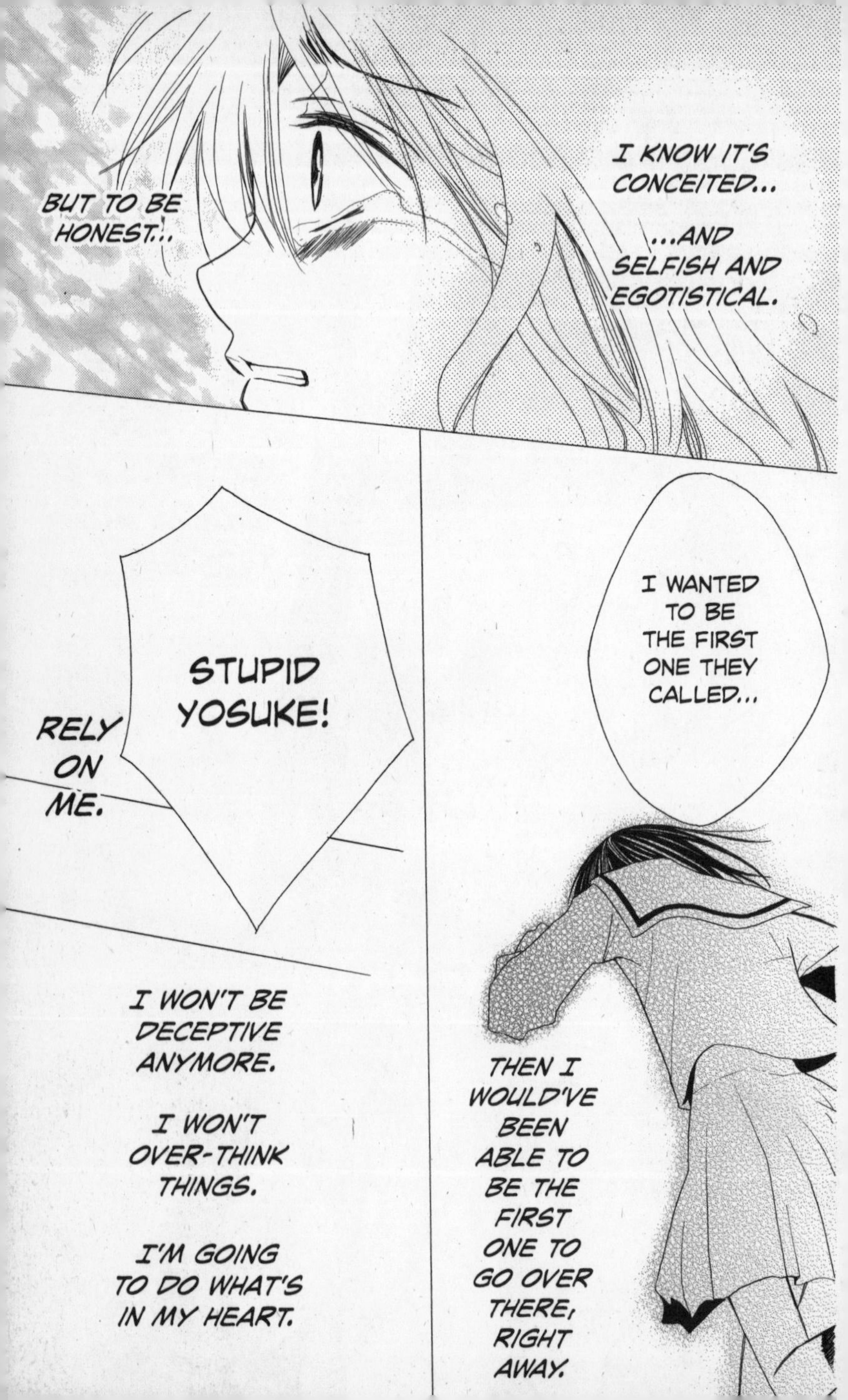
I KNOW IT'S CONCEITED...
...AND SELFISH AND EGOTISTICAL.
BUT TO BE HONEST...
I WANTED TO BE THE FIRST ONE THEY CALLED...
THEN I WOULD'VE BEEN ABLE TO BE THE FIRST ONE TO GO OVER THERE, RIGHT AWAY.
STUPID YOSUKE!
RELY ON ME.
I WON'T BE DECEPTIVE ANYMORE.
I WON'T OVER-THINK THINGS.
I'M GOING TO DO WHAT'S IN MY HEART.

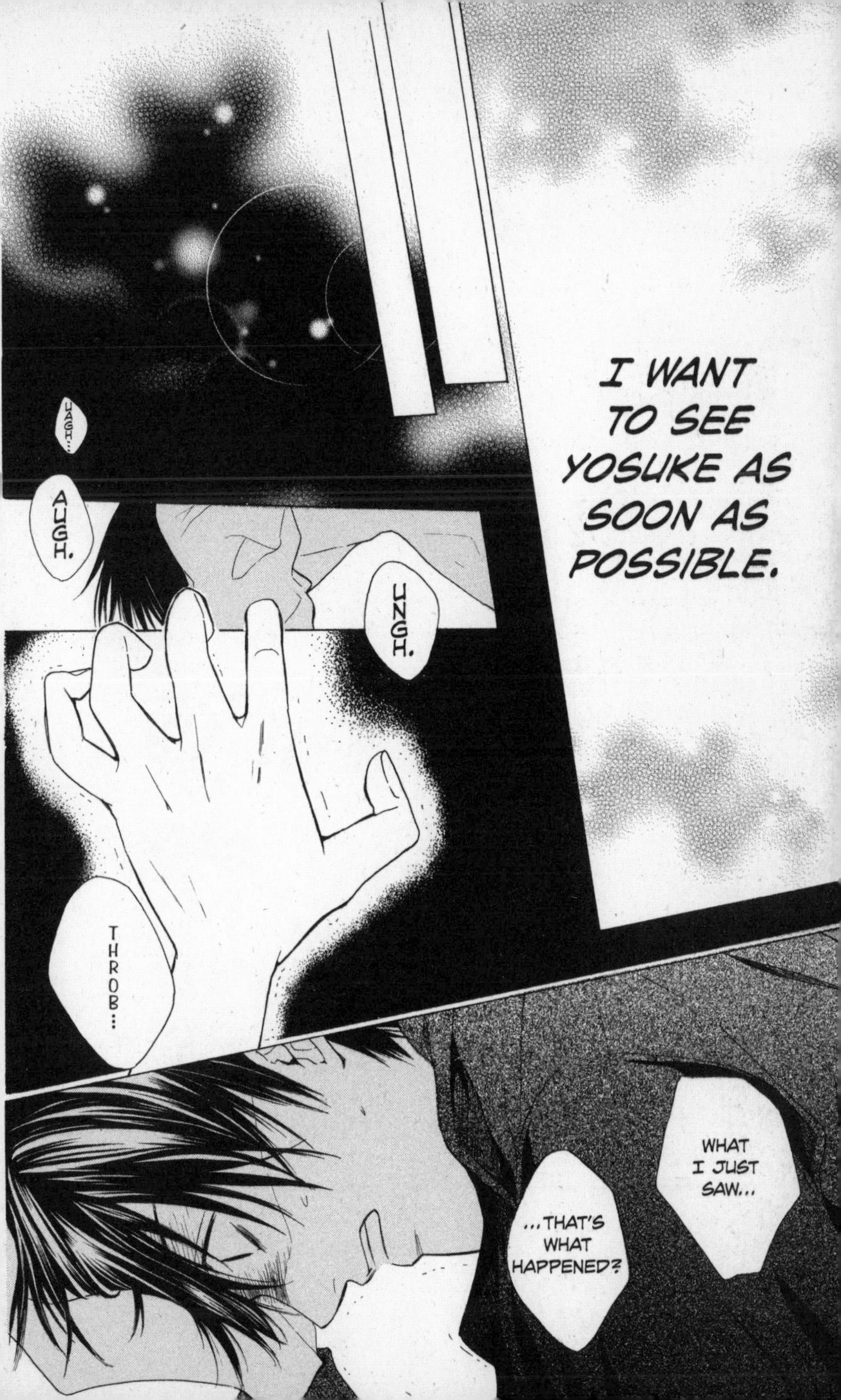
I WANT TO SEE YOSUKE AS SOON AS POSSIBLE.
UAGH...
UNGH.
AUGH.
THROB...
WHAT I JUST SAW...
...THAT'S WHAT HAPPENED?

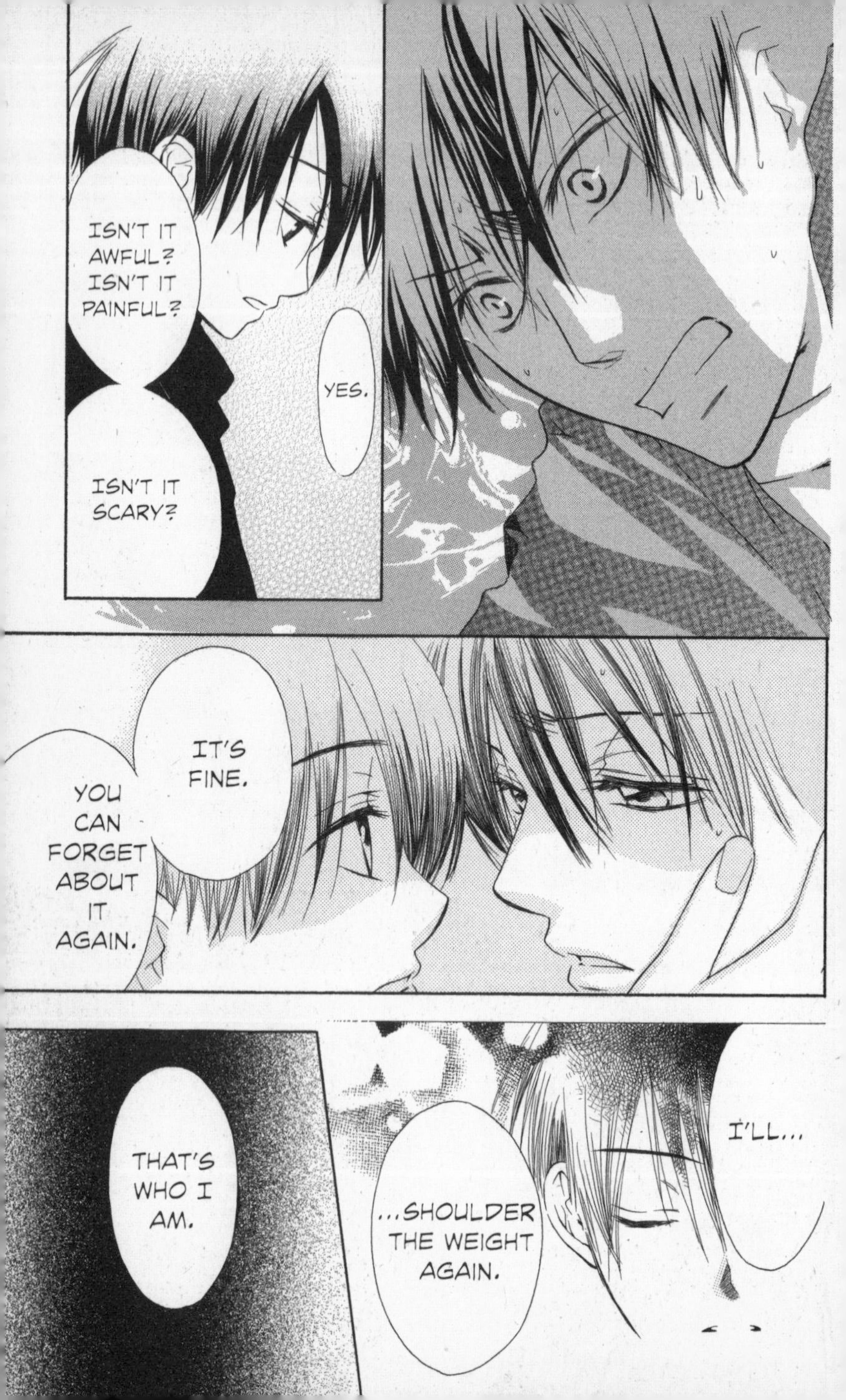
ISN'T IT AWFUL? ISN'T IT PAINFUL?
YES.
ISN'T IT SCARY?
IT'S FINE.
YOU CAN FORGET ABOUT IT AGAIN.
I'LL...
...SHOULDER THE WEIGHT AGAIN.
THAT'S WHO I AM.

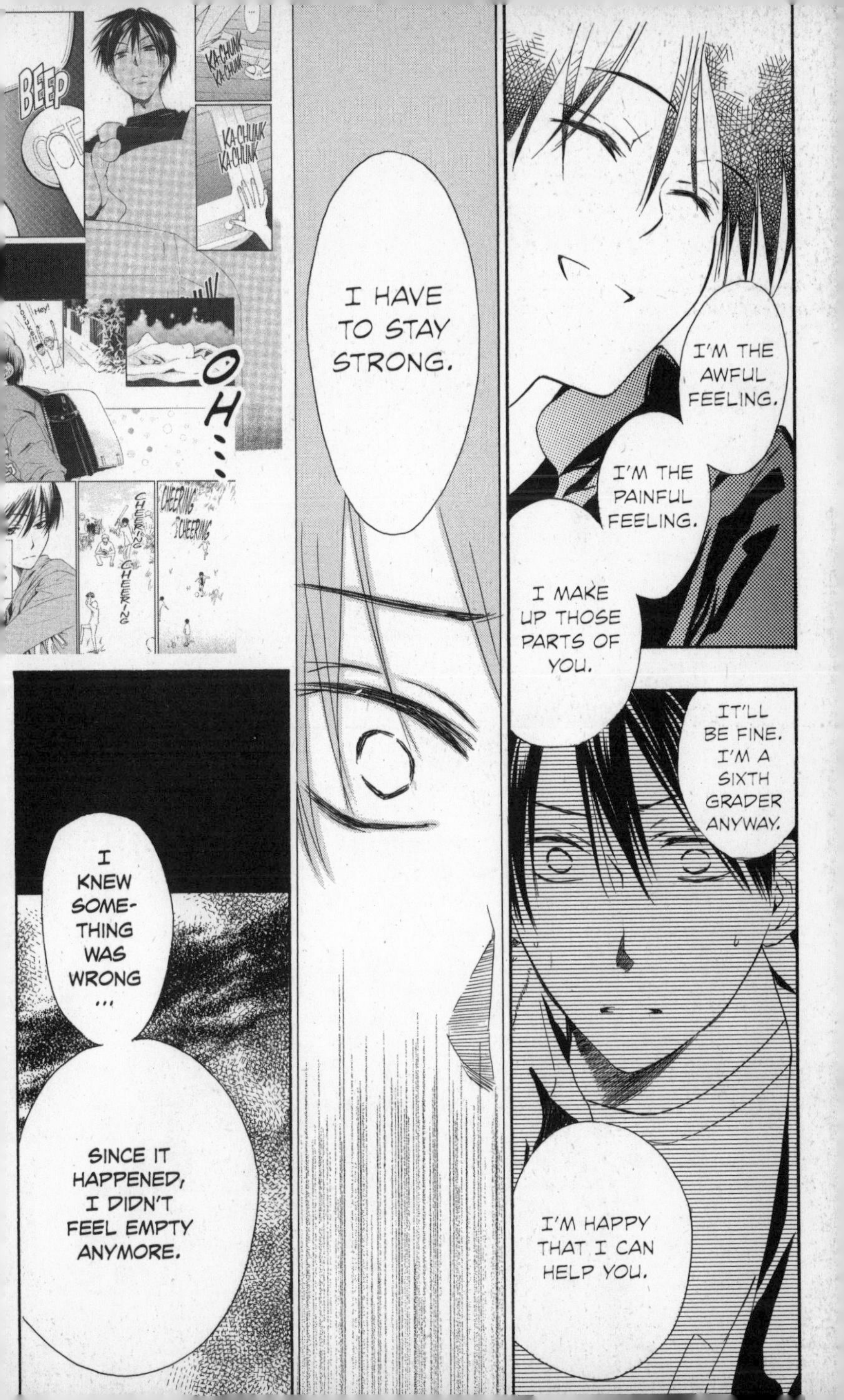
I'M THE AWFUL FEELING.
I'M THE PAINFUL FEELING.
I MAKE UP THOSE PARTS OF YOU.
IT'LL BE FINE. I'M A SIXTH GRADER ANYWAY.
I'M HAPPY THAT I CAN HELP YOU.
I HAVE TO STAY STRONG.
KA-CHUNK KA-CHUNK
KA-CHUNK KA-CHUNK
BEEP
Hey!
OH...
CHEERING CHEERING
CHEERING CHEERING
I KNEW SOME-THING WAS WRONG...
SINCE IT HAPPENED, I DIDN'T FEEL EMPTY ANYMORE.

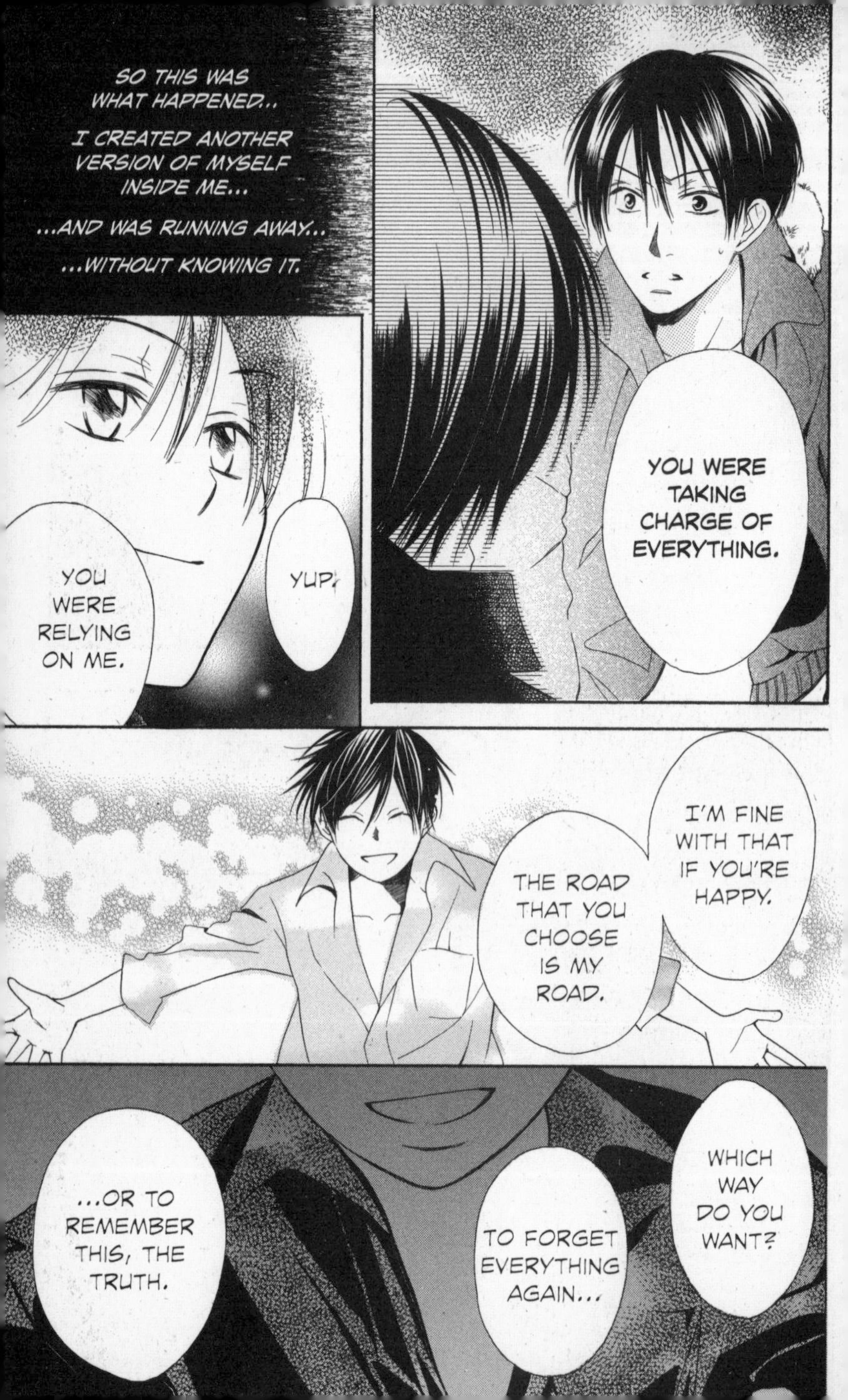
YOU WERE TAKING CHARGE OF EVERYTHING.
SO THIS WAS WHAT HAPPENED...
I CREATED ANOTHER VERSION OF MYSELF INSIDE ME...
...AND WAS RUNNING AWAY...
...WITHOUT KNOWING IT.
YUP.
YOU WERE RELYING ON ME.
I'M FINE WITH THAT IF YOU'RE HAPPY.
THE ROAD THAT YOU CHOOSE IS MY ROAD.
WHICH WAY DO YOU WANT?
TO FORGET EVERYTHING AGAIN...
...OR TO REMEMBER THIS, THE TRUTH.

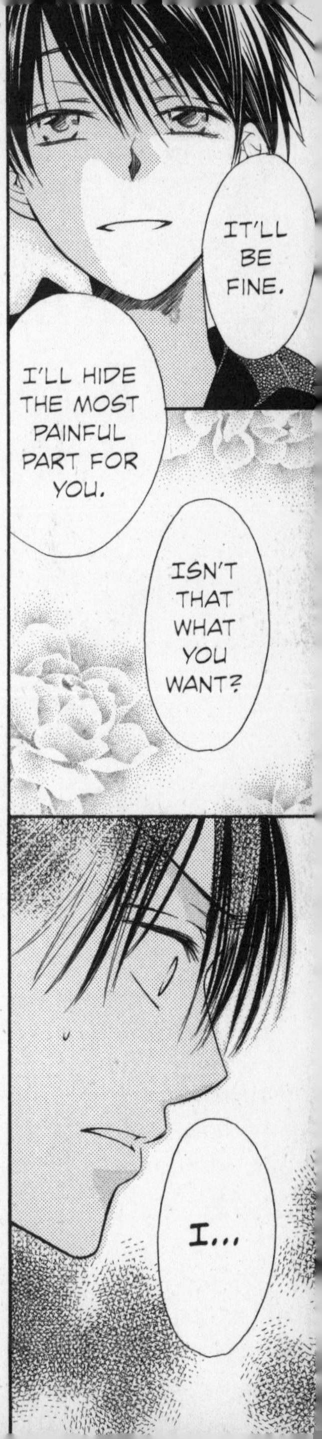
IT'LL BE FINE.
I'LL HIDE THE MOST PAINFUL PART FOR YOU.
ISN'T THAT WHAT YOU WANT?
I...

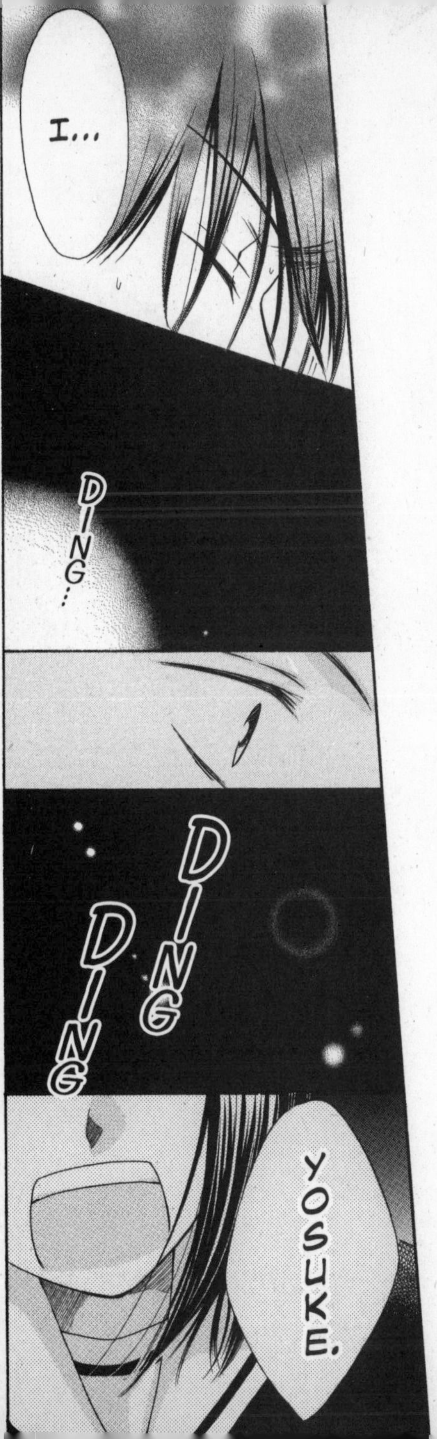
I...
DING...
DING
DING
YOSUKE.

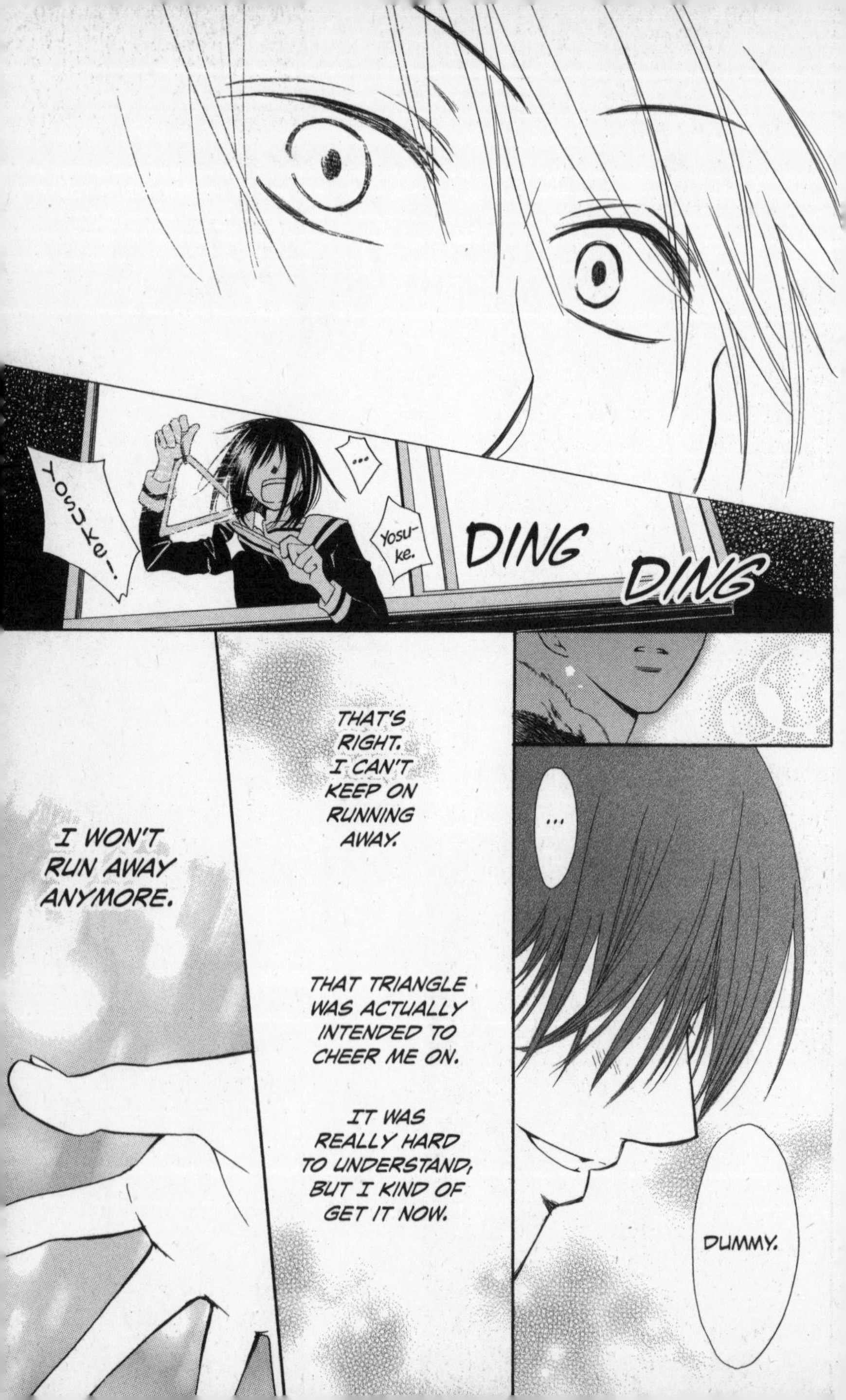
DING DING
Yosu-ke.
...
Yosuke-!
...
DUMMY.
THAT'S RIGHT. I CAN'T KEEP ON RUNNING AWAY.
THAT TRIANGLE WAS ACTUALLY INTENDED TO CHEER ME ON.
IT WAS REALLY HARD TO UNDERSTAND, BUT I KIND OF GET IT NOW.
I WON'T RUN AWAY ANYMORE.

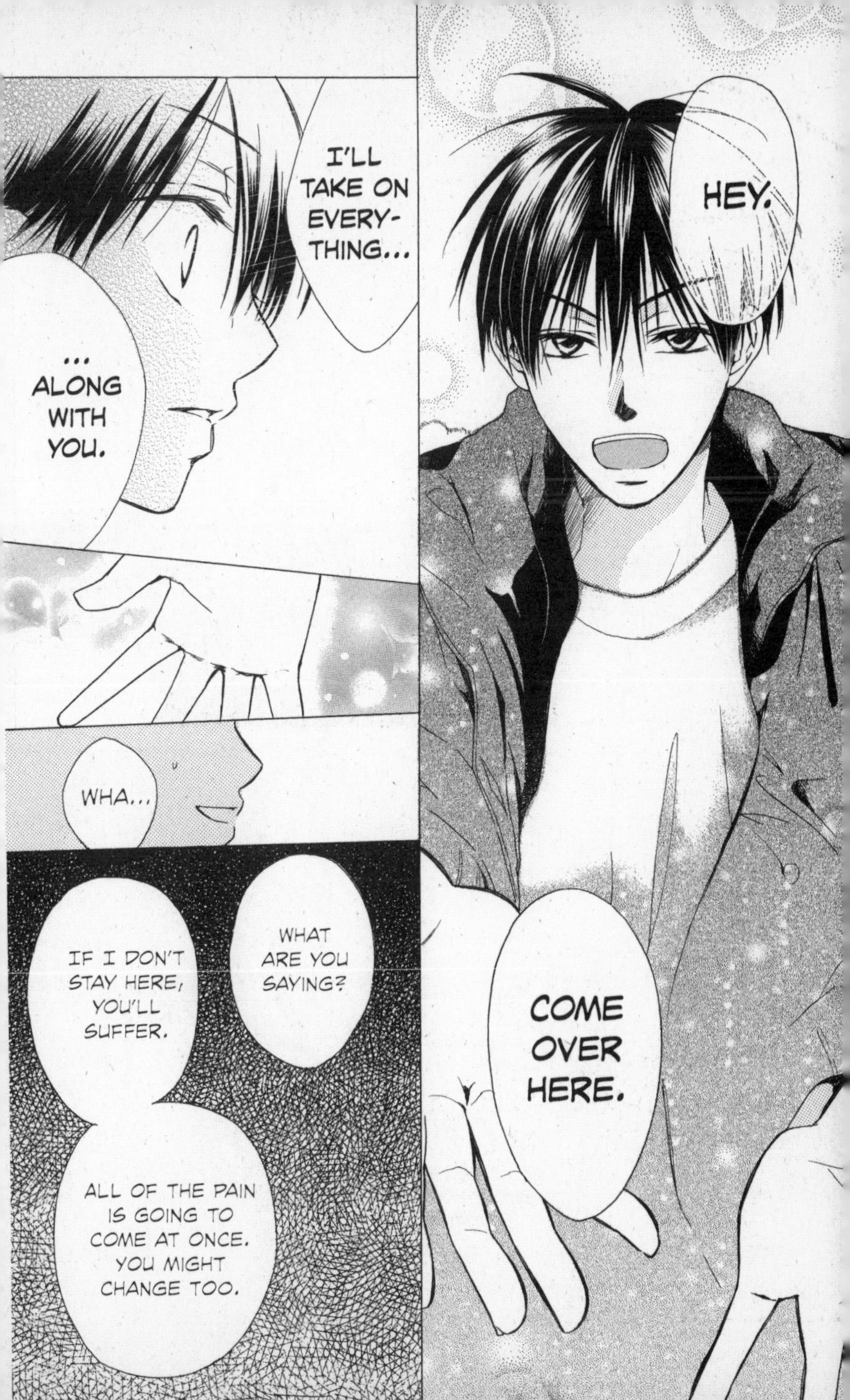
HEY.
COME OVER HERE.
I'LL TAKE ON EVERY-THING...
... ALONG WITH YOU.
WHA...
WHAT ARE YOU SAYING?
IF I DON'T STAY HERE, YOU'LL SUFFER.
ALL OF THE PAIN IS GOING TO COME AT ONCE. YOU MIGHT CHANGE TOO.

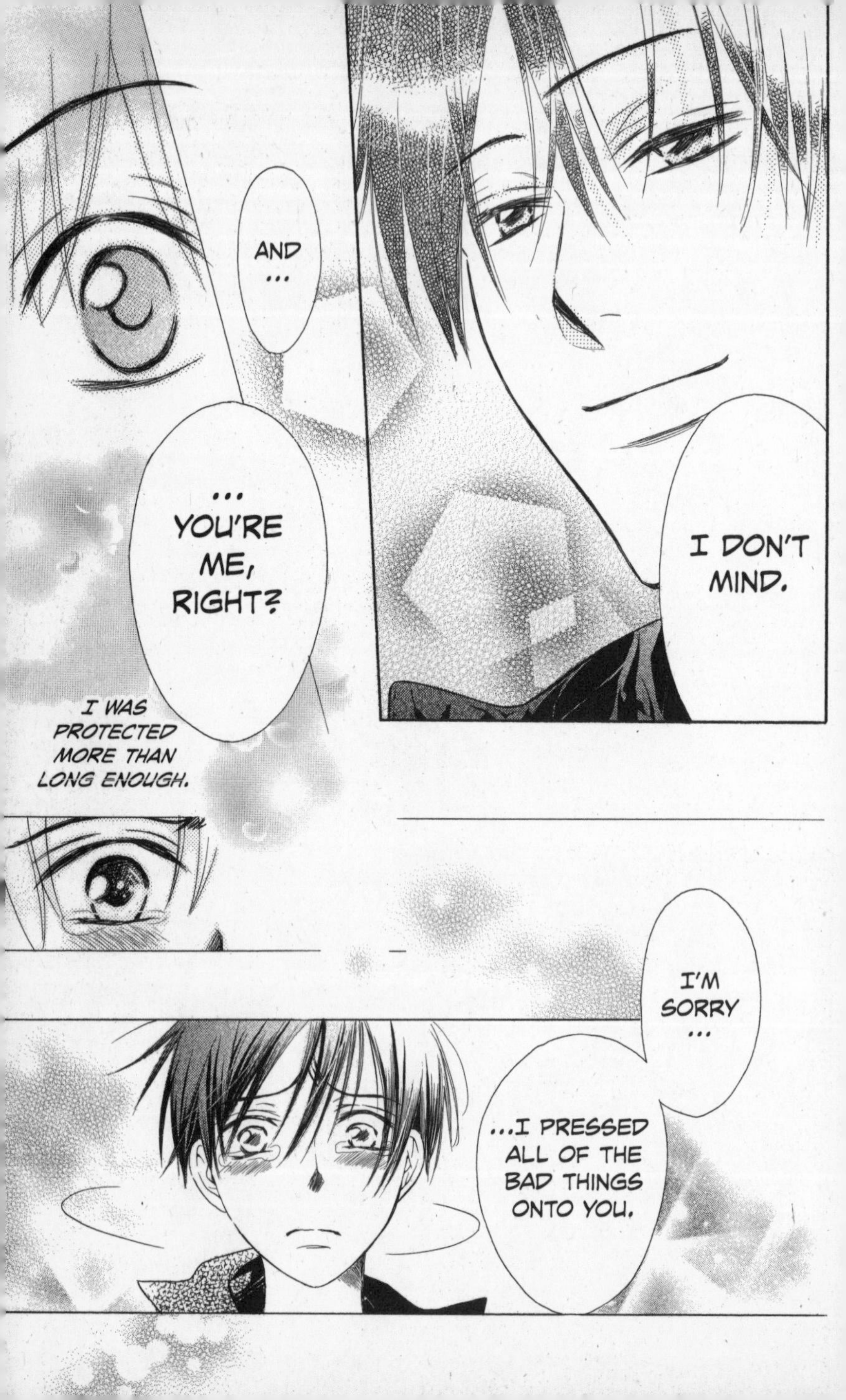
I DON'T MIND.
AND ...
... YOU'RE ME, RIGHT?
I WAS PROTECTED MORE THAN LONG ENOUGH.
I'M SORRY ...
...I PRESSED ALL OF THE BAD THINGS ONTO YOU.

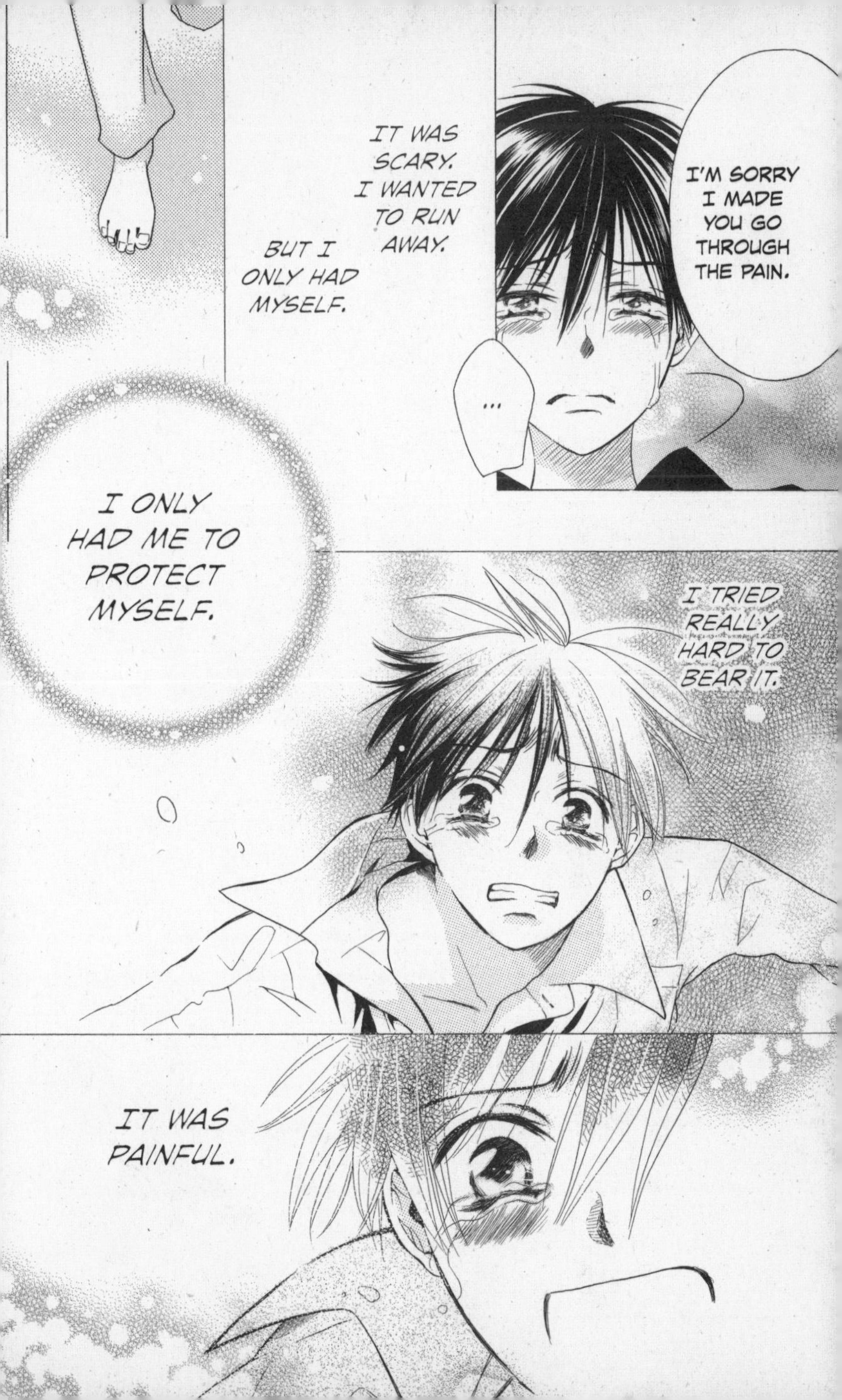

I'M SORRY I MADE YOU GO THROUGH THE PAIN.
...
IT WAS SCARY. I WANTED TO RUN AWAY.
BUT I ONLY HAD MYSELF.
I ONLY HAD ME TO PROTECT MYSELF.
I TRIED REALLY HARD TO BEAR IT.
IT WAS PAINFUL.

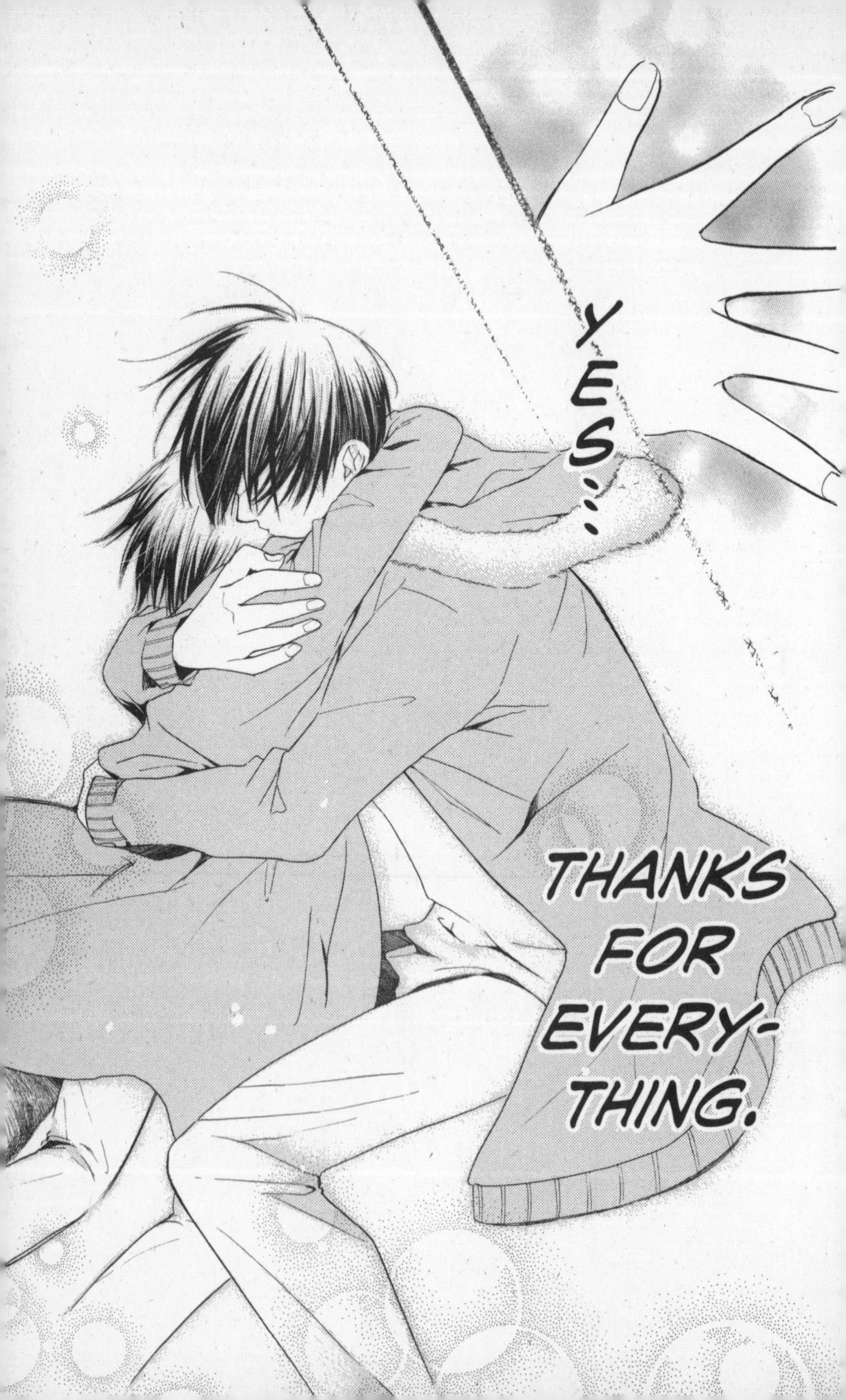
YES...
THANKS FOR EVERY-THING.

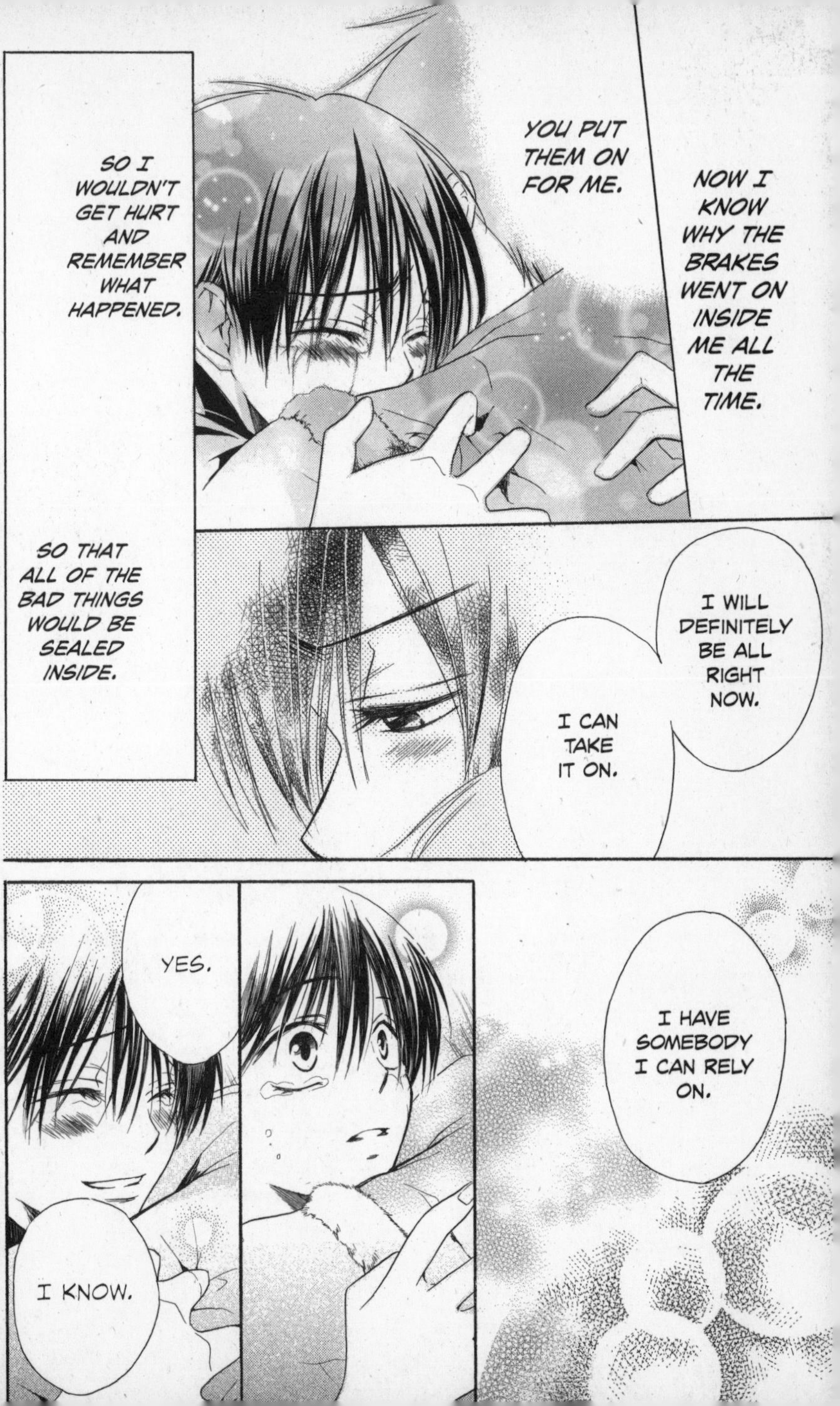
NOW I KNOW WHY THE BRAKES WENT ON INSIDE ME ALL THE TIME.
YOU PUT THEM ON FOR ME.
I WILL DEFINITELY BE ALL RIGHT NOW.
I CAN TAKE IT ON.
SO I WOULDN'T GET HURT AND REMEMBER WHAT HAPPENED.
SO THAT ALL OF THE BAD THINGS WOULD BE SEALED INSIDE.
I HAVE SOMEBODY I CAN RELY ON.
YES.
I KNOW.

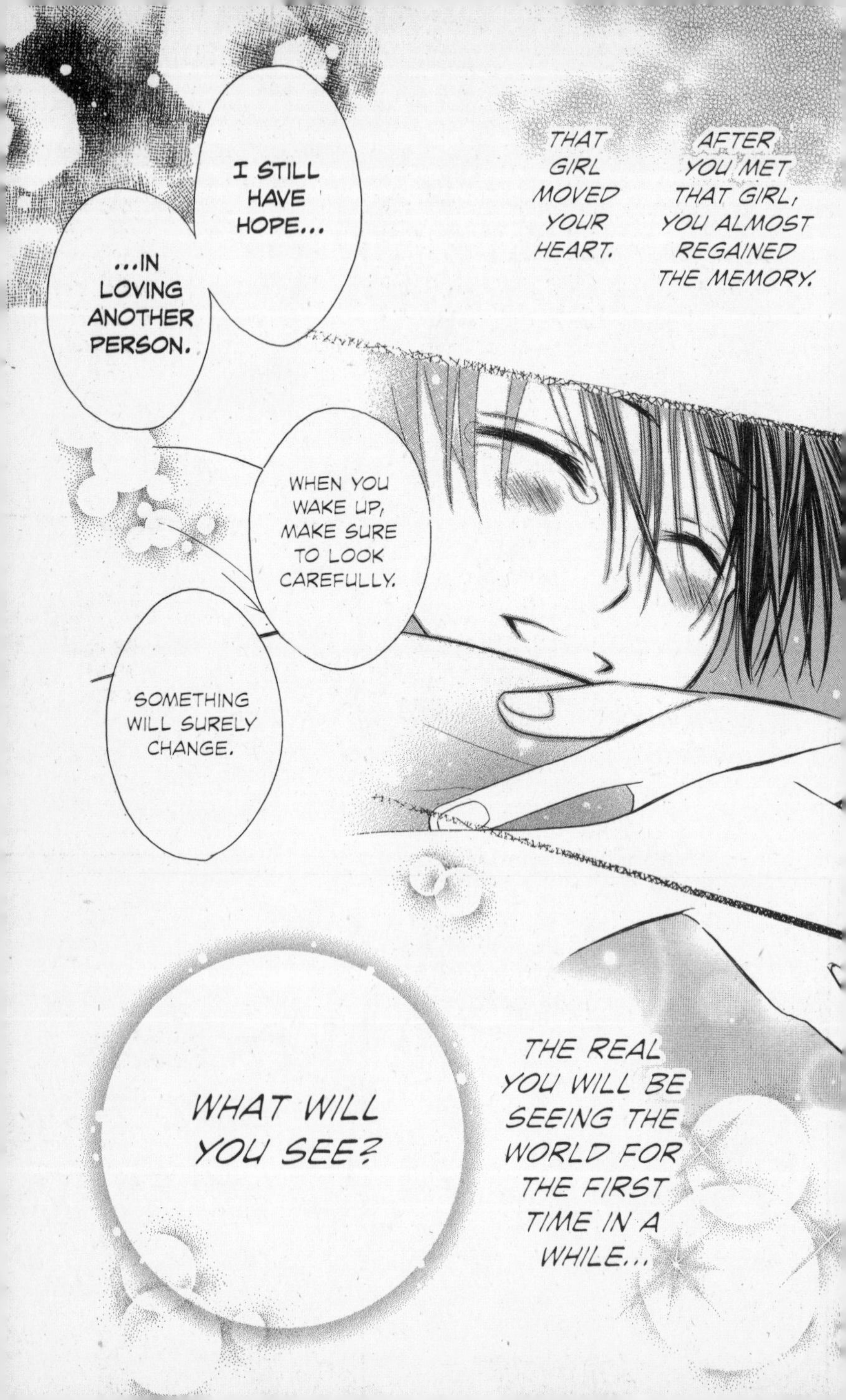
AFTER YOU MET THAT GIRL, YOU ALMOST REGAINED THE MEMORY.
THAT GIRL MOVED YOUR HEART.
I STILL HAVE HOPE...
...IN LOVING ANOTHER PERSON.
WHEN YOU WAKE UP, MAKE SURE TO LOOK CAREFULLY.
SOMETHING WILL SURELY CHANGE.
THE REAL YOU WILL BE SEEING THE WORLD FOR THE FIRST TIME IN A WHILE...
WHAT WILL YOU SEE?

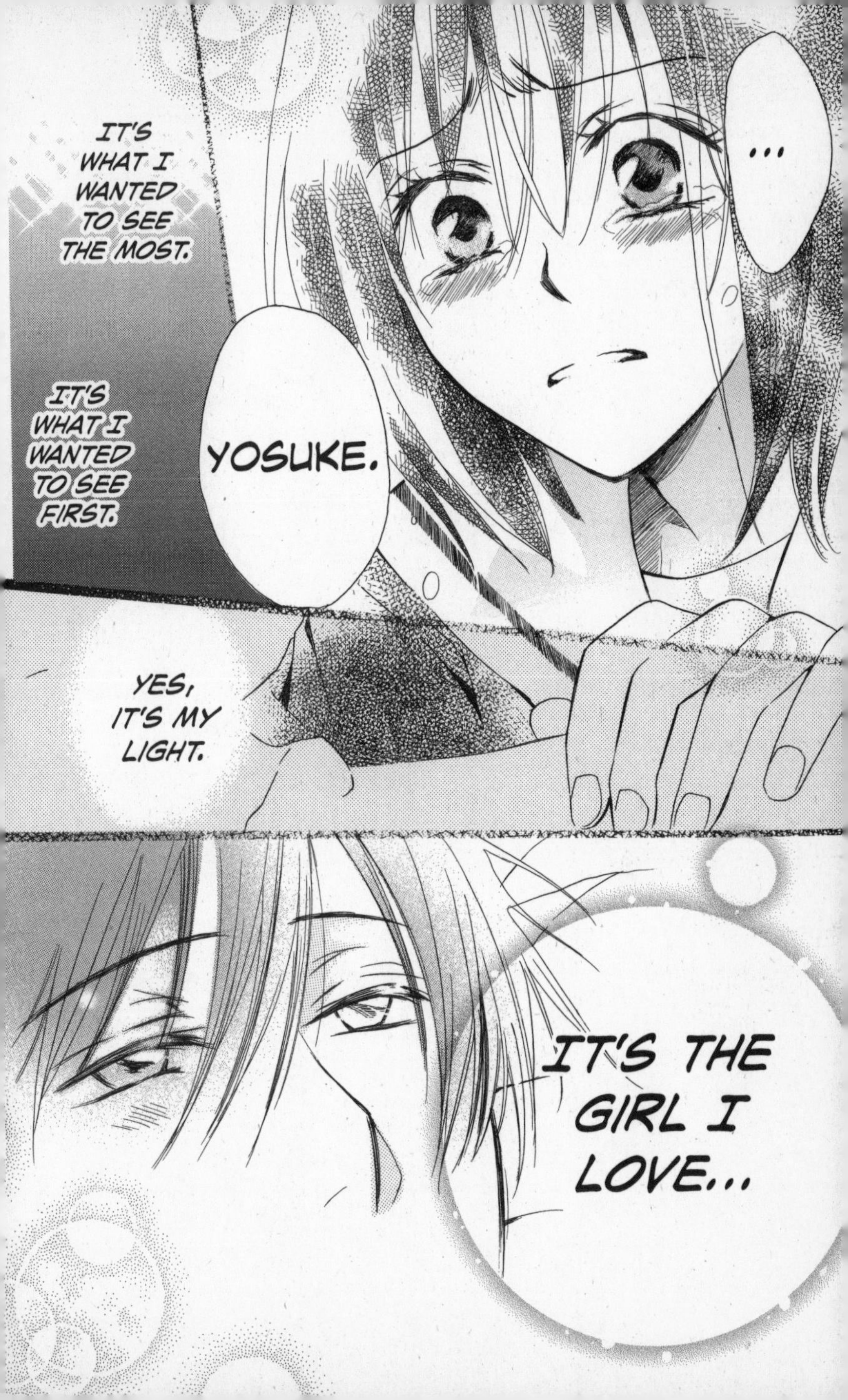
...
IT'S WHAT I WANTED TO SEE THE MOST.
YOSUKE.
IT'S WHAT I WANTED TO SEE FIRST.
YES, IT'S MY LIGHT.
IT'S THE GIRL I LOVE...

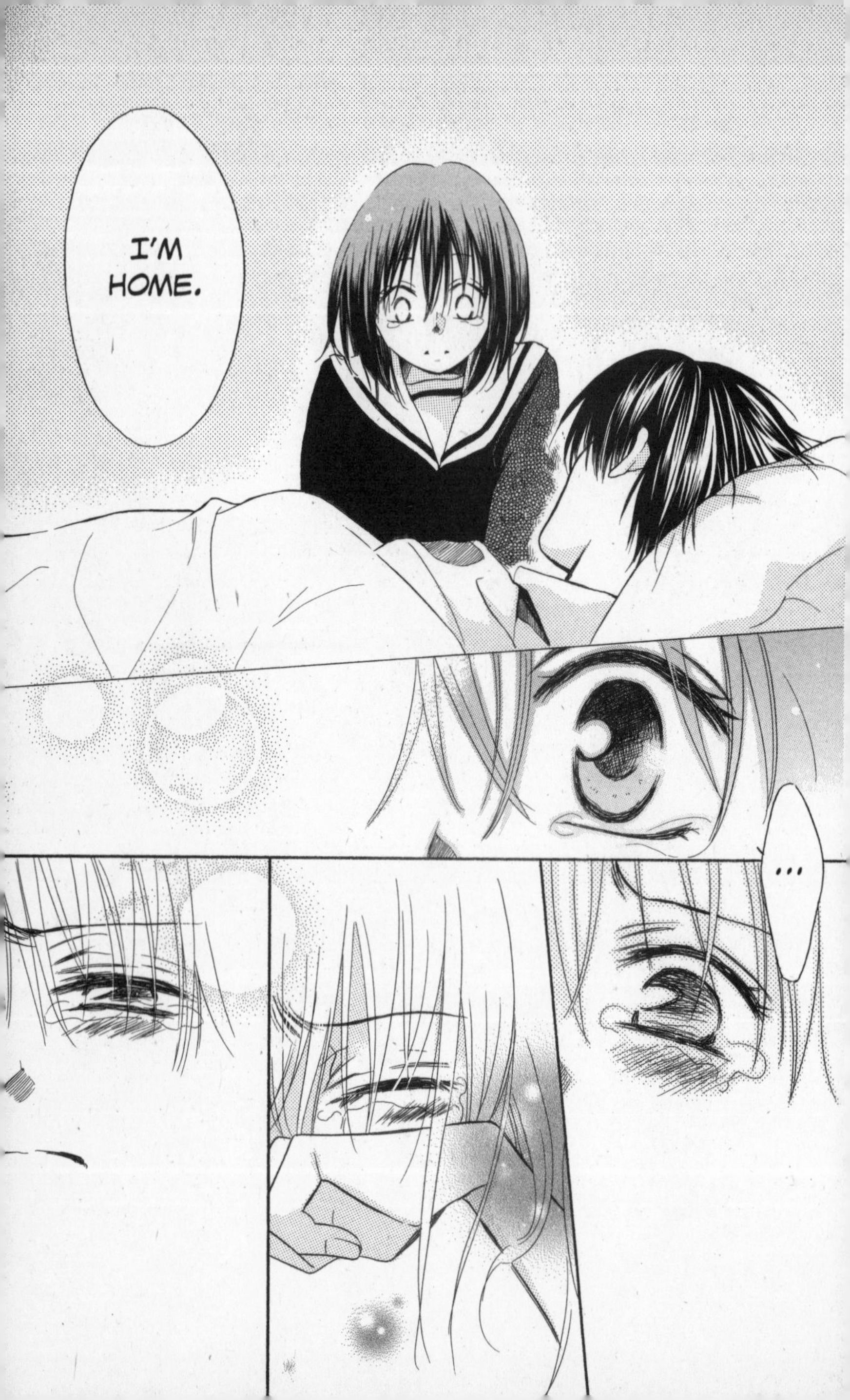
I'M HOME.
...

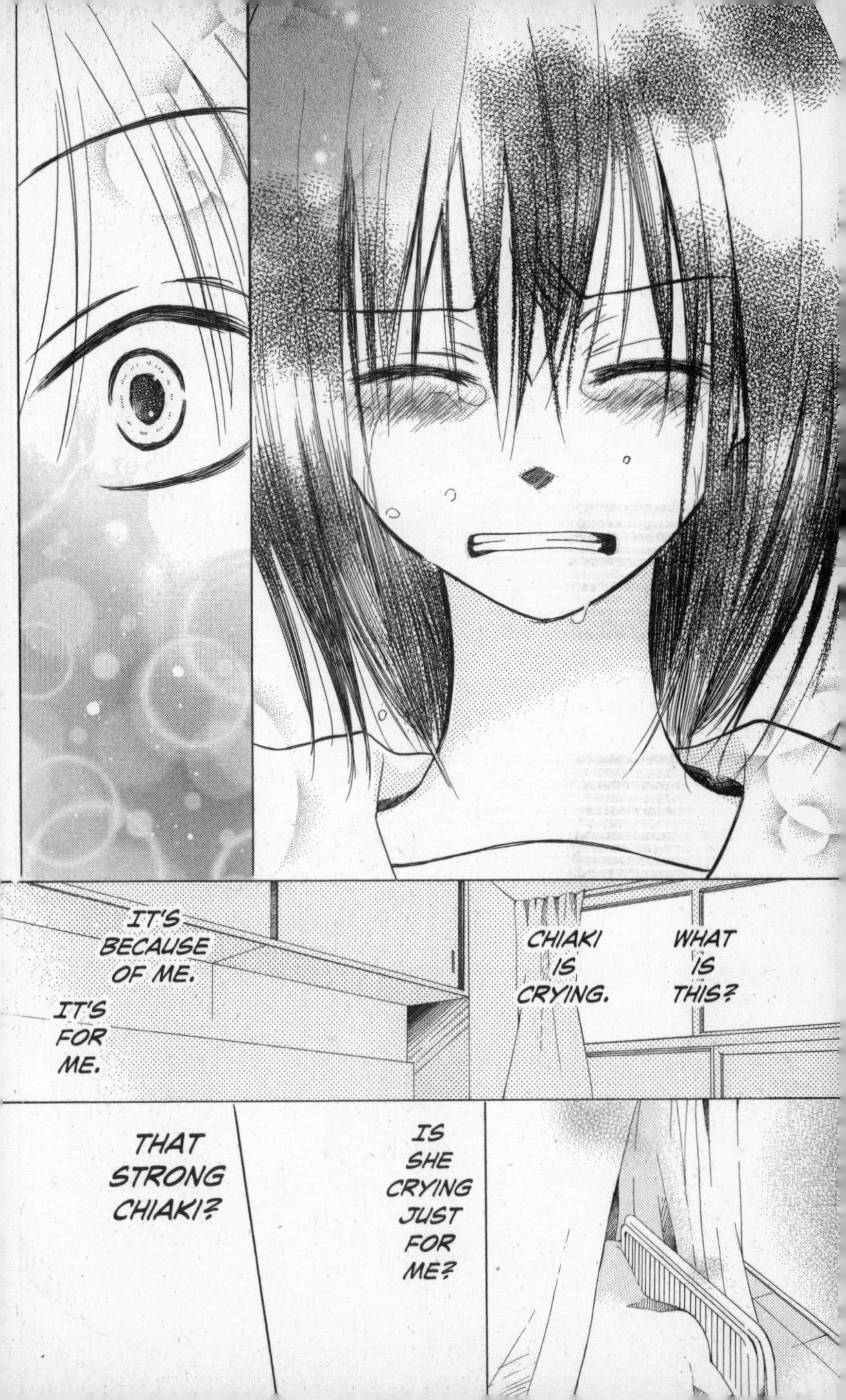
WHAT IS THIS?
CHIAKI IS CRYING.
IT'S BECAUSE OF ME.
IT'S FOR ME.
IS SHE CRYING JUST FOR ME?
THAT STRONG CHIAKI?

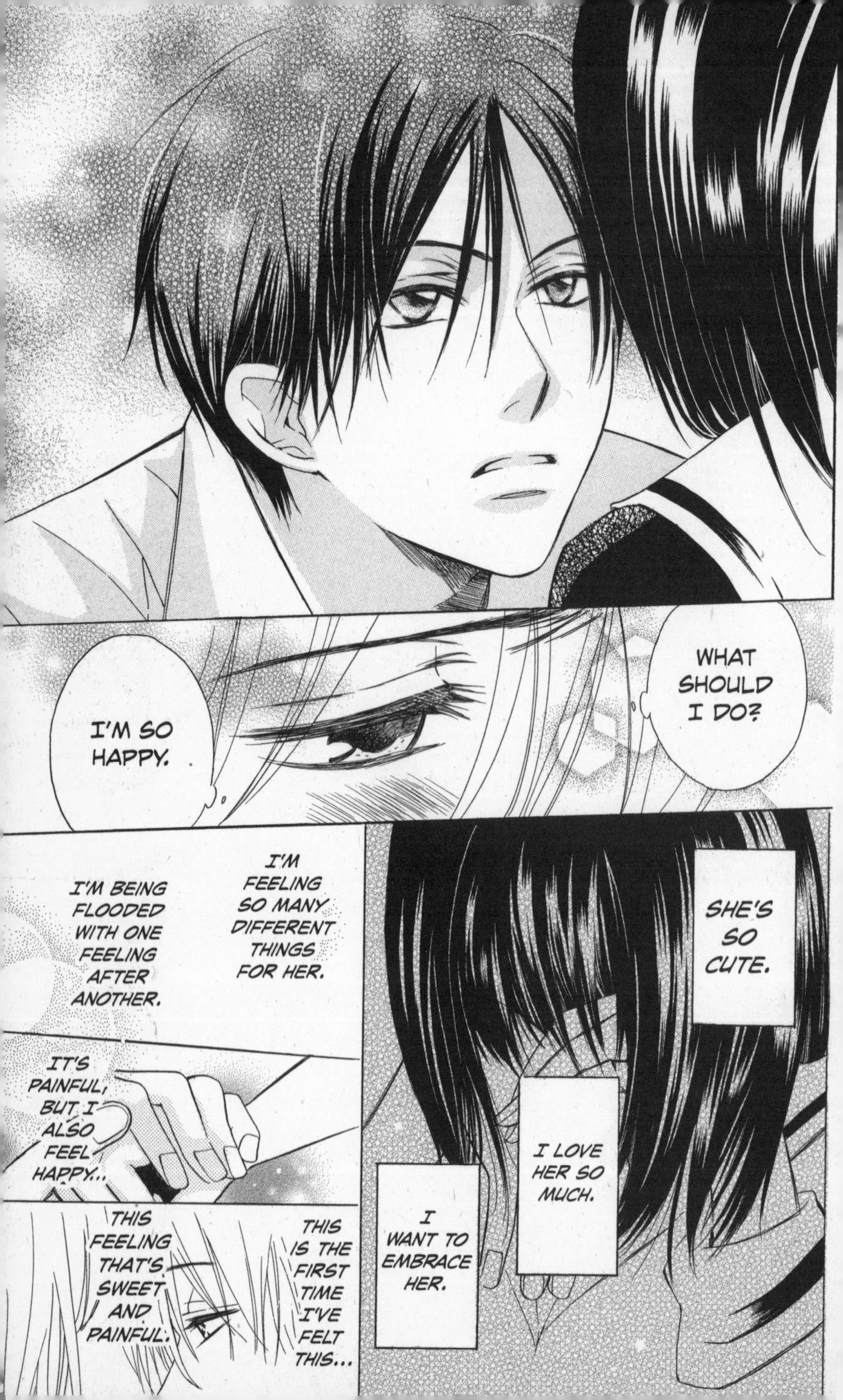
WHAT SHOULD I DO?
I'M SO HAPPY.
SHE'S SO CUTE.
I LOVE HER SO MUCH.
I WANT TO EMBRACE HER.
I'M FEELING SO MANY DIFFERENT THINGS FOR HER.
I'M BEING FLOODED WITH ONE FEELING AFTER ANOTHER.
IT'S PAINFUL, BUT I ALSO FEEL HAPPY...
THIS IS THE FIRST TIME I'VE FELT THIS...
THIS FEELING THAT'S SWEET AND PAINFUL.

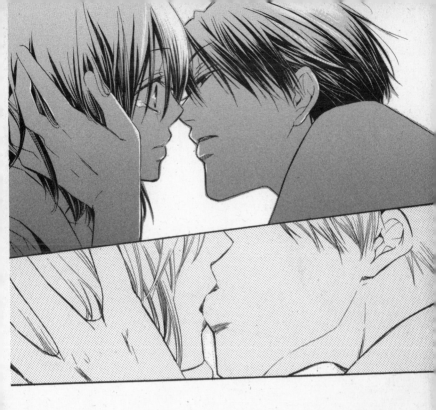

I LOVE HER.

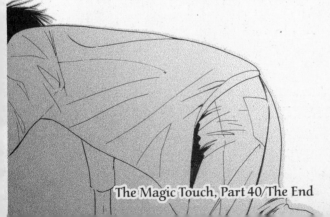

The Magic Touch, Part 40/The End

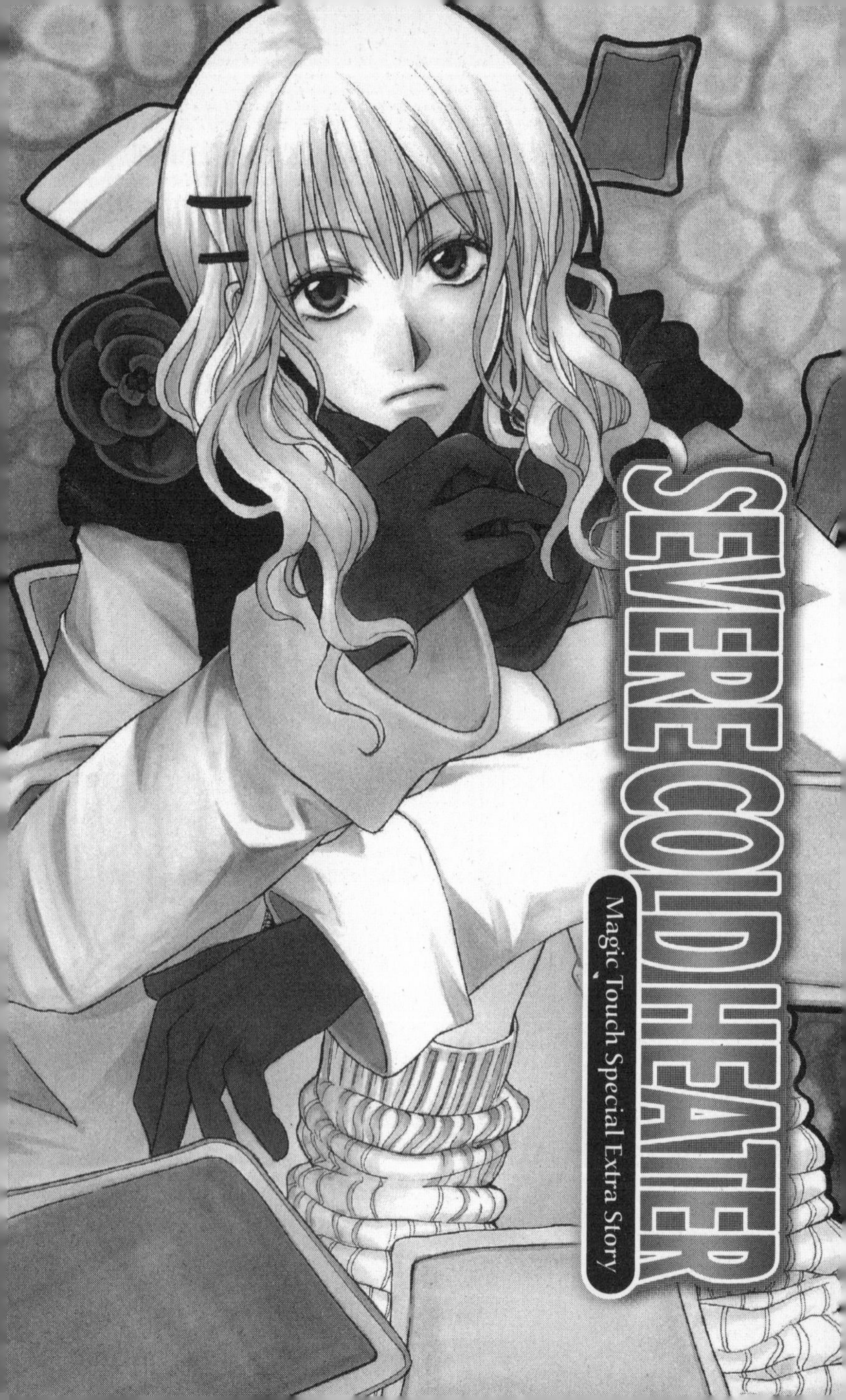
SEVERE COLD HEATER
Magic Touch Special Extra Story

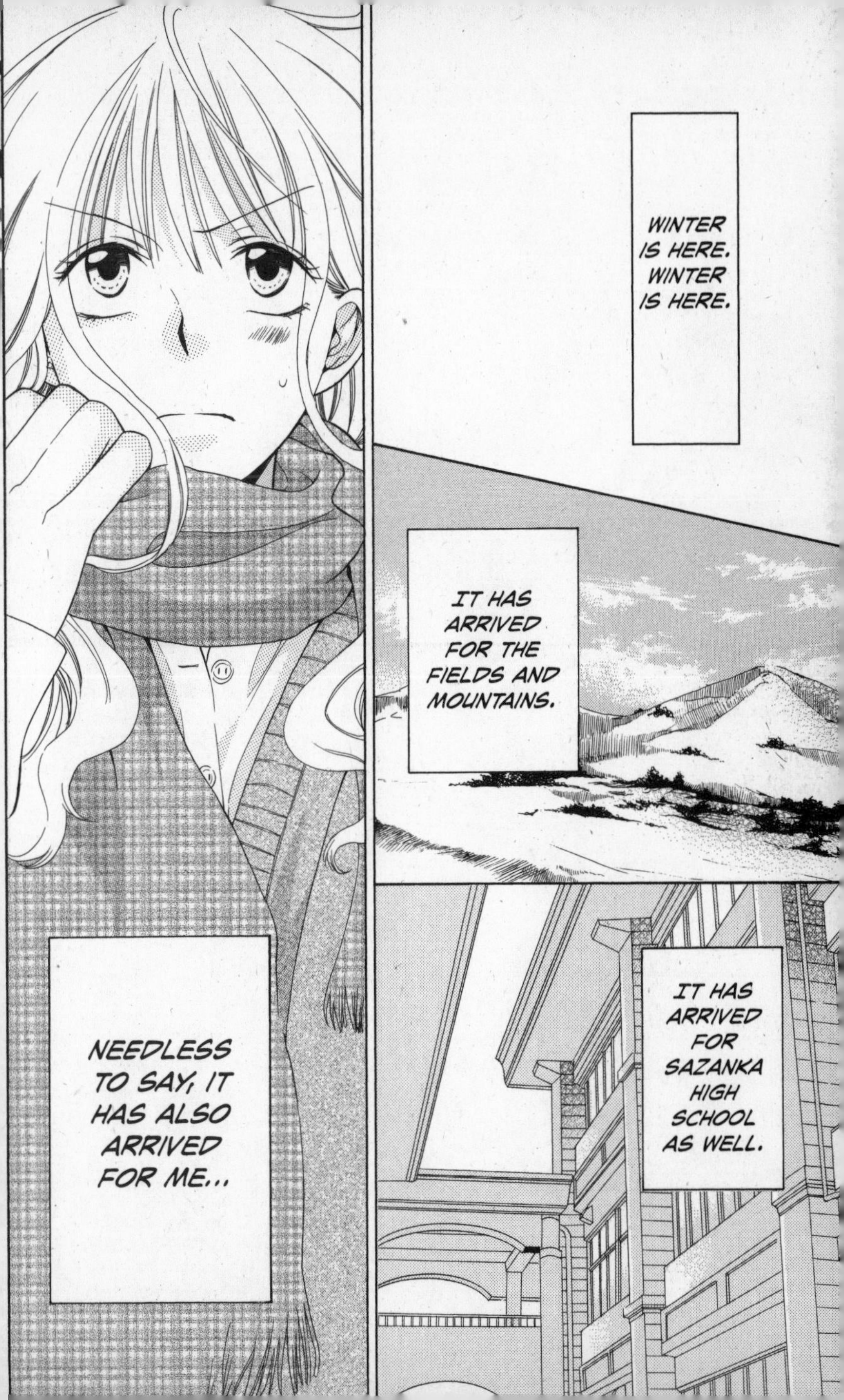
WINTER IS HERE. WINTER IS HERE.
IT HAS ARRIVED FOR THE FIELDS AND MOUNTAINS.
IT HAS ARRIVED FOR SAZANKA HIGH SCHOOL AS WELL.
NEEDLESS TO SAY, IT HAS ALSO ARRIVED FOR ME...

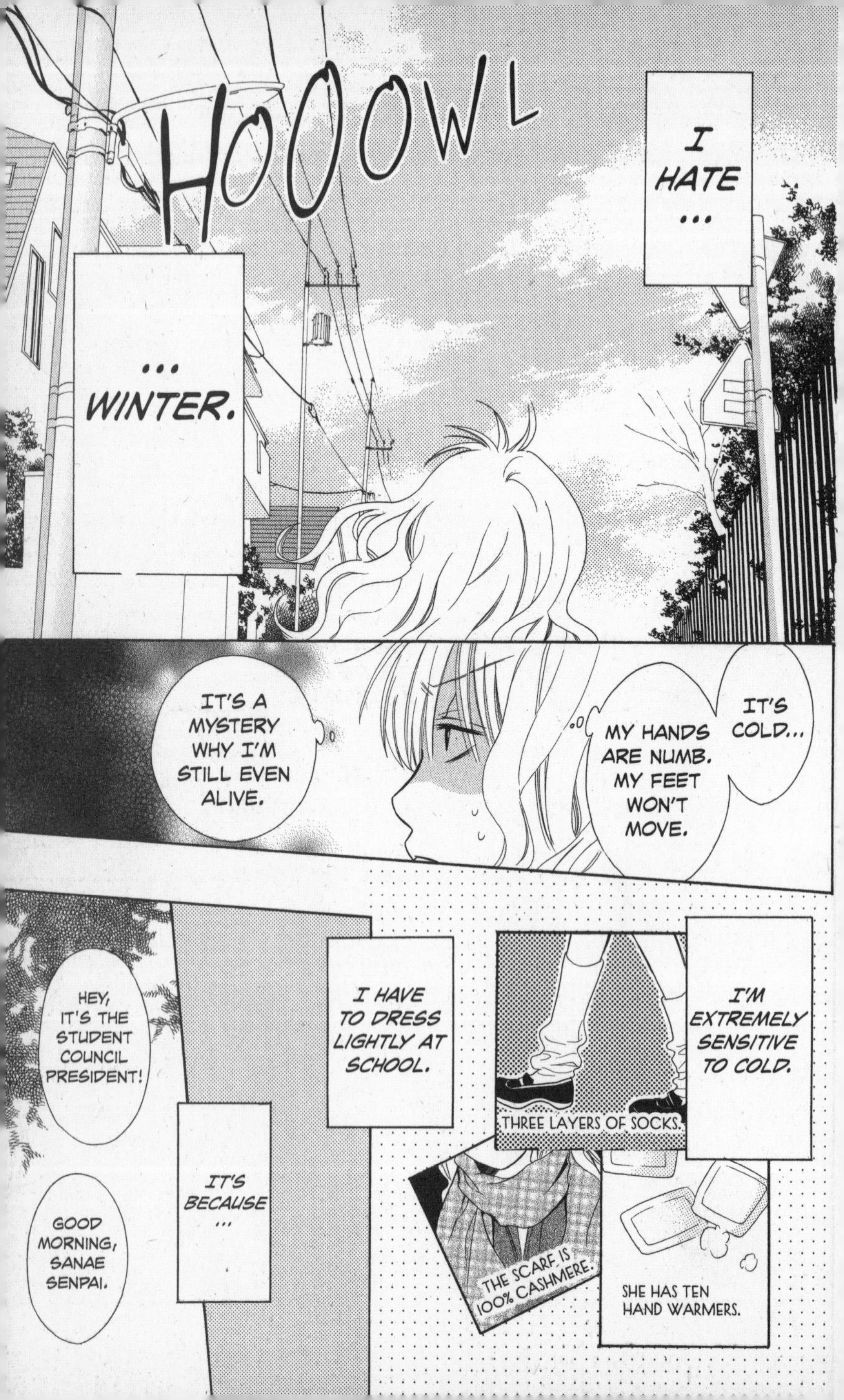
I HATE ...
HOOOWL
... WINTER.
IT'S COLD...
MY HANDS ARE NUMB. MY FEET WON'T MOVE.
IT'S A MYSTERY WHY I'M STILL EVEN ALIVE.
I'M EXTREMELY SENSITIVE TO COLD.
THREE LAYERS OF SOCKS.
SHE HAS TEN HAND WARMERS.
THE SCARF IS 100% CASHMERE.
I HAVE TO DRESS LIGHTLY AT SCHOOL.
IT'S BECAUSE ...
HEY, IT'S THE STUDENT COUNCIL PRESIDENT!
GOOD MORNING, SANAE SENPAI.

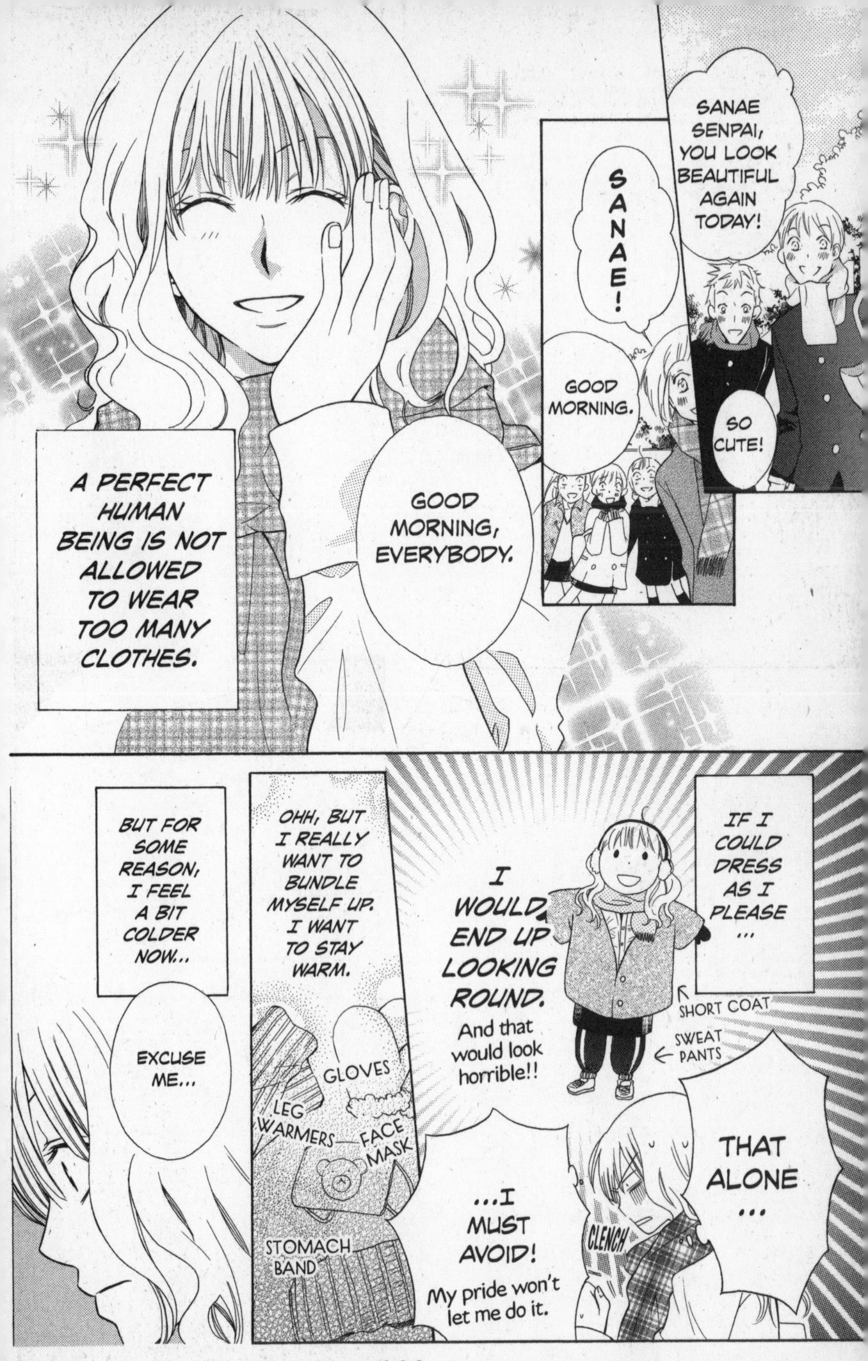
SANAE SENPAI, YOU LOOK BEAUTIFUL AGAIN TODAY!
SO CUTE!
SANAE!
GOOD MORNING.
GOOD MORNING, EVERYBODY.
A PERFECT HUMAN BEING IS NOT ALLOWED TO WEAR TOO MANY CLOTHES.
IF I COULD DRESS AS I PLEASE...
I WOULD END UP LOOKING ROUND.
And that would look horrible!!
SHORT COAT
SWEAT PANTS
THAT ALONE...
CLENCH
...I MUST AVOID!
My pride won't let me do it.
OHH, BUT I REALLY WANT TO BUNDLE MYSELF UP. I WANT TO STAY WARM.
GLOVES
LEG WARMERS
FACE MASK
STOMACH BAND
BUT FOR SOME REASON, I FEEL A BIT COLDER NOW...
EXCUSE ME...

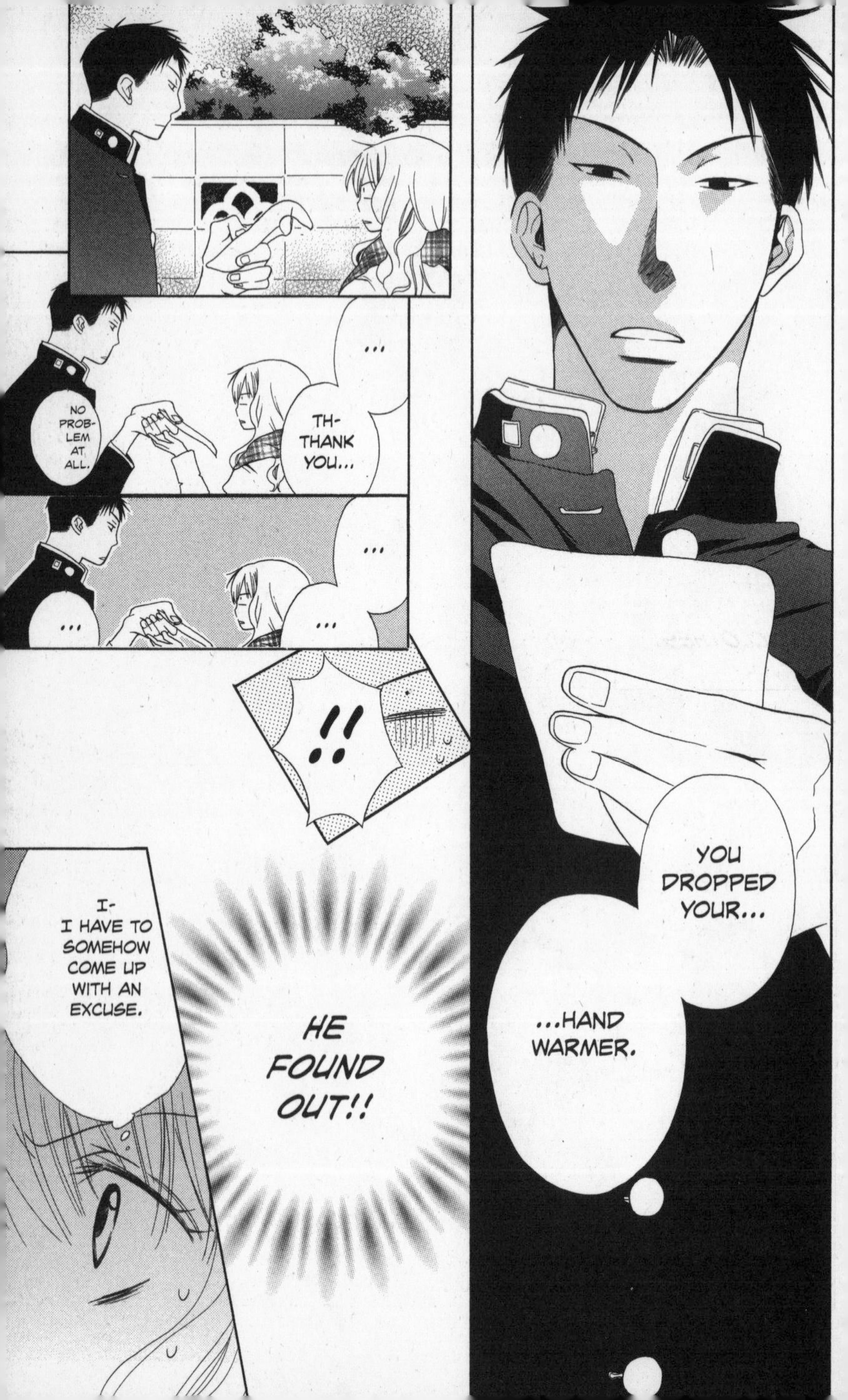

YOU DROPPED YOUR...
...HAND WARMER.
...
TH-THANK YOU...
NO PROB-LEM AT ALL.
...
...
...
!!
HE FOUND OUT!!
I- I HAVE TO SOMEHOW COME UP WITH AN EXCUSE.

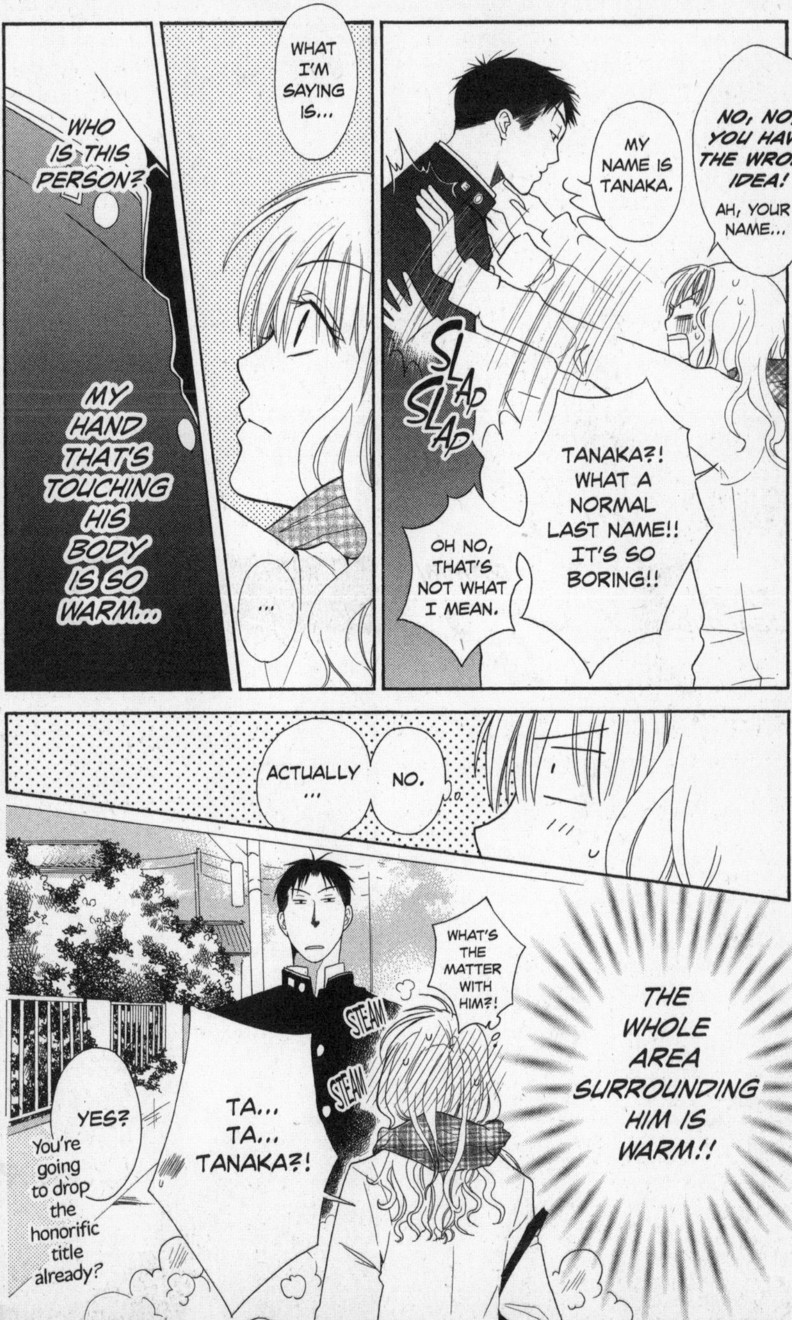
NO, NO, YOU HAVE THE WRONG IDEA!
AH, YOUR NAME...
MY NAME IS TANAKA.
SLAP SLAP
TANAKA?! WHAT A NORMAL LAST NAME!! IT'S SO BORING!!
OH NO, THAT'S NOT WHAT I MEAN.
WHAT I'M SAYING IS...
...
WHO IS THIS PERSON?
MY HAND THAT'S TOUCHING HIS BODY IS SO WARM...
NO.
ACTUALLY ...
THE WHOLE AREA SURROUNDING HIM IS WARM!!
WHAT'S THE MATTER WITH HIM?!
STEAM
STEAM
TA... TA... TANAKA?!
YES?
You're going to drop the honorific title already?

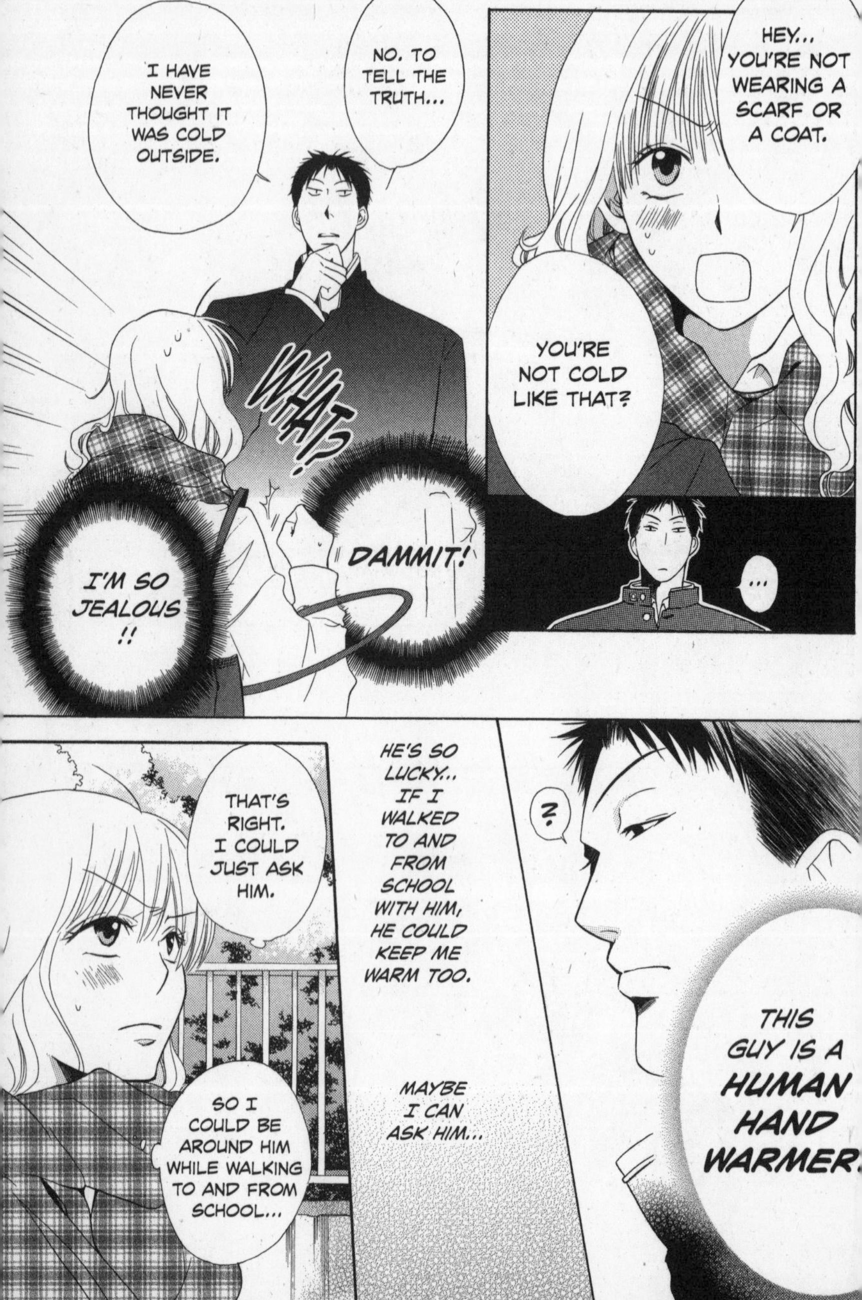
HEY... YOU'RE NOT WEARING A SCARF OR A COAT.
YOU'RE NOT COLD LIKE THAT?
...
NO. TO TELL THE TRUTH...
I HAVE NEVER THOUGHT IT WAS COLD OUTSIDE.
WHAT?!
DAMMIT!
I'M SO JEALOUS!!
?
THIS GUY IS A HUMAN HAND WARMER.
HE'S SO LUCKY... IF I WALKED TO AND FROM SCHOOL WITH HIM, HE COULD KEEP ME WARM TOO.
MAYBE I CAN ASK HIM...
THAT'S RIGHT. I COULD JUST ASK HIM.
SO I COULD BE AROUND HIM WHILE WALKING TO AND FROM SCHOOL...

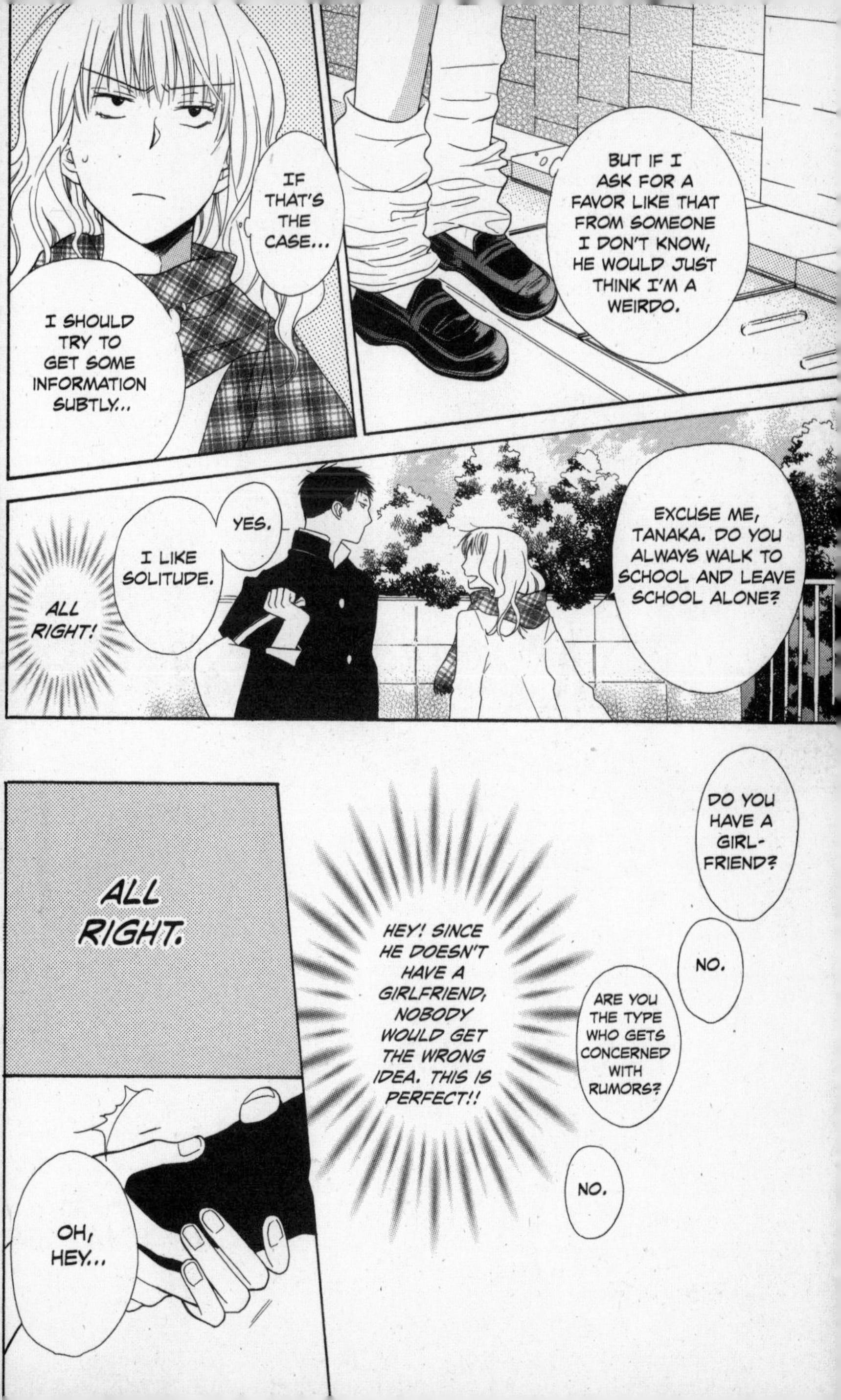
BUT IF I ASK FOR A FAVOR LIKE THAT FROM SOMEONE I DON'T KNOW, HE WOULD JUST THINK I'M A WEIRDO.
IF THAT'S THE CASE...
I SHOULD TRY TO GET SOME INFORMATION SUBTLY...
EXCUSE ME, TANAKA. DO YOU ALWAYS WALK TO SCHOOL AND LEAVE SCHOOL ALONE?
YES.
I LIKE SOLITUDE.
ALL RIGHT!
DO YOU HAVE A GIRL-FRIEND?
NO.
ARE YOU THE TYPE WHO GETS CONCERNED WITH RUMORS?
NO.
HEY! SINCE HE DOESN'T HAVE A GIRLFRIEND, NOBODY WOULD GET THE WRONG IDEA. THIS IS PERFECT!!
ALL RIGHT.
OH, HEY...

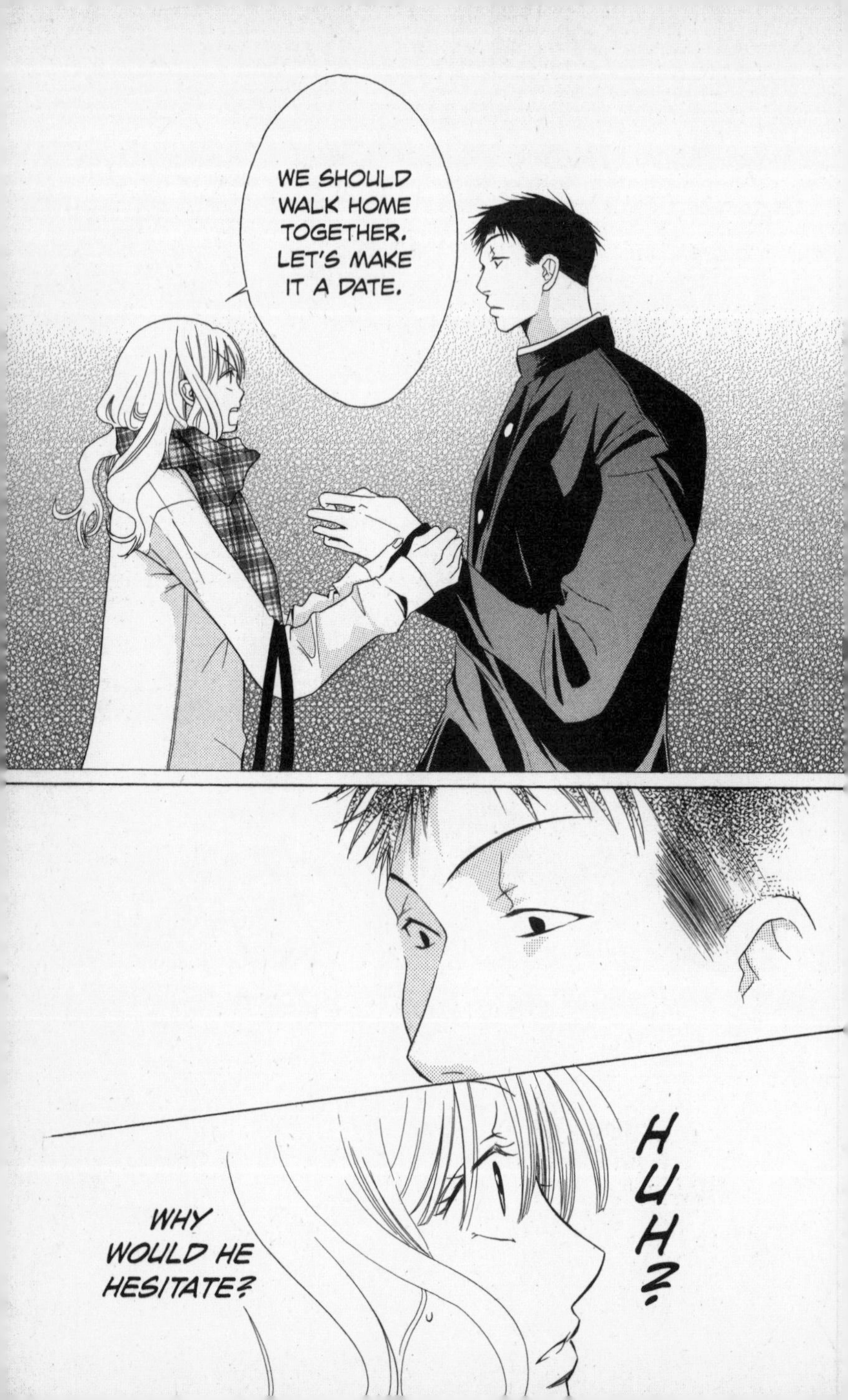
WE SHOULD WALK HOME TOGETHER. LET'S MAKE IT A DATE.
HUH?
WHY WOULD HE HESITATE?

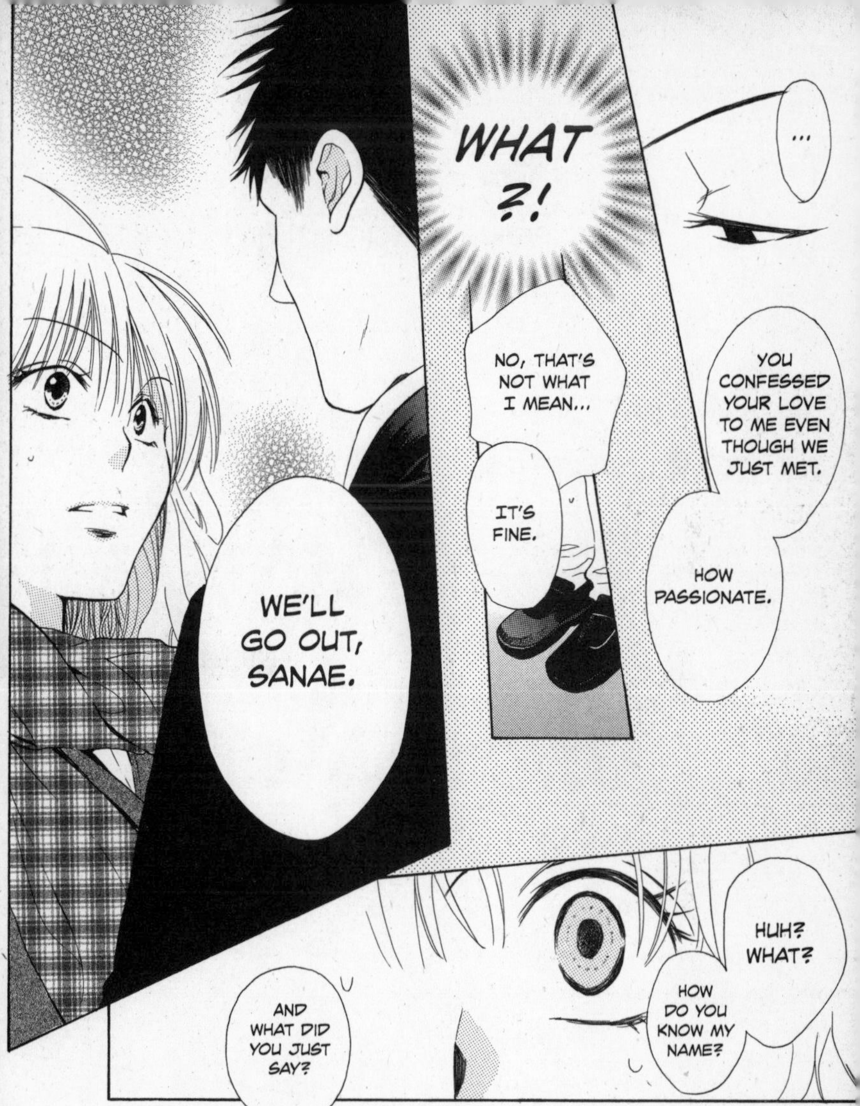
...
YOU CONFESSED YOUR LOVE TO ME EVEN THOUGH WE JUST MET.
HOW PASSIONATE.
WHAT ?!
NO, THAT'S NOT WHAT I MEAN...
IT'S FINE.
WE'LL GO OUT, SANAE.
HUH? WHAT?
HOW DO YOU KNOW MY NAME?
AND WHAT DID YOU JUST SAY?

I JUST SAID IT THE WAY I WAS THINKING IT.

BUT...

...SOMETHING IS WRONG.

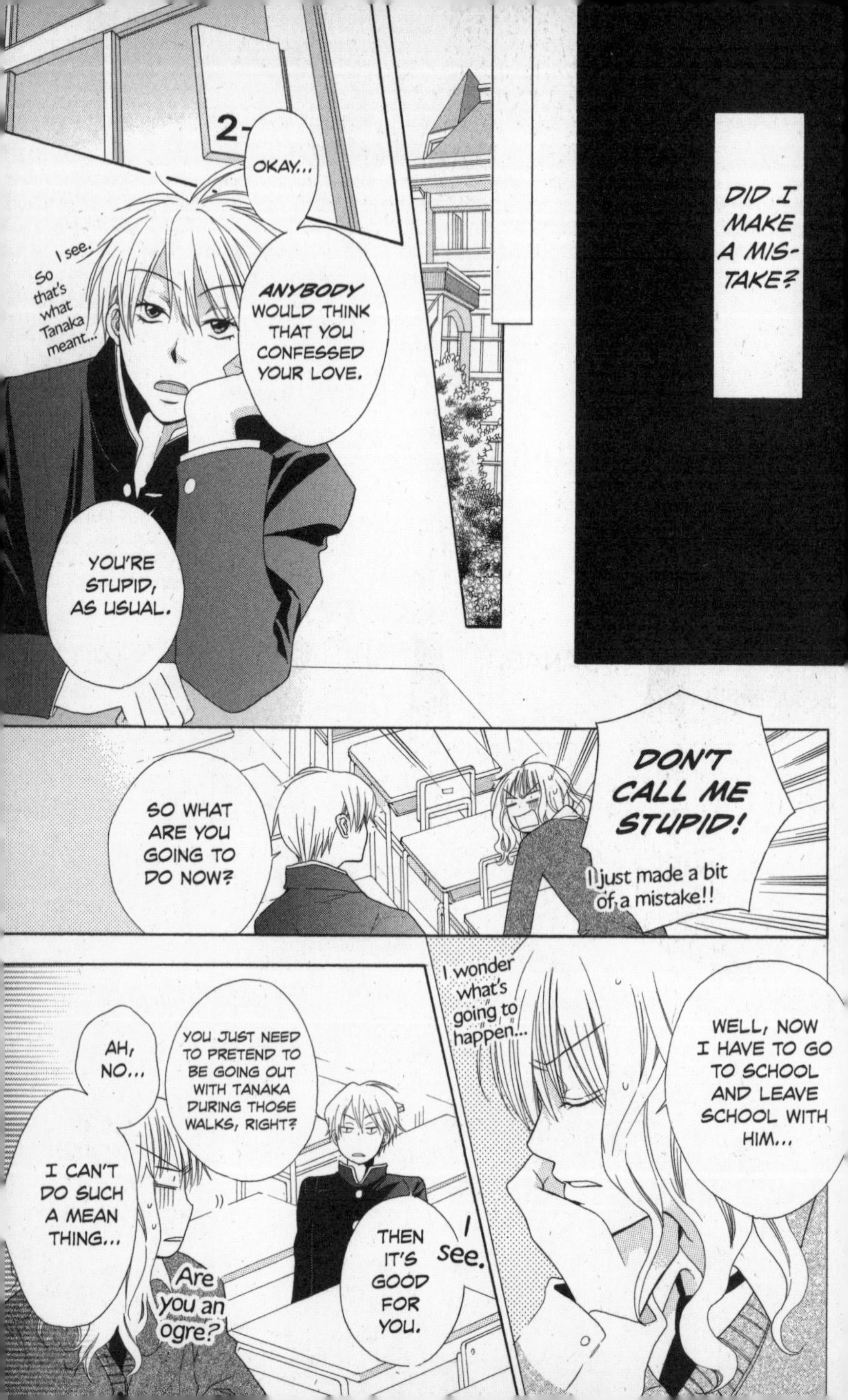
DID I MAKE A MISTAKE?
2-
OKAY...
ANYBODY WOULD THINK THAT YOU CONFESSED YOUR LOVE.
I see. So that's what Tanaka meant...
YOU'RE STUPID, AS USUAL.
DON'T CALL ME STUPID!
I just made a bit of a mistake!!
SO WHAT ARE YOU GOING TO DO NOW?
WELL, NOW I HAVE TO GO TO SCHOOL AND LEAVE SCHOOL WITH HIM...
I wonder what's going to happen...
YOU JUST NEED TO PRETEND TO BE GOING OUT WITH TANAKA DURING THOSE WALKS, RIGHT?
AH, NO...
I CAN'T DO SUCH A MEAN THING...
I see.
THEN IT'S GOOD FOR YOU.
Are you an ogre?

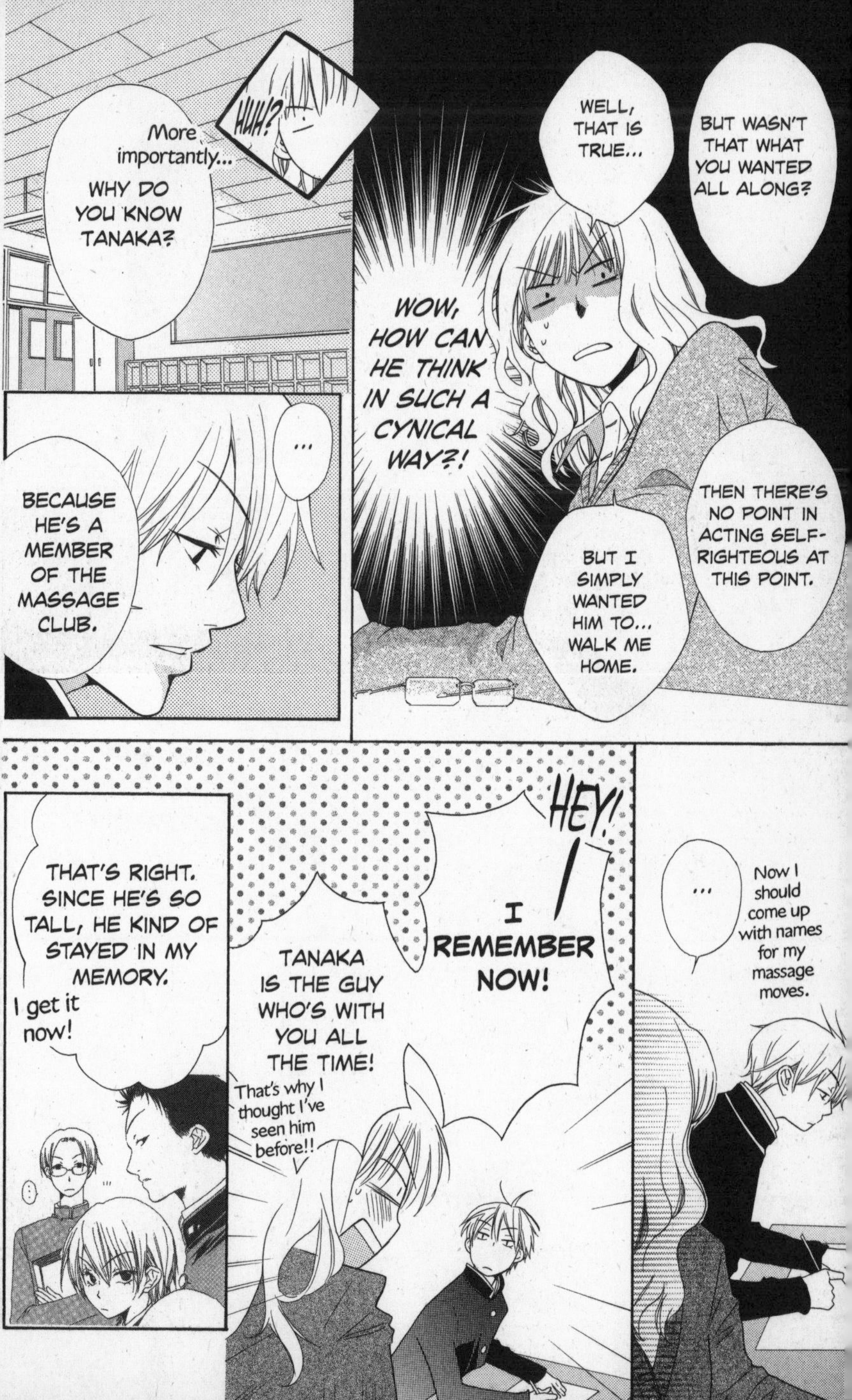
BUT WASN'T THAT WHAT YOU WANTED ALL ALONG?
WELL, THAT IS TRUE...
WOW, HOW CAN HE THINK IN SUCH A CYNICAL WAY?!
THEN THERE'S NO POINT IN ACTING SELF-RIGHTEOUS AT THIS POINT.
BUT I SIMPLY WANTED HIM TO... WALK ME HOME.
HUH?
More importantly...
WHY DO YOU KNOW TANAKA?
...
BECAUSE HE'S A MEMBER OF THE MASSAGE CLUB.
Now I should come up with names for my massage moves.
...
HEY!
I REMEMBER NOW!
TANAKA IS THE GUY WHO'S WITH YOU ALL THE TIME!
That's why I thought I've seen him before!!
THAT'S RIGHT. SINCE HE'S SO TALL, HE KIND OF STAYED IN MY MEMORY.
I get it now!

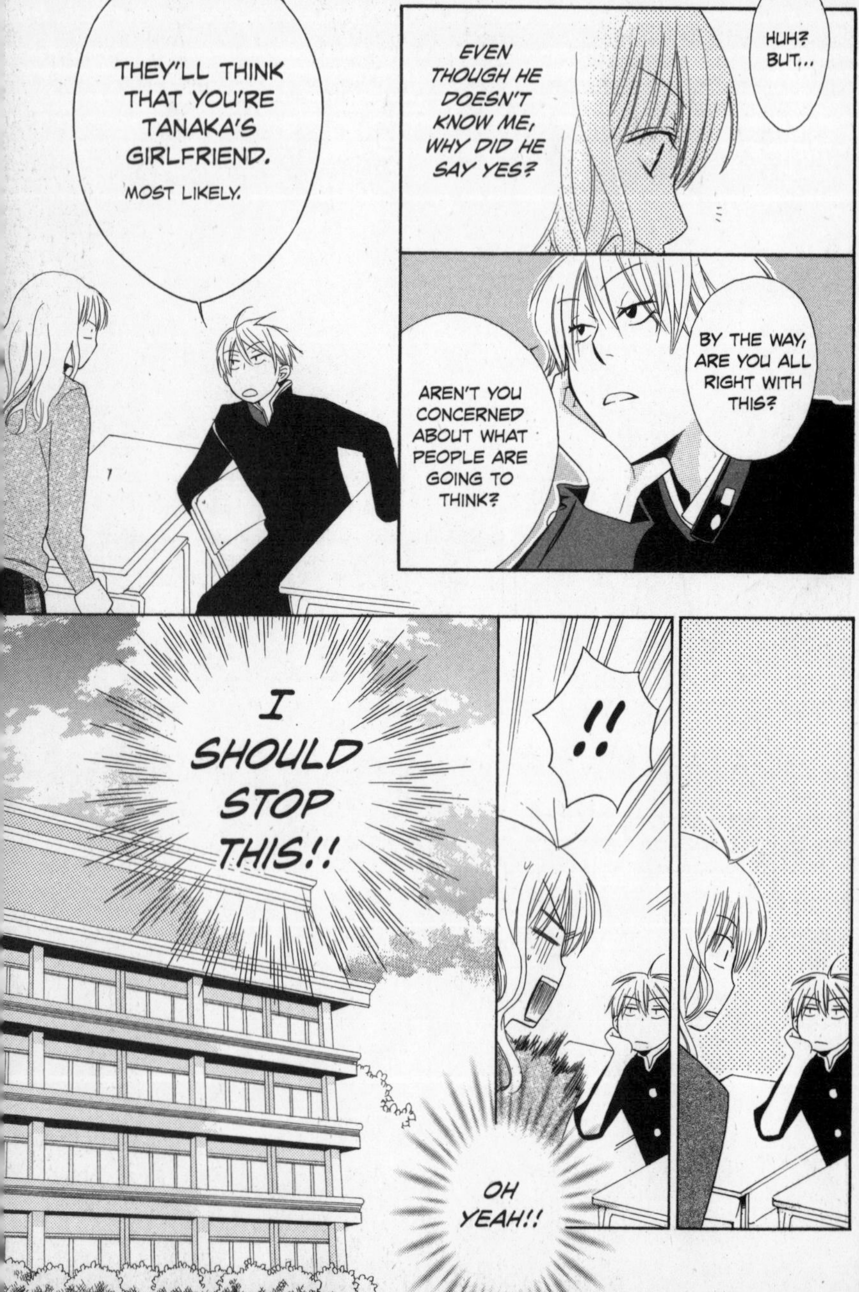
HUH? BUT...
EVEN THOUGH HE DOESN'T KNOW ME, WHY DID HE SAY YES?
BY THE WAY, ARE YOU ALL RIGHT WITH THIS?
AREN'T YOU CONCERNED ABOUT WHAT PEOPLE ARE GOING TO THINK?
THEY'LL THINK THAT YOU'RE TANAKA'S GIRLFRIEND.
MOST LIKELY.
!!
I SHOULD STOP THIS!!
OH YEAH!!

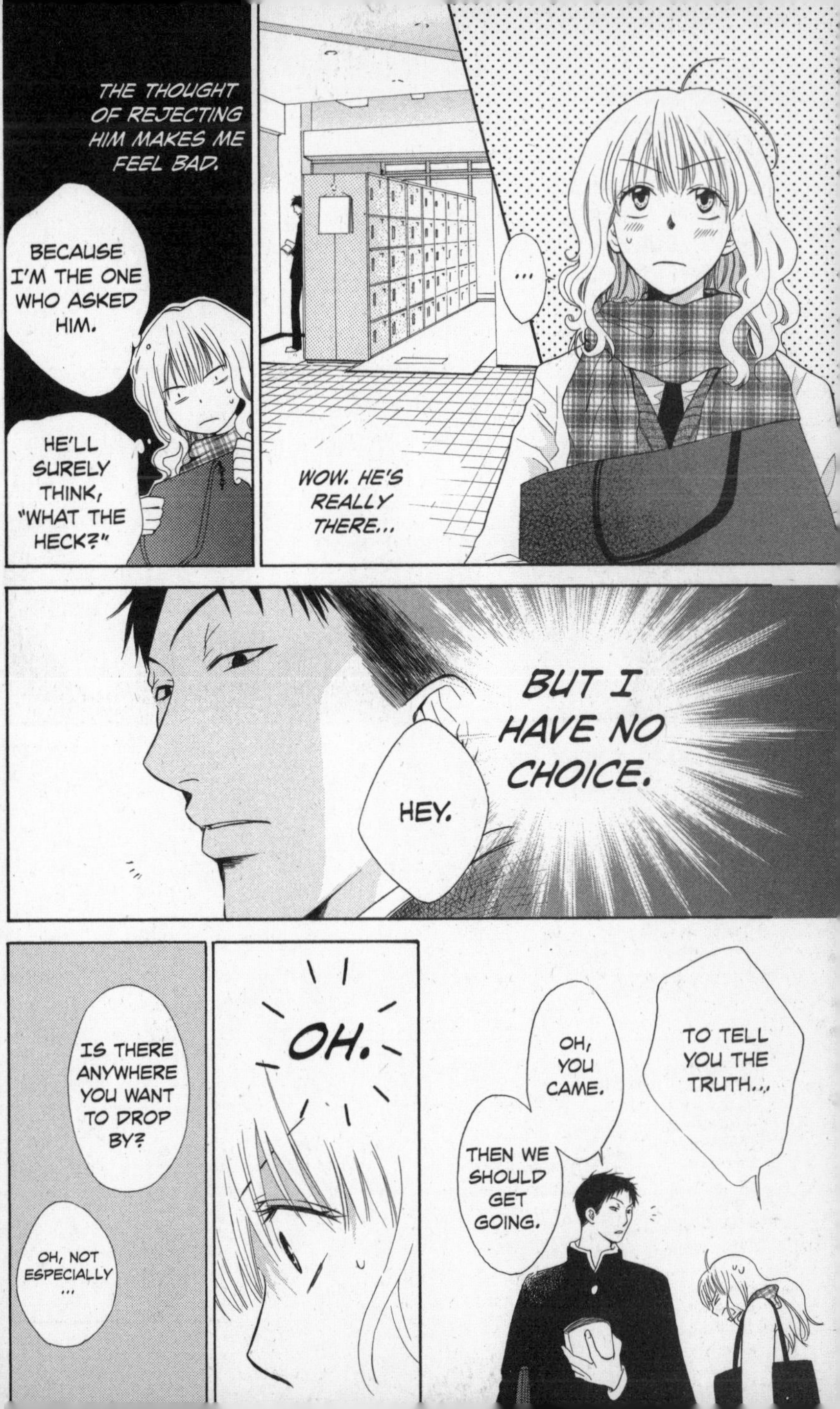
...
WOW. HE'S REALLY THERE...
THE THOUGHT OF REJECTING HIM MAKES ME FEEL BAD.
BECAUSE I'M THE ONE WHO ASKED HIM.
HE'LL SURELY THINK, "WHAT THE HECK?"
BUT I HAVE NO CHOICE.
HEY.
TO TELL YOU THE TRUTH...
OH, YOU CAME.
THEN WE SHOULD GET GOING.
OH.
IS THERE ANYWHERE YOU WANT TO DROP BY?
OH, NOT ESPECIALLY...

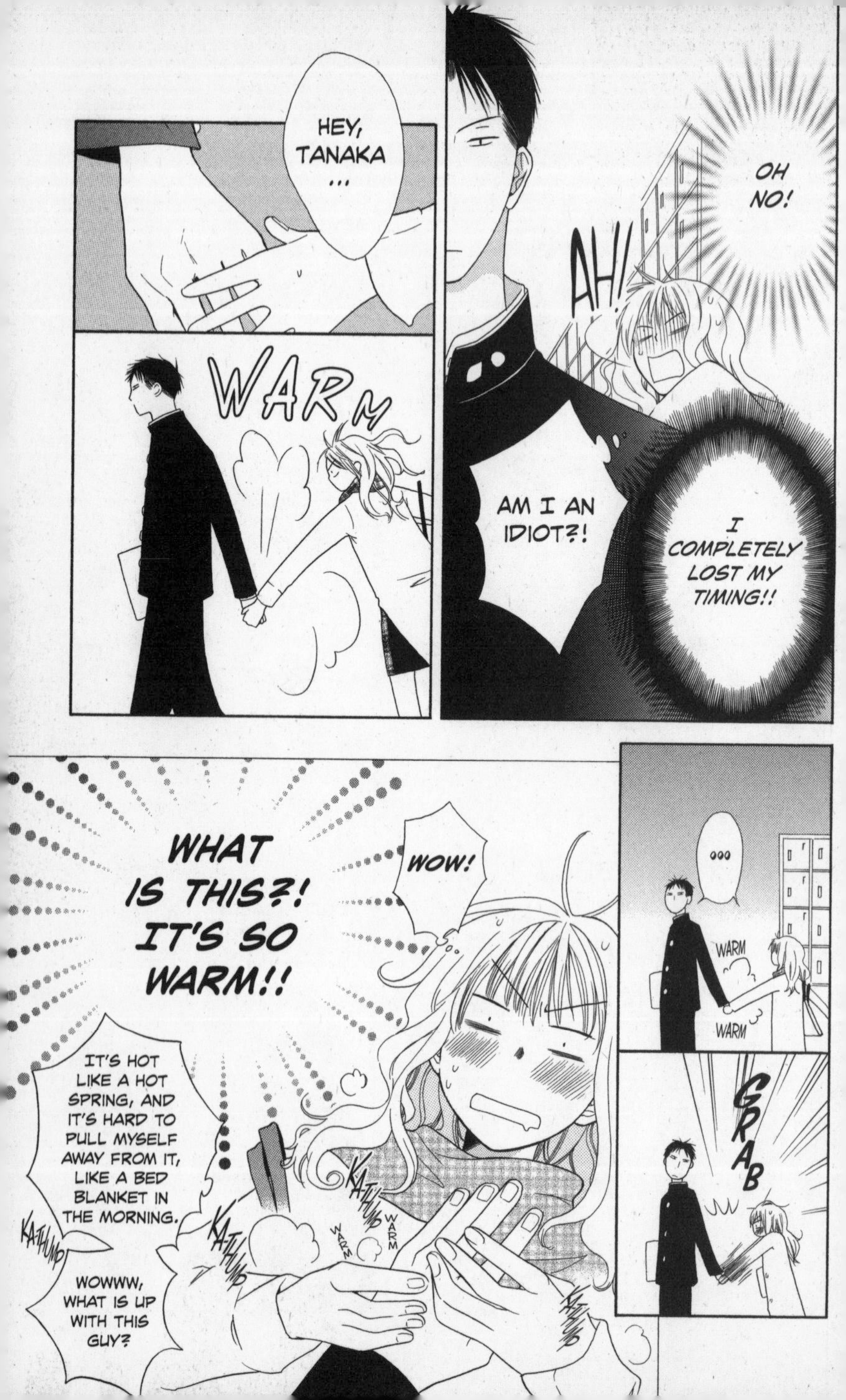
OH NO!
AH!
I COMPLETELY LOST MY TIMING!!
AM I AN IDIOT?!
HEY, TANAKA...
WARM
...
WARM
WARM
GRAB
WOW!
WHAT IS THIS?! IT'S SO WARM!!
IT'S HOT LIKE A HOT SPRING, AND IT'S HARD TO PULL MYSELF AWAY FROM IT, LIKE A BED BLANKET IN THE MORNING.
KA-THUMP
WARM
WARM
KA-THUMP
KA-THUMP
WOWWW, WHAT IS UP WITH THIS GUY?
KA-THUMP

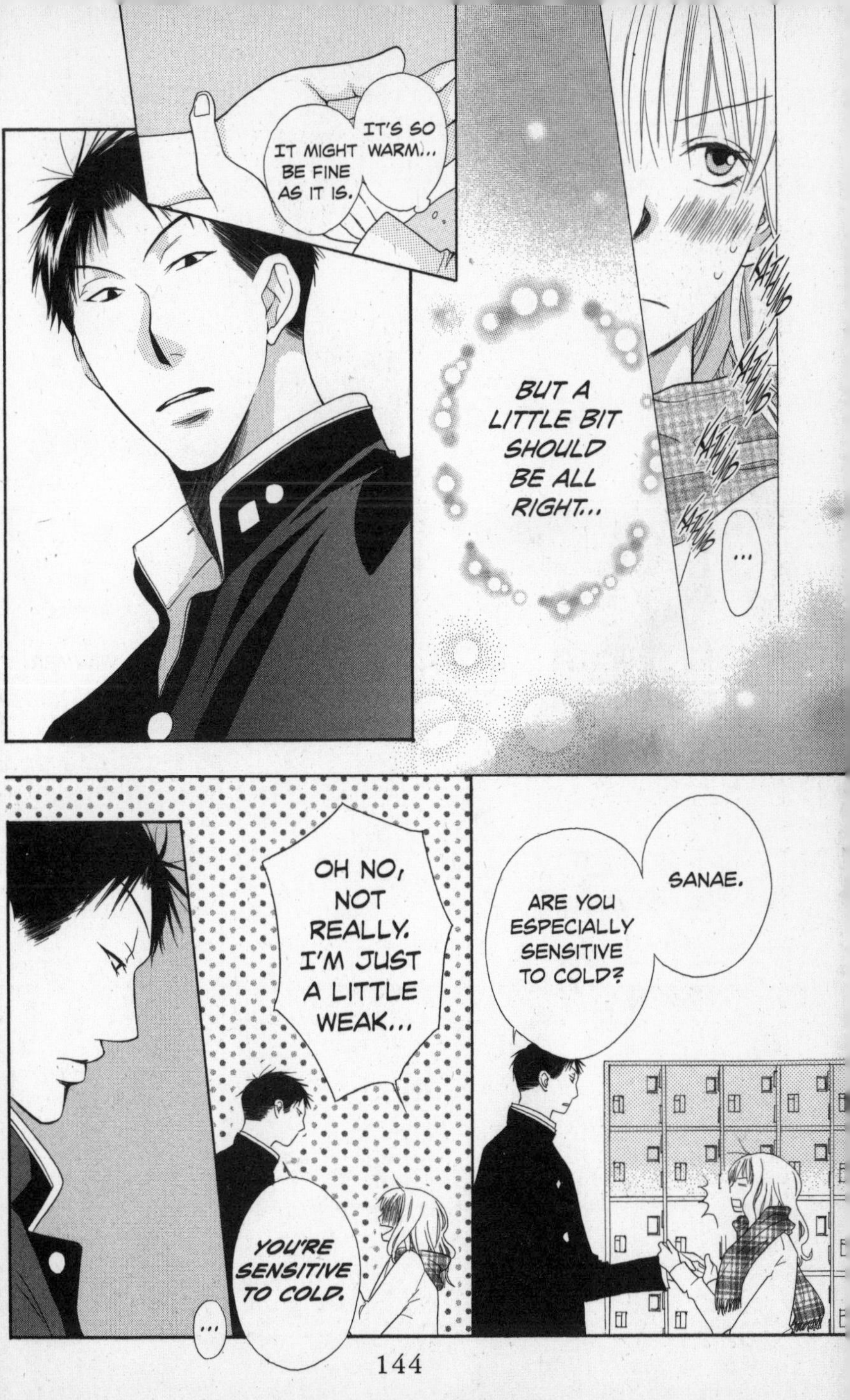
IT'S SO WARM...
IT MIGHT BE FINE AS IT IS.
BUT A LITTLE BIT SHOULD BE ALL RIGHT...
...
SANAE.
ARE YOU ESPECIALLY SENSITIVE TO COLD?
OH NO, NOT REALLY. I'M JUST A LITTLE WEAK...
YOU'RE SENSITIVE TO COLD.
...

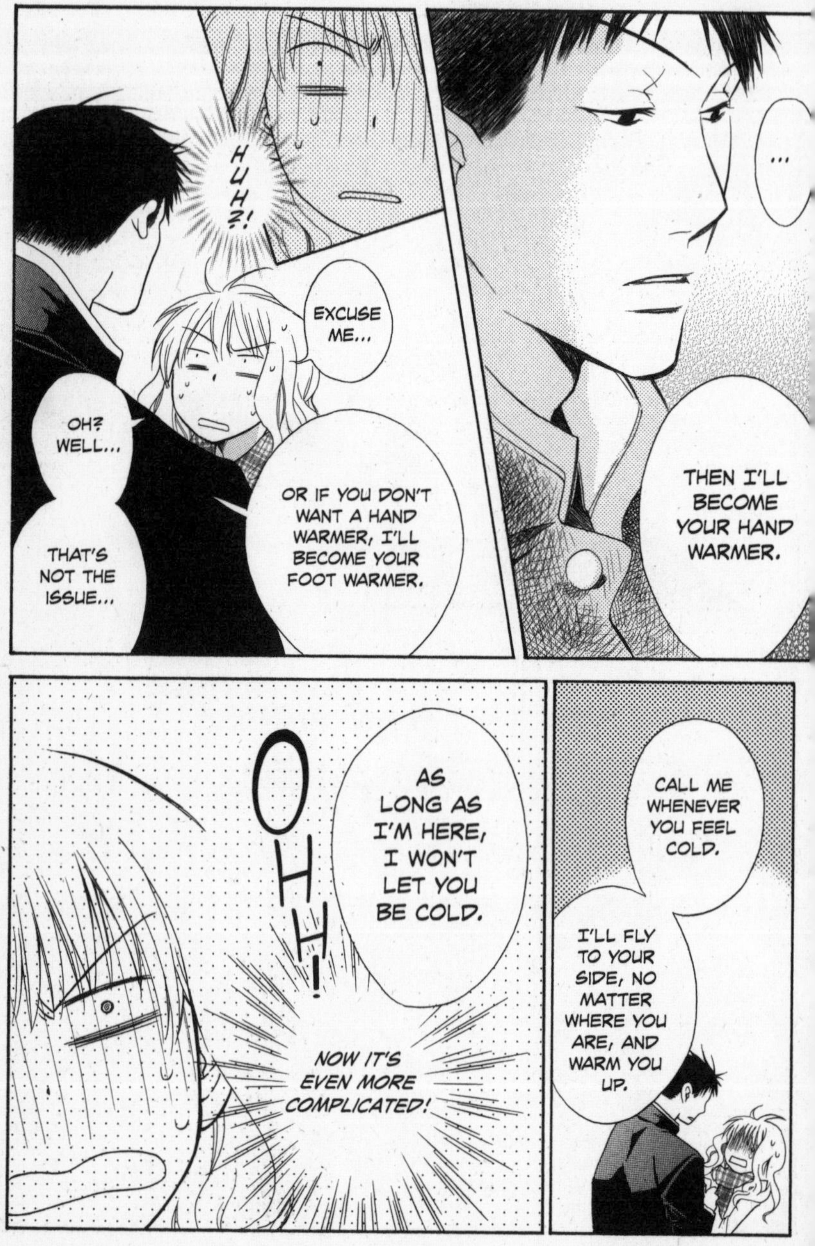
...
THEN I'LL BECOME YOUR HAND WARMER.
HUH?!
EXCUSE ME...
OR IF YOU DON'T WANT A HAND WARMER, I'LL BECOME YOUR FOOT WARMER.
OH? WELL...
THAT'S NOT THE ISSUE...
CALL ME WHENEVER YOU FEEL COLD.
I'LL FLY TO YOUR SIDE, NO MATTER WHERE YOU ARE, AND WARM YOU UP.
AS LONG AS I'M HERE, I WON'T LET YOU BE COLD.
OHH!
NOW IT'S EVEN MORE COMPLICATED!

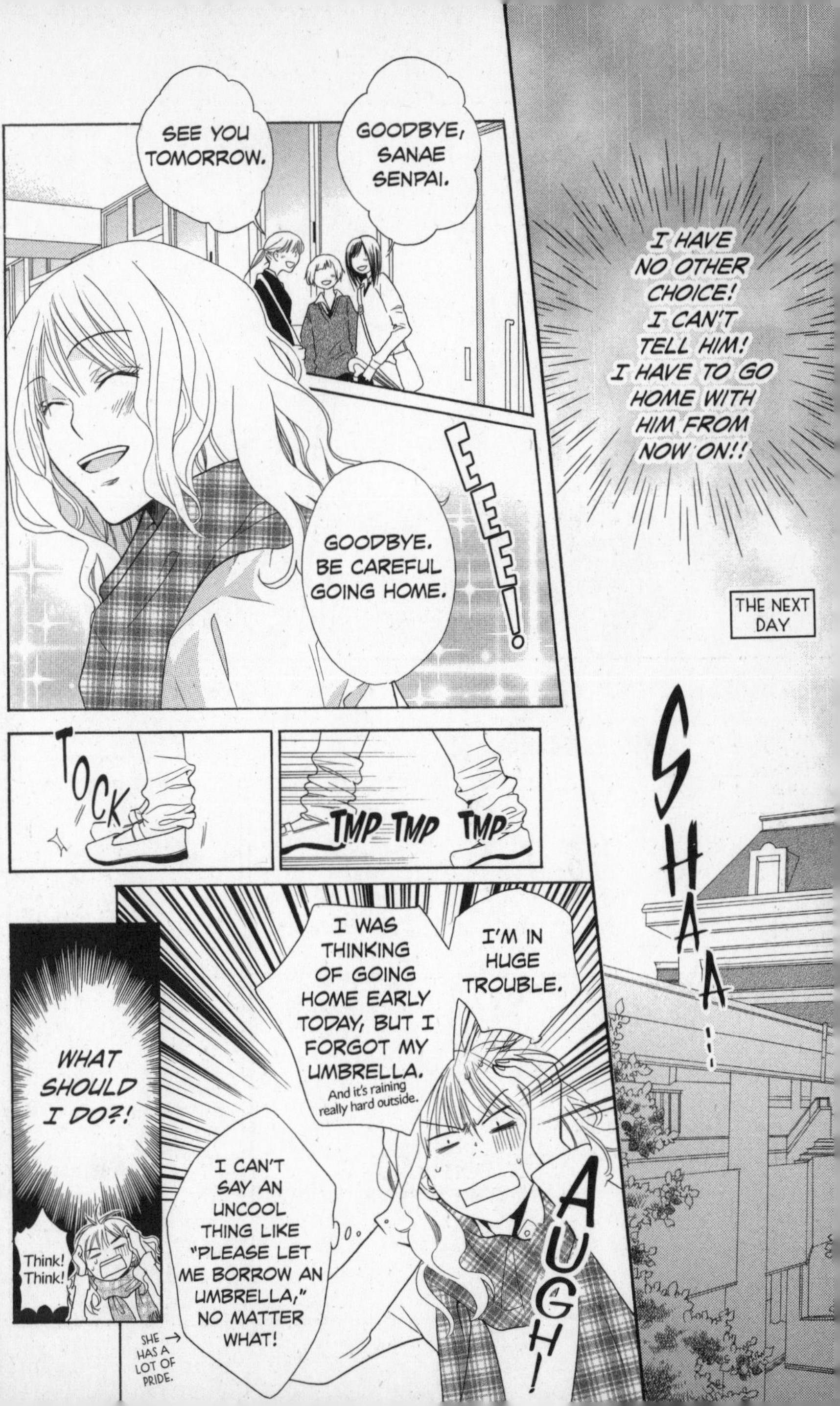
I HAVE NO OTHER CHOICE! I CAN'T TELL HIM! I HAVE TO GO HOME WITH HIM FROM NOW ON!!
GOODBYE, SANAE SENPAI.
SEE YOU TOMORROW.
EEEE!
GOODBYE. BE CAREFUL GOING HOME.
TMP TMP TMP
TOCK
THE NEXT DAY
SHAA...!!
I'M IN HUGE TROUBLE.
I WAS THINKING OF GOING HOME EARLY TODAY, BUT I FORGOT MY UMBRELLA.
And it's raining really hard outside.
AUGH!
I CAN'T SAY AN UNCOOL THING LIKE "PLEASE LET ME BORROW AN UMBRELLA," NO MATTER WHAT!
SHE HAS A LOT OF PRIDE.
WHAT SHOULD I DO?!
Think! Think!

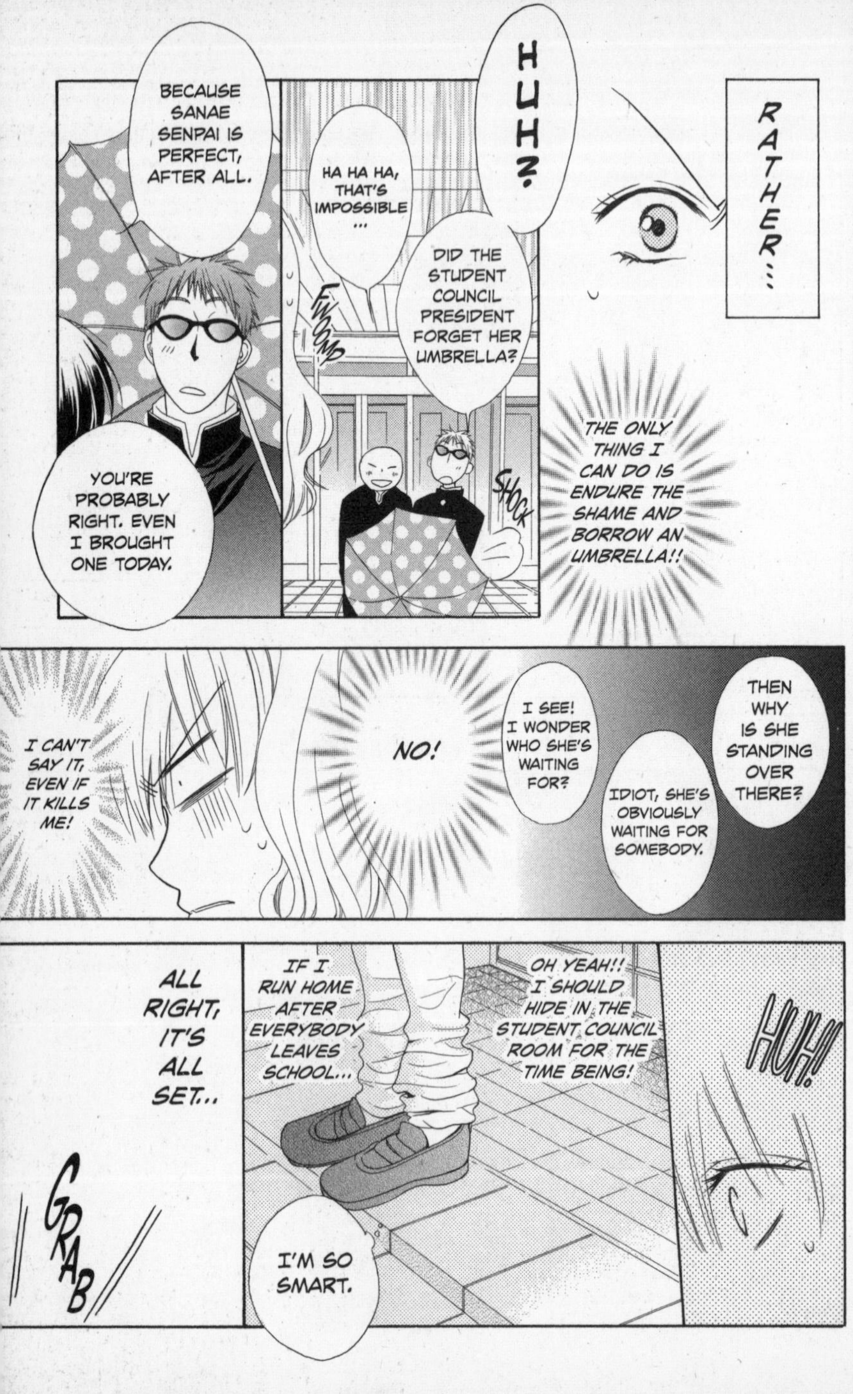
RATHER...
THE ONLY THING I CAN DO IS ENDURE THE SHAME AND BORROW AN UMBRELLA!!
HUH?
DID THE STUDENT COUNCIL PRESIDENT FORGET HER UMBRELLA?
HA HA HA, THAT'S IMPOSSIBLE...
FWOOMP
SHOCK
BECAUSE SANAE SENPAI IS PERFECT, AFTER ALL.
YOU'RE PROBABLY RIGHT. EVEN I BROUGHT ONE TODAY.
THEN WHY IS SHE STANDING OVER THERE?
IDIOT, SHE'S OBVIOUSLY WAITING FOR SOMEBODY.
I SEE! I WONDER WHO SHE'S WAITING FOR?
NO!
I CAN'T SAY IT, EVEN IF IT KILLS ME!
HUH!
OH YEAH!! I SHOULD HIDE IN THE STUDENT COUNCIL ROOM FOR THE TIME BEING!
IF I RUN HOME AFTER EVERYBODY LEAVES SCHOOL...
I'M SO SMART.
ALL RIGHT, IT'S ALL SET...
GRAB

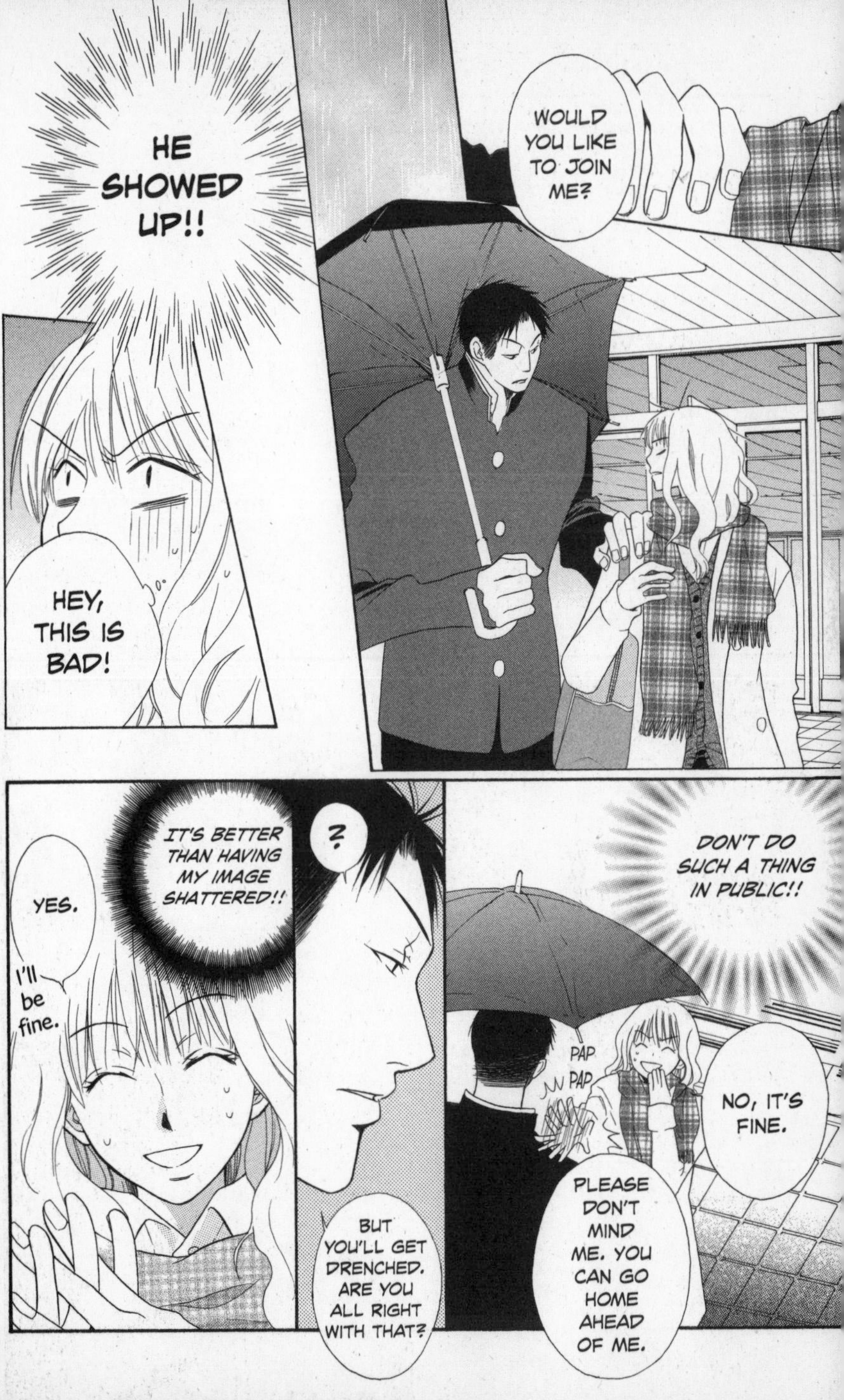
WOULD YOU LIKE TO JOIN ME?
HE SHOWED UP!!
HEY, THIS IS BAD!
DON'T DO SUCH A THING IN PUBLIC!!
NO, IT'S FINE.
PAP PAP
PLEASE DON'T MIND ME. YOU CAN GO HOME AHEAD OF ME.
?
BUT YOU'LL GET DRENCHED. ARE YOU ALL RIGHT WITH THAT?
IT'S BETTER THAN HAVING MY IMAGE SHATTERED!!
YES.
I'll be fine.

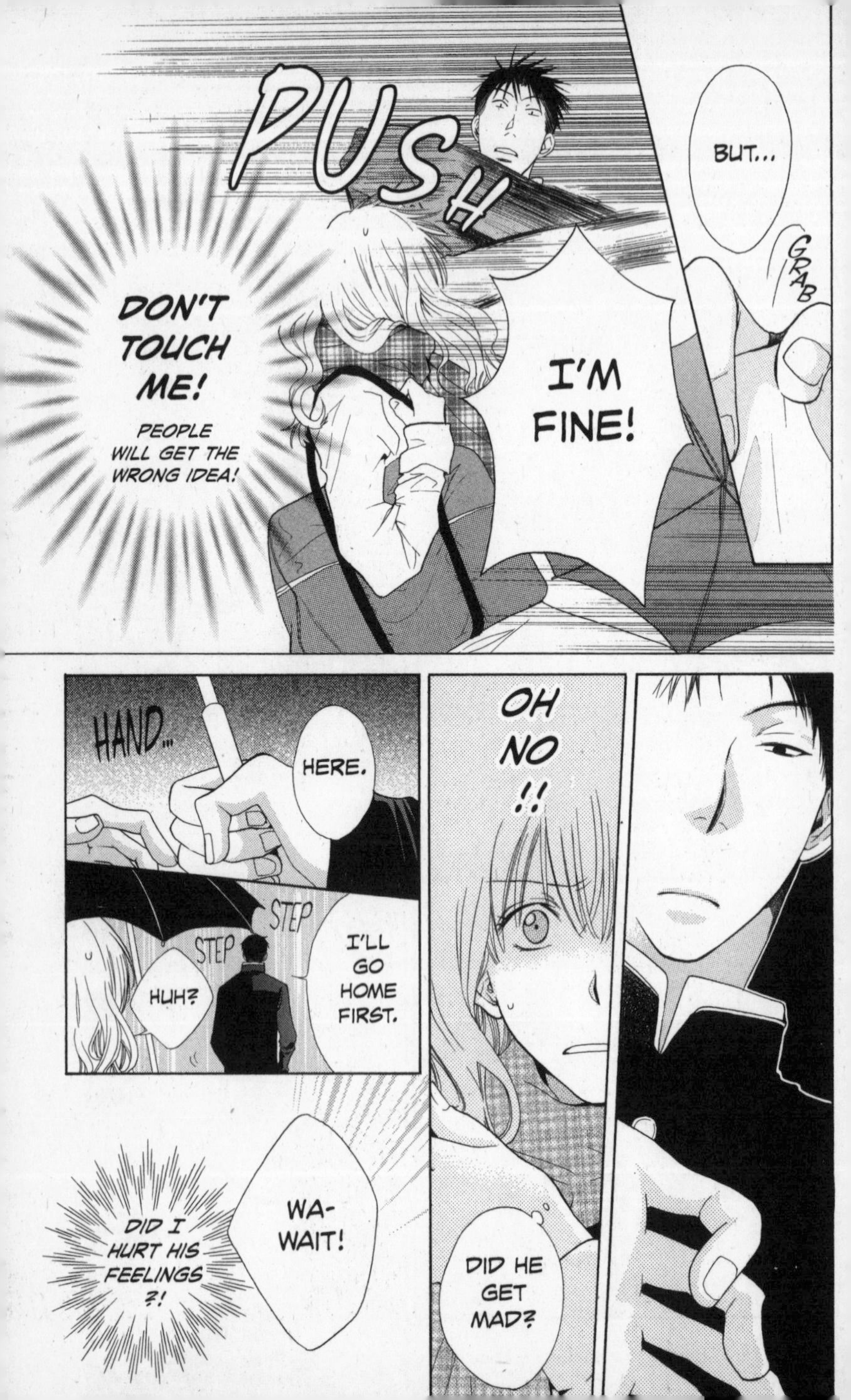
BUT...
GRAB
PUSH
I'M FINE!
DON'T TOUCH ME!
PEOPLE WILL GET THE WRONG IDEA!
OH NO !!
DID HE GET MAD?
HAND...
HERE.
STEP
STEP
I'LL GO HOME FIRST.
HUH?
WA-WAIT!
DID I HURT HIS FEELINGS ?!

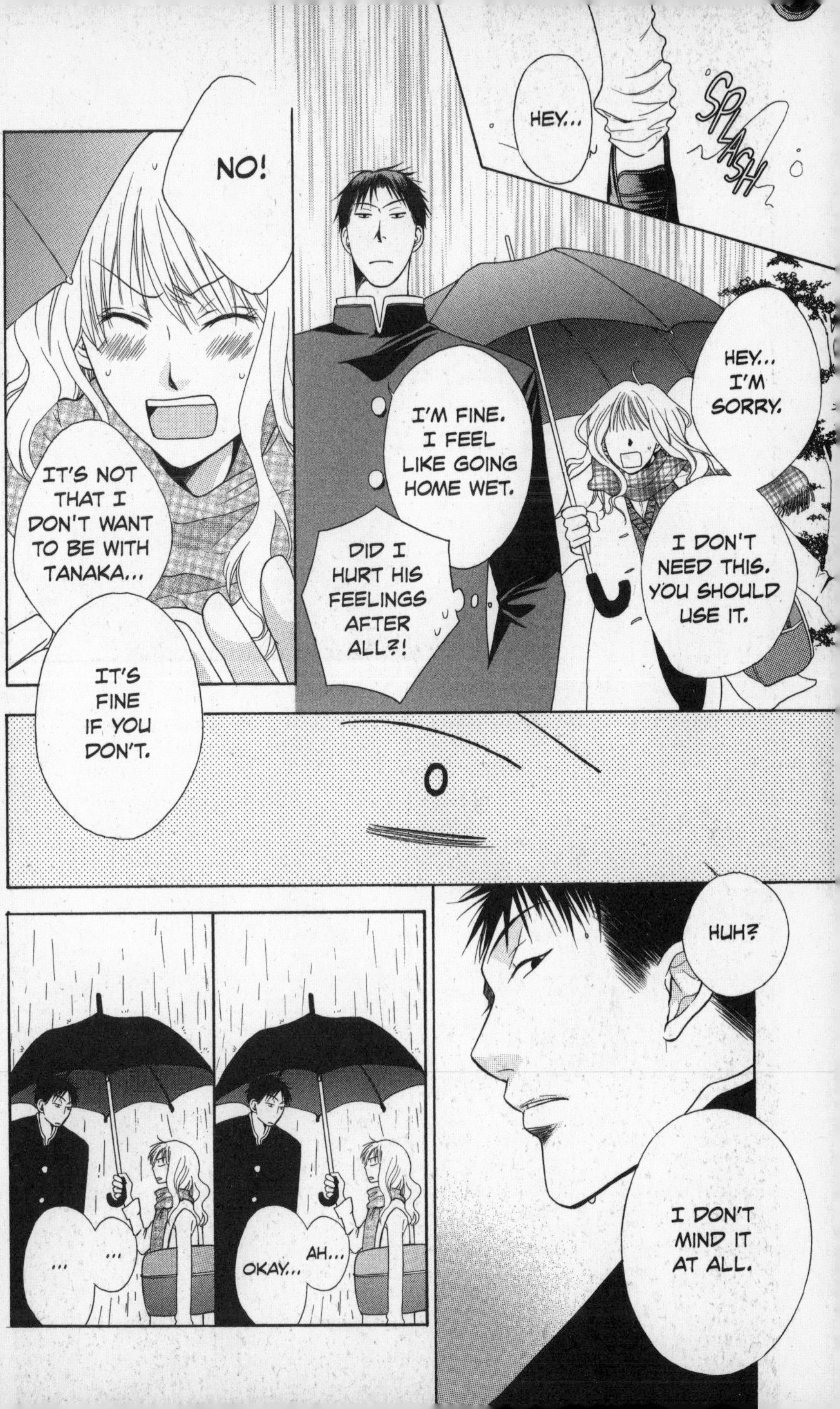
HEY...
SPLASH
HEY... I'M SORRY.
I DON'T NEED THIS. YOU SHOULD USE IT.
I'M FINE. I FEEL LIKE GOING HOME WET.
DID I HURT HIS FEELINGS AFTER ALL?!
NO!
IT'S NOT THAT I DON'T WANT TO BE WITH TANAKA...
IT'S FINE IF YOU DON'T.
HUH?
I DON'T MIND IT AT ALL.
AH...
OKAY...
...
...

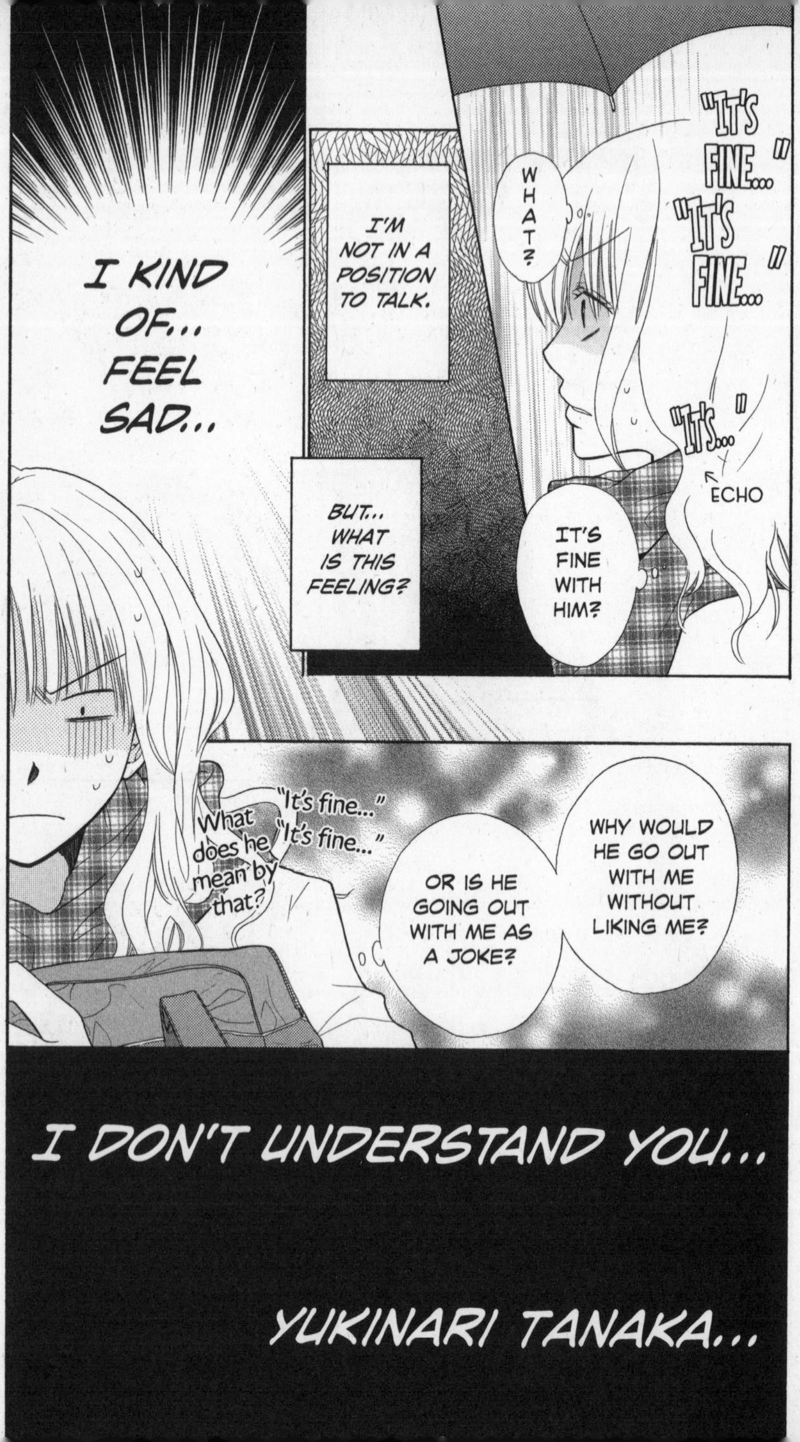
"IT'S FINE..." "IT'S FINE..."
"IT'S..."
ECHO
WHAT?
IT'S FINE WITH HIM?
I'M NOT IN A POSITION TO TALK.
BUT... WHAT IS THIS FEELING?
I KIND OF... FEEL SAD...
WHY WOULD HE GO OUT WITH ME WITHOUT LIKING ME?
OR IS HE GOING OUT WITH ME AS A JOKE?
"It's fine..." "It's fine..."
What does he mean by that?
I DON'T UNDERSTAND YOU...
YUKINARI TANAKA...

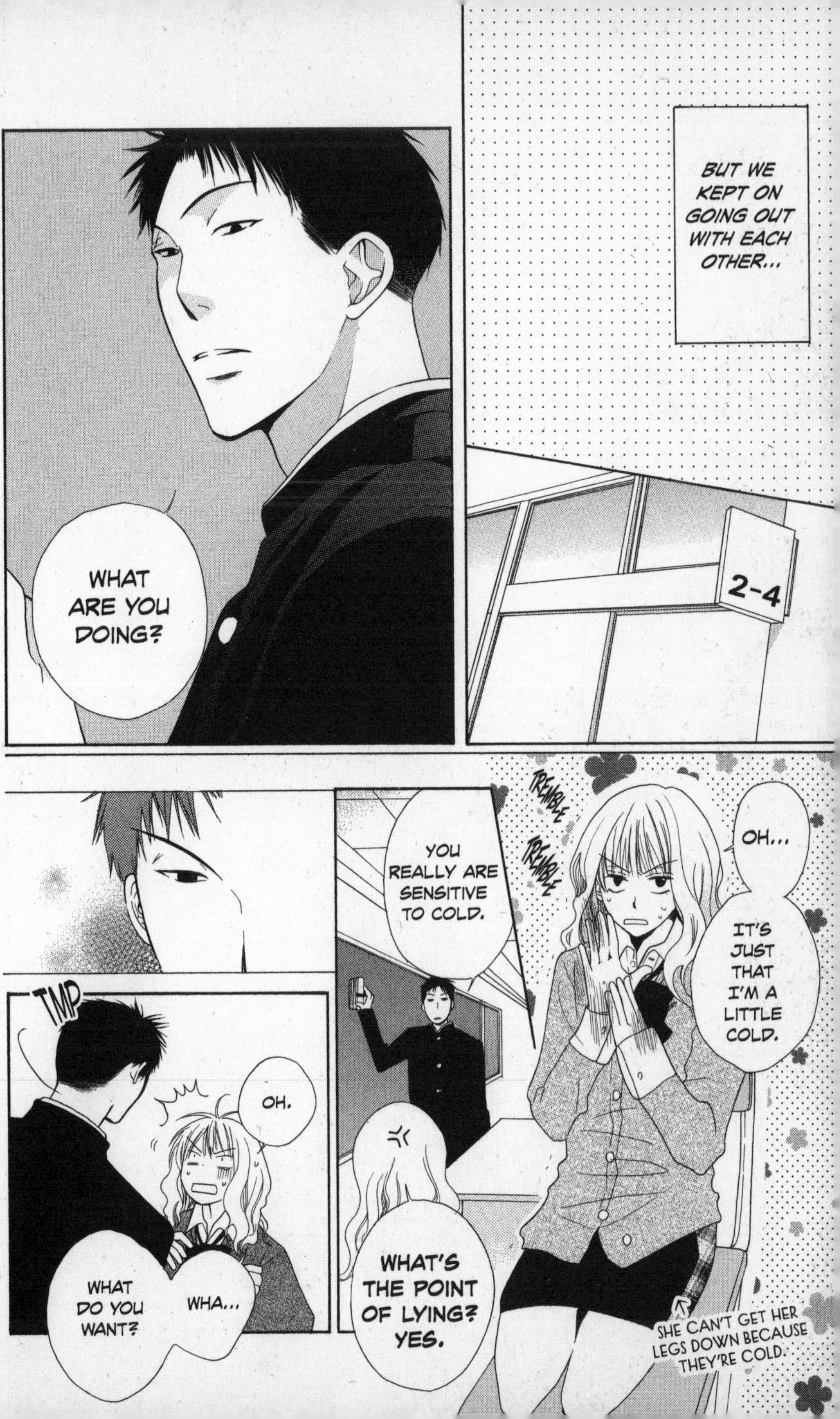
BUT WE KEPT ON GOING OUT WITH EACH OTHER...
2-4
WHAT ARE YOU DOING?
TREMBLE
TREMBLE
OH...
IT'S JUST THAT I'M A LITTLE COLD.
SHE CAN'T GET HER LEGS DOWN BECAUSE THEY'RE COLD.
YOU REALLY ARE SENSITIVE TO COLD.
WHAT'S THE POINT OF LYING? YES.
TMP
OH.
WHA...
WHAT DO YOU WANT?

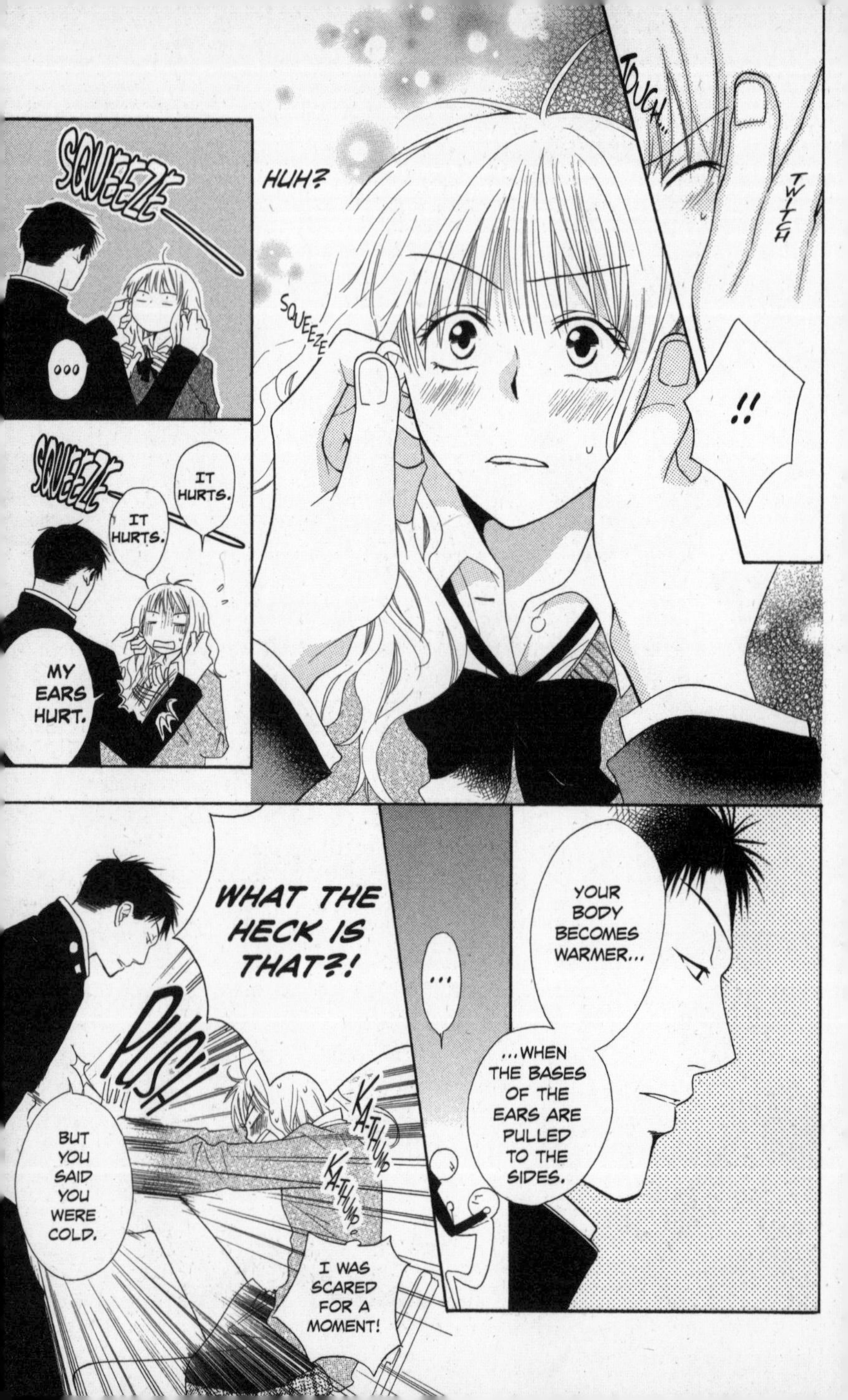
TOUCH...
TWITCH
!!
HUH?
SQUEEZE
SQUEEZE
...
SQUEEZE
IT HURTS.
IT HURTS.
MY EARS HURT.
YOUR BODY BECOMES WARMER...
...WHEN THE BASES OF THE EARS ARE PULLED TO THE SIDES.
...
WHAT THE HECK IS THAT?!
PUSH
KA-THUMP
KA-THUMP
I WAS SCARED FOR A MOMENT!
BUT YOU SAID YOU WERE COLD.

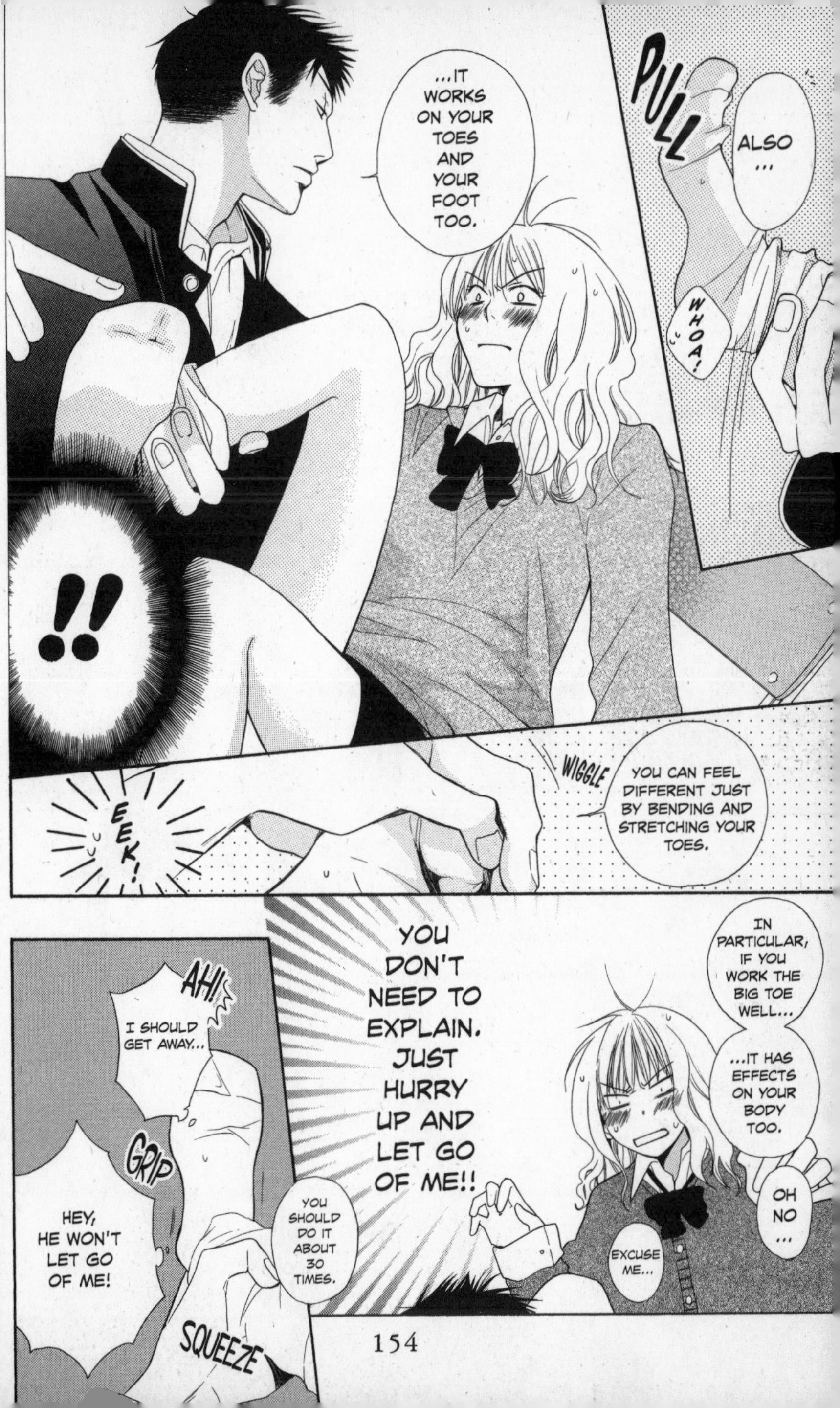
PULL
ALSO ...
WHOA!
...IT WORKS ON YOUR TOES AND YOUR FOOT TOO.
!!
WIGGLE
YOU CAN FEEL DIFFERENT JUST BY BENDING AND STRETCHING YOUR TOES.
EEK!
IN PARTICULAR, IF YOU WORK THE BIG TOE WELL...
...IT HAS EFFECTS ON YOUR BODY TOO.
OH NO ...
EXCUSE ME...
YOU DON'T NEED TO EXPLAIN. JUST HURRY UP AND LET GO OF ME!!
YOU SHOULD DO IT ABOUT 30 TIMES.
AH!
I SHOULD GET AWAY...
GRIP
HEY, HE WON'T LET GO OF ME!
SQUEEZE

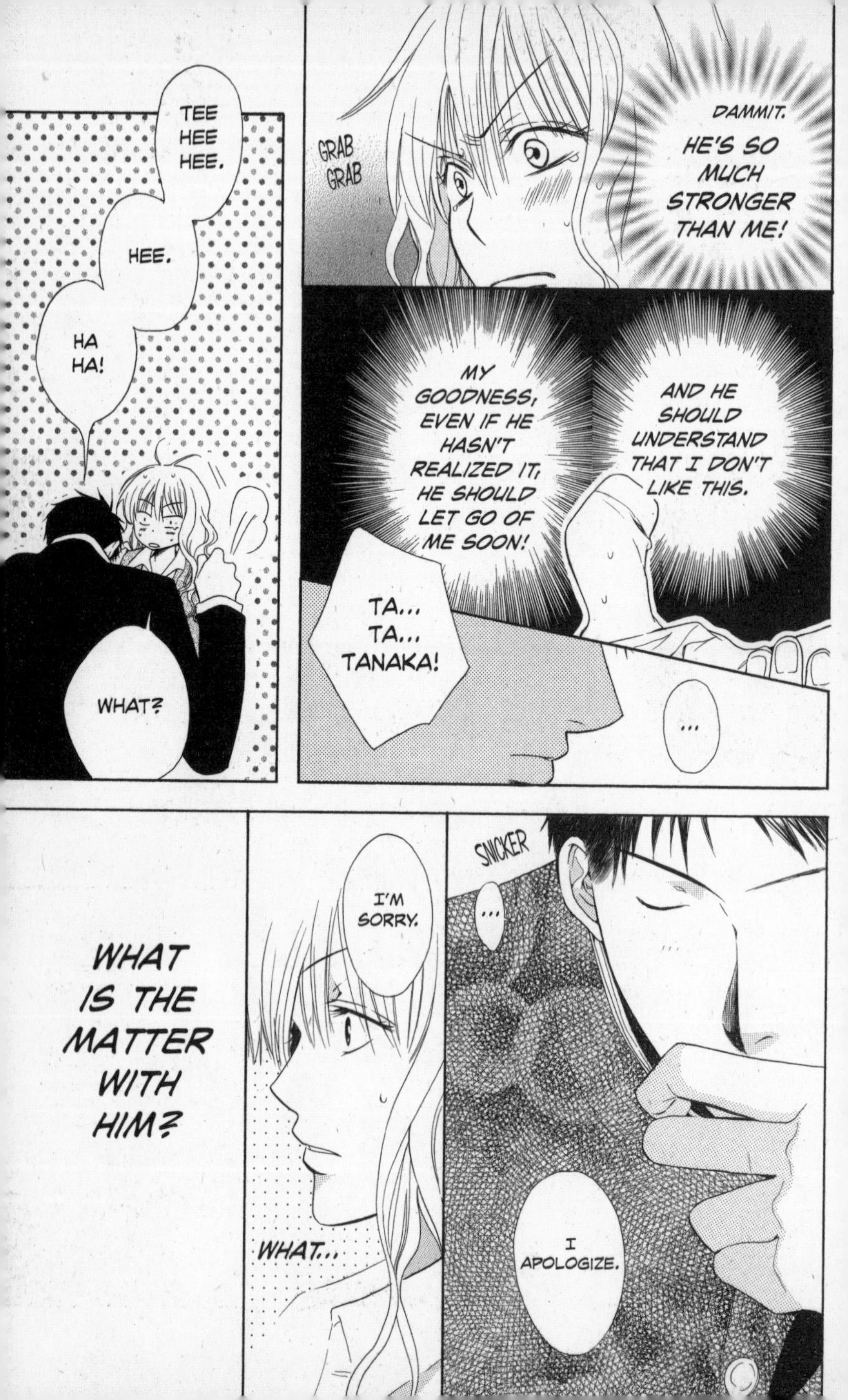
DAMMIT.
HE'S SO MUCH STRONGER THAN ME!
GRAB GRAB
MY GOODNESS, EVEN IF HE HASN'T REALIZED IT, HE SHOULD LET GO OF ME SOON!
AND HE SHOULD UNDERSTAND THAT I DON'T LIKE THIS.
TA... TA... TANAKA!
...
TEE HEE HEE.
HEE.
HA HA!
WHAT?
SNICKER
...
I APOLOGIZE.
I'M SORRY.
WHAT...
WHAT IS THE MATTER WITH HIM?

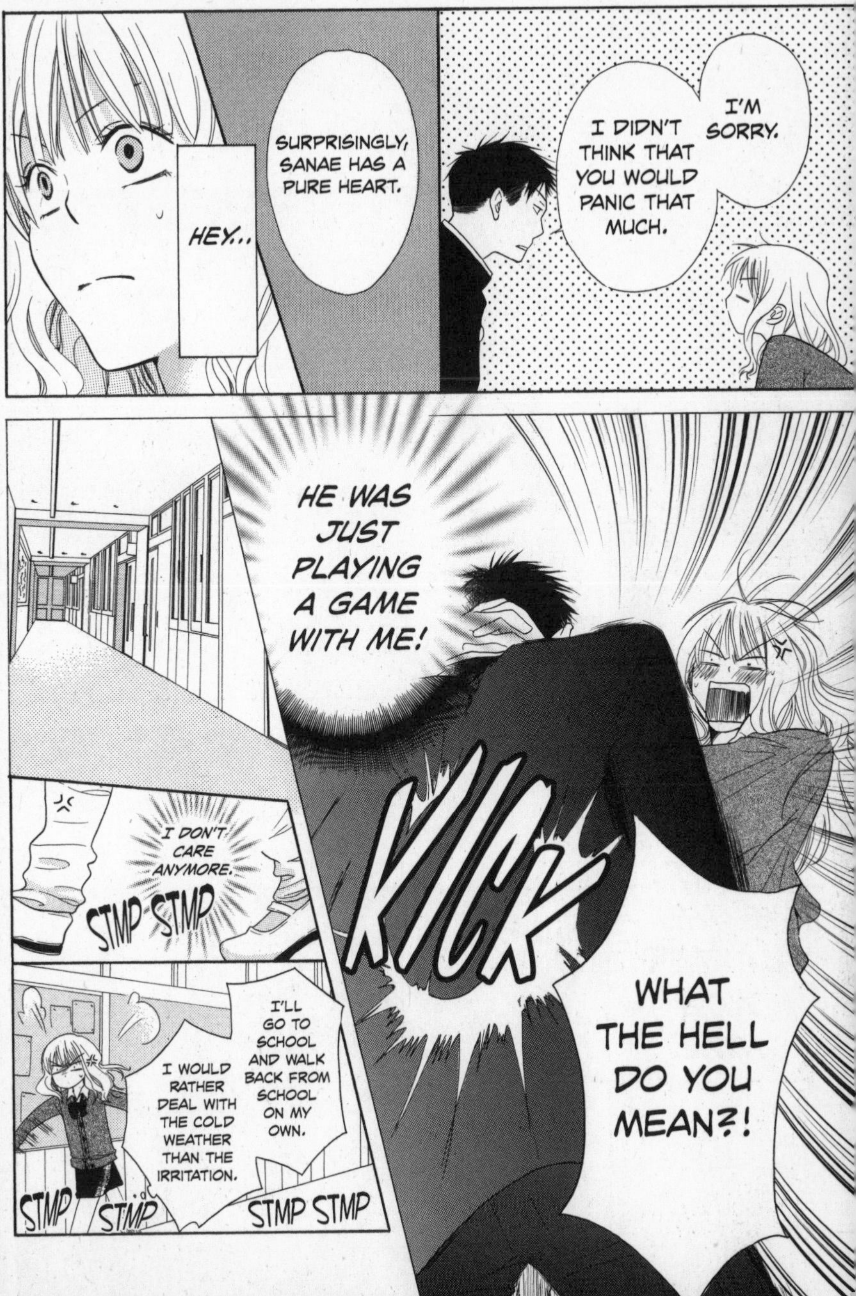
I'M SORRY.
I DIDN'T THINK THAT YOU WOULD PANIC THAT MUCH.
SURPRISINGLY, SANAE HAS A PURE HEART.
HEY...
HE WAS JUST PLAYING A GAME WITH ME!
KICK
WHAT THE HELL DO YOU MEAN?!
I DON'T CARE ANYMORE.
STMP STMP
I'LL GO TO SCHOOL AND WALK BACK FROM SCHOOL ON MY OWN.
I WOULD RATHER DEAL WITH THE COLD WEATHER THAN THE IRRITATION.
STMP STMP
STMP STMP

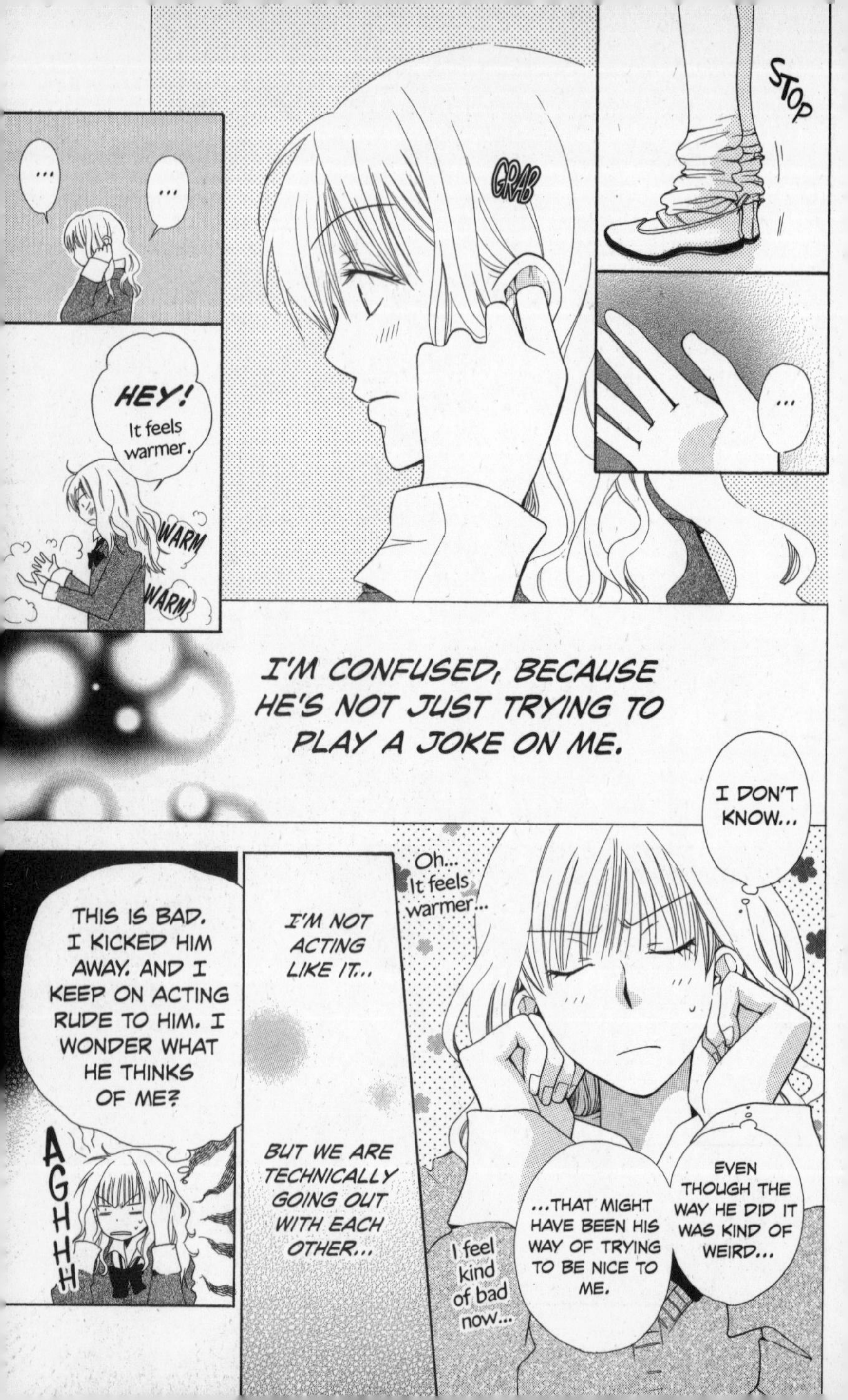
STOP
...
GRAB
...
...
HEY! It feels warmer.
WARM WARM
I'M CONFUSED, BECAUSE HE'S NOT JUST TRYING TO PLAY A JOKE ON ME.
I DON'T KNOW...
Oh... It feels warmer...
EVEN THOUGH THE WAY HE DID IT WAS KIND OF WEIRD...
...THAT MIGHT HAVE BEEN HIS WAY OF TRYING TO BE NICE TO ME.
I feel kind of bad now...
I'M NOT ACTING LIKE IT...
BUT WE ARE TECHNICALLY GOING OUT WITH EACH OTHER...
THIS IS BAD. I KICKED HIM AWAY. AND I KEEP ON ACTING RUDE TO HIM. I WONDER WHAT HE THINKS OF ME?
AGHHH

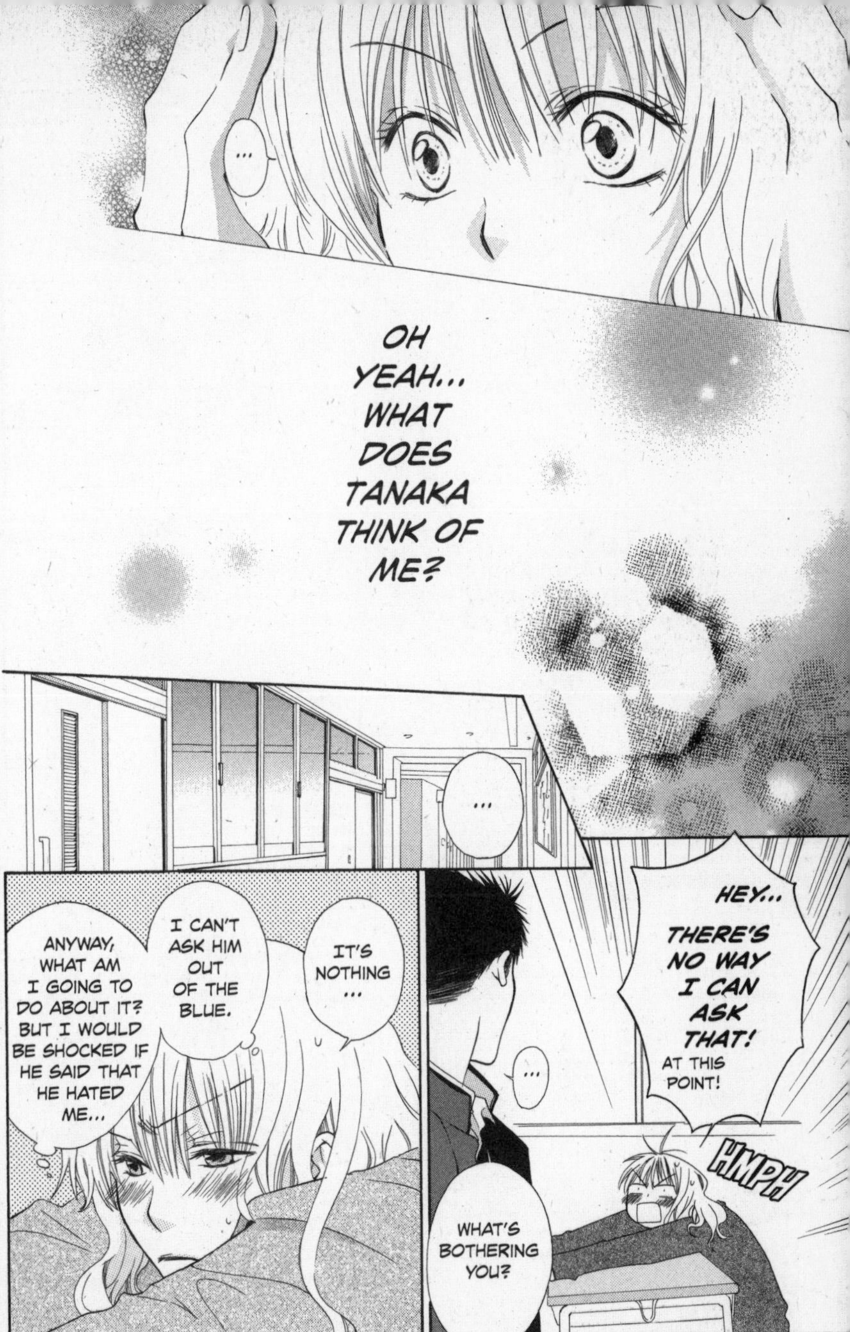
...
OH YEAH... WHAT DOES TANAKA THINK OF ME?
...
HEY... THERE'S NO WAY I CAN ASK THAT! AT THIS POINT!
HMPH
...
WHAT'S BOTHERING YOU?
IT'S NOTHING...
I CAN'T ASK HIM OUT OF THE BLUE.
ANYWAY, WHAT AM I GOING TO DO ABOUT IT? BUT I WOULD BE SHOCKED IF HE SAID THAT HE HATED ME...

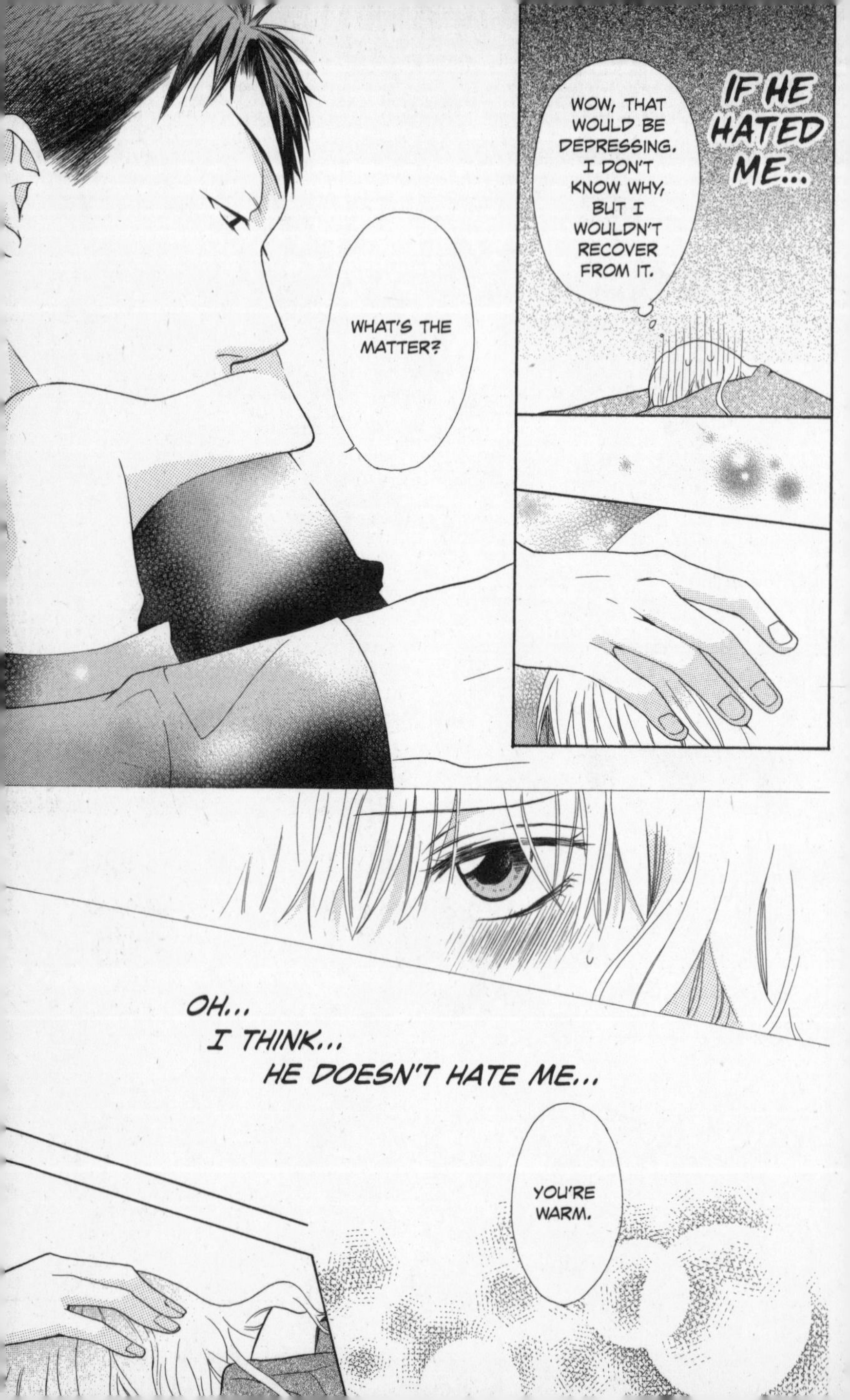
IF HE HATED ME...
WOW, THAT WOULD BE DEPRESSING. I DON'T KNOW WHY, BUT I WOULDN'T RECOVER FROM IT.
WHAT'S THE MATTER?
OH... I THINK... HE DOESN'T HATE ME...
YOU'RE WARM.

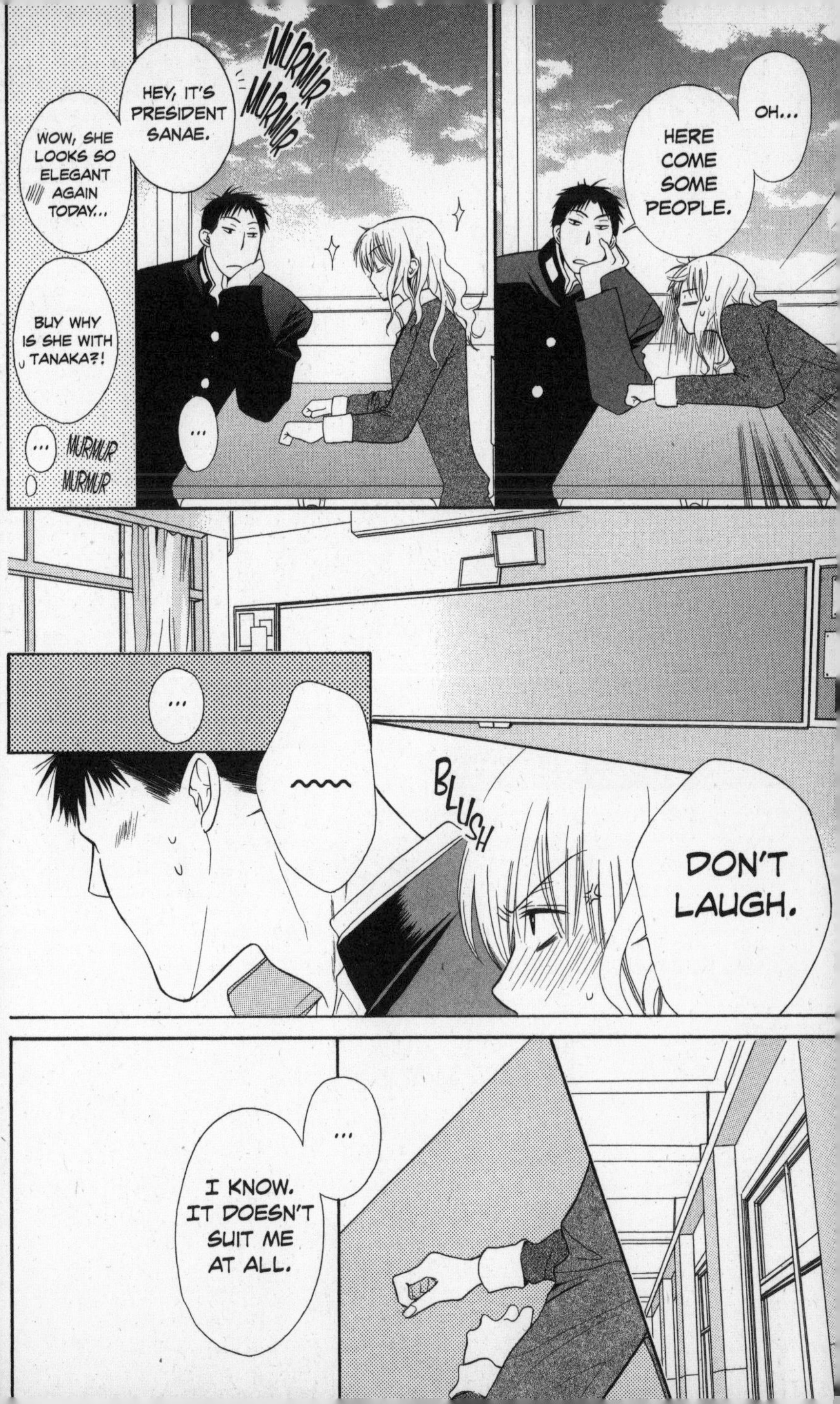
OH...
HERE COME SOME PEOPLE.
MURMUR MURMUR
HEY, IT'S PRESIDENT SANAE.
WOW, SHE LOOKS SO ELEGANT AGAIN TODAY...
BUY WHY IS SHE WITH TANAKA?!
...
...
MURMUR MURMUR
DON'T LAUGH.
BLUSH
~~~
...
...
I KNOW. IT DOESN'T SUIT ME AT ALL.
~~~

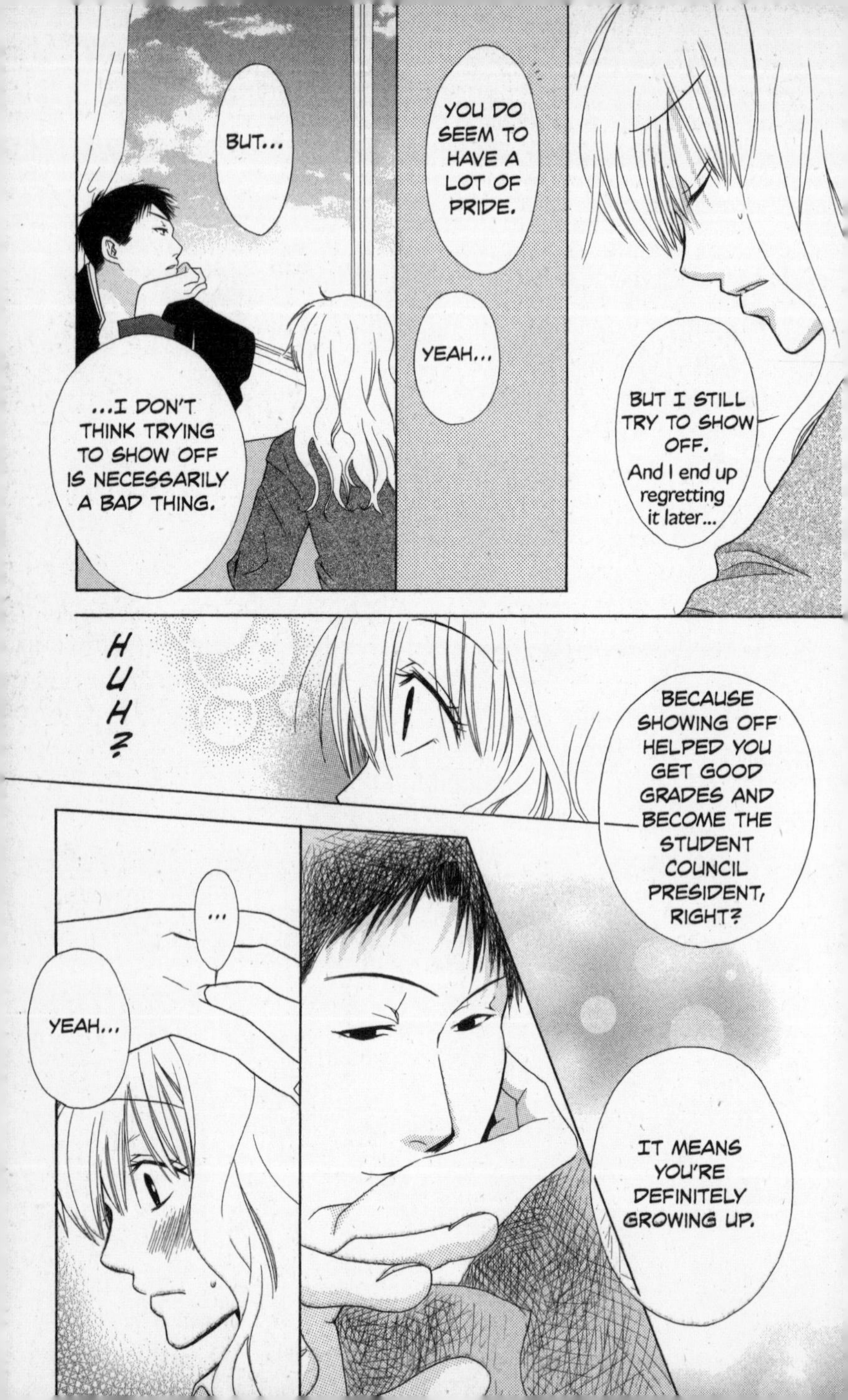
BUT I STILL TRY TO SHOW OFF. And I end up regretting it later...
YOU DO SEEM TO HAVE A LOT OF PRIDE.
YEAH...
BUT...
...I DON'T THINK TRYING TO SHOW OFF IS NECESSARILY A BAD THING.
BECAUSE SHOWING OFF HELPED YOU GET GOOD GRADES AND BECOME THE STUDENT COUNCIL PRESIDENT, RIGHT?
HUH?
IT MEANS YOU'RE DEFINITELY GROWING UP.
...
YEAH...

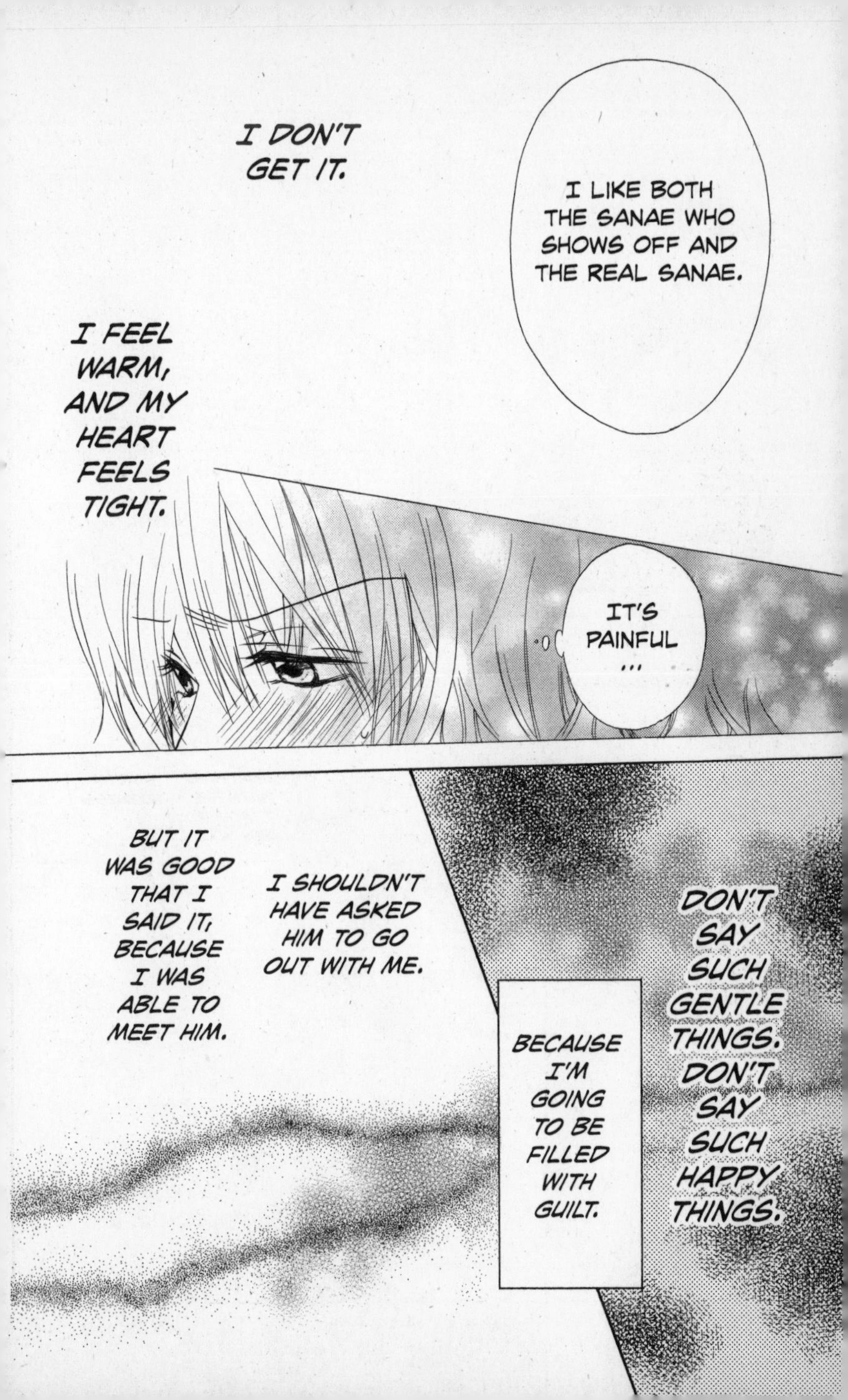
I LIKE BOTH THE SANAE WHO SHOWS OFF AND THE REAL SANAE.
I DON'T GET IT.
I FEEL WARM, AND MY HEART FEELS TIGHT.
IT'S PAINFUL ...
DON'T SAY SUCH GENTLE THINGS. DON'T SAY SUCH HAPPY THINGS.
BECAUSE I'M GOING TO BE FILLED WITH GUILT.
I SHOULDN'T HAVE ASKED HIM TO GO OUT WITH ME.
BUT IT WAS GOOD THAT I SAID IT, BECAUSE I WAS ABLE TO MEET HIM.

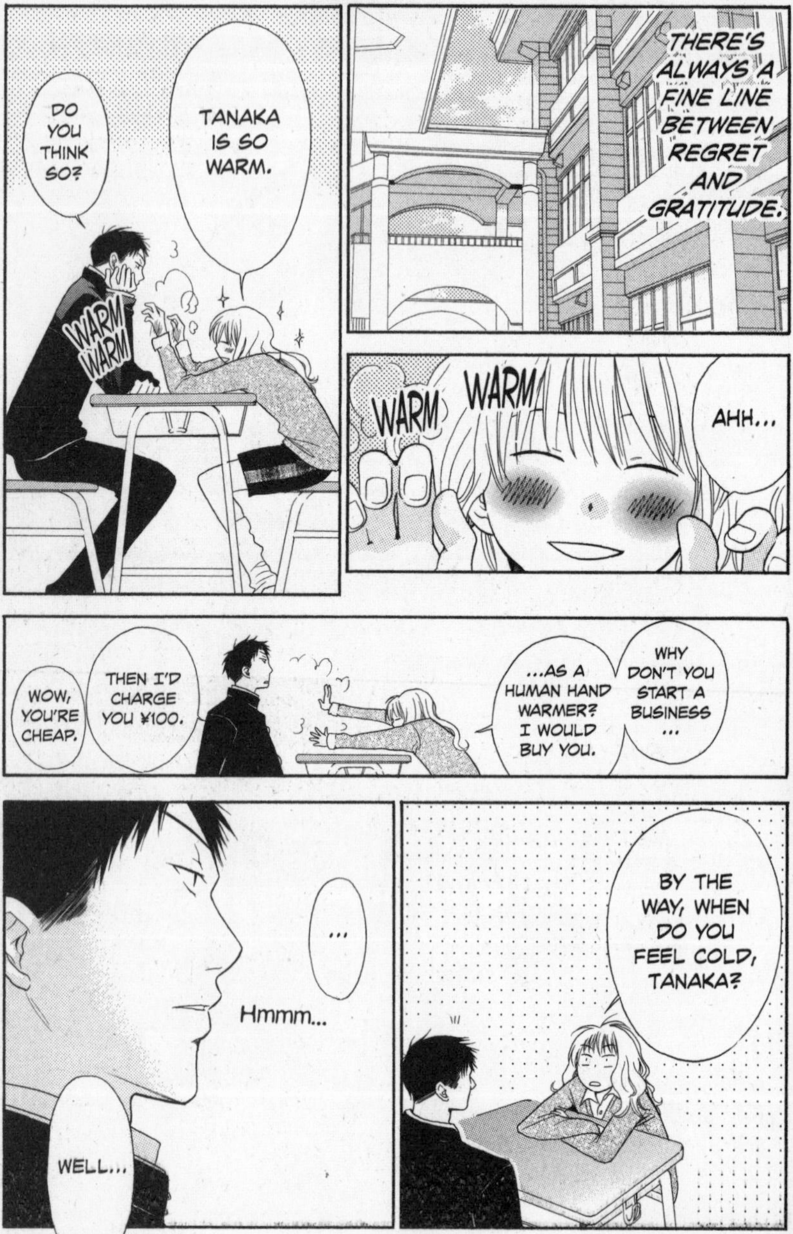
THERE'S ALWAYS A FINE LINE BETWEEN REGRET AND GRATITUDE.
AHH...
WARM
WARM
TANAKA IS SO WARM.
DO YOU THINK SO?
WARM WARM
WHY DON'T YOU START A BUSINESS...
...AS A HUMAN HAND WARMER? I WOULD BUY YOU.
THEN I'D CHARGE YOU ¥100.
WOW, YOU'RE CHEAP.
BY THE WAY, WHEN DO YOU FEEL COLD, TANAKA?
...
Hmmm...
WELL...

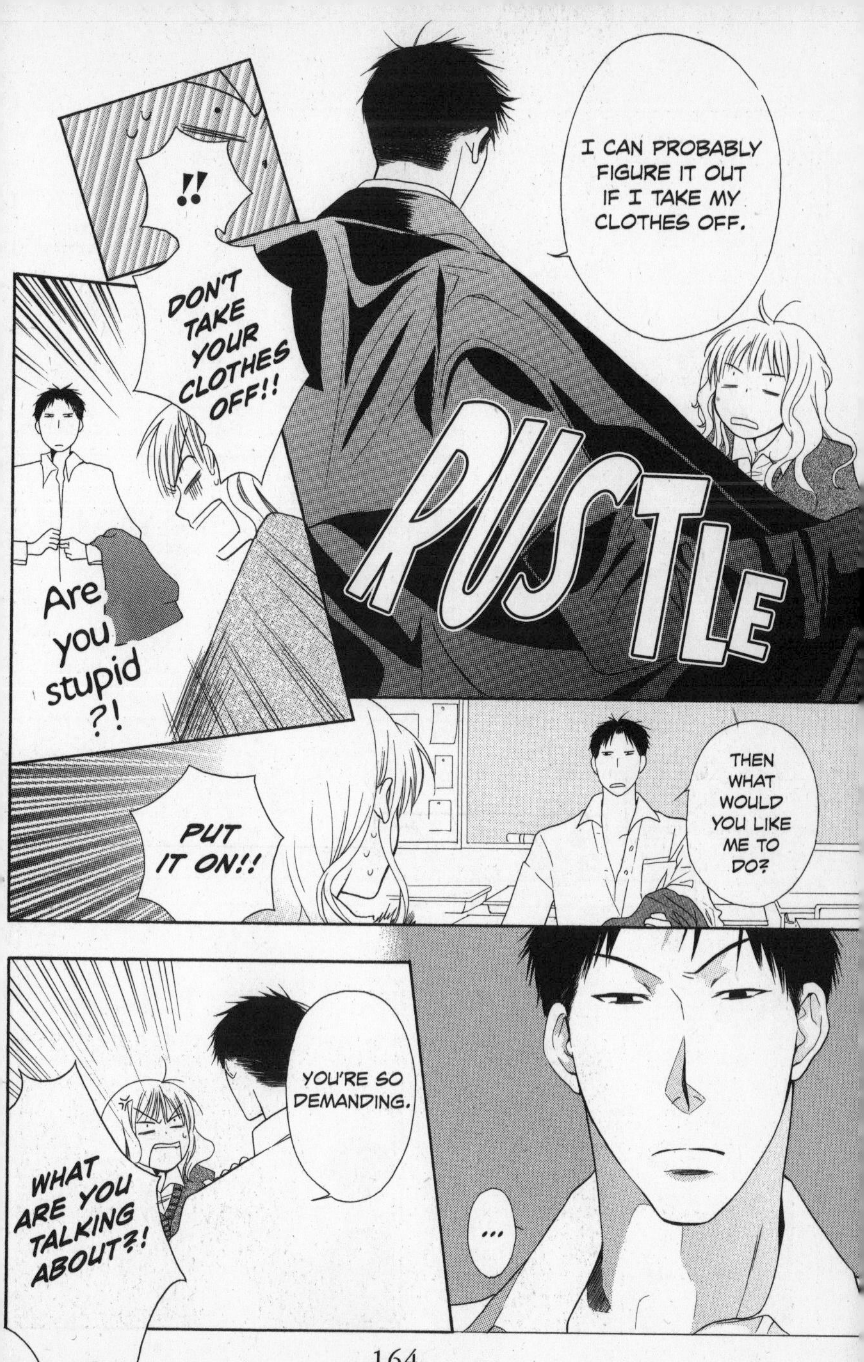
I CAN PROBABLY FIGURE IT OUT IF I TAKE MY CLOTHES OFF.
RUSTLE
!!
DON'T TAKE YOUR CLOTHES OFF!!
Are you stupid?!
THEN WHAT WOULD YOU LIKE ME TO DO?
PUT IT ON!!
...
YOU'RE SO DEMANDING.
WHAT ARE YOU TALKING ABOUT?!

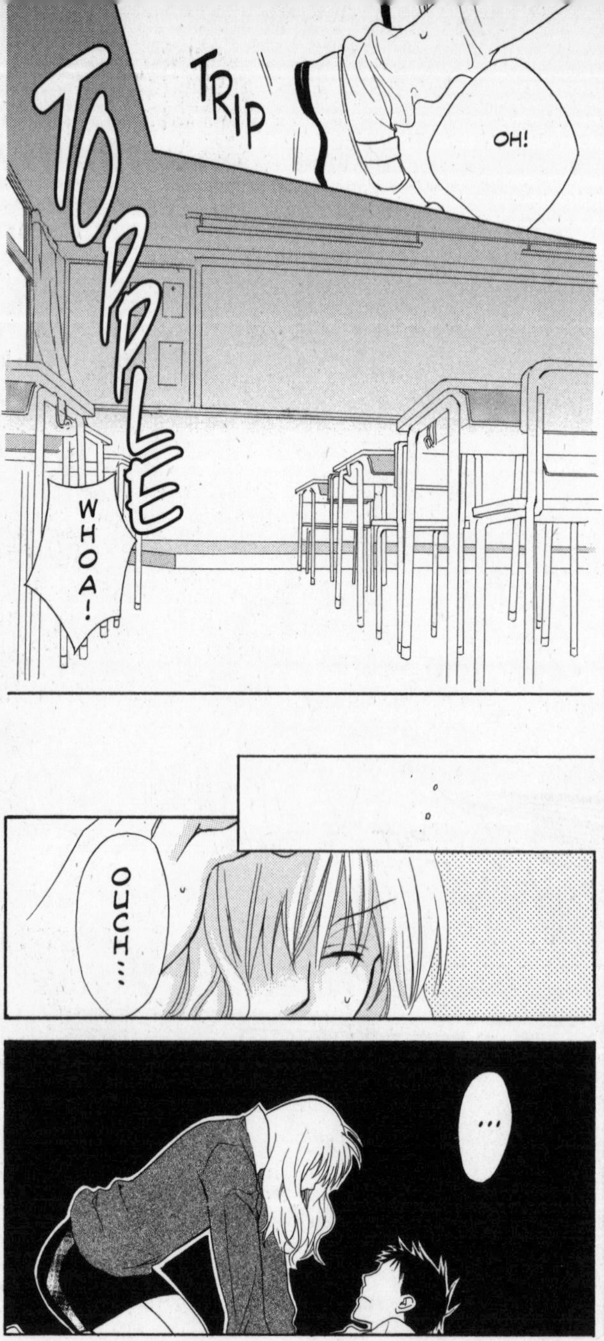
OH!
TRIP
TOPPLE
WHOA!
OUCH...
...

Continuation of the Story

And the hero will be the prince of the balance ball world.
(Is there such a person?)

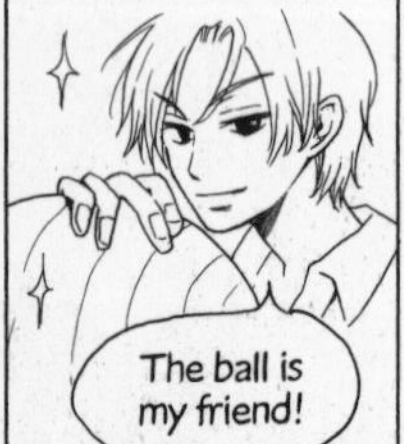
The ball is my friend!

Even though they become rivals, they also become attracted to each other.

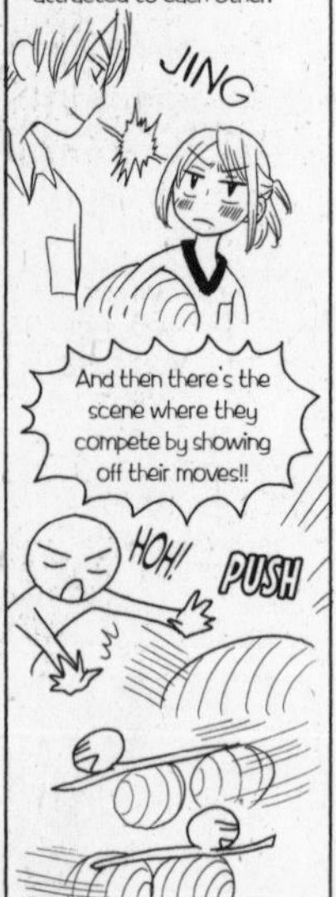
JING
And then there's the scene where they compete by showing off their moves!!
HOH!
PUSH
ROLLROLL ROLLROLL

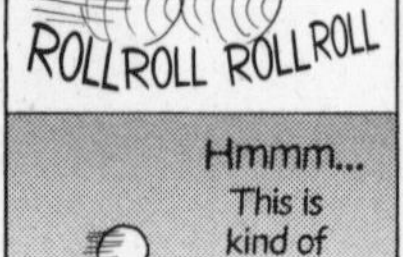
Hmmm... This is kind of awkward...

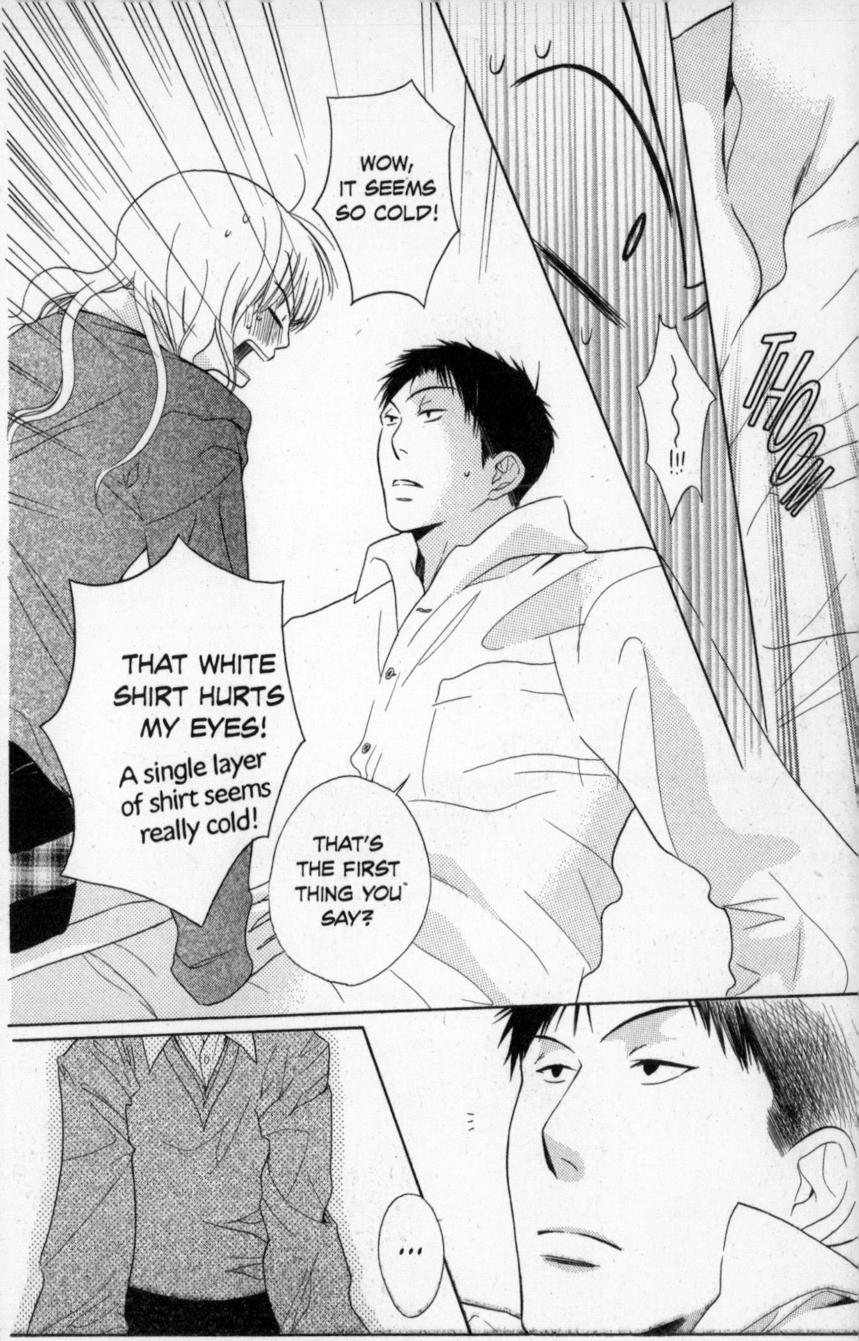
THOOM
!!!
WOW, IT SEEMS SO COLD!
THAT WHITE SHIRT HURTS MY EYES!
A single layer of shirt seems really cold!
THAT'S THE FIRST THING YOU SAY?
...

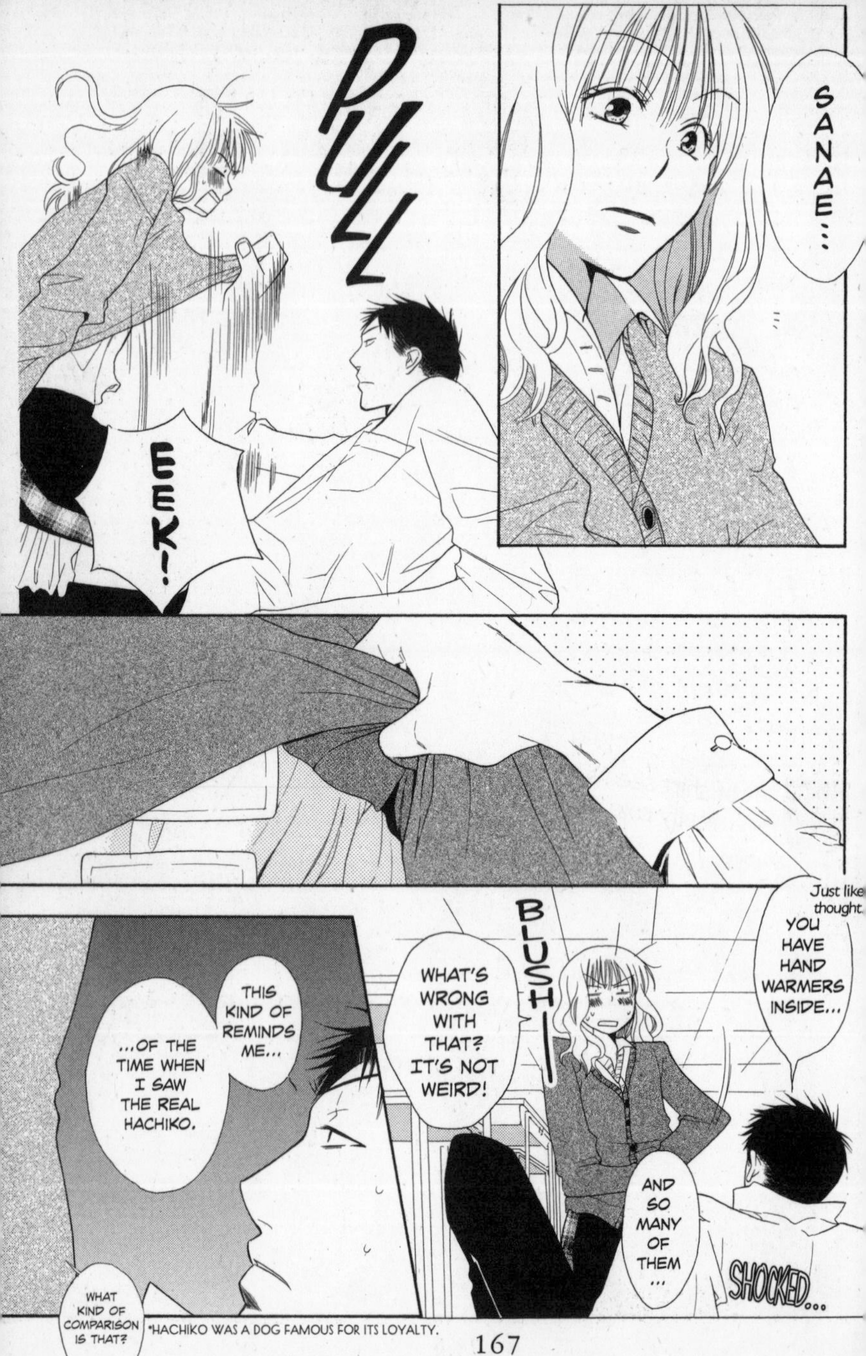
SANAE...
PULL
EEK!
Just like thought.
YOU HAVE HAND WARMERS INSIDE...
BLUSH
WHAT'S WRONG WITH THAT? IT'S NOT WEIRD!
AND SO MANY OF THEM...
SHOCKED...
THIS KIND OF REMINDS ME...
...OF THE TIME WHEN I SAW THE REAL HACHIKO.
WHAT KIND OF COMPARISON IS THAT?

*HACHIKO WAS A DOG FAMOUS FOR ITS LOYALTY.

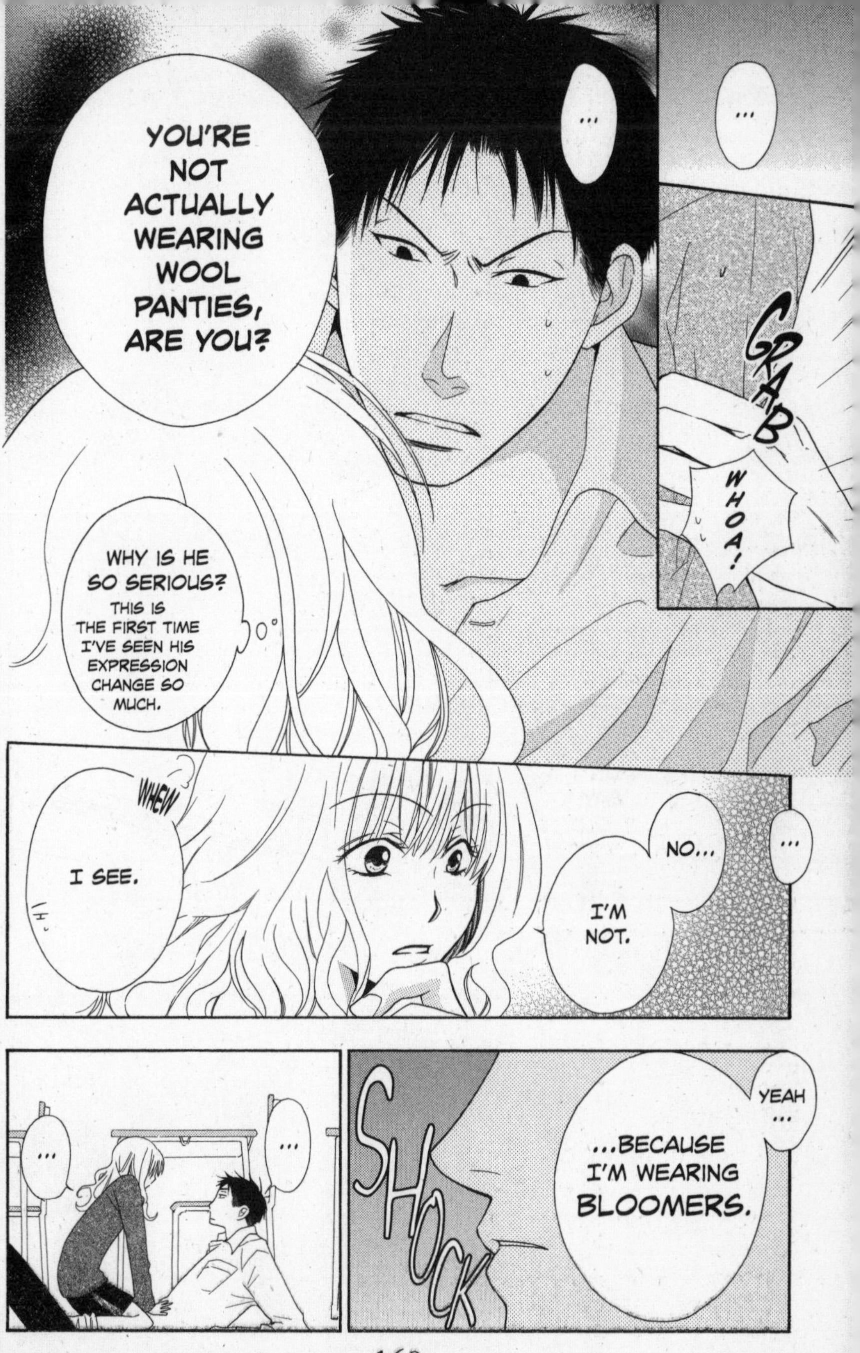
...
GRAB
WHOA!
...
YOU'RE NOT ACTUALLY WEARING WOOL PANTIES, ARE YOU?
WHY IS HE SO SERIOUS? THIS IS THE FIRST TIME I'VE SEEN HIS EXPRESSION CHANGE SO MUCH.
...
NO... I'M NOT.
WHEW
I SEE.
YEAH...
...BECAUSE I'M WEARING BLOOMERS.
SHOCK
...
...

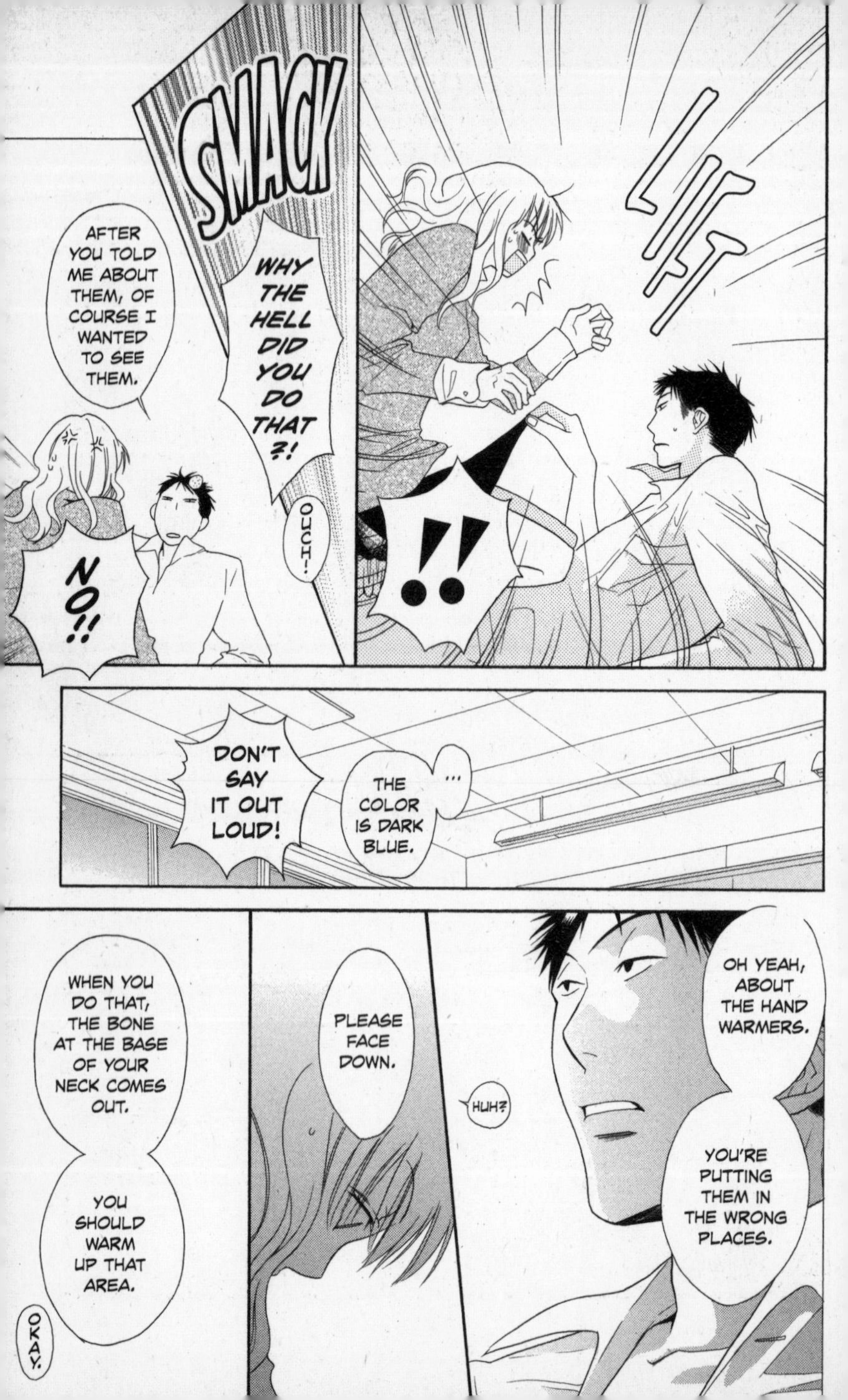
LIFT
!!
SMACK
WHY THE HELL DID YOU DO THAT?!
AFTER YOU TOLD ME ABOUT THEM, OF COURSE I WANTED TO SEE THEM.
OUCH!
NO!!
...
THE COLOR IS DARK BLUE.
DON'T SAY IT OUT LOUD!
OH YEAH, ABOUT THE HAND WARMERS.
YOU'RE PUTTING THEM IN THE WRONG PLACES.
HUH?
PLEASE FACE DOWN.
WHEN YOU DO THAT, THE BONE AT THE BASE OF YOUR NECK COMES OUT.
YOU SHOULD WARM UP THAT AREA.
OKAY.

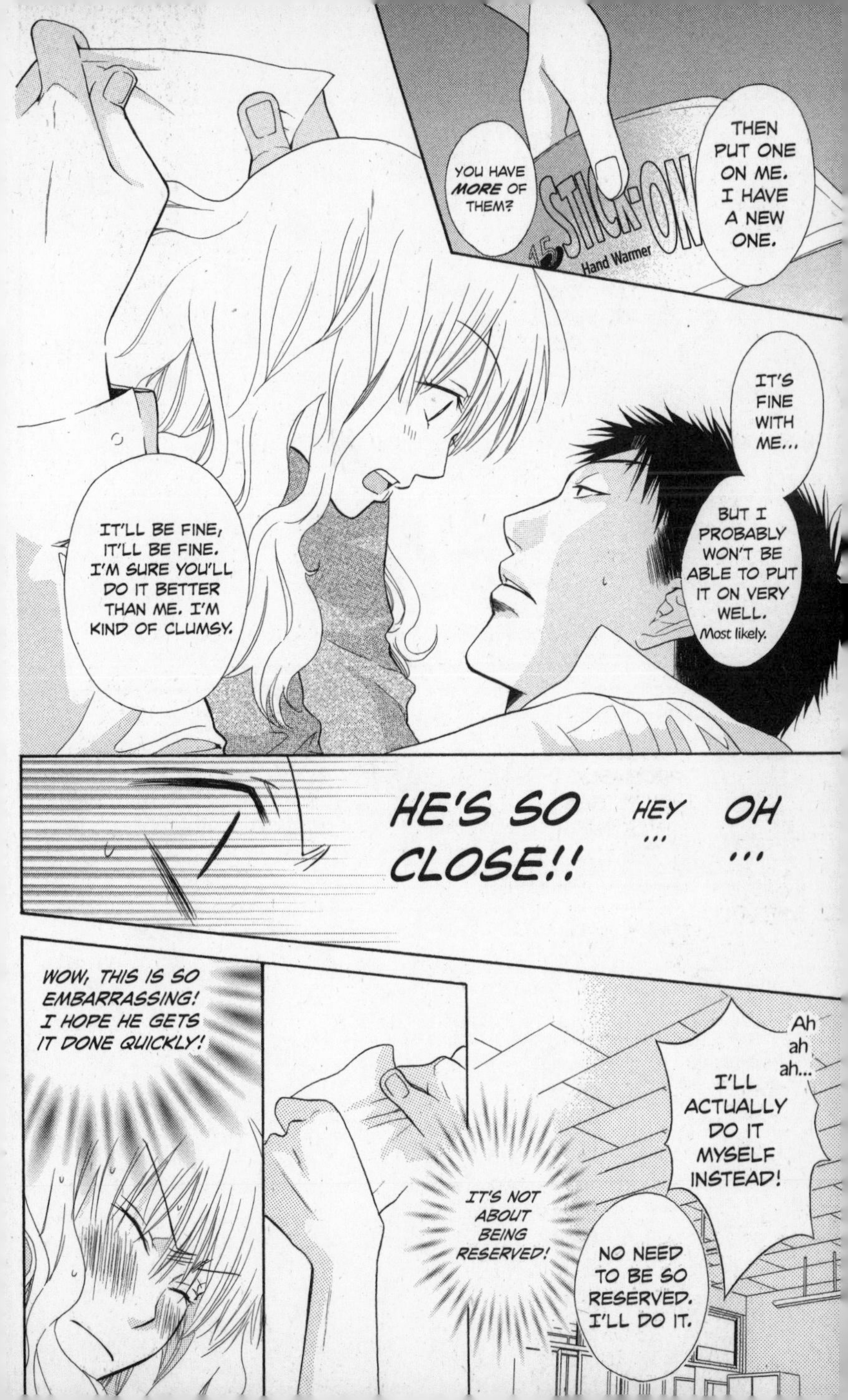
THEN PUT ONE ON ME. I HAVE A NEW ONE.
YOU HAVE *MORE* OF THEM?
STICK-ON Hand Warmer
IT'S FINE WITH ME...
BUT I PROBABLY WON'T BE ABLE TO PUT IT ON VERY WELL. Most likely.
IT'LL BE FINE, IT'LL BE FINE. I'M SURE YOU'LL DO IT BETTER THAN ME. I'M KIND OF CLUMSY.
OH ...
HEY ...
HE'S SO CLOSE!!
Ah ah ah...
I'LL ACTUALLY DO IT MYSELF INSTEAD!
NO NEED TO BE SO RESERVED. I'LL DO IT.
IT'S NOT ABOUT BEING RESERVED!
WOW, THIS IS SO EMBARRASSING! I HOPE HE GETS IT DONE QUICKLY!

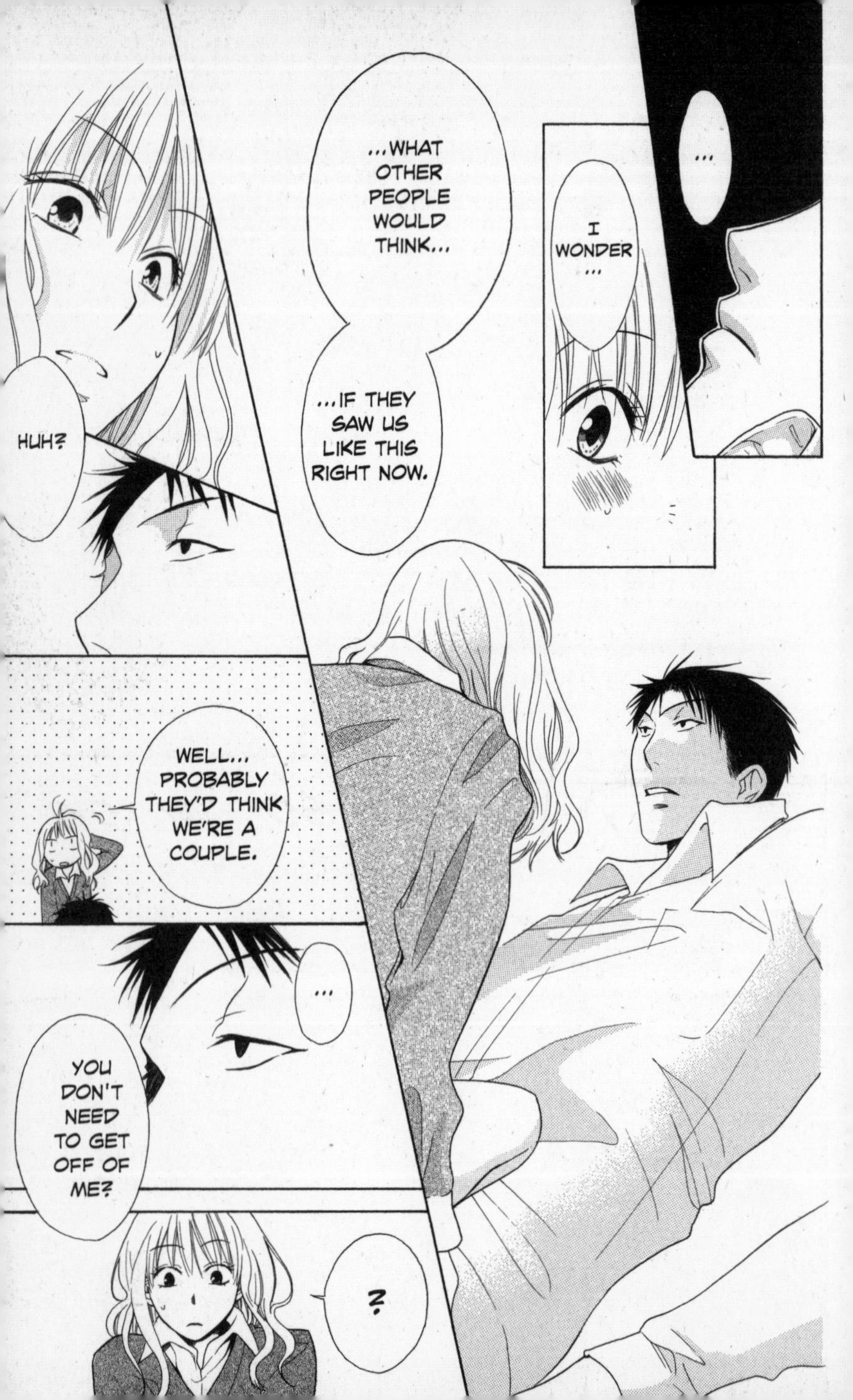
...
I WONDER...
...WHAT OTHER PEOPLE WOULD THINK...
...IF THEY SAW US LIKE THIS RIGHT NOW.
HUH?
WELL... PROBABLY THEY'D THINK WE'RE A COUPLE.
...
YOU DON'T NEED TO GET OFF OF ME?
?

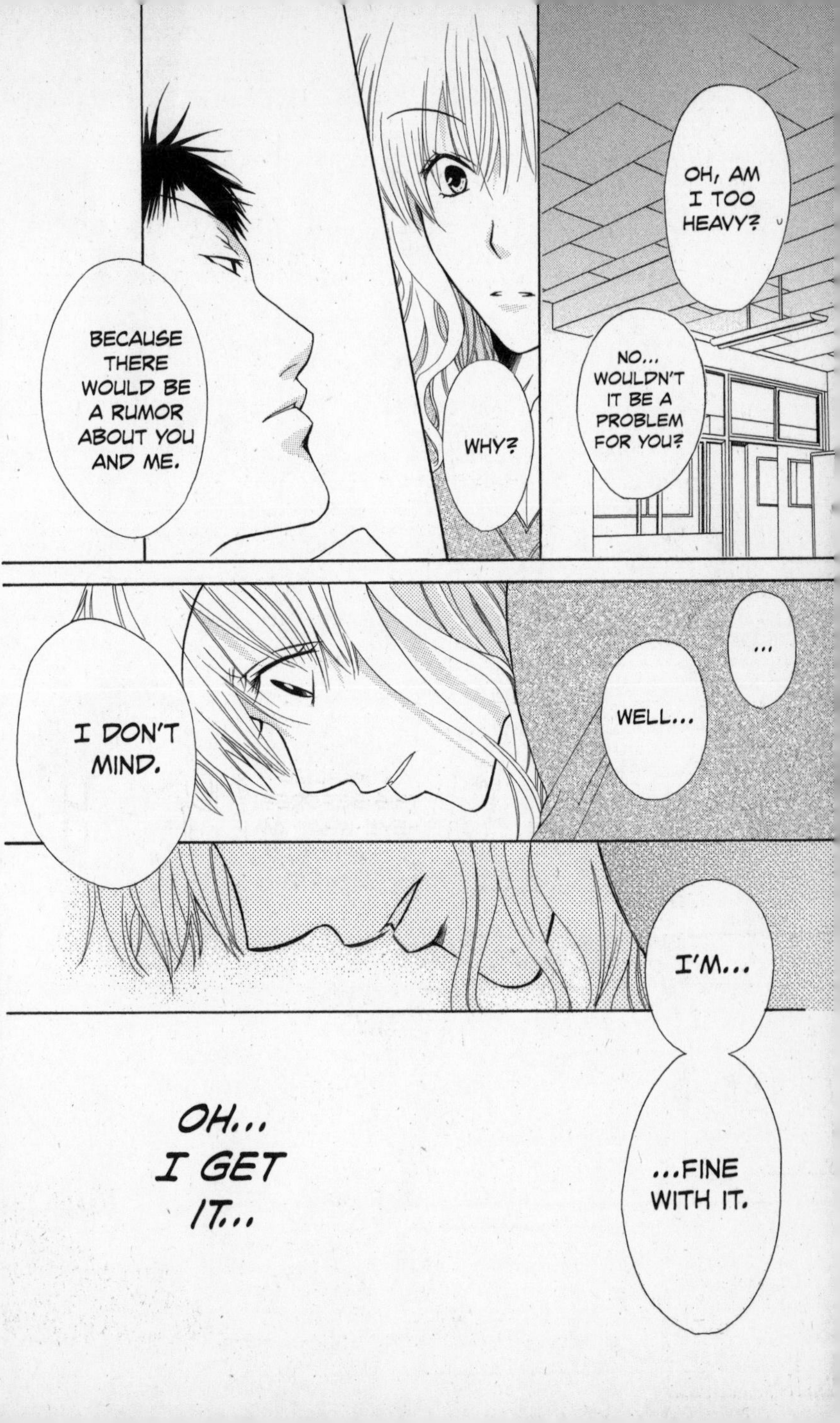
OH, AM I TOO HEAVY?
NO... WOULDN'T IT BE A PROBLEM FOR YOU?
WHY?
BECAUSE THERE WOULD BE A RUMOR ABOUT YOU AND ME.
...
WELL...
I DON'T MIND.
I'M...
...FINE WITH IT.
OH... I GET IT...

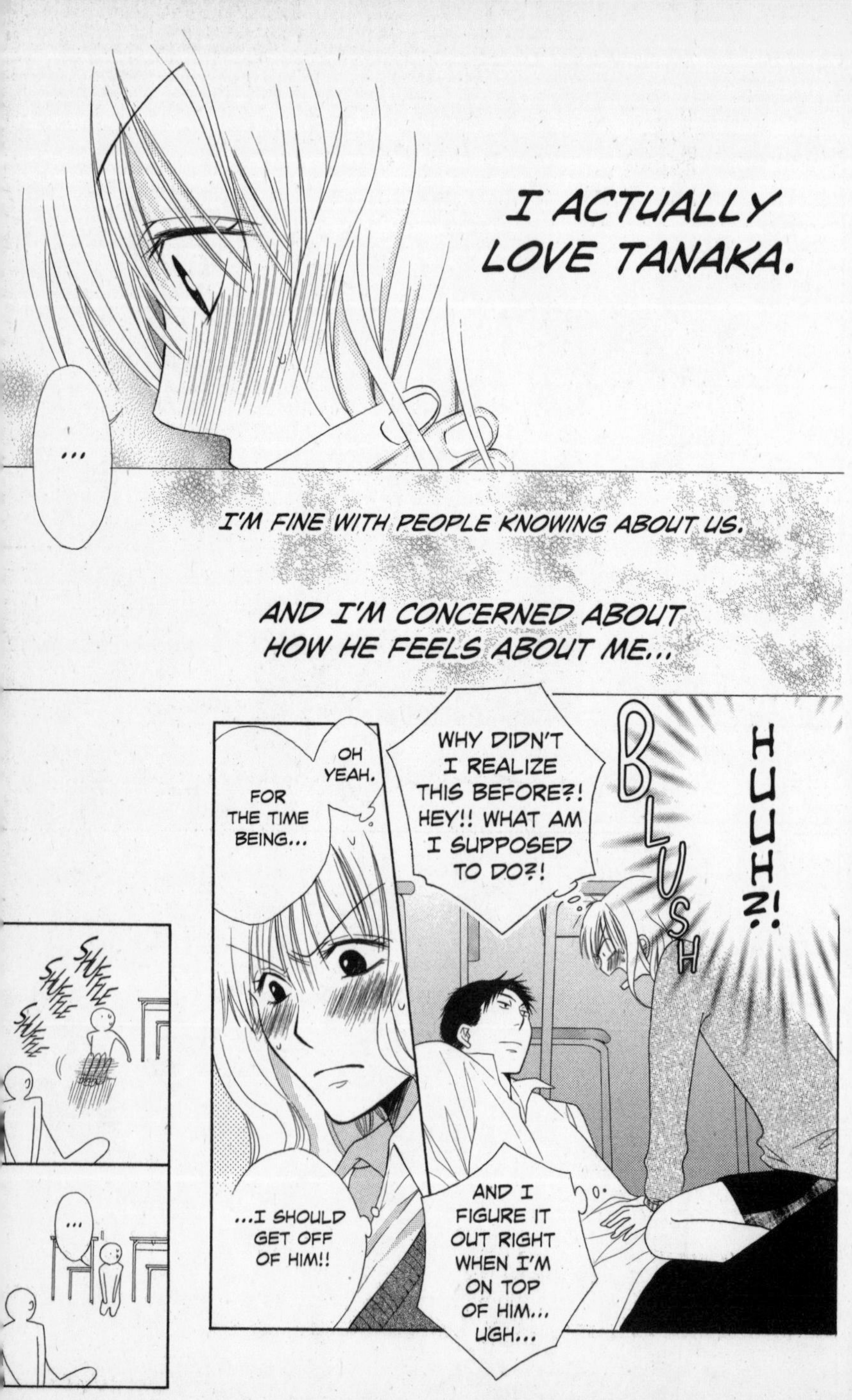

I ACTUALLY LOVE TANAKA.
...
I'M FINE WITH PEOPLE KNOWING ABOUT US.
AND I'M CONCERNED ABOUT HOW HE FEELS ABOUT ME...
HUUUH?!
BLUSH
WHY DIDN'T I REALIZE THIS BEFORE?! HEY!! WHAT AM I SUPPOSED TO DO?!
AND I FIGURE IT OUT RIGHT WHEN I'M ON TOP OF HIM... UGH...
OH YEAH.
FOR THE TIME BEING...
...I SHOULD GET OFF OF HIM!!
SHUFFLE
SHUFFLE
SHUFFLE
...

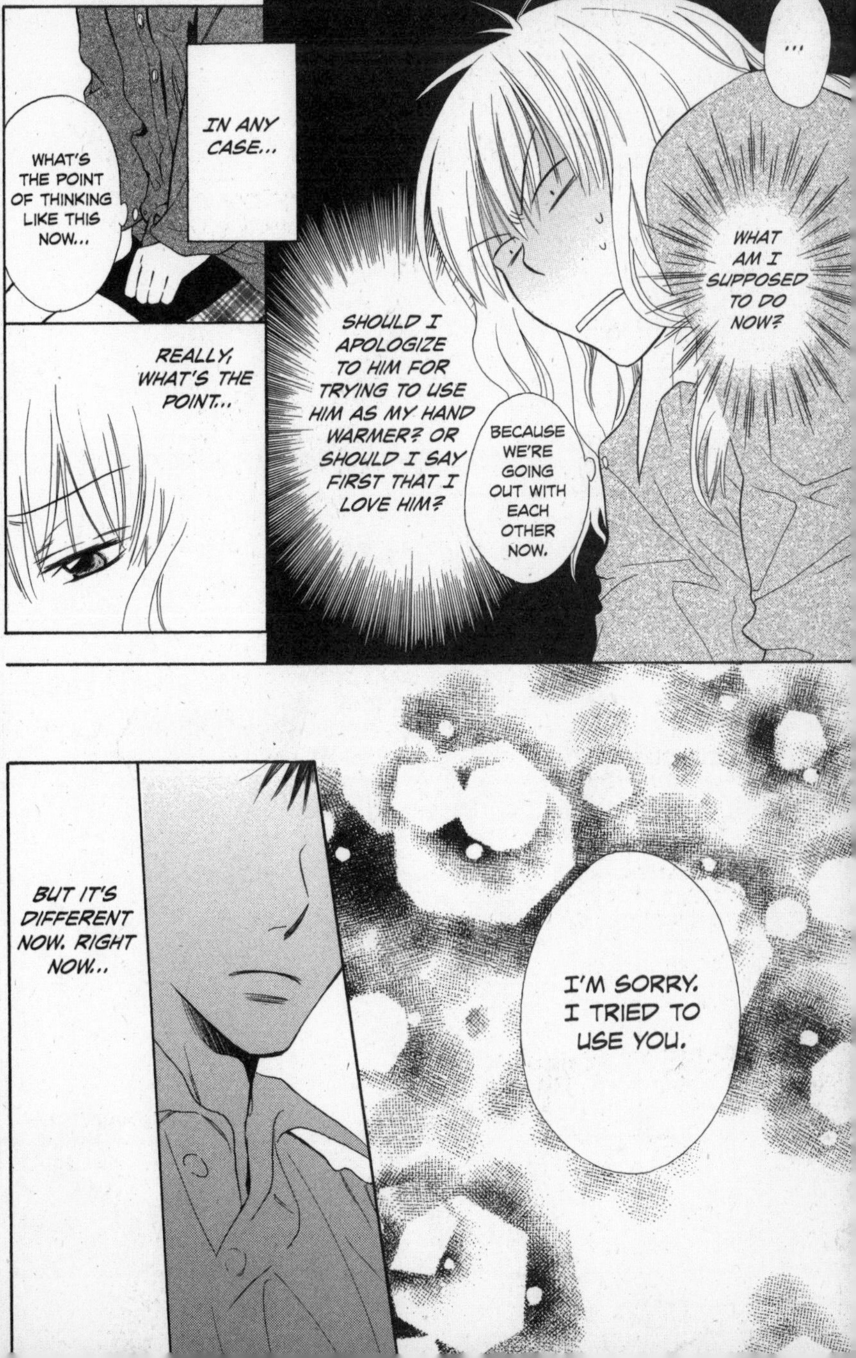
...
WHAT AM I SUPPOSED TO DO NOW?
SHOULD I APOLOGIZE TO HIM FOR TRYING TO USE HIM AS MY HAND WARMER? OR SHOULD I SAY FIRST THAT I LOVE HIM?
BECAUSE WE'RE GOING OUT WITH EACH OTHER NOW.
IN ANY CASE...
WHAT'S THE POINT OF THINKING LIKE THIS NOW...
REALLY, WHAT'S THE POINT...
I'M SORRY. I TRIED TO USE YOU.
BUT IT'S DIFFERENT NOW. RIGHT NOW...

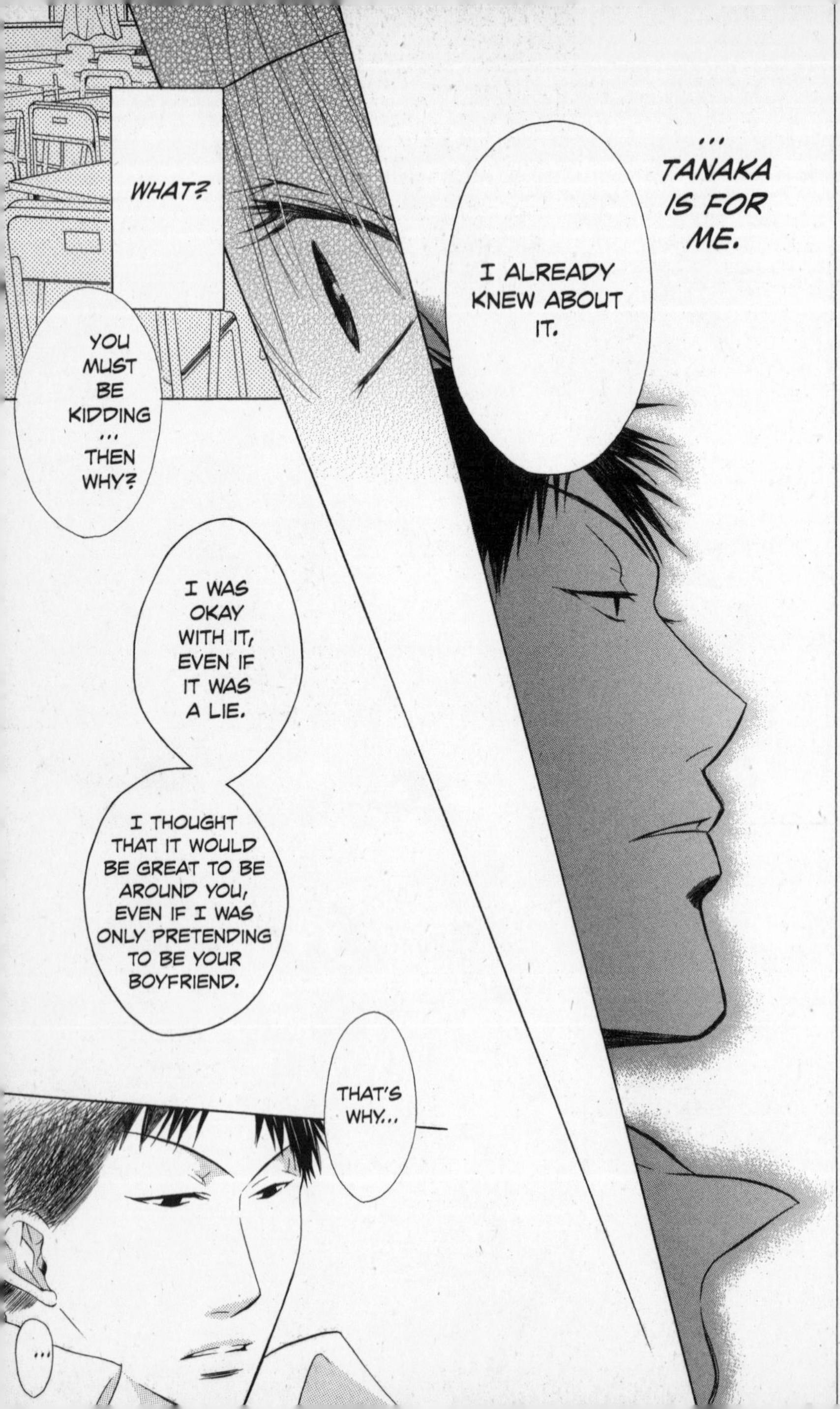

...TANAKA IS FOR ME.
I ALREADY KNEW ABOUT IT.
WHAT?
YOU MUST BE KIDDING... THEN WHY?
I WAS OKAY WITH IT, EVEN IF IT WAS A LIE.
I THOUGHT THAT IT WOULD BE GREAT TO BE AROUND YOU, EVEN IF I WAS ONLY PRETENDING TO BE YOUR BOYFRIEND.
THAT'S WHY...
...

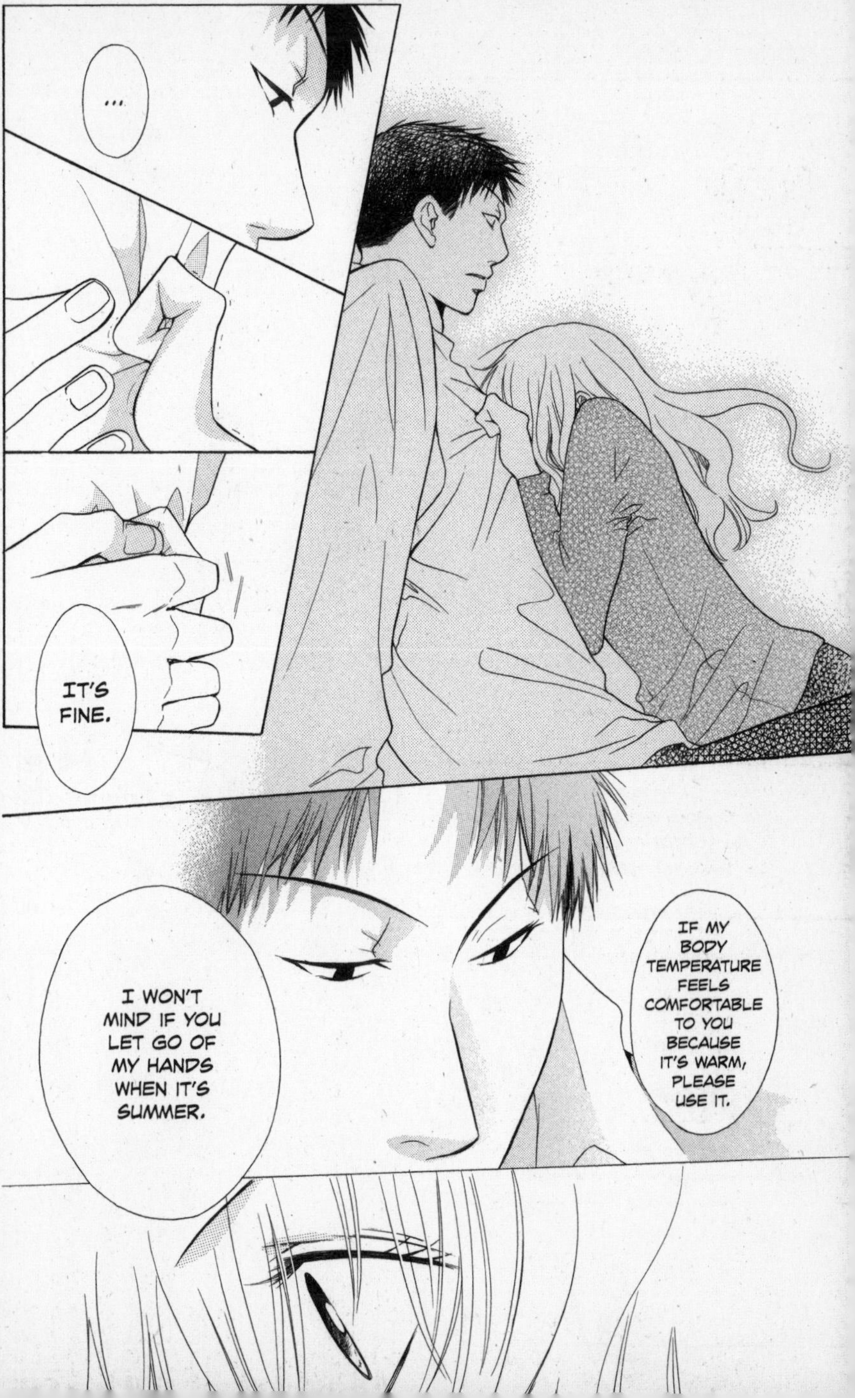
...
IT'S FINE.
IF MY BODY TEMPERATURE FEELS COMFORTABLE TO YOU BECAUSE IT'S WARM, PLEASE USE IT.
I WON'T MIND IF YOU LET GO OF MY HANDS WHEN IT'S SUMMER.

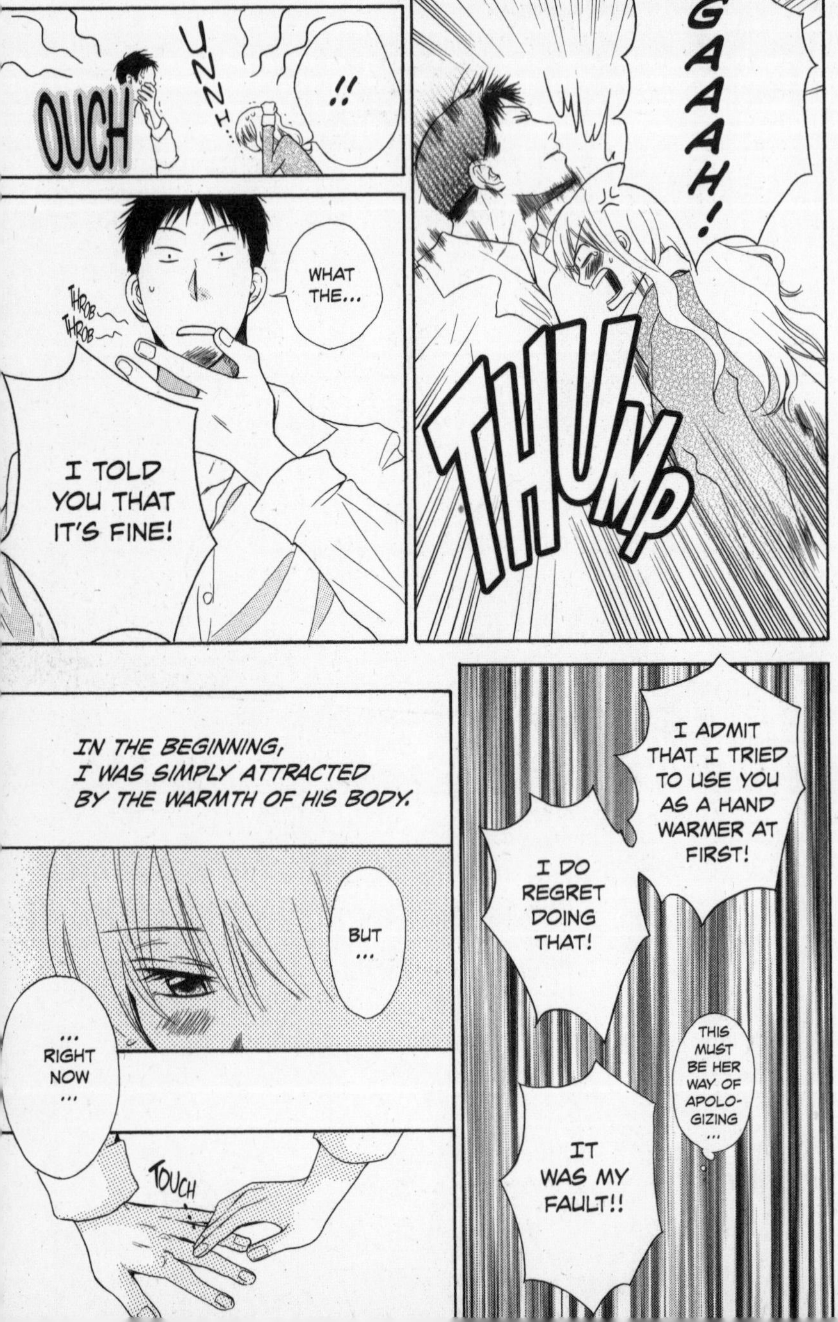
GAAAH!
THUMP
!!
UNNI...
OUCH
WHAT THE...
THROB THROB
I TOLD YOU THAT IT'S FINE!
I ADMIT THAT I TRIED TO USE YOU AS A HAND WARMER AT FIRST!
I DO REGRET DOING THAT!
THIS MUST BE HER WAY OF APOLO-GIZING...
IT WAS MY FAULT!!
IN THE BEGINNING, I WAS SIMPLY ATTRACTED BY THE WARMTH OF HIS BODY.
BUT...
...RIGHT NOW...
TOUCH

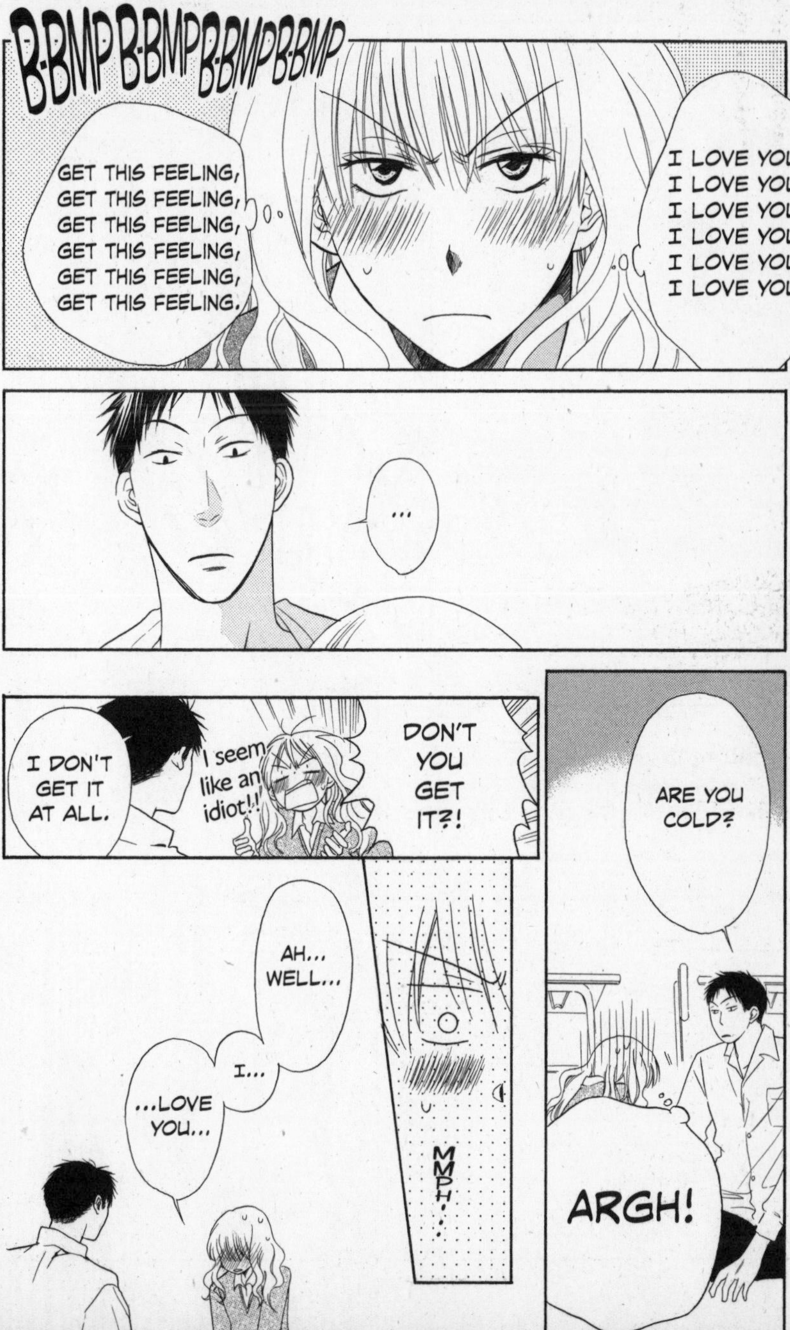
B-BMP B-BMP B-BMP B-BMP
I LOVE YOU, I LOVE YOU, I LOVE YOU, I LOVE YOU, I LOVE YOU, I LOVE YOU.
GET THIS FEELING, GET THIS FEELING, GET THIS FEELING, GET THIS FEELING, GET THIS FEELING, GET THIS FEELING.
...
ARE YOU COLD?
ARGH!
DON'T YOU GET IT?!
I seem like an idiot!!
I DON'T GET IT AT ALL.
MMPH...
AH... WELL...
I...
...LOVE YOU...

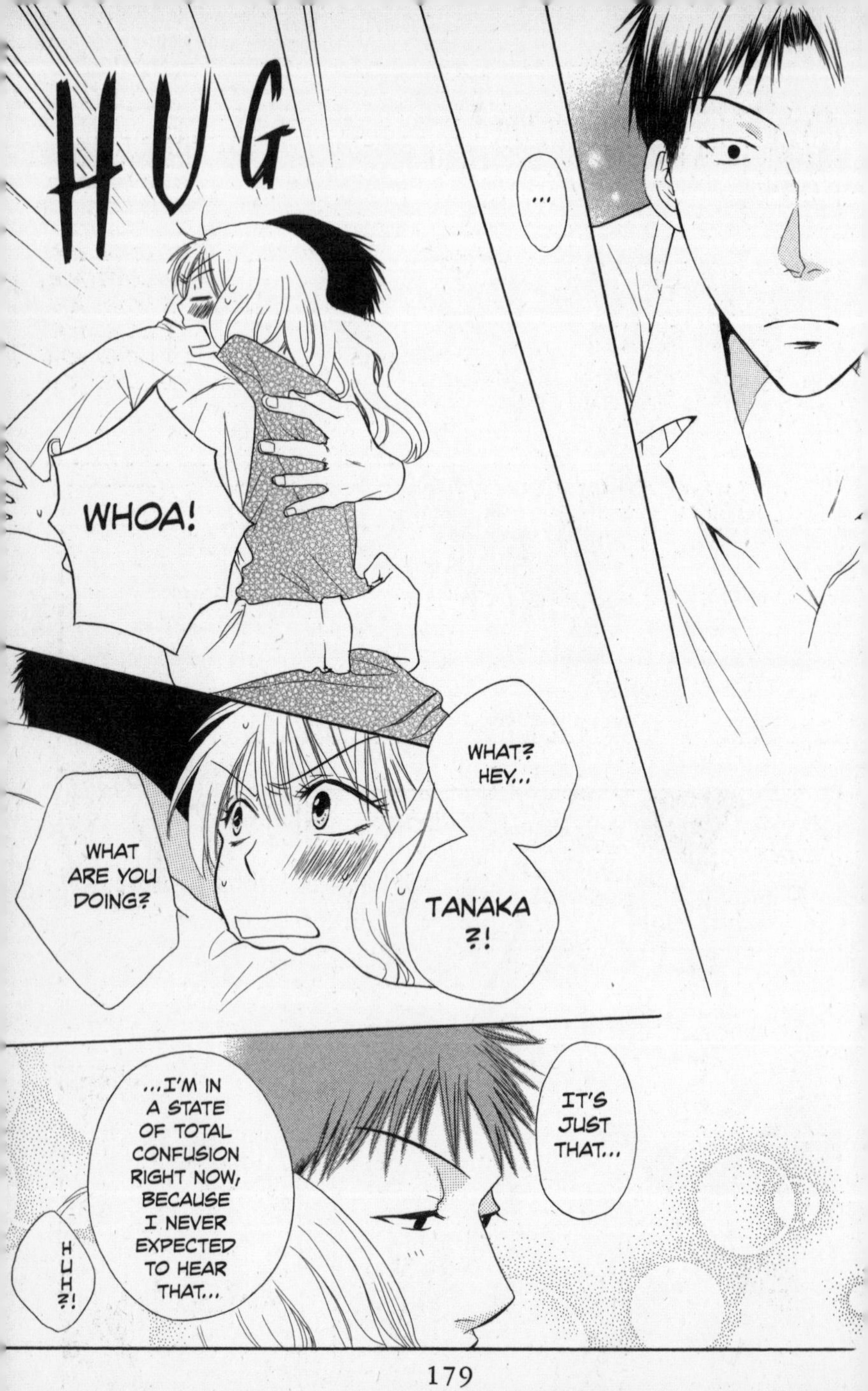
...
HUG
WHOA!
WHAT? HEY...
TANAKA?!
WHAT ARE YOU DOING?
IT'S JUST THAT...
...I'M IN A STATE OF TOTAL CONFUSION RIGHT NOW, BECAUSE I NEVER EXPECTED TO HEAR THAT...
HUH?!

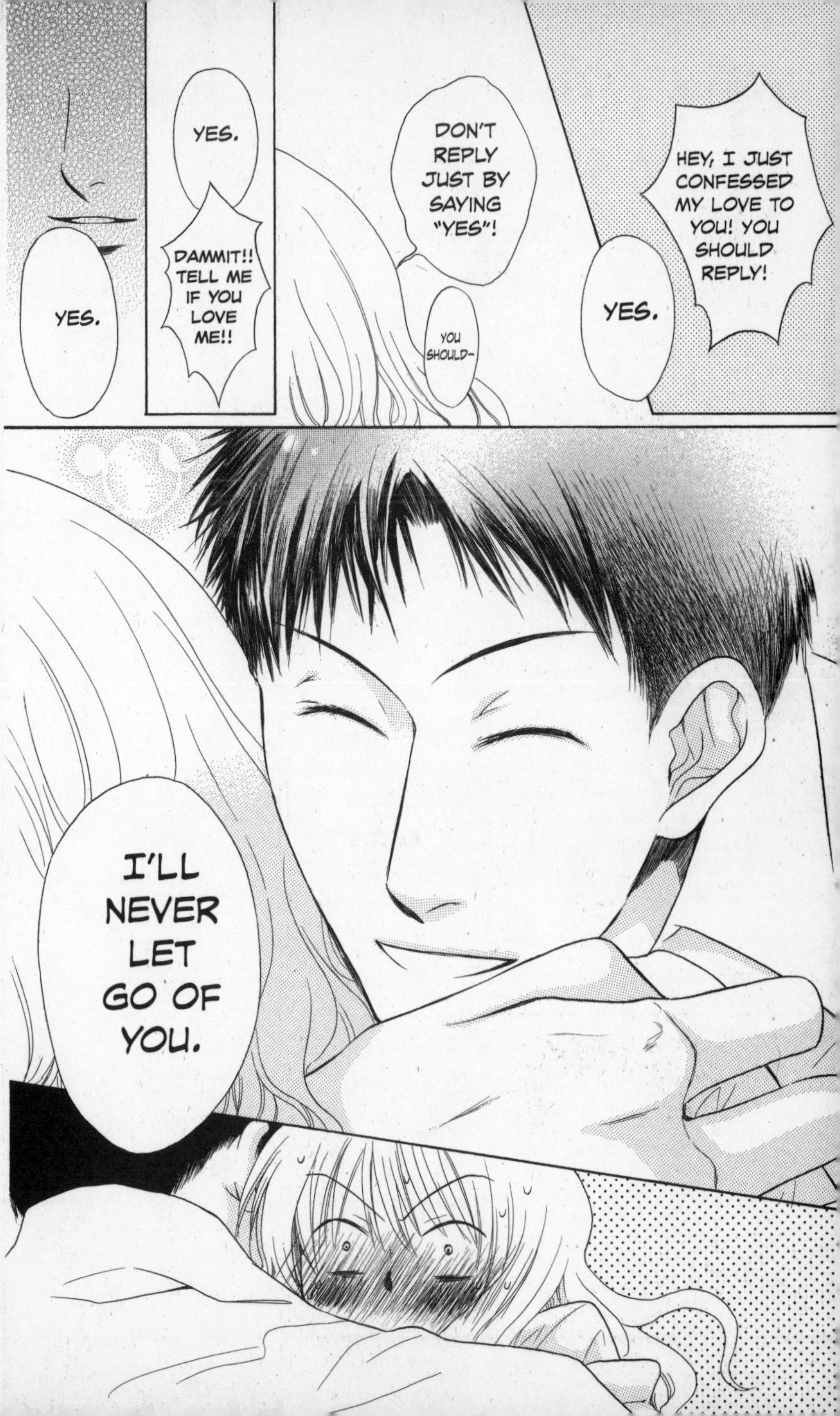
HEY, I JUST CONFESSED MY LOVE TO YOU! YOU SHOULD REPLY!
YES.
DON'T REPLY JUST BY SAYING "YES"!
YOU SHOULD-
YES.
DAMMIT!! TELL ME IF YOU LOVE ME!!
YES.
I'LL NEVER LET GO OF YOU.

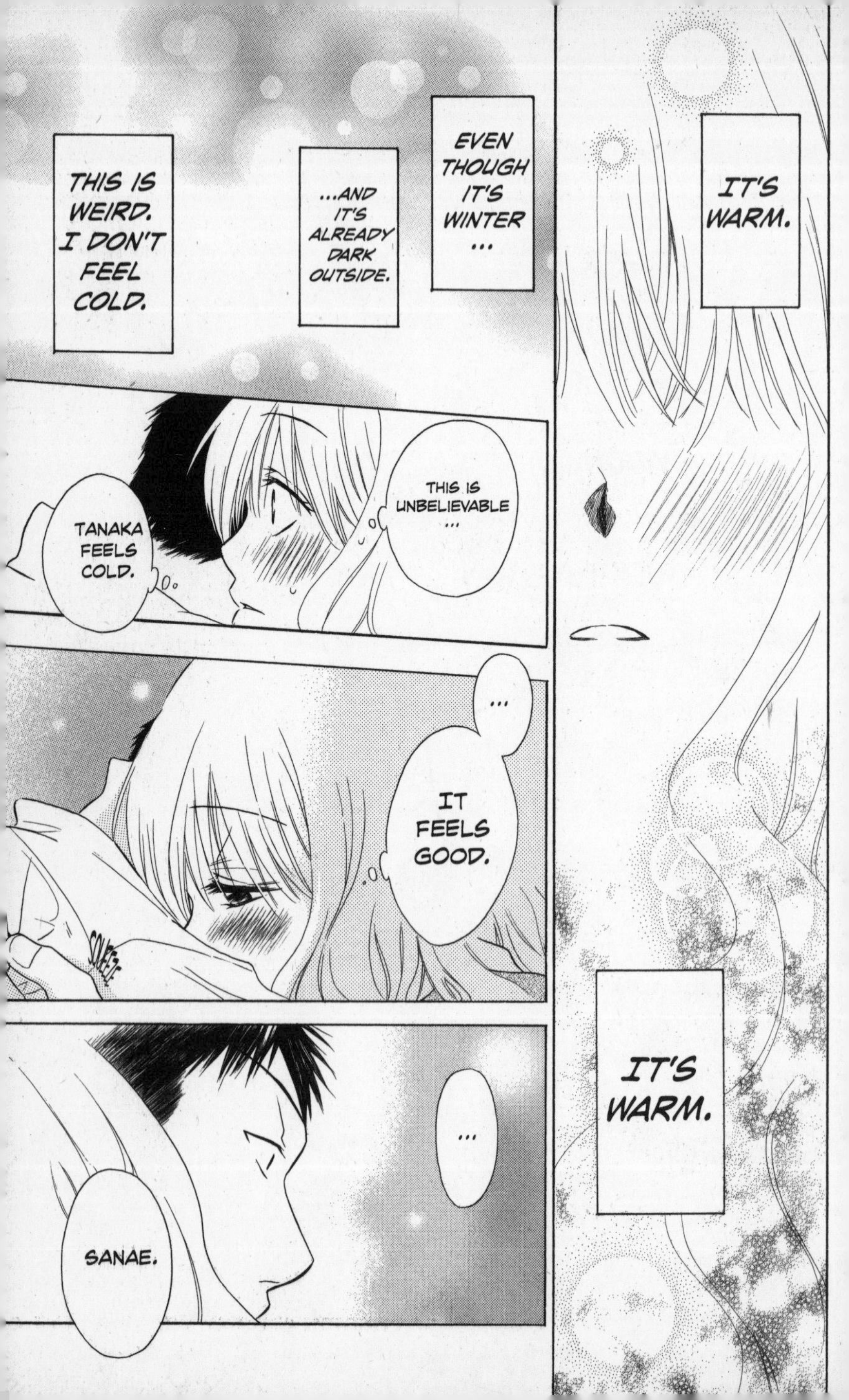
IT'S WARM.
IT'S WARM.
EVEN THOUGH IT'S WINTER...
...AND IT'S ALREADY DARK OUTSIDE.
THIS IS WEIRD. I DON'T FEEL COLD.
THIS IS UNBELIEVABLE...
TANAKA FEELS COLD.
...
IT FEELS GOOD.
...
SANAE.

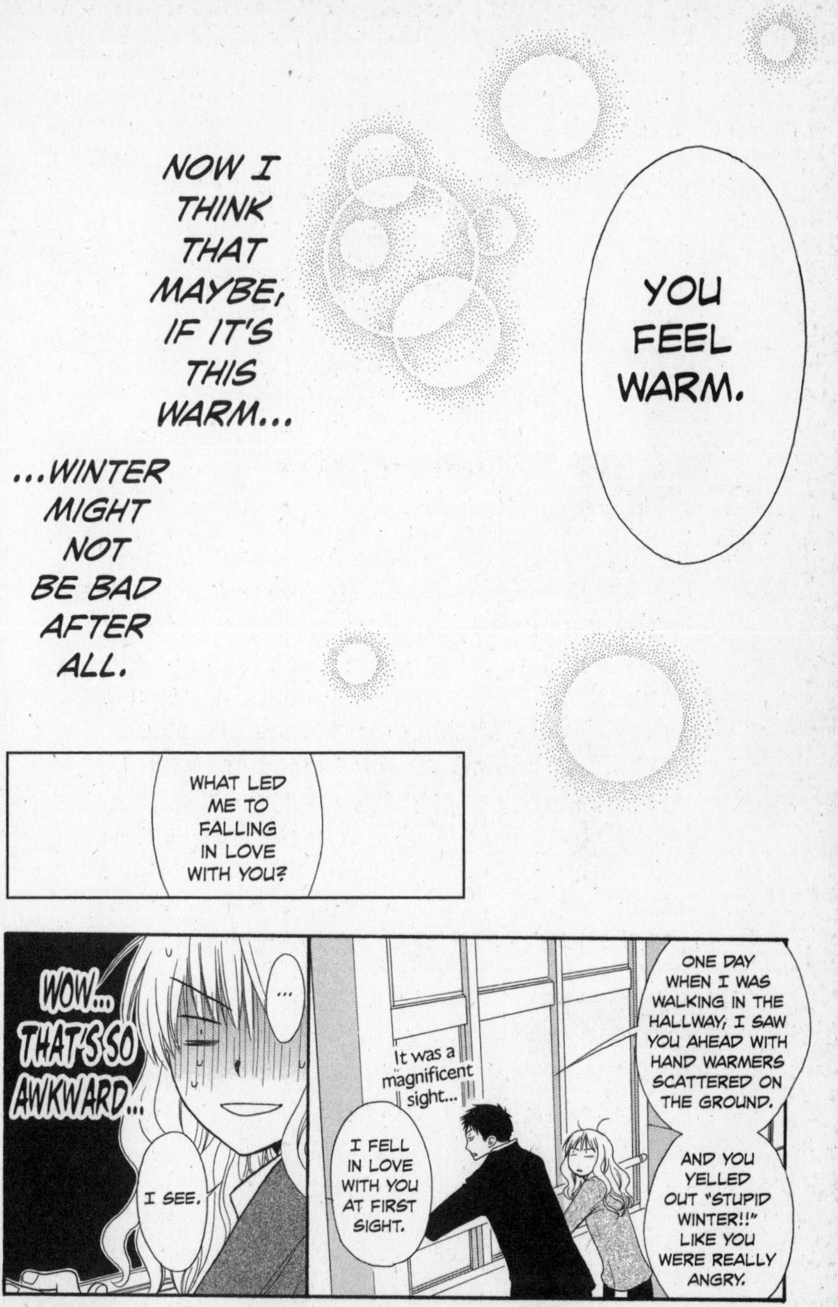
YOU FEEL WARM.
NOW I THINK THAT MAYBE, IF IT'S THIS WARM...
...WINTER MIGHT NOT BE BAD AFTER ALL.
WHAT LED ME TO FALLING IN LOVE WITH YOU?
ONE DAY WHEN I WAS WALKING IN THE HALLWAY, I SAW YOU AHEAD WITH HAND WARMERS SCATTERED ON THE GROUND.
AND YOU YELLED OUT "STUPID WINTER!!" LIKE YOU WERE REALLY ANGRY.
It was a magnificent sight...
I FELL IN LOVE WITH YOU AT FIRST SIGHT.
...
WOW... THAT'S SO AWKWARD...
I SEE.

Severe Cold Heater/The End

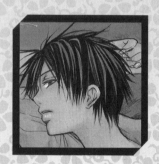

Izumi Tsubaki began drawing manga in her first year of high school. She was soon selected to be in the top ten of *Hana to Yume*'s HMC (Hana to Yume Mangaka Course) and subsequently won *Hana to Yume*'s Big Challenge contest. Her debut title, *Chijimete Distance* (Shrink the Distance), ran in 2002 in *Hana to Yume* magazine, issue 17. In addition to *The Magic Touch* (originally published in Japan as *Oyayubi kara Romance*, or "Romance from the Thumbs"), she is currently working on the manga series *Oresama Teacher* (I'm the Teacher).

Tsubaki Sensei hails from Saitama Prefecture, her birthday is December 11 and she confesses that she enjoys receiving massages more than she enjoys giving them.

THE MAGIC TOUCH
Vol. 7
Shojo Beat Edition

STORY AND ART BY
IZUMI TSUBAKI

English Adaptation/Lorelei Laird
Translation/Nori Minami
Touch-up Art & Lettering/James Gaubatz
Design/Sean Lee
Editor/Eric Searleman

VP, Production/Alvin Lu
VP, Sales & Product Marketing/Gonzalo Ferreyra
VP, Creative/Linda Espinosa
Publisher/Hyoe Narita

Oyayubi kara Romance by Izumi Tsubaki © Izumi Tsubaki 2006
All rights reserved. First published in Japan in 2006 by HAKUSENSHA, Inc., Tokyo.
English language translation rights arranged with HAKUSENSHA, Inc., Tokyo.

Printed in Canada

Published by VIZ Media, LLC
P.O. Box 77010
San Francisco, CA 94107

10 9 8 7 6 5 4 3 2 1
First printing, April 2010

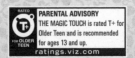

PARENTAL ADVISORY
THE MAGIC TOUCH is rated T+ for
Older Teen and is recommended
for ages 13 and up.
ratings.viz.com

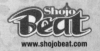

www.viz.com

www.shojobeat.com

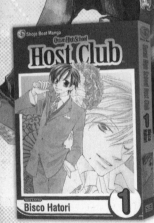
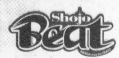

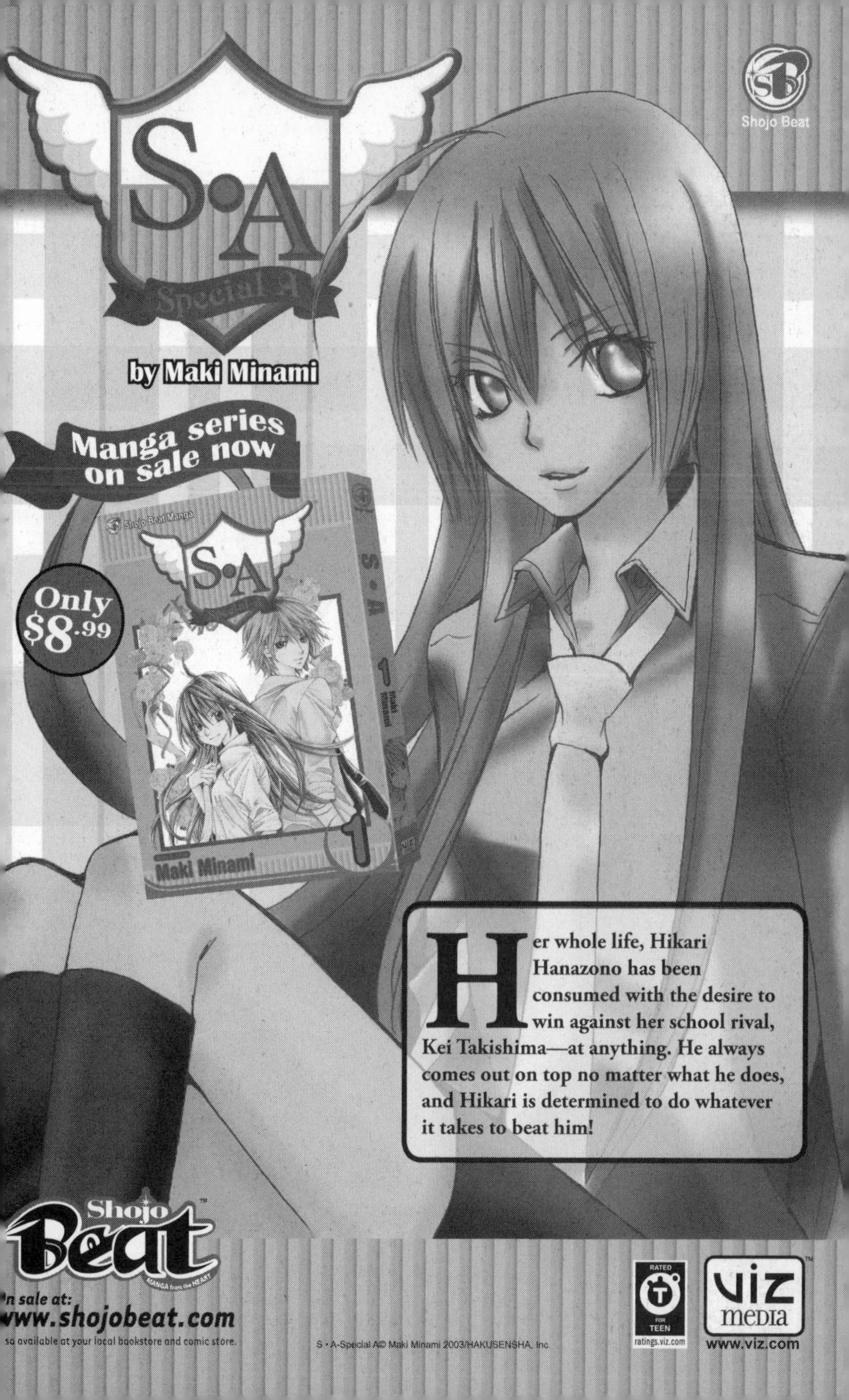
Shojo Beat
S•A
Special A
by Maki Minami
Manga series on sale now
Only $8.99
Her whole life, Hikari Hanazono has been consumed with the desire to win against her school rival, Kei Takishima—at anything. He always comes out on top no matter what he does, and Hikari is determined to do whatever it takes to beat him!
Shojo Beat
MANGA from the HEART
'n sale at:
www.shojobeat.com
so available at your local bookstore and comic store.
S • A-Special A© Maki Minami 2003/HAKUSENSHA, Inc.
RATED T FOR TEEN
ratings.viz.com
VIZ media
www.viz.com

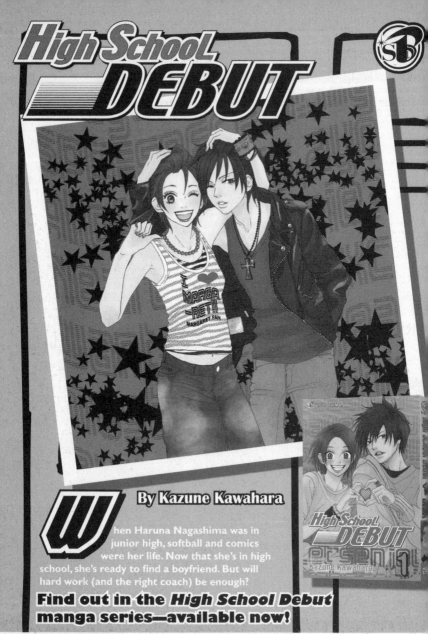
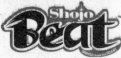

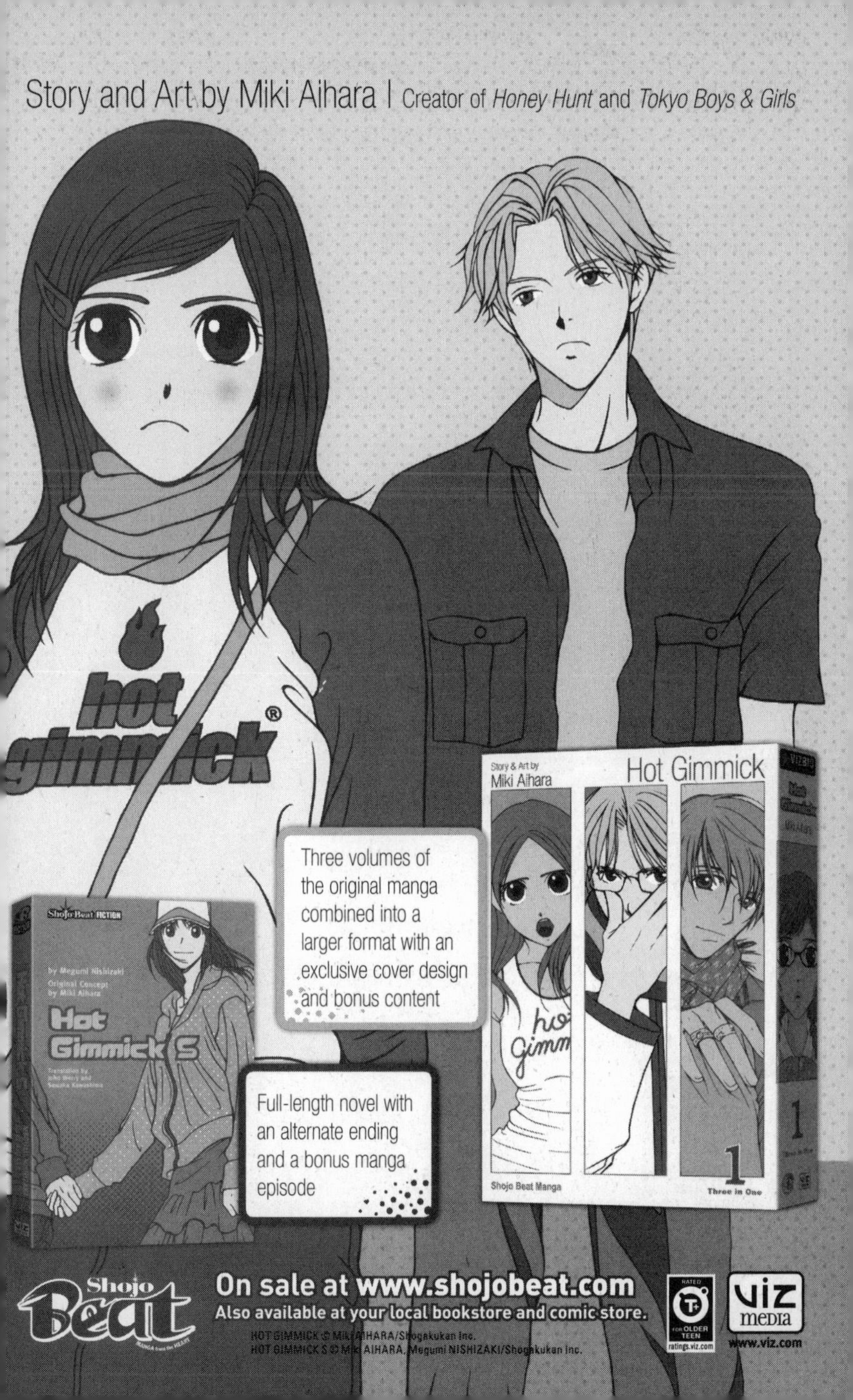
Story and Art by Miki Aihara | Creator of *Honey Hunt* and *Tokyo Boys & Girls*
hot gimmick®
Shojo Beat FICTION
by Megumi Nishizaki
Original Concept by Miki Aihara
Hot Gimmick S
Three volumes of the original manga combined into a larger format with an exclusive cover design and bonus content
Full-length novel with an alternate ending and a bonus manga episode
Story & Art by Miki Aihara
Hot Gimmick
Shojo Beat Manga
1
Three in One
Shojo Beat
On sale at www.shojobeat.com
Also available at your local bookstore and comic store.
HOT GIMMICK © MIKI AIHARA/Shogakukan Inc.
HOT GIMMICK S © Miki AIHARA, Megumi NISHIZAKI/Shogakukan Inc.
RATED T+ FOR OLDER TEEN
ratings.viz.com
VIZ MEDIA
www.viz.com

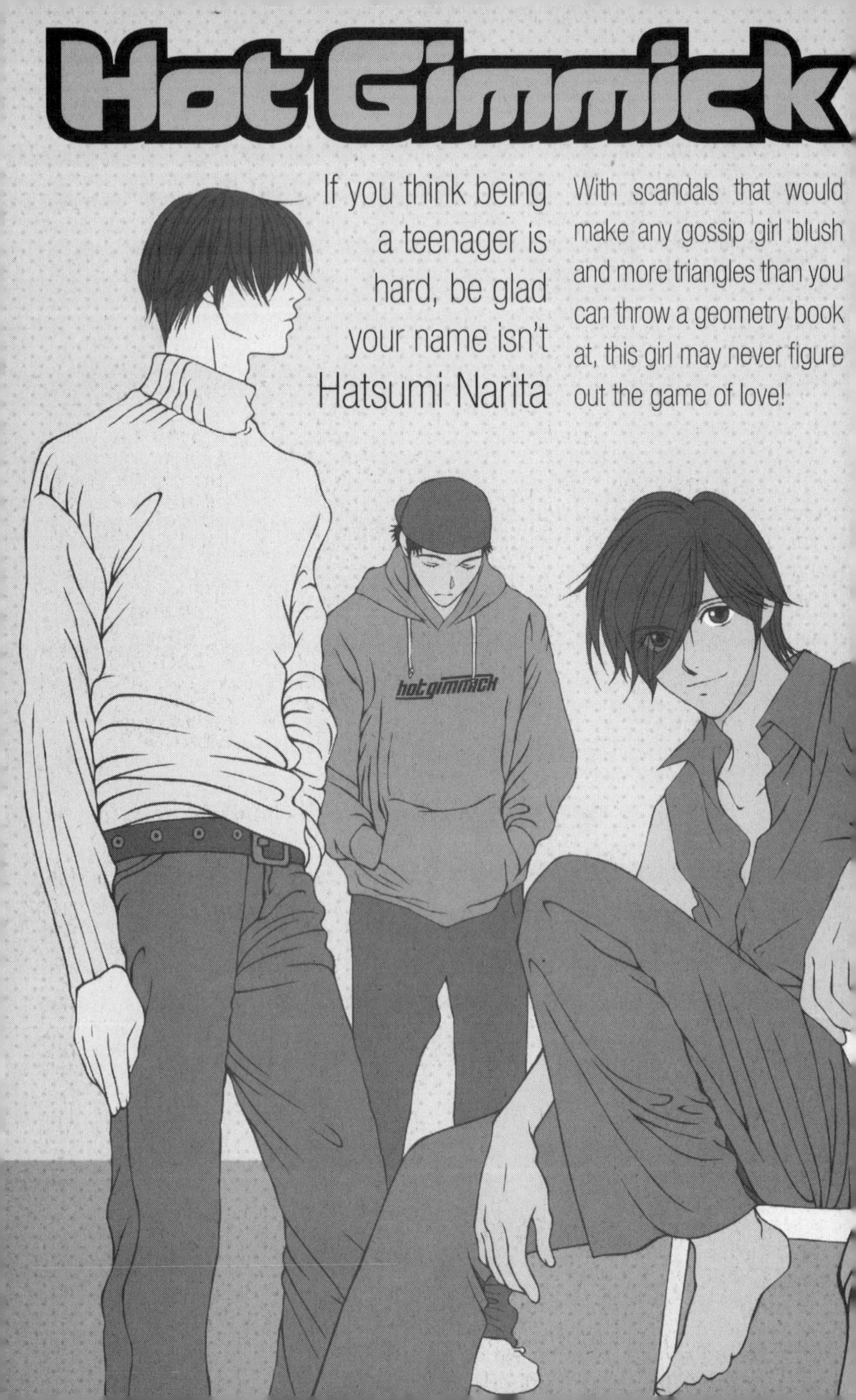
Hot Gimmick
If you think being a teenager is hard, be glad your name isn't Hatsumi Narita
With scandals that would make any gossip girl blush and more triangles than you can throw a geometry book at, this girl may never figure out the game of love!
hotgimmick

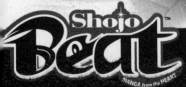

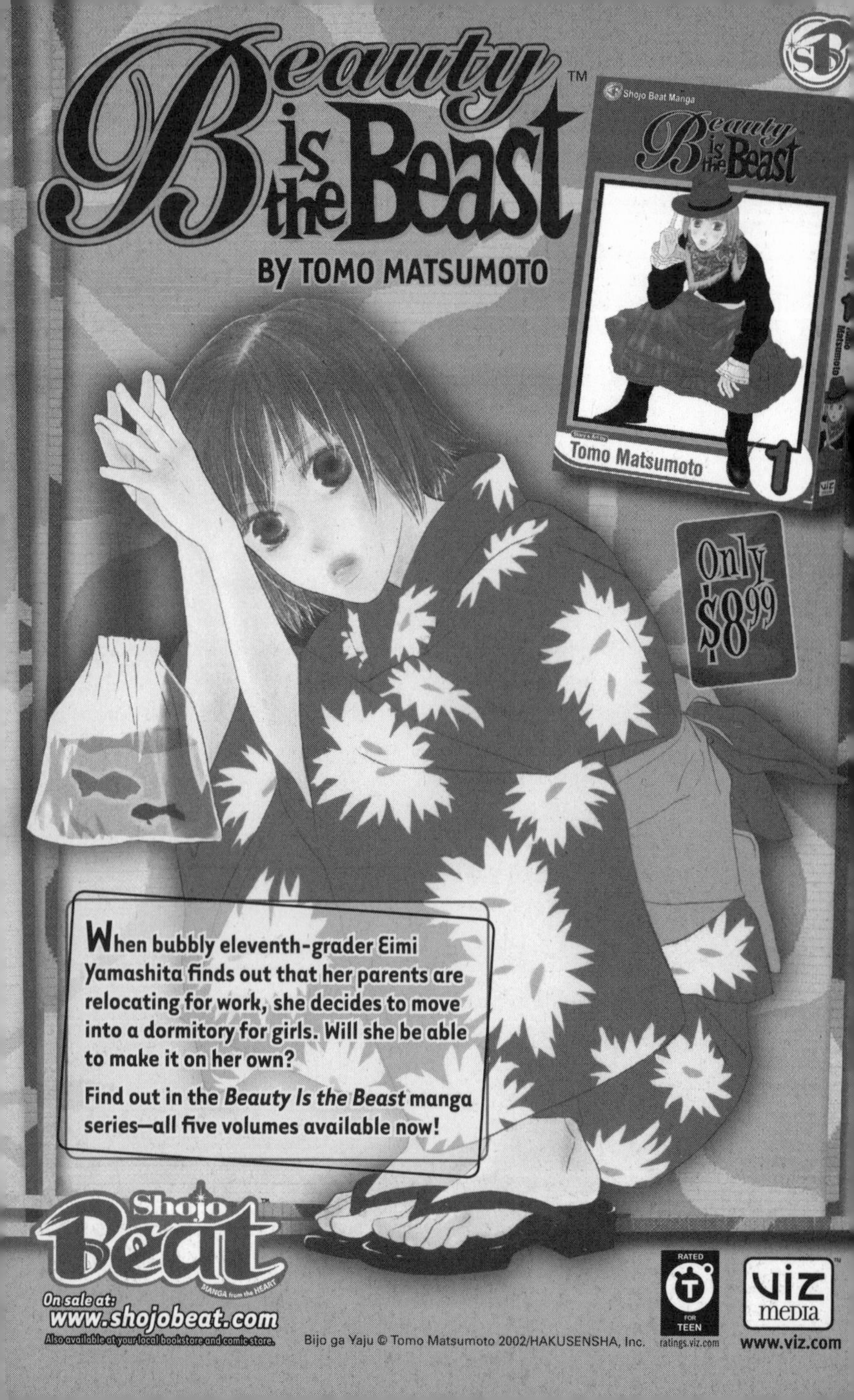
Beauty is the Beast™
BY TOMO MATSUMOTO
Shojo Beat Manga
Beauty is the Beast
Tomo Matsumoto
1
Only $8.99
When bubbly eleventh-grader Eimi Yamashita finds out that her parents are relocating for work, she decides to move into a dormitory for girls. Will she be able to make it on her own?
Find out in the *Beauty Is the Beast* manga series—all five volumes available now!
Shojo Beat™
MANGA from the HEART
On sale at:
www.shojobeat.com
Also available at your local bookstore and comic store.
Bijo ga Yaju © Tomo Matsumoto 2002/HAKUSENSHA, Inc.
RATED T FOR TEEN
ratings.viz.com
VIZ media
www.viz.com

Tell us what you think about Shojo Beat Manga!

S0-ARD-588

Our survey is now available online. Go to:

shojobeat.com/mangasurvey

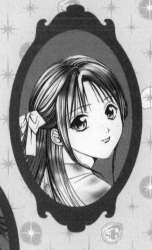

Help us make our product offerings better!

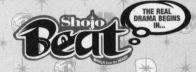